Edited with an Introduction by
Thomas G. Paterson

Cold War Critics
Alternatives to American Foreign Policy in the Truman Years

Chicago
Quadrangle Books
1971

Library of Congress Catalog Card Number: 70–116083

SBN Cloth 8129–0163–0

SBN Paper 8129–6140–4

Designed by Chestnut House/Miles Zimmerman

Contents

Cold War Critics

by Thomas G. Paterson

Introduction:
American Critics
of the Cold War
and Their Alternatives

American foreign policy and the wars it has helped to initiate or failed to avert have always had their largely unwelcome and unappreciated critics. Scholars have recounted, for example, the troubled stories of the anti-imperialists of the 1890's, the dissenters from American entry into World War I, the isolationists of the 1930's, and the doves of the 1960's. Their dissent marked them in the popular and even official mind as either deluded or uninformed, yet loyal, citizens, conscious troublemakers, irrational misfits, or dangerous traitors. Their suggested policy alternatives, in the turbulent atmospheres of war crisis, were seldom examined carefully for merit. Rather, defenders of official policy superficially dismissed them as outside the majority and hence most important opinion, and as a potential threat to the nation itself. Thus Senator Robert M. LaFollette, Jr., according to Theodore Roosevelt in 1917, was "loyally and efficiently serving one country—Germany," by questioning American participation in the First World War, and critics of the Vietnam War have been charged by the administrators of that conflict with assisting, through their vociferous dissent, the cause of an aggressive North Vietnam.[1] Critics, in asking questions and proposing alternatives which often differed radically from official policy, refused to accept the consensus that leaders have al-

3

ways sought in crises, and hence became conspicuous targets for verbal abuse, sometimes even physical attacks.

During the early years of the Cold War, many American critics of the Truman administration's foreign policies had to endure this pattern of international crisis, consensus, dissent, and intolerance. Although the Cold War was not an engaged military conflict but rather a "prolonged armed truce," [2] many of the features of war were evident: embellished rhetoric, national self-righteousness, mindless patriotism, military build-up, and anxiety fed especially by the awesome power of atomic weapons. Present, too, in the years after World War II were the elements of intolerance, fear, and political repression, characterized by popular name-calling, red-baiting political campaigns, new internal security measures, and political ostracism.

Although most critics of the Cold War have received little scholarly attention, the traditional and prevailing view is that they were unrealistic, misguided, wrong, and, in some cases, even duped and disloyal. A common theme, too, is that the more ardent dissenters apologized for and excused the brutalities and offenses of Stalinist foreign policy. This unfavorable assessment has been sustained by the entrenched official explanation that the coming of the Cold War was inevitable; by the power of bipartisan foreign policy and consensus in the Truman years; by the apparent life-or-death struggle with communism which called forth extreme support for the administration; and by the widespread belief in the righteousness of the American world role. Finally, the carelessness, contradictions, and strained rhetoric of some of the dissenters themselves have contributed to the traditional portrait.

The Cold War critics were, of course, never organized into one group; they were quite divergent in backgrounds and attitudes, and sometimes in vigorous disagreement with one another. The critics discussed in this book are a few of the many, and demonstrate the mixed character of dissent from the Cold War. What united most of them was not their desire for peace (for almost every American wanted that), but their generally shared belief that reconciliation with the Soviet Union was possible without sacrificing the national interest, that American foreign policy and its misconceptions were helping to aggravate Soviet-American friction, that the Cold War should not be increasingly militarized, and that the conflict threatened American institutions and cherished principles at home. These critics recognized the intense ideological differences between Russia and the United States, but believed that some kind of *modus vivendi* or coexistence without military escalation could be realized diplomatically. Many of them also denied that Russia was such an aggressive monster that the United States should avoid negotiations.[3]

Three of the critics discussed here were United States senators. Robert A. Taft, "Mr. Republican," seldom agreed with his colleagues Claude Pepper of Florida and Glen Taylor of Idaho, for their liberalism challenged his conscious conservatism on domestic issues, and their often shrill language, excited oratorical performances, and acquaintances with blunt dissenters of the left offended the sedate legislator from Ohio. Their contrasts were evident in 1948, for example: Taft supported Thomas Dewey; Pepper, a Democrat, reluctantly backed Truman; and Taylor left the Democratic party to run as the vice-presidential candidate for the Progressive party which was pledged to Henry A. Wallace.

The two journalists treated in this book, Walter Lippmann and I. F. Stone, also separated on a number of issues. Lippmann was a long-established respectable commentator with a regular syndicated column. Limited by his identification with many American foreign policy goals, he sometimes slapped at official policy rather than battering it down. Stone, on the other hand, was brazen, insistent, and unorthodox, and was never accepted into the journalistic elite. Lippmann was often admired by policy-makers, whereas Stone was viewed with distrust and suspicion. Lippmann published his many books with eager houses like Harper's and Little, Brown; Stone in the early fifties had to scratch around before finding the Monthly Review Press.

Two other critics, James Paul Warburg and Henry A. Wallace, could not have been much more different from one another in temperament, style, and background. Maverick Warburg, member of a wealthy Wall Street family and confrere of leading administration figures, was always an independent characterized by a dispassionate, carefully reasoned criticism of Truman administration policies, especially toward Germany, and of policy-makers, especially his long-time friend Dean Acheson. Wallace had traveled many political routes from agricultural Iowa to Washington, liked dramatic public attention, and styled himself one of the apostles of the "common man." Less guarded and reflective than Warburg, Wallace had a lively tongue which alienated him from the political establishment and often led his listeners to ask for clarification. Truman clumsily removed Wallace from his post as Secretary of Commerce in 1946 for criticizing American foreign policy, and Wallace then went on to run very poorly as the Progressive party candidate for the presidency in 1948.

Several not so well-known critics are also represented in this book. A wide spectrum of black critics, with a perspective different from that of any of the other dissenters, questioned aspects of policy and centered their attention on colonialism and Africa. There was a remarkable unity in their dissent, but there was disagreement between the radical Council on African Affairs and the more cautious National Association for the Advancement of Colored People. Walter White and *The Crisis* were less hostile to American foreign policy than W.E.B. DuBois, Horace Cayton, Rayford Logan, and the *Pittsburgh Courier*. Finally, some critics close to and within the administration were deeply concerned with the question of internal security and the initiation of a federal loyalty program, both matters exacerbated by the Cold War. Herbert Gaston, Stephen Spingarn, Harry Mitchell, C. Girard Davidson, Robert Carr, and Donald Hansen worked quietly to head off some of the more blatant Justice Department infringements of civil liberties.

Any list of critics and criticisms of the Cold War would include many more than are discussed in this book, and would further demonstrate the heterogeneity of the group. Deserving historical investigation are Corliss Lamont, son of the elite Lamonts of J. P. Morgan and Company, and active spokesman for reconciliation with Russia through the National Council of Soviet-American Friendship. The latter body published *Soviet Russia Today,* edited by Jessica Smith, one of whose contributors was Frederick L. Schuman, Professor of Political Science at Williams College, who gave scholarly treatment to the origins of the Cold War. Another scholar, William Appleman Williams, wrote one of the first "revisionist" and questioning studies, *American-Russian Relations, 1781–1947* (1952).[4] Historians have studied the movement of a number of prominent scientists who were alarmed by the moral and political consequences of the atomic bomb they had helped to create. Leo Szilard, James Franck, and Eugene Rabinowitch, among others, tried to prevent use of the atomic bomb against Japan to avert a postwar arms race. After the dropping of the bomb, they organized the Federation of Atomic Scientists and founded the *Bulletin of Atomic Scientists*. Albert Einstein, Harold Urey, and Linus Pauling also worked to explain the dangers of American monopoly of the bomb and the military's control of it, and the need to approach Russia directly for negotiations rather than brandishing the bomb as a diplomatic weapon.[5]

Political commentators Freda Kirchwey of *The Nation* and Vera Micheles Dean, a regular contributor to *Foreign Policy Reports*, offered tempered criticisms of and suggested alternative policies to American diplomacy in the early years of the Cold War. In 1946 Mrs. Dean asked: "Is it possible that we may be expecting of Russia higher standards of international conduct than our own?"[6] Critics of varying degrees, interests, and consistency included pacifists A. J. Muste, David Dellinger, and the American Friends Service Committee; Grenville Clark, respected lawyer and United World Federalist; Ernest C. Ropes, a low-echelon Department of Commerce official who actively sought a large postwar loan for and trade with Russia; and Franklin A. Lindsay, executive assistant to Bernard Baruch and a member of the American delegation to the United Nations Atomic Energy Commission who, among his other suggestions, wrote a perceptive memorandum in 1947 arguing against the use of loans as diplomatic pressure on Russia and Eastern Europe.[7]

A more controversial critic was Vito Marcantonio, congressman from East Harlem. A member and leader of the declining American Labor party, Marcantonio consistently and sometimes flamboyantly lashed out at American actions abroad, business and military influences in Washington, and American capitalism, which so many other critics accepted.[8] Like Marcantonio, Carl Marzani, former OSS officer and alleged communist spy, insisted that *We Can Be Friends* (1952) with Russia. Conspicuous, but much less radical,

was the colorful director of the United Nations Relief and Rehabilitation Administration in 1946, Fiorello LaGuardia. He chastised the Truman administration for terminating UNRRA and refusing
to consider LaGuardia's alternative Food Fund. The brusque
former mayor of New York City blasted Truman's "use of food
relief as a weapon of foreign policy. . . ." [9] Richard Scandrett,
establishment lawyer from New York, shared LaGuardia's sentiment on relief. Scandrett served as chief of the UNRRA mission in
Byelorussia and as an assistant to Edwin Pauley in the Allied
Reparations Commission, and he was a close friend of Robert A.
Taft. He scored American foreign policy for its oversimplified notions of an aggressive and totalitarian Soviet Union and particularly
chided Pauley for his inept attempts to win points against the
Russians rather than to achieve successful reparations negotiations.[10]

Conspicuous in his criticism of an increasingly uncompromising
American stance toward Russia at the Potsdam conference was
Joseph Davies, former Ambassador to Russia.[11] H. Stuart Hughes,
a low-ranking officer in the State Department's Division of Research for Europe, reminds us that there were some quieter, less
dramatic critics of the Cold War. He recently recounted that he
and others in the depths of the State Department opposed unsuccessfully American self-righteousness and argued a case for spheres
of influence because the United States was powerless to dislodge
Russia from Eastern Europe.[12] Another man who tended to accept
spheres of influence was George F. Kennan, the elusive and ambiguous architect of the containment doctrine, who focused his
criticism on Acheson's penchant for military containment—an emphasis Kennan's own imprecision in 1947 had helped foster.[13]
Elliott Roosevelt, son of President Franklin D. Roosevelt, raised a
stir when he charged in *As He Saw It* (1946) that Truman and his
State Department advisers were shoving America away from Big
Three unity, away from President Roosevelt's charted peace, and
were doing it "grievously" and "deliberately." [14] Henry Morgenthau, Jr., shared the view that Truman had reversed Roosevelt's
foreign policy. The former Secretary of the Treasury, removed by
Truman in 1945, thought Truman too uncompromising toward
Russia and concentrated his attention on Germany. He lamented

that the Truman administration seemed intent upon rebuilding that defeated country, to the detriment of Soviet-American relations and the future peace of the world.[15] Finally, Norman Thomas, perennial presidential candidate for the Socialist party, considered himself to be a moderate and reasonable critic of the United States, and he attacked both Wall Street and Henry Wallace. Although his anti-communism was often as virulent as Truman's, Thomas offered alternatives to the administration's emphasis on a military response to communism.[16]

Despite the critics' diversity and the varied intensity of their criticism, they had in common some characteristics besides their drive to find viable solutions to the Cold War deadlock. Most of them were political independents, seldom bound fast to any one party or leader, and in the case of politicians they were usually unpopular with the major party leadership. They were loners, letting their ideas take them to the men and institutions they thought best able to extricate America from immediate crisis. Thus Pepper flirted with Eisenhower as a presidential candidate in 1948, and Taylor and Wallace left the Democratic party for the Progressives. For the most part, the critics remained outside official Washington circles and were only occasionally listened to. Even for high officeholders such as Wallace and Taft, it was difficult to affect policy. It was Senator Arthur Vandenberg, not Taft, whom the Truman administration invited to attend international conferences and to further the cause of bipartisanship.

Most dissenters were not "isolationists" or "neo-isolationists" who supposedly were withdrawing from foreign involvements. Rather, many of them were anti-imperialists who advocated disengagement from empire, not from international relations, and less reliance on the military; most of them had favored intervention in World War II. Easily refuted are the unsubstantiated charges that Cold War dissenters like Pepper and Wallace were simply apologists for the Soviet Union. It is no longer tenable to assume that because one criticizes American foreign policy he is condoning or endorsing the foreign policy of Russia. And most Cold War critics eschewed a missionary zeal to carry American institutions abroad forcibly or to insist on American interpretations of international treaties and events. Rather, they chided American self-righteousness in diplomacy and stressed the importance of domestic priorities to a healthy world image of the United States.

Then, too, many of these critics possessed the fallibility of the men they criticized. Neither superhumans nor heroes, they demonstrated instances of contradiction, sometimes imagined conspiracies, often stressed one factor to the exclusion of others and hence slighted complexities, and under pressure sometimes failed to press their views vigorously. Because so few were listening to them, and because of their deep conviction, they occasionally shouted to be heard. Few of them constructed a well-conceived, thorough, and systematic critique of American foreign policy, in part because they shared many of the Truman administration's values and goals. Instead, some dissenters nibbled at those issues which bothered them most and avoided clear-cut philosophical critiques. Thus Wallace, although an ardent critic on specific questions such as the Truman Doctrine, the use of the atomic bomb, and NATO, shared the basic American goal of the Open Door abroad—unrestricted multilateral trade, whose benefits, he believed, included improved political relations. Given the traditionalism of many of the critics and the rapidity and shifting nature of international crises, it is not surprising that their suggested policy alternatives were related more to tactics than to grand schemes or strategies.

The Cold War critics, contrary to their detractors, were not fuzzy-minded idealists clinging to illusory hopes or out of touch with power politics. They recognized that postwar Soviet-American competition was unavoidable and that relations would not be free of troublesome dispute. But they refused to accept the idea that a growing militarism, heated verbiage, and actual military skirmishes were inevitable. The word "realist" is usually applied to the defenders of Cold War diplomacy. But the word has been much abused in its application, because it has at least the dual meanings of (1) tough-mindedness and (2) awareness of what diplomacy might achieve. "Tough-mindedness" defies careful measurement, and if the policies recommended by some of the critics had been followed and had worked, the realism of the second meaning would seem to lie with them. The policies actually pursued by the Truman administration failed to cool Soviet-American tension, and generally helped draw tight lines around the world. Since the critics' alternatives were rejected and Truman's policies faltered, we really do not know where realism rests. Did realism lie more in an accommodation with the Soviet Union on the basis of post-war reconstruction aid and recognition of the *fait accompli* in Eastern Europe, or did it lie in the blatant use of economic power to coerce the Russians, and blustering, challenging American moves in Eastern Europe? Perhaps Warburg was more the "realist" in arguing against a rearmed Germany because it would revive Russia's fears, however exaggerated, of another German onslaught. Also, any term which supposedly includes Lippmann, Kennan, and Acheson cannot provide careful definition. In short, the American Cold War debate cannot be explained simply as a clash between realists and nonrealists.[17]

The long-accepted idea that the Cold War was inevitable and that the United States could have done nothing to change it has perhaps obscured the history of its critics more than has any other factor. It has also allowed those persons who adhere to this view of inevitability to give scant attention to the critics' alternative proposals and to assume that there were very few choices before official Washington *at that time*. In the traditional view, it follows that the Truman administration made decisions which were largely forced upon it from abroad, especially by an aggressive and destructive Russia, and that the dissenters' alternative suggestions were irrelevant. Such an interpretation, of course, is too straitjacketed to make historical sense. It suggests that American policy-makers were not free to change events, did not have the chance, power, or will to make different decisions. The complexity of Cold War history and the significance of American participation in spawning some of the crises of the Cold War years is thus overlooked for a heavy emphasis on Soviet intransigence, Stalin's brutalities, communist ideology, and Moscow's obstructionist international conspiracy. Recently Arthur M. Schlesinger, Jr., after writing of some of the errors and stubbornness of American foreign policy, easily shifted to argue that what really counted, what really brought on the Cold War, were messianic Leninist ideology and totalitarian Stalinist paranoia, neither of which the United States could do anything about and before which it was largely helpless.[18] Professor Adam Ulam of Harvard University finds an "air of inevitability" in the Cold War and tends to place the burden on Russia, because of its intense suspicion of the West growing out of Russian internal questions— Stalin's fear of his political opponents and "cosmopolitan" writers, the devastation of the Soviet economy, and the Soviet drive for national unity.[19]

As the following essays suggest, the Cold War was not cut and dried, foreordained, or inexorable. To argue against the traditional story is difficult, because it has become deeply enshrined among our national myths. And to a certain extent we are dealing in "might-have-been" history; that is, attempting to *indicate* how the Cold War might have been avoided, as well as delineating the mistakes that were made. But such history—a history of critics and policy alternatives—offers new questions to scholarship, sends students to new sources, and reveals the complexity of events and decisions. In pointing out alternatives, we improve our understanding of the reasons for the Truman administration's rejection of them and thereby sharpen our study of the administration's "mind" and diplomatic behavior. As Ulam has recently observed, scholars' emphasis on the questions "Who started it all?" and "Who was responsible?" have caused us to overlook "those occasions where tenacious, well-informed diplomacy could have made a difference and where hard bargaining rather than posturing might have brought partial solutions and lowered the international tension."[20] We cannot be certain that the alternatives were viable and would have made a difference in international relations, but adherents to the traditional account must now give attention to the alternatives and try to explain, not assume, that such options were unsound and unworkable.

The alternatives discussed below range from specific proposals relating to single issues, such as Germany and the Greek civil war, to more general calls for world federalism. There are recommendations on the atomic bomb and its control, international organizations, foreign aid and trade, the Truman Doctrine and Greece, Germany and its postwar occupation, the Marshall Plan, NATO, colonialism, Eastern Europe, China, internal security programs, and the Korean War. Some of the suggestions are simply the negatives or the opposites of declared policies: Do not abandon UNRRA. Do not rearm Germany. Avoid the simplistic language and concept of the Truman Doctrine. Do not attempt to use the atomic bomb for diplomatic bargaining. Do not support European imperialism in Africa and Asia.

In their alternatives and criticisms, the critics exposed an international double standard applied by Washington and American abuse and sidestepping of international institutions. They pointed out uncompromising American positions which obstructed negotiations, the United States' desire to use its power to shape an American-oriented world, and American support for traditional European imperialism. They attempted to allay exaggerated and sometimes hysterical American fears of Soviet communism and its expansion, and stressed the dangers of the Cold War to domestic well-being.

In their thinking and activities, the critics challenged the conscious bipartisanship in Washington, which the Truman administration wanted so as to free the President's hand as much as possible in diplomacy and to quiet criticism in the nation. Most of those critics who ardently bucked this trend found themselves at the receiving end of calculated distortion and charges ranging from idiocy to conspiracy. In a memorandum prepared for the President in 1947, his White House assistant Clark Clifford explained how Truman could defeat the upstart Wallace: "Every effort must be made *now* jointly and at one and the same time—although of course, by different groups—to dissuade him and also to identify him and isolate him in the public mind with the Communists." [21] Social critic Dwight Macdonald believed unfairly and wrongly that Wallace was the "mouthpiece of American communism." [22]

These attempts to tag critics with communist labels were popular long before Joseph McCarthy gave ostentatious drama to the practice. Athan Theoharis has demonstrated well that the Truman administration itself, employing a language of immediate crisis and fear to move its programs through Congress and to allay public criticism, helped prepare the way for McCarthy's more explosive diatribes. It was Attorney General J. Howard McGrath in 1949 who said that "there are today many Communists in America. They are everywhere—in factories, offices, butcher stores, on street corners, in private businesses. And each carries in himself the germ of death for society." [23] Pepper, Taylor, and Wallace were vilified

as Soviet apologists, the Council of African Affairs was placed on
the Attorney General's subversive list, and W. E. B. DuBois was
indicted in 1951 for refusing to register as an agent of a foreign
government (Marcantonio successfully defended DuBois). Conservative critics such as Taft, on the other hand, were criticized as
"isolationists." [24] Defenders of official policy refurbished the words
"appeasement" and "Munich" to belittle alternative approaches.[25]
Wallace understood the effectiveness of such attitudes and treatment in 1948, when he gathered in 1,157,000 votes or only about
2 per cent of the total cast—less than the Southern-based Dixie-
crats received. The mild critic Richard Scandrett summarized the
plight of dissenters in 1948: "Even to suggest in a whisper here
nowadays that every Russian is not a cannibal is to invite incar-
ceration for subversive activities." Scandrett lamented that "that is
the American way. Things are either pure black or pure white.
There are no greys." [26]

The favorable popular response to the Marshall Plan as an example of American generosity and selflessness, and the widespread
and horrified American reaction to the *coup* in Czechoslovakia and
the Berlin Blockade of 1948, further tainted dissent. And a number
of critics themselves were shocked by the communist subjugation
of Czechoslovakia. The crushing blow for many critics was the
Korean War. This war, which appeared to be a clear-cut case of
Soviet aggression and intransigence, fit the "we-told-you-so" cate-
gory. Seemingly disarmed, many critics met defeat at the polls in
1950 or succumbed finally to the Cold War consensus. Pepper lost
his Senate seat after a vicious campaign by George Smathers. Taylor and Marcantonio met a similar fate. Wallace and many other
critics endorsed American intervention in Korea. As imperfect men
under considerable and unrelenting pressure, some of the critics
crumbled under the weight of the hostility against them. The power
of consensus was extensive, and it eventually forced men, some of
whom were not thoroughgoing in their critiques and who had only
nibbled at issues, to fall in line.

In sum, most of the critics made little immediate impact upon
American foreign policy. Some were harassed, and dismissed as
misguided aberrations; others received polite if cool attention. For
the most part their alternatives were not given a careful hearing. As

one student of the Truman Doctrine has concluded: "The rather shocking fact which emerges when considering the United States assumption of the British role in Greece and Turkey, and elsewhere, is the lack of discussion at the highest levels of meaningful policy alternatives." [27] In 1946 Wallace appealed to Truman to initiate new economic talks with Russia to reduce Soviet-American tension. The President later facilely recalled that "I ignored this letter of Wallace's." [28] Indeed, there are few clear instances in which the critics changed national policies or initiated new ones. Yet their questioning, their vigilance, their suggestions, and their interest were checks of varying degrees upon the Truman administration in the first few years of the Cold War. Some of their questions to the administration were perceptive and occasionally uncovered the tangled yet powerful roots of American Cold War foreign policy. And it is important, for example, that Senator Taft's critique of NATO, according to Senator Vandenberg, "has given me a first class headache. . . ."—that is, a longer debate on the issue than Vandenberg wanted.[29]

In their bequeathing of questions and ideas to later scholars, the Cold War critics made a contribution to last beyond their own time. Building upon those questions and ideas, bringing new research materials and perspectives to bear upon the answers, and willing to shatter many of the assumptions of traditional Cold War history, the authors of the following essays point out the strengths and weaknesses of the Cold War critics who preceded them.

Notes

1. Quoted in H. C. Peterson and Gilbert C. Fite, *Opponents of War, 1917–1918* (Seattle, 1968; copyright 1957), p. 14.

2. Words of Maxim Litvinov, May 23, 1946, Department of State, *Foreign Relations of the United States, 1946: Eastern Europe; The Soviet Union* (Washington, D.C., 1969), VI, 763n.

3. Two groups of critics have been excluded from this collection: (1) those whose policy alternatives would have augmented Soviet-American tension (Arthur Bliss Lane and Joseph McCarthy, for example); and (2) those who owed allegiance to a foreign government (the Communist Party of America).

4. For Frederick L. Schuman, see his *Soviet Politics at Home and Abroad* (New York, 1946); "Designs for Democracy," *Current History,* IX (December 1945), 497–502; "East Europe and Two Worlds," *ibid.,* XI (November 1946), 357–364; "The Soviet Union: Cordon Sanitaire," *ibid.,* XI (December 1946), 459–468; "Diagnosis of the Big Three Problem," *New York Times Magazine,* June 30, 1946, pp. 6ff; "The Devil and Jimmy Byrnes," *Soviet Russia Today,* XVI (December 1947), 7ff; *Russia Since 1917: Four Decades of Soviet Politics* (New York, 1957); and *The Cold War: Retrospect and Prospect* (rev. ed., Baton Rouge, 1967); William A. Williams, *American-Russian Relations, 1781–1947* (New York, 1952); and *The Tragedy of American Diplomacy* (rev. ed., New York, 1962).

5. Lawrence S. Wittner, *Rebels Against War: The American Peace Movement, 1941–1960* (New York, 1969), pp. 143–150, 165–169; Otto Nathan and Heinz Norden, eds., *Einstein on Peace* (New York, 1960); Alice Kimball Smith, *A Peril and a Hope: The Scientists' Movement in America, 1945–47* (Chicago, 1965); Leo Szilard, "Reminiscences," ed. by Gertrud Weiss Szilard and Kathleen R. Winsor, in *Perspectives in American History,* II (1968), 94–151.

6. Quoted from Vera Micheles Dean, "Is Russia Alone to Blame?" *Foreign Policy Reports,* XXV (March 8, 1946). See also Freda Kirchwey, "Manifest Destiny," *Nation,* CLXIV (March 22, 1947), 317–319, and "To the Greeks, Bearing Gifts," *ibid.,* CLXIV (March 29, 1947), 347–349.

7. Wittner, *Rebels Against War;* Nat Hentoff, *Peace Agitator: The Story of A. J. Muste* (New York, 1963); American Friends Service Committee, *The United States and the Soviet Union: Some Quaker Proposals for Peace* (New Haven, 1949); Grenville Clark, *A Plan for Peace* (New York, 1950); "Statesman Incognito [on Clark]," *Fortune,* XXXIII (February 1946), 110–115; Ernest C. Ropes, "American-Soviet Trade: 1917–1947," *Soviet Russia Today,* XVI (November 1947), 14ff; Ropes, "Opportunities for Russian-American Trade Expansion," *Dun's Review,* LV (May 1947), 11, 58; Ropes, *Doing Business with Russia* (Washington, D.C., June 1945); Franklin A. Lindsay, "American Foreign Policy in the Balkans," January 9, 1947, Part XI:1, Bernard Baruch Papers, Princeton University Library. J. Garry Clifford of the University of Connecticut is preparing a study of Grenville Clark from the Clark Papers at Dartmouth College.

8. Alan Schaffer, *Vito Marcantonio: Radical in Congress* (Syracuse, 1966); Norman Kaner, "Towards a Minority of One: Vito Marcantonio and American Foreign Policy," unpublished Ph.D. dissertation, Rutgers University, 1968.

9. Quoted in Petition, November 13, 1946, UNRRA Files, Herbert Lehman Papers, Columbia University. See also George Woodbridge, *et al., The History of the United Nations Relief and Rehabilitation Administration* (3 vols., New York, 1950).

10. Scandrett's collection of papers is in the Cornell University Library.

11. See his papers in the Manuscript Division, Library of Congress, and his *Mission to Moscow* (New York, 1941).

12. "Our contention had been that if each side would stay out of the other's sphere, then each could tolerate substantial dissent within that sphere. . . . We believed that one could find an intermediate course between armed antagonism and a cordial *modus vivendi.*" H. Stuart Hughes, "The

Second Year of the Cold War: A Memoir and an Appreciation," *Commentary*, XLVIII (August 1969), 27–32.

13. George F. Kennan, *Memoirs, 1925–1950* (New York, 1967).

14. Elliott Roosevelt, *As He Saw It* (New York, 1946), p. xviii.

15. Henry Morgenthau, Jr., *Germany Is Our Problem* (New York, 1945); John M. Blum, *From the Morgenthau Diaries*, Vol. III, *Years of War, 1941–1945* (3 vols., Boston, 1967); Thomas G. Paterson, "The Abortive American Loan to Russia and the Origins of the Cold War, 1943–1946," *Journal of American History*, LVI (June 1969), 70–92.

16. Murray Seidler, *Norman Thomas, Respectable Rebel* (rev. ed., Syracuse, 1967); Harry Fleischman, *Norman Thomas: A Biography* (New York, 1964); Bernard K. Johnpoll, *Pacifist's Progress: Norman Thomas and the Decline of American Socialism* (Chicago, 1970); Norman Thomas, *Appeal to the Nations* (New York, 1947).

17. See the difficulties of Alonzo Hamby, "Henry A. Wallace, the Liberals, and Soviet-American Relations," *Review of Politics*, XXX (April 1968), 153–169.

18. Arthur M. Schlesinger, Jr., "Origins of the Cold War," *Foreign Affairs*, XLVI (October 1967), 22–52.

19. Adam B. Ulam, *Expansion and Coexistence: The History of Soviet Foreign Policy, 1917–67* (New York, 1968), pp. 398–404.

20. Adam B. Ulam, "On Modern History: Re-reading the Cold War," *Interplay Magazine*, II (March 1968), 53.

21. Clark Clifford, "Memorandum for the President," November 19, 1947, Clark Clifford Papers, Harry S. Truman Library, Independence, Missouri.

22. Quoted in Wittner, *Rebels Against War*, p. 196.

23. Quoted in Athan Theoharis, "The Rhetoric of Politics: Foreign Policy, Internal Security, and Domestic Politics in the Truman Era, 1945–1950," in Barton J. Bernstein, ed., *Politics and Policies of the Truman Administration* (Chicago, 1970), p. 215.

24. See Norman Graebner, *The New Isolationism: A Study in Politics and Foreign Policy Since 1950* (New York, 1956).

25. Les K. Adler and Thomas G. Paterson, "Red Fascism: The Merger of Nazi Germany and Soviet Russia in the American Image of Totalitarianism, 1930's–1950's," *American Historical Review*, LXXV (April 1970), 1057–1058.

26. Richard Scandrett to Phyllis Auty, October 25, 1948, Vol. 20-A, Scandrett Papers.

27. Bernard Weiner, "The Truman Doctrine: Background and Presentation," unpublished Ph.D. dissertation, Claremont Graduate School, 1967, p. 255.

28. Harry S. Truman, *Memoirs* (2 vols., Garden City, N.Y., 1955), I, 556.

29. Arthur H. Vandenberg, Jr., ed., *The Private Papers of Senator Vandenberg* (Boston, 1952), p. 498 (entry for July 11, 1949).

by Barton J. Bernstein

Walter Lippmann and the Early Cold War

Well before the bombing of Hiroshima and Winston Churchill's call at Fulton, Missouri, for an Anglo-American alliance against the Soviet Union, Walter Lippmann, the widely acclaimed philosopher-journalist, had been formulating policies for a postwar world order designed to avert or reduce Soviet-American antagonism. In his columns, speeches, and books, he lectured the educated citizenry, including policy-makers, on the mistakes of the past and the dangers and possibilities of the present and future. Unlike many other critics of American foreign policy, he was usually dispassionate and restrained, never a proselytizer or partisan. Perhaps because of his distrust of popular passions, as well as his hope of counseling policy-makers, he seldom condemned or even attacked American leaders, and he usually contented himself with focusing upon policies, not personalities. To the problems of public affairs he brought a reflective intelligence, a keen sense of history, and a deep commitment to the powers of analysis.[1]

For these qualities, as well as his reputation and experience, Lippmann commanded the attention and respect of American leaders and foreign statesmen. A prominent commentator on the American scene since the Progressive years, he had been an editor of the

I am grateful to Allen J. Matusow of Rice University, Thomas G. Paterson of the University of Connecticut, Jeff Preefer of Rutgers University, John S. Rosenberg of Stanford University, and Martin Sherwin of the University of California at Berkeley for their generous counsel. I am indebted to George H. Knoles, director of the Institute of American History at Stanford University, for encouragement and financial assistance.

18

early *New Republic,* a member of the distinguished committee that sought to prepare Wilson's delegation for the Versailles peace conference, the chief editor of the *New York World,* and the author of influential books on modern politics and social thought and the widely syndicated column "Today and Tomorrow." No mere journalist, he was a man of demonstrated achievements who might well have merited the title of unofficial—and often uninvited—public adviser to the makers of American foreign policy. Even when they disagreed with him, they could not easily ignore his arguments. More than any other man outside the government, he influenced the dialogue in "official" Washington. Indeed, he had "already attained the settled status of a public monument" by the time of the New Deal, Harry Ashmore later recalled. An intimate of the powerful but nonetheless independent-minded, Lippmann, unlike Henry Wallace, never moved outside the orbit of "responsible" criticism or jeopardized his prestige. To a nation in quest of guidance, Lippmann offered the counsel of power and morality in a fluid combination that few could easily dismiss.[2]

Ultimately Lippmann sought a world order based upon liberal democratic principles and the innate dignity of man, but in the short run he was willing to settle for less. Despite his commitment to democratic values, for example, he often counseled acceding to undemocratic conditions in order to avoid conflict or war. It was the tension between the universal principles he desired and the policies he offered for a *modus vivendi* between East and West that created some of the inconsistencies and ambiguities in his thought.

In criticizing American foreign policy, he deplored Wilsonian diplomacy, opposed national self-righteousness, distrusted ideological *crusades* for democracy and capitalism, emphasized the limitations of American power, eschewed isolationism and pacifism, and rejected a peace based upon the United Nations. Instead he offered the counsel of realism: the use of power to serve the national interest, which meant at minimum the maintenance of national security, territorial integrity, national independence, and the democratic form of government at home. In outlining policies to protect the national interest and to achieve a *modus vivendi,* he relied upon military preparedness and power politics, endorsed regional alliances, uneasily accepted spheres of influence, and always affirmed the need for diplomatic negotiations. He never banished idealism (including the extension of democracy abroad) from his prescription, but he did seek to limit American energies to the quest for the possible, and especially the likely. So flexible was this intellectual framework that it permitted Lippmann, under the pressure of events, to revise—sometimes even to reverse—his recommendations on the major Cold War issues—Eastern Europe, Germany, the Mediterranean, and the atomic bomb.

Like most Americans, Lippmann did not believe that American policy-makers had an "ideology" and a well-defined conception of the national interest. Where he saw innocence there was often, in fact, design; where he saw ignorance or blundering there was often purpose. In offering the counsel of realism, he failed to understand fully how much he ultimately shared of the vision of policy-makers and how much his dissent was limited to means and tactics, not goals and ends. As a defender of Western civilization, and particularly Anglo-American democratic standards, Lippmann sought to create a world quite similar to the one American policy-makers struggled to establish. He differed from them primarily in that he was prepared in the short run to accede to Soviet influence while they sought to roll it back.

I

In publishing *U.S. Foreign Policy: Shield of the Republic* (1943), Lippmann declared that it marked the end of his age of innocence. The book represented the distillation of his thought during the early war years, and emphasized his repudiation of Wilsonian principles in favor of new standards of realism. Twentieth-century America, Lippmann complained, had failed to base its policy upon the national interest and to recognize that commitments must be balanced with power. Policy-makers had subverted the national interest to idealism and, in so doing, had lost sight of the nation's needs. Wilson, for example, in offering moral and legal reasons for entering World War I, had misled the nation and failed to explain that America had gone to war not to preserve democracy elsewhere but to stop Germany and defend Britain in order to protect American security. Policy-makers should be "enlightened nationalists"; because he believed in American innocence, for Lippmann power politics in the service of the American national interest, and thus national security, became moral acts. In turn, in what seemed a blanket assault on Wilsonian idealism, he warned against building a foreign policy on an "abstract theory of our rights and duties"—that was like "building castles in the air." [3]

The American people would not defend such policies Lippmann warned, and the "acid" test of a foreign policy was whether it could unite the American people. The national interest, then, was a geopolitical matter which also took account of popular attitudes toward foreign peoples and recognized as acceptable commitments the protection of nations which the American people wished to support. By the logic of Lippmann's analysis (which he did not then pursue), policy-makers should act upon American idealism if it was rooted in deeply held popular attitudes, but not if it simply rested upon "abstract theories of rights and duties." Put bluntly, idealism, if widely accepted, was a basis for sound policy; ideal-ism, if not widely accepted, was a basis for error, perhaps tragedy. [4]

In his first sustained effort to formulate a design for the postwar world, Lippmann built his conception on a continuation of the wartime alliance: the three great powers—the United States, Great Britain, and the Soviet Union—would enforce the peace and guar-antee that Germany and Japan would not disrupt the postwar world. An Anglo-American alliance, based upon "complementary and inseparable" interests and a similar culture, was at the core of his design for this new world order and essential to the protection of American interests in both the Atlantic and the Pacific. Linked to this alliance would be the many countries within the geopolitically defined "Atlantic Community"—the other American nations and the Western European states, as well as their overseas empires. [5]

In examining Soviet-American affairs, Lippmann found historical evidence to indicate that national interest, not ideology, which he casually distinguished, might shape relations. Both powers, he con-tended, had a "common interest in a European settlement which will maintain itself without bringing them into conflict." The prob-lem, he shrewdly foresaw, would be the borderland between the Atlantic Community and Russia—Finland, Sweden, Poland, the Danube Valley, the Balkans, Turkey, and Germany—where the United States was weakest and Russia strongest. Because this area was beyond effective American military power, any attempt to re-create a *cordon sanitaire* was doomed to failure: Russia could break through it and the United States could not defend it. The only hope for Poland, the Balkans, and the Danubian states was the chance that the Soviet Union would allow them to be neutralized from power politics. In this way they would be secure, Lippmann reasoned, and the Soviet Union would be protected against their becoming "spearheads of a western coalition." But if the Russians were to menace the "national liberties" of her neighbors, he pre-dicted that Britain and the U.S. would regard the action as a threat and encourage resistance. The Soviets could not establish a sphere of influence, he argued, because it would overlap British inter-ests; the idea of overlapping spheres was impractical and self-contradictory.[6]

While seeking to minimize ideological differences, Lippmann had in fact subtly intruded an ideological standard for judging Russian behavior: the preservation of "national liberties." Unless the great powers maintained "liberty through law" and respected the liberties of other peoples, the alliance would crumble. As was so often the case, Lippmann sought to rest his idealistic conclusions on a prag-matic base and to identify what he and American policy-makers desired with what was necessary. Rather than questioning whether preservation of these "liberties" was in America's national interest, Lippmann had accepted Western demands, not Soviet fears, as the primary basis for defining a policy in Eastern Europe. His analysis relied upon a double standard that he would later repudiate: his strictures against Soviet control in Eastern Europe were unmatched by similar strictures about United States power in Latin America. In 1943 he was unwilling to acknowledge that this American sphere of influence existed, perhaps partly because he neglected the entire issue of noncolonial imperialism. He also ignored rivalries for markets and raw materials, or the struggle for competing visions of the world economic order. Even his definition of America's vital interests disregarded the needs of her economy, and therefore neg-lected questions of Soviet-American—as well as Anglo-American

—conflict on these matters. So numerous were the defects of his analysis that his hope of a continuing alliance with the Soviet Union seemed unduly optimistic, for it rested upon conditions which required far more of the Soviets than of the United States.[7]

II

A year later, in *U.S. War Aims,* a sequel to *U.S. Foreign Policy,* Lippmann modified and extended this marred analysis. He outlined a system of regional alliances that would rely upon power politics and ultimately, in some vague way, would be transformed into the world order he desired. By subordinating the foreign policy (but not internal policy) of the small states to that of the large powers, he aimed to avoid the shifting alliances that disrupted international affairs and led to dangerous rivalry between power blocs. Lippmann therefore retreated from his earlier call for neutrality of the Balkans and placed them within a Soviet-dominated regional alliance, where he hoped that "non-aggression, co-operation, and good will would prevail." Implicitly he thus accepted spheres of influence, and predicted that world peace could be achieved only if each of the great powers stayed in its own orbit and all reached a settlement on Japan and Germany.[8]

Reversing Wilsonian practice, Lippmann placed little faith in a world organization to keep the peace. Great powers, rather than entrusting their security or vital interests to the collective security of the United Nations, should rely "first upon . . . armed power and national strength, then upon . . . natural allies, and then upon a world organization." Alliances and peace treaties ought to create the conditions for peace. Put bluntly, the great powers must recognize vital interests, allow mutual accommodations, and thereby prevent future wars. The world organization could not "police the policemen," but it could contribute to the definition of world law and thereby help to define a desirable world order.[9]

Focusing on relations between the United States and the Soviet Union, Lippmann explained that the two different philosophical systems could not hope to trust each other until they endorsed the same "standards of value": liberal democratic principles. Harmonious relations awaited the creation of "basic political and human liberties" in the Soviet Union. "Only then will there be full confidence and a free intercourse on the basis of full equality. For between states that do have free institutions and those that do not . . . , international relations must necessarily be special and restricted." Guided by this principle, Lippmann found some evidence for optimism in Russia's recent behavior: during the war, Stalin affirmed democratic principles in dealing with his neighbors within the Russian orbit. Lippmann also hoped that Russia would implement the democratic constitution of 1936.[10]

He was correct that a different Soviet policy would have allayed Western fears in the postwar years. But had he not been wedded to advancing Western values he might also have seen good reason for a change of attitude in the West, also a source of likely problems. Once again Lippmann had used a double standard. "It does not follow," explained Vera Dean, a political scientist, "that the United States can ask Russia to alter its way of life as the price of our collaboration. What if Russia turned the tables . . . ?" [11]

Lippmann's own conception of realism permitted, even encouraged, development of this ideological test. By his supple definition of the national interest, its primary component, national security, could mean more than physical protection; in this instance it also meant the preservation of values, ideals, and a way of life that in the case of America included the attempt to project democracy abroad. Rather than objecting to this impulse, as some of his strictures against Wilsonianism suggested, he ended by endorsing it. "This persistent evangel of America in the outer world . . . reflects the fact that no nation, and certainly not this nation, can endure in a politically alien and morally hostile environment; . . . [it] is a profound and abiding truth that a people which does not advance its faith has already begun to abandon it." The danger, he warned, was that American efforts to expand democracy should not exceed American resources. In his own terms he was calling not for a crusade for the impossible or the unlikely (which he always decried) but for the careful expenditure of energy to achieve the possible. In short, the effort to extend democracy was wise if it could be successful.[12]

Despite his disclaimers, Wilson's principles still dominated much of Lippmann's thought. Although he seemed to endorse a plurality of ideologies and forms of government, in calling for the "accept-ance and avowal of the same standards of value" he created a universal value: liberal democracy. "Only the inviolability of the human spirit can ever be the criterion," he explained. "Nothing else unites all men beneath their differences. The outward and visible sign of faith in this inviolability is, in the realm of politics, to guar-antee freedom of thought and expression, and thus found govern-ment upon the consent of the governed. When these guarantees are effective, a national state is affirming its adherence to the only con-ceivable standard of morals which can be universal. And without a universal standard of morals, a universal society does not exist." Already at work on *The Public Philosophy,* which he would not publish until 1955, Lippmann was basing his conclusion on the doctrine of natural law that he was to develop in that book.[13]

By his formulation of the issues in *U.S. War Aims,* Lippmann stressed the importance of the very ideological differences and ideal-istic aims he often sought to minimize in shaping a foreign policy for America. Yet, while he made a democratic Russia the *sine qua non* for *harmonious* relations between the two states, he still be-lieved that an undemocratic Russia and the United States could at least achieve a *modus vivendi:* not true collaboration but "compro-mises, bargains, specific agreements, only a diplomacy of checks and counter-checks." [14]

Unlike some advocates of realism who would use virtually un-limited power to serve the national interest, Lippmann was not an aggressive nationalist. To Europeans and Americans in the war years, he preached a genial realism—based upon a loosely defined national interest, regional alliances, the dominance of great powers, and continued armaments—which he hoped would bring peace. He opposed the visionaries—the prophets of world federation or of European federalism. On the important issue of Soviet-American relations, his analysis moved in two directions: in much of *U.S. War Aims* he did rely upon standards of liberal democracy, but else-where he also offered an alternative which demanded less of the Soviet Union. This alternative proposal minimized ideological dif-ferences and suggested that Soviet policy would be based upon her vital interests, not on an ideological impulse for expansion or spreading revolution. He denied that Soviet vital interests included the export of communist ideology and implied that he was willing, despite earlier calls for America's extending liberal democracy, to accept Soviet dominance in her orbit, even if it meant rejection of liberal democratic standards there. In this case the strategy of realism appeared to lead to the conclusion that America's vital interests were not endangered by Soviet control in Eastern Europe.

III

As the war moved toward a close, Lippmann began to focus on specific problems and sought to formulate policies consistent with his principle of regional defense systems. Because he was always primarily concerned about Europe and only occasionally interested in Asia, he emphasized the dispute over Eastern Europe and the need for a strengthened Atlantic community and a settlement on Germany. Watching American policy unfold, he slowly clarified his own position, particularly on Eastern Europe, and the conditions for a *modus vivendi* with the Soviet Union.

In the last months of Roosevelt's administration, Lippmann was optimistic that the great powers could reach a settlement. He endorsed Roosevelt's decision in October 1944 to let Stalin and Churchill divide Eastern Europe into spheres of influence. Appraising Yalta, Lippmann concluded that this conference, like those at Moscow and Teheran, showed that the military alliance was becoming the "core of a new international order." Roosevelt had abandoned the policy of postponing the settlement of political issues until after the war, Lippmann declared, and the Big Three had compromised to maintain unity: the Soviet Union had agreed to a reorganization of the Polish government and to free elections in that country; in turn, the United States had acceded to the Curzon line for the Soviet-Polish border and thereby wisely stopped encouraging the Polish government in exile to delay reconciliation with the Lublin government.[15]

In the late winter of 1945 Lippmann could not foresee that the Yalta agreement would founder in part on the very issues he had not comfortably and explicitly resolved: should the United States accept a permanent settlement that did not clearly contribute to the establishment of democracy in Eastern Europe? Because he believed that the reorganization of the Polish government would be followed by free elections, Lippmann was able to avoid this problem. In accepting a Soviet sphere in Eastern Europe, he had not given up the hope that this area would become democratic. Yet he wisely recognized that if democracy were established there it would be created, not restored. In his optimistic appraisal of Yalta, he also overlooked the joined issues of reparations from Germany and American aid to the Soviet Union—issues which Yalta had left unresolved and which would disrupt future Soviet-American relations.[16]

Shortly after Truman's accession to the presidency, as the hopes inspired by Yalta began to falter, several actions of the State Department distressed Lippmann and led him to criticize the administration for heavy-handed diplomacy and violation of the principles of great-power regional responsibility. In the dispute over reorganization of the Polish government, he pointed out correctly that there were "two interpretations" of this procedure in the Yalta agreement, and warned the United States not to force its own interpretation. (Privately, Admiral William Leahy, who had previously discussed the issue with Roosevelt, had also told Truman that the agreement "was susceptible of two interpretations." General George C. Marshall and Secretary of War Henry L. Stimson had supported a policy of caution, with Stimson observing "that the Russians perhaps were being more realistic than we . . . in regard to their own security.") Lippmann also opposed American tactics at the United Nations conference in San Francisco, where, he claimed, the U.S. eschewed diplomacy and shoved through the seating of Argentina—thereby repudiating Roosevelt's pledge to Stalin and embittering the Soviets. As the great power in the hemisphere, the United States, Lippmann concluded, should have restrained the Latin American nations and served as a mediator. Instead it was clear that the United Nations "will be dominated by the American republics with the help of British votes whenever the United States draws upon its political credit in the British countries." At San Francisco, according to Lippmann, the United States, without any vital interests at issue with Russia, unwisely abandoned its earlier role under Roosevelt of "mediator and

stabilizer" between Britain and Russia. For Lippmann, the United
States could serve both as a "mediator" between the other two
great powers and as a close ally of Britain in the Atlantic community; the primary interests of the Atlantic community were not
incompatible with those of the Soviet Union.[17]

Often he warned the State Department that it was confusing priorities: it should not concentrate its efforts on Eastern Europe,
which was beyond the vital interests and effective power of the
United States. "No nation, however strong," Lippmann wrote, "has
the universal world power which reaches everywhere. The realm
in which each state has the determining influence is limited by
geography and circumstances. Beyond that realm it is possible to
bargain and persuade but not to compel, and no foreign policy
is well conducted which does not recognize these invisible realities." The United States ought to concentrate on a settlement in
Germany and on the creation of harmony in the Atlantic community.[18]

When the London conference of foreign ministers failed in September 1945, Lippmann explained that specific agreements were
impossible until the great powers decided "how far and for what
purpose each of the leading nations is to exert influence beyond its
own borders." His own solution, recognizing the limitations of
American power, included regional alliances and spheres of influence. Looking at the expansion of Soviet influence to the Oder
in Europe and American influence to Okinawa and Saipan in Asia,
he emphasized that "no power . . . on earth could compel either
the Soviet Union or the United States to draw back from their new
military frontiers." He warned repeatedly that the United States
could not continue to operate on a double standard: it could not
demand unilateral authority in its own sphere of influence and deny
the Soviets the same authority in theirs. "We cannot, for example,
declare as we have . . . [in Japan] that 'in the event of any differences among the principal Allied Powers the policies of the United
States will govern,' and then expect to persuade Mr. Molotov that
it is wrong for the Soviet Union to act 'unilaterally' in Rumania
and Bulgaria." [19]

For the State Department, Lippmann thought, the crucial issue
in Eastern Europe was whether the area was being organized "for

the defense of Soviet security or for the expansion of the Soviet power." Free elections and civil liberties thus became overriding issues. But to the Soviet Union this emphasis "appears as British-American protection of those East European and Balkan factions which are hostile to the Soviet Union . . . [and likely to] become the political spearheads of all the anti-Soviet forces of the western world." Because Eastern Europe was essential to Soviet security, the Russians wanted to know whether American interest in the Soviet orbit was a "cover" for Western intervention. They were beginning to fear that the United States "is drifting, or perhaps deliberately moving toward becoming the center of an anti-Soviet coalition." [20]

Such fears and anxieties, Lippmann concluded, could only be allayed by a direct and frank discussion of intentions. Otherwise the great powers would simply blunder into conflict. Undoubtedly he based his optimism on the belief that each power would follow its realistic interests (as he had defined them), and therefore would understand that there was no reason for conflict.[21]

In effect, Lippmann counseled the State Department to accept the *fait accompli*—Soviet authority in Eastern Europe, even in the internal affairs of the various states. Though the Soviet Union would not generally permit in Eastern Europe conditions that conformed to Western ideals, Stalin was pursuing a cautious policy and seeking accommodation with the West. He was willing to permit capitalism but was suspicious of American efforts at economic penetration which might lead to political dominance. The Soviets had allowed free elections in Hungary, where the Communist party was defeated, and in Bulgaria, where, despite American protests, a single ticket (representing most of the parties) had triumphed. Eastern European governments were subservient to the Soviet Union in foreign policy, but they varied in form and in degree of independence—democracy in Czechoslovakia (the only country in the area with a democratic tradition), free elections and the overthrow of the Communist party in Hungary, a Communist-formed coalition government in Poland, and a Soviet-imposed government in Rumania (the most anticommunist of these nations). In 1945, then, the pattern in Eastern Europe indicated that nations within the Soviet orbit could enjoy a

degree of independence in their domestic policies as long as Russia
could be sure that anti-Soviet forces would not move into positions
of power and thereby threaten Soviet security.[22]

Contrary to Lippmann's analysis, American policy-makers generally did not fear Soviet military expansion. Their main efforts
were toward rolling back Soviet influence and repudiating the agreement on spheres of influence—established by agreement between
Stalin and Churchill and ratified at Yalta and by the armistice
agreements on the Balkans—which conceded Eastern Europe to
the Soviets. Had Lippmann not defined vital interests so narrowly
at this time, he would have understood that at the root of the
emerging conflict was the American view that the future of Eastern
Europe affected the national interest. He did not understand that
policy-makers, in trying to pry the Eastern bloc away from the
Soviets, were operating within an implicit "ideology" to promote a
special conception of the national interest: American democracy
and prosperity at home depended upon an expanding world economy and the extension of democracy abroad. In short, the "open
door" was economically and politically essential to America's welfare. Like Henry Wallace, Lippmann criticized only tactics, not
"ideology"; but unlike Wallace, who was more in bondage to this
"ideology" and unable to accept the closed economic "door" along
with the political one, Lippmann could countenance a Soviet economic *and* political sphere in Eastern Europe.[23]

Troubled that the Truman administration was being diverted
from such paramount issues as Germany and the building of the
Atlantic community, he charged that it was not in control of its
policy. One group, for example, was making policy for Japan and
China, and another for Eastern Europe; sometimes contradictory
decisions were pushing the United States into an armaments race;
American policy-makers, he still believed, were innocently caught
in the "whip saw" between Russian and British imperialism and
could not understand that the United States must remain a mediator, not an adversary, in that conflict.[24]

By late November 1945, as he watched the policy of "drift,"
Lippmann revealed for the first time his long-time doubt of achieving harmonious cooperation with the Soviet Union. But he thought
"an accommodation, a *modus vivendi*" was still possible. The
cultural division between Russia and the West, stretching back

nearly a thousand years, was "too old and too deep" for intimate
cooperation, but not for agreement. "The right course is not to
assume that this is 'one world' nor yet to believe that this division
. . . means inevitable and moral conflict: the right course is to seek
a *modus vivendi* by which the Russians and ourselves, neither fearing they are predestined enemies nor believing they are members
of a single society, are able to live and let live by practical adjust-
ments around the edge where their power and influence meet." [25]

In line with this analysis, Lippmann soon noted with approval
that the United States and Russia had agreed in December at the
Moscow meeting of foreign ministers to recognize their respective
spheres of influence (primary but not exclusive power) in North-
east Asia and Eastern Europe. The United States had wisely given
up in the short run the hope that liberal, democratic capitalism
could be established in Eastern Europe; the Soviets had recognized
that Japan, China, and South Korea were within the military orbit
of the United States; and the United States had accepted Soviet
control of Manchuria and North Korea. Believing wrongly that the
two powers had resolved the major issues threatening a *modus
vivendi,* Lippmann looked forward to U.S. efforts to help Great
Britain, France, and the Soviet Union in reaching agreements on
Germany, the Mediterranean, and the Middle East.[26]

IV

Early in 1946 Lippmann's cautious optimism briefly collapsed. Like
many in Washington, he was alarmed by Stalin's speech of February
9, which predicted future wars between capitalist powers and called
for a Five-Year Plan of industrial and military expansion. (Privately,
Justice William O. Douglas called it "The Declaration of World
War III," and Secretary of the Navy James Forrestal seized upon it
as confirmation of the Soviet "menace.") Lippmann concluded that
the Soviet Union had defined its "central purpose" as the development of military strength, not improvement of its domestic standard
of living. He advised that the United States must rebuild the industrial plant of Western Europe and at the same time develop
Asia in order to compete militarily with the Soviet Union in ten
or fifteen years.[27]

Stressing British weakness in the Mediterranean and fearing Russian designs in Greece, Turkey, Iran, and Tripoltania, he counseled the United States to resist Soviet efforts to become a rival sea power and thereby a direct threat to America's vital interests. The Soviet Union was already a great land power; if it also gained strength at sea, the balance of power in the world would be seriously upset. For Lippmann it was not a matter of backing up British imperialism but rather of asserting America's independent interests in the Mediterranean, which included maintaining the balance of power there and retaining access to Middle East oil. Still hopeful of a settlement, he suggested a discussion of naval armaments with the Russians. They were the "real issues," of which the disputes over Trieste, the Italian Colonies, Greece, and the Dodacanese Islands were only the manifestations. It was not communism but Soviet power that Lippmann sought to restrain, and it was not democracy or liberty abroad but American security (narrowly defined) that he sought to protect.[28]

A year before the global crusade of the Truman Doctrine, Lippmann warned repeatedly that America would be squandering its limited resources if it sought to check Soviet pressure *at every point* by "underwriting" all nations who opposed it. Such a policy would also entangle the United States with "reactionary and obsolete forces." Instead of a global policy, he outlined a strategy of focused resistance to the Soviets. To replace the weakened British in the Mediterranean, the United States should establish its own power there by reconstituting a Mediterranean fleet, then negotiate a settlement which would allow Soviet participation in control of the Dardanelles, make Trieste independent, and settle the problem of Greece. Recognizing Soviet concern about her security, he also granted to Russia "legitimate" but not exclusive interest in the Balkans, Turkey, and Iran. Lippmann's suggestions were broad rather than precise, but unlike the State Department he did not wish entirely to eliminate Soviet influence in the Mediterranean. Indeed, his strategy was devised to maintain the balance of power there while pushing for a settlement in Europe.[29]

The painful alternative to a settlement, he warned, was the Anglo-American, anti-Soviet alliance that had been proposed by Churchill at Fulton, Missouri, and temporarily rejected by the American people. Nevertheless, it might well become American policy at each of the trouble spots—in the Middle East, in Germany, and in China—if Russia made "collaboration so inordinately difficult that there is nothing to show for it but disappointment and frustration." Lippmann feared that the United States and Russia were at that dangerous "line where, though there is yet no formal diplomatic rupture, the process of diplomatic negotiations is believed in less and less seriously." With his faith still in diplomacy, he continued to call upon the American government to resist Soviet pressure by picking a point, preferably in the eastern Mediterranean, where a buildup of American power would lead to negotiations. In September he again explained, "We must want the discussion so much that we are willing to take the risk of acting to convince the Russians that their power and our power are in balance and at a point which is so vitally important that it is no longer possible to evade negotiation." Unlike other observers, Lippmann was not arguing that negotiations had to wait until America achieved superior power; he was not calling for "negotiations from strength," though he was opposing negotiations from weakness. The proper combination of power and diplomacy would improve, not impair, Soviet-American relations.[30]

In Eastern Europe, however, Lippmann counseled not confrontation but caution. The United States was wrong in assuming that Russia's attempts to dominate its zone would succeed "unless we intervened ostentatiously to prevent them." In fact, Russia could not succeed, and so the United States was simply justifying Russia's own "dangerous measures in attempting to dominate." Using the case of Poland to demonstrate his point, Lippmann emphasized that, as long as tensions persisted between Russia and the West, any effort to raise to power a government beholden to the West would mean suppression of the Polish democracy. "The best way we can support the Polish democracy is not to intervene in Polish politics, not even by talking . . . about our interest in it at dinner tables . . . and [to] journalists." Later that year, in a shift of emphasis, he explained that the way to liberate Eastern Europe was not by focusing on that area but by starting to build a whole European system which Eastern Europe could join. He seemed to be reverting to the goals he had outlined in 1943 and 1944 and hoping that American policy might achieve at least the independence of Eastern Europe.[31]

At the heart of Lippmann's program was Germany. Ever since

the war years, when he had proposed a disarmed, unallied Germany integrated into the Atlantic community, he had insisted that a German settlement precede other agreements on a European peace: Germany was the key to the peace. In 1945 and 1946 he chided Secretary of State James F. Byrnes for neglecting this principle and for getting bogged down in "peripheral" matters, especially Eastern Europe. Great Britain and France, he had foreseen in 1945, must reach agreement on the western frontier of Germany and also resolve their differences on Germany's postwar strength. While the Western allies were still divided on such matters as the Rhineland, the Saar, and the Ruhr, Lippmann thought (incorrectly) that the Russians had clear policies for Germany.[32]

During the spring and summer of 1946 Lippmann began to move publicly to formulate a solution to the German problem. First he proposed a plan for the political reconstruction of all of Germany—but one which the Western powers could, if necessary, initiate without Russian participation. The plan called for a federal union in which the states, not the weak central government, would have most of the power. Rather than seeking to maintain a low level of German industry according to the Potsdam agreement, thus depriving other European nations of needed goods, Lippmann's plan allowed full production but kept powerful industries outside the control of the central government. Such an arrangement would keep the industrial Ruhr, for example, under local authority and thereby meet many of the demands of the French, who, like the Soviets, feared the revival of a powerful Germany and its heavy industry. Lippmann, without proposing specific tactics, called upon Secretary Byrnes to "induce" France and Britain to reconcile their differences and accept this plan.[33]

Although these measures would integrate Germany into the Western European economy and thereby advance European unity, Lippmann emphasized that he was not calling for a Western bloc against the Soviet Union. The Soviets could always bring their zone into the new Germany. A settlement in nearly two-thirds of Germany would "act as a powerful lever" on the Soviet portion. "Not to participate in the control of this state would be to cede to the western powers the hegemony of the strongest and richest part of the whole European continent," and that the Russians could not afford. What Lippmann failed to see was that Western hegemony would not be significantly altered if the Soviets allowed their zone to participate on the terms he had outlined. Contrary to his expectations, Soviet influence would probably have been inadequate to keep Germany out of the Atlantic community.[34]

In July 1946 Lippmann saw "plenty of signs, not all a product of . . . [unfounded Soviet] suspicions, that the British, with the Americans following, were . . . toying with the idea of controlling Germany to use . . . against Russia." Perhaps, he suggested, this explained why the Soviets had abruptly reversed their expressed policy favoring a weak economy in Germany; now they condemned the West for seeking pastoralization of the economy and dismemberment of the defeated nation. Lippmann feared that the Soviets actually were appealing to German nationalists by promising a Russian-German alliance and the restoration to Germany of her lost eastern provinces, then in the possession of Poland. In effect, he suggested, the Soviets were once more proposing an alliance with Germany for the partitioning of Poland. The Soviet Union was making Germany, rather than the nations of Eastern Europe, the "pivot of her policy." [35]

Two months later, Secretary Byrnes sought to regain German support by outlining a program for German unity. Calling for expanded economic production and economic unity under the four occupying powers, he also held out the hope ultimately of political unification, including restoration of the Rhine and Ruhr, which were in Western zones, and of the eastern territory occupied by Poland. Lippmann chided Byrnes for three errors: first, for promising the Germans the eastern provinces, which the West did not control, and thereby playing into Soviet hands by stressing that only the Soviets, not the West, could restore this area; second, for promising to return the Rhine and Ruhr to a central German government, not a federal government, and thereby yielding his advantage to German nationalists without adequate concessions on the future of Germany; third, for assuming that the economy could be safely reorganized without placing the German states in a decentralized, federal structure. According to Lippmann, Byrnes was only making a Soviet-German alliance more attractive to the Germans, for the Soviets, not the West, withheld what the German nationalists still wanted. Moreover, Lippmann warned, a centralized government was more susceptible to control by the Communist party and more likely to move into partnership with the Soviet Union. Throughout his entire analysis of the German "problem," Lippmann never lost sight of one dominant principle: a united and centralized Germany would be a menace to Europe, to the Soviet Union, and ultimately to the United States.[36]

Unlike the problem of Germany, the subject of international control of atomic energy only occasionally attracted Lippmann's interest. Shortly after Hiroshima he had briefly feared an arms race and warned against using the bomb as a diplomatic weapon. Policymakers, he believed, did not understand the "grave political importance" of the bomb. Apparently he did not know that Secretary Byrnes had already tried to use atomic diplomacy to frighten the Soviets out of Eastern Europe, and that Byrnes hoped to delay negotiations on the international control of atomic energy until he could secure the peace he wanted. Lippmann did suspect, however, that the United States and Britain "have not been acting as trustees of this great weapon, but have been disposed to regard it as a military asset to be used in weighing the balance of power decidedly in their favor." [37]

His fears were partially allayed by the American promise in November 1945 to make available to all nations "the basic scientific information essential to the development of atomic energy for peaceful purposes." Lippmann went further to propose that the secret of the bomb be made public, so that scientists could detect efforts to develop atomic energy for military purposes. His loosely wrought plan, based upon notions then current in America's scientific community, assumed that scientists would serve as agents of peace and report evidence of violations. His plan did not require inspections or open access to the world's laboratories, for a nation —the Soviet Union, for example—would have difficulty isolating its scientists and concealing their work if knowledge of the bomb was widely shared.[38]

In the summer of 1946, when the Baruch plan for control of atomic weapons was before the United Nations, Lippmann briefly commented upon the tangled issues in dispute. The United States wished to abolish the veto in the Security Council on issues of atomic energy so that the Soviet Union would not be able to block sanctions. But Lippmann supported the Soviet position on retaining the veto, correctly pointing out that America's plan, by its series of stages, guaranteed an American atomic monopoly until the final stage of control, and in effect gave the United States a veto by permitting withdrawal from the plan. There was, moreover, no need to worry about a formal veto on punishment of violators, Lippmann explained, for the ultimate sanction (war) would be determined by independent nations and not by the UN. Privately he complained that the Baruch plan "has not only aroused the Russians, more than is necessary, but . . . has hardened American opinion behind ideas that really, at bottom, make no sense." [39]

Assessing the Soviet plan, Lippmann was at first optimistic that the two nations could agree; but he stressed that the Soviets, by calling for nuclear disarmament and disclosure of information *before* the establishment of controls, failed to provide an effective guarantee against a nuclear arms race. When negotiations reached an impasse in the early autumn, he warned the United States not to push matters to a vote and force the Soviets into a defensive minority. The vote, he accurately foresaw, would be a hollow victory. Instead, obliquely criticizing Baruch, he called for an unspecified modification of the American proposal in order to gain Soviet approval. The alternative, he warned, was to accept the arms race and wait for the Soviets to get the bomb, for America's nuclear monopoly could not compel the Soviets to accept the present United States plan.[40]

Lippmann's criticism and analysis, as far as they went, were astute. In failing to devise a clear alternative to the Baruch plan, he stumbled on the very problem that troubled some other critics of American policy. Perhaps the United States should have gambled and moved boldly to accept the Soviet plan, despite the absence of an agreement on controls. At worst, even if the Soviets did not later offer such an agreement, the U.S. would have forfeited its nuclear monopoly for only about two or three years before the Soviets were expected to (and did) develop the weapon. At best, a positive American response would have ended the stalemate and moved the nations toward accommodation. But such a bold policy was politically impossible for the Truman administration, for the Republicans

would have charged "sell-out" and citizens would have feared betrayal. Moreover, the administration would have been compelled to
abandon its hopes of using the bomb to secure diplomatic victories,
and thus might also have forced it to rebuild its armies—which had
been recently demobilized partly because the atomic monopoly had
seemed to make them less important.[41]

Analyzing the strategic limitations of the bomb, Lippmann emphasized that it was not a *decisive* weapon. It could not *guarantee*
victory: it was of limited value in preventive war or even in halting Soviet expansion, once begun, into Western Europe. An American nuclear attack against a large nation like the Soviet Union
could not be decisive because, among other factors, the Soviets had
a widely dispersed population and industry. In addition, the Soviets,
if attacked, could always retaliate by sending their soldiers into the
West. "Against the Red Army in Europe it would be impossible to
use the atomic bomb without exterminating hundreds, perhaps
thousands, of Europeans for every soldier killed." Europe would
become a fortress for Soviet armies.[42]

In the autumn of 1946, as the impasse on atomic energy continued and Lippmann called for an American demonstration of
naval power in the Mediterranean, he came around to the view
that the United States needed the bomb to offset Soviet land armies.
His strategic analysis, though fragmentary, seemed to rest not upon
the possibilities of preventive war or of halting aggression once begun, but rather of deterring the *initiation* of Soviet aggression: the
U.S. could threaten serious retaliation at the Soviet heartland.
Therefore, recognizing that atomic talks had failed, he reversed his
earlier position of seeking a separate agreement on atomic energy
and counseled that the United States should yield its nuclear monopoly *only* as part of a general postwar settlement. If the Soviet
government claimed that the U.S. was using its temporary monopoly
to exert pressure for a settlement, he recommended that the United
States reply that "it is a sensible, civilized, and wholly necessary
thing for us to do." Always a proponent of power politics and
armed preparedness, Lippmann now endorsed a moderate form of
atomic diplomacy. He concluded, without adequate evidence, that
the Soviets were not intimidated by America's nuclear monopoly,
for "they know we shall not use . . . [the bomb] against them unless

they do what they do not intend to do—precipitate a general war."
He did not spell out his meaning, but he seemed to imply that the
Soviet Union did not intend to expand militarily into Western
Europe. He did not see that, by the logic of his strategic analysis
and his diplomatic prescription, the Soviets should tighten their
grip on Eastern Europe in order to maintain distant military frontiers and make it easier to launch armies into Western Europe—this
capability being the most effective deterrent against an American-
directed preventive war.[43]

V

As hopes for a Soviet-American settlement waned, the American
government, when informed in February 1947 that Great Britain
could no longer bear the financial burdens of a stewardship in
Greece and Turkey, decided to provide large doses of economic
and military aid to these beleaguered nations. On March 12, 1947,
President Truman appeared before Congress to request assistance
for these nations and to offer a global promise: "It must be the
policy of the United States to support free peoples who are resisting
attempted subjugation by armed minorities or by outside pressures." [44]

Lippmann, long an advocate of containing Soviet expansion by
concentrating power and influence at "key points" such as Germany, Western Europe, and Turkey, promptly opposed both Truman's tactics and strategy. Shortly before the Truman Doctrine
speech, Lippmann had proposed an alternative policy of power
politics which focused directly on Turkey as the strategically key
country in the Middle East: economic aid and a military guarantee
of security under Article 51 of the UN charter. This would provide adequate protection, allow demobilization of much of Turkey's
costly army, and permit a concentration of resources on economic
recovery. The specific guarantee would not expand American commitments, Lippmann contended, only make them more explicit.
Greece, in contrast, was on the periphery: as a "rear area" to the
Middle East, Greece could be defended from Turkey and therefore
did not warrant the same action. Instead the United States should
ask—first privately, then, if necessary, in the UN—the Soviet

Union to halt Tito's aid to the guerrillas and thereby "act as guardian of the peace in her own sphere of influence." It was a policy of risk, he acknowledged, but better than being entangled in a Balkan war or subsidizing a questionable government and squandering American power without effectively restraining Soviet expansion.[45]

After Truman's speech, Lippmann endorsed aid to Turkey and Greece, but he regretted that the United States had not addressed the Soviet Union directly. He called for a declaration that America wanted a Turkish-Soviet agreement "negotiated and not imposed by force." In the case of Greece, he wanted the United States to declare that the seizure of power by a "Greek Tito" would bring an American military response, including possibly a blockade or the amputation of the Peloponnesus and Greek islands from the Greek government. After such declarations, the United States, he thought, could demand that the civil strife in Greece be settled by political, not military, means. For Lippmann, Truman's major mistake was that he had initiated a crusade for democracy, not a limited defensive action for American security. In place of Truman's global crusade Lippmann favored a controlled policy, a specific Mediterranean strategy which avoided the risks of squandering prestige and power and allowed the United States to concentrate on strengthening Western Europe.[46]

In September he continued this analysis in a penetrating and important critique of George F. Kennan's influential essay on "The Sources of Soviet Conduct." Kennan, also a realist, was then head of the State Department's Policy Planning Staff. His essay, published anonymously in *Foreign Affairs* under the name "Mr. X," was widely regarded as the rationale for the Truman Doctrine and the most complete statement of American foreign policy. Lippmann agreed with Kennan that Soviet power would expand unless it was confronted by American power, but he objected on pragmatic grounds to Kennan's plan for the next ten or fifteen years: resistance with "counterforce" *wherever* the Soviets threatened, until the pressure caused the collapse of the Soviet system.[47]

For Lippmann, Kennan's proposal was unworkable and dangerous; indeed, it was a "strategic monstrosity." It rested, by Kennan's own admission, on the unproven, optimistic assumption that "Soviet power . . . bears within itself the seeds of decay," and that pressure on Soviet society might cause it to collapse. Rejecting a policy that offered success by "hoping for the best," Lippmann contended that strategy must be based upon the "worst and hardest" case. The United States lacked the resources for Kennan's open-ended policy: America had neither the efficiency, the patience, the economic strength, nor the armed forces to contain the Soviet Union *wherever* it showed signs of encroaching and *until* it collapsed. Nor could the United States afford to yield the military initiative to the Soviets who could choose the area—usually closer to Soviet strength—for confrontation. In short, American sea and air power could redress the balance of power but not for a strategy of "containing, waiting, countering, blocking, with no more specific objective than the eventual 'frustration' of the opponent." Americans, Lippmann feared, might well become frustrated by this policy long before the Russians.[48]

Lippmann found other serious defects in Kennan's program. If it were followed, Lippmann complained, the United States would have to recruit and organize a "heterogeneous array of satellites, clients, dependents, and puppets" to make up for its inadequate military strength. Such a coalition of weak allies would be most difficult to establish and maintain, and easy for the Soviet Union to disrupt. And these client states, as Lippmann wisely foresaw, might act on their own judgment or initiative and confront the United States with *faits accomplis,* thereby compelling the United States to disown them, "which would be tantamount to appeasement and defeat and loss of face, or . . . support them at an incalculable cost" in unforeseen ventures. Even worse, Kennan's policy, in seeking to make "unassailable barriers" out of the states bordering the Soviet Union, required an unnatural alliance of weak states in an area of great Soviet, not Western, strength. The United States, Lippmann saw perceptively, was having enough trouble organizing the Atlantic community; how could it be more successful in the Soviet sphere? By conducting a campaign in these borderlands, the U.S. would continue foolishly to neglect its natural alliance with the Atlantic community and to threaten it with the specter of a Third World War. Caught between the Soviet Union and the United States, the other members of the Atlantic community would either retreat into isolation or seek to become mediators between the two great powers.[49]

On the grounds of efficiency and practicality, not ideology or morality, Lippmann shrewdly proposed different and more limited tactics for restraining the Soviet Union and achieving a settlement in Europe. Unlike Kennan, he did not find Soviet expansion irrational or ideological, but rather motivated by traditional Russian drives for long-coveted territory and now made possible by the Russian army. It was the army, not ideology, that gave the Soviets power within their sphere and also constituted a threat to Western Europe. Though he steadfastly opposed and wished to outlaw Communist parties in Western Europe, Lippmann stressed that alone they were not very dangerous—no more than a fifth column, unlikely to gain power without the aid of the Soviet army. The withdrawal of the Soviet army was the central issue. Lippmann lamented that the United States had conducted the wrong kind of campaign—on elections, forms of government, and ideology, instead of on the army—to liberate Eastern Europe from alien forces.[50]

He proposed a policy—known as "disengagement" when Kennan advocated it a decade later—for the withdrawal from continental Europe of the armies of the United States, the Soviet Union, and Great Britain. By means of peace treaties covering Germany and Austria and specifying the terms for ending the military occupation, Lippmann hoped to liberate Europe and move toward a *modus vivendi* with the Soviet Union. An agreement to evacuate armies, he explained, unlike promises of democracy or free elections, on which nations could disagree honestly, required a specific act on which there could be no disagreements, no quarrels over interpretation. Military evacuation from the continent would mean a "strategic change in the balance of power." Still convinced that American policy-makers feared Soviet military expansion into Western Europe, he pointed out that the withdrawal of the Soviet army would be the "acid test" of Soviet purpose. If the United States followed his policy, it could accurately assess Soviet intentions and probably succeed in liberating Europe. The price of Soviet withdrawal could be high, but success was worth the possible cost —American economic aid for the Soviet reconstruction program and security guarantees written into the German settlement. Even if the policy failed in the short run, it might succeed in the longer run: alien armies were sure to provoke hostility in occupied countries, and rising nationalism might ultimately compel the withdrawal of these armies. In the interim, American policy would no longer frighten allies. The United States would be the "champion of the vital interests of all the peoples of Europe." [51]

This was no crusade for democracy, Lippmann explained; he simply wanted the restoration of *independence* in Eastern Europe, which he had earlier granted to the Soviet sphere. By outlining a policy of negotiations looking forward to a settlement, he explicitly sought to reverse the Truman Doctrine, as well as Kennan's program. Unlike the Truman administration and Henry Wallace, he proposed to keep disruptive issues out of the United Nations. That fragile organization ought to be protected from "the burdens, the discredit, of having to deal with issues that it is not designed to deal with." (This he advised just six months after counseling policymakers to take to the Security Council the issue of Tito's assistance of the Greek guerrillas.) Lippmann was distressed to see that the British and American delegates, in discussing the Greek affair, "appear to be acting on instructions which treat the U.N. as expendable in our conflict with the Soviet Union." Because the containment policy looked forward to victory rather than settlement, some policy-makers, he wrote, had perhaps already concluded that the United Nations was purposeless: they would destroy the world organization either by casting it aside like the League or by transforming it into an anti-Soviet coalition.[52]

For Lippmann, the Truman Doctrine and Kennan's prescription represented the dangerous alternative to two mutually compatible policies which he saw struggling for survival within the State Department: support of the United Nations and what he called the "Marshall line," represented by the Marshall Plan. Unlike the Truman Doctrine, the Marshall Plan, Lippmann contended, avoided globalism, did not treat nations as "instruments" of American policy but as independent nations, and allowed the Europeans to save themselves. In his concern for the initiative and independence of nations in the Atlantic community, he departed from his wartime formulation of rules for regional alliances (subordination of the

small powers' foreign policy). European nationalism, he acknowledged, was a fact, and so was the growing desire of European
nations to shape their own future. The Marshall Plan was based
loosely upon Lippmann's own recommendations in the spring of
1947 that the United States should provide financial aid for
European reconstruction and also benefit its own economy by
creating new export markets. Then, as well as in the summer
after the Soviets had refused participation in the program, Lippmann believed that the Marshall Plan would ultimately end the
division of Europe by reviving east-west trade on the continent
and luring the satellites out of the Soviet orbit.[53]

In the long run, perhaps the Marshall Plan, and the economic
revival it created in Western Europe, did contribute to the establishment of better European relations. But in the short run Lippmann was quite wrong. American policy-makers had not expected
the Soviet Union to join the plan. They understood what Lippmann
did not: the Soviet Union would reject the plan because it required
disclosure of secret economic data, maintenance of Eastern Europe
as a subordinate agricultural area, penetration by Westerners of the
loosely bound Soviet sphere, and a decisive American voice in how
aid would be used. Rejecting any important distinction between
the Truman Doctrine and the Marshall Plan, President Truman
described both as "two halves of the same walnut." As policy-
makers expected, the Soviets feared that the United States was
trying to challenge the Soviet Union and also to impose economic
and political terms as conditions of aid.[54]

In some ways Soviet fears were identical to Lippmann's hopes:
the Marshall Plan might attract the satellite states to Western
Europe and thereby pressure the Soviets to relax their grip on Eastern Europe. As a champion of European unity, Lippmann sought
to use economic aid directly to achieve political goals, including
the breakdown of the Soviet bloc. He even suggested that the United
States might barter aid to Russia for an easing of political control
in Eastern Europe (a policy the United States had already tried—
without success—by suggesting a large loan to Russia). Yet, despite
his earlier warnings that the West must not seek power in the
Soviet orbit, he did not anticipate the Russian reaction to the Marshall Plan: fear and the hardening of policies in the Soviet sphere.[55]

Perhaps had Lippmann understood more fully the relationship

of politics and economics in international life, his analysis would not have been so flawed. He might have understood the Soviet argument that American aid meant control of Europe, not independence. Though he condemned Soviet imperialism, he did not believe that the United States sought economic dominance in the world, and therefore he was unable or unwilling to see that American economic power could mean the extension of American political authority into foreign lands.[56]

Throughout the war and postwar years, Lippmann had minimized the relationship of economics and politics in international affairs. But he agreed with American policy-makers that an expanding and relatively free trade was essential to the United States. Like them, he concluded that the American economy would be endangered by a contraction of trade or the rise of state-trading; the United States, as well as other nations, would then have to retreat from free enterprise to controlled economies. Unlike the policy-makers, however, Lippmann did not see depression, war, and the demise of American liberties flowing from a fettered trade. He believed that a relatively free trade in part of the world (sterling and dollar areas) was sufficient to maintain American free enterprise. In contrast, the State Department, especially in analyzing Europe, feared that a world economy half composed of state-trading would so disrupt markets that a catalog of atrocities—upset world trade patterns, contracting economies, state-trading, and the end of American free enterprise—could hardly be avoided.[57]

Largely because Lippmann's dissent from this analysis was so oblique, he could never understand why Byrnes concentrated on a settlement in Eastern Europe and focused upon free elections and the Open Door there. To Byrnes and other policy-makers, the closing of this sector of the world economy as well as the suppression of civil liberties there endangered the American system. Their "ideology," rooted in a specific conception of political economy, linked peace and prosperity with the Open Door and political liberties. Contrary to Lippmann's analysis, they were not acting in innocence but out of ideology. They were acting to promote the conditions they regarded as essential to the national interest. Where he differed from them was not on the need to pursue the national interest but on the very definition of that interest.[58]

Because he never understood their conception, Lippmann failed

to meet their argument on its own terms. Nor could he clearly
analyze American policy or offer to policy-makers an explicit alternative assumption: that American prosperity *and* democracy did
not depend upon an expanding economic system overseas; or at
least that the control of Eastern Europe by the Soviets did not
threaten these values in the United States. Because of his own
wavering concern about expanding American democracy, he could
not consistently agree that the political restrictions in the Soviet
sphere did not imperil the American political faith. Yet tucked
within his fragmentary analysis was the belief that the severance of
Eastern Europe from the international economy was of restricted
significance.[59]

VI

In this limited sense, then, Walter Lippmann challenged—but never
realized he was challenging—a central conception of American
practice and ideology: that Eastern Europe was vital to American
security and well-being. By his own analysis he believed he was
engaged in a more limited endeavor: correcting blunders, noting
inconsistencies, redefining priorities, questioning crusades, emphasizing the limitation of American resources, defining the national
interest—in short, offering realism as a guide to achieve accommodation with the Soviet Union.

Only in limited ways did Lippmann offer alternatives to American Cold War policies. Despite his call for democracy in the Soviet
Union and her orbit, he had also proposed in 1944 a less am-
bitious and demanding test for a Soviet-American *modus vivendi*.
In 1945, when the United States sought to liberate Eastern Europe
with "atomic diplomacy," Lippmann subtly warned policy-makers
against using the bomb as a diplomatic weapon, pointed to the
sham of America's double standards on spheres of influence, and
opposed a major effort to roll back the Soviet Union from this area.
Repeatedly he warned that the Soviets had justifiable worries about
Eastern Europe, and he emphasized that American policy increased
Russian fears that the U.S. was seeking to restore a *cordon sanitaire* and to back anti-Soviet, even fascist, groups on Soviet borders.
American policies, he concluded, were likely to provoke antago-

nism without achieving success. Had American policy-makers followed Lippmann's advice they might well have avoided pushing the Soviets into a hardening of their policies in Eastern Europe in 1947. For those who look back upon the origins of the Cold War, the disputes over Eastern Europe loom large, and the alternative tactics proposed by Lippmann in 1945 (but not the Marshall Plan in 1947) would certainly have reduced Soviet-American antagonisms and perhaps salvaged some independence for the Eastern European states.[60]

Lippmann saw clearly that Germany was the key to a settlement in Europe. Perhaps his proposal for a disarmed, decentralized Germany oriented economically to the Atlantic community was too unfavorable to the Soviet Union to win acceptance, but he was correct in calling upon the United States to focus on this problem and in emphasizing the danger of a united, centralized Germany.

In the Mediterranean he was more sympathetic than American policy-makers to Russia's attempts to increase its influence, but he did counsel the United States to intervene on grounds of national security to halt the extension of Soviet power in some key situations. Explicitly he admonished policy-makers for conducting a crusade for democracy when only the balance of power was a matter of vital interest to the United States.

In dealing with the tangled issues of international control of atomic energy, Lippmann often displayed shrewd intelligence. As he struggled to raise the understanding of policy-makers on this critical subject, his analysis of the strategic limitations and possibilities of the atomic bomb was penetrating. Unlike most American observers, he saw many weaknesses in the Baruch plan for international control and he wisely criticized its emphasis on sanctions and suspension of the veto. At crucial junctures he also warned the United States against forcing issues to a vote and pushing the Russians into a corner. When many despaired of a Soviet-American agreement on international control, he still briefly retained hope and proposed that the United States modify its position.

Even though his alternative to containment included support for the Marshall Plan—which he did not expect to harden Soviet policies in Eastern Europe—his analysis of America's flawed tactics was masterful and his proposal of disengagement was bold. He understood the dangers of alliances with "puppets," the perils of overcommitting American power, the likelihood of national frustration with containment, and European fears of being trapped in a Soviet-American war. In focusing on the withdrawal of Soviet and allied armies from the continent, he grasped the central issue that could alter the balance of power and stabilize relations in Europe.

In the years of the early Cold War, Lippmann's realism, resting upon an elastic definition of the national interest, was so flexible that it accommodated widely varied, even contradictory, proposals within his own thought. Indeed, as a working guide, realism could sustain such a broad range of policies that its adherents could easily disagree. As a result, Lippmann was able to formulate policies that other realists, such as George Kennan and Dean Acheson, could neither share nor endorse. All were dedicated to pursuing the national interest, and all distrusted excessive moralism and crusades for democracy, though more of each crept into their analyses than any of them would care to admit. But Acheson could never accept the division of Eastern Europe, and neither he nor Kennan could retain a belief in the efficacy of diplomacy. In 1947, concluding his critique of Kennan's X-article and the Truman Doctrine, Lippmann wrote a strong rebuke that signifies much of the difference between him and these members of the State Department: "The history of diplomacy is the history of relations among rival powers, which did not enjoy political intimacy, and did not respond to appeals to common purposes. Nevertheless, there have been settlements. . . . For a diplomat to think that rival and unfriendly powers cannot be brought to a settlement is to forget what diplomacy is all about." [61]

By such counsel Lippmann kept alive the possibilities of a Soviet-American accommodation when many other critics of the Cold War were becoming suspect or marginal, if not discouraged. Unlike Henry Wallace, Vito Marcantonio, Claude Pepper, or Glen Taylor, for example, Lippmann was never shrill, never given to dramatics, never subject to vicious attacks. Unlike them, he was regarded as a gentleman and usually as a serious, constructive critic of American policy. Unlike I. F. Stone, for example, Lippmann had no difficulty finding publishers, no problems gaining the attention of America's educated citizenry and policy-makers. They never questioned his loyalty, and many were impressed by his wisdom and judgment, his penetrating criticism, and his keen sense of history. A moderate critic of the Cold War, Lippmann commanded respect for his intellect and experience, and for these reasons, among others, he sometimes compelled Americans to re-examine their understanding of Soviet-American relations and to entertain the possibility of different arrangements.

Notes

1. For studies of Walter Lippmann and foreign policy, see Marquis Childs and James Reston, eds., *Walter Lippmann and His Times* (New York, 1959), pp. 111–188; Francine C. Cary, *The Influence of War on Walter Lippmann, 1914–1944* (Madison, Wisc., 1967); Edward L. and Frederick H. Schapsmeier, *Walter Lippmann: Philosopher-Journalist* (Washington, D.C., 1969); Anwar Syed, *Walter Lippmann's Philosophy of International Politics* (Philadelphia, 1968); and Jeff Preefer, "Walter Lippmann and the Cold War" (unpublished manuscript, 1970). For harsh estimates of Lippmann's thought, see Fred Rodell, "Walter Lippmann," *American Mercury,* LX (March 1945), 263–273; and Amos Pinchot, "Obfuscator DeLuxe," *Nation,* CXXXVII (July 19, 1933), 67–70.

2. Ashmore, "Apostle of Excellence: The View from Afar," in Childs and Reston, eds., *Lippmann,* p. 157. For evidence of Lippmann's influence, see also Joseph Jones, *The Fifteen Weeks* (New York, 1955), pp. 226–229; James Forrestal to Walter Lippmann, January 7, 1946, Forrestal Papers, Princeton University; James Conant to Walter Lippmann, December 14, 1945, Conant Papers, Library of Congress; Chester I. Barnard to Walter Lippmann, June 20 and 24, 1946, David Lilienthal Papers, Princeton University; Henry L. Stimson to Lippmann, March 21, 1950, Stimson Papers, Yale University. On realism, see Robert Osgood, *Ideals and Self-Interest in America's Foreign Relations* (Chicago, 1953).

3. Walter Lippmann, *U.S. Foreign Policy: Shield of the Republic* (Boston, 1943), pp. 3–73 and quotations at p. 137. For a more astute view of Wilson, see N. Gordon Levin, *Woodrow Wilson and World Politics* (New York, 1968). For Lippmann's later views, see his *Isolation and Alliances: An American Speaks to the British* (Boston, 1952), pp. 10, 22–23.

4. *U.S. Foreign Policy,* pp. 81–86 and quotation at p. 81.

5. *U.S. Foreign Policy,* pp. 119–127, 161–177, and quotation at p. 124. He also anticipated the rise of China as a great power (pp. 155–160). See also Lippmann, "Can We Win the Peace?," *Ladies Home Journal,* LXI (January 1944), 22–23. "As for my use of the term 'alliance,' all I can say is that I deliberately chose the word which has the maximum resistance to the public mind, feeling that if I used some softer word I might be giving people a chance to evade what I think is the real issue." Lippmann to Sidney Fay, September 4, 1943, "Fan Letters," Lippmann Papers, Yale University.

6. *U.S. Foreign Policy*, pp. 138–154 and quotations at pp. 147 and 152.

7. *U.S. Foreign Policy*, pp. 169–173, 130, 124, 158, 44–45, and quotations at pp. 170–171. Also see Jacques Maritain to Lippmann, June 29, 1943, and reply, July 1, 1943, Lippmann Papers.

8. Walter Lippmann, *U.S. War Aims* (Boston, 1944), pp. 80–85, 91, 136–141. See also *Washington Post*, April 13, 1945.

9. *U.S. War Aims*, pp. 157–169 and quotation at p. 160.

10. *U.S. War Aims*, pp. 134–154 and quotation at p. 148. See also "U.S. War Aims" (draft), pp. 25–26, Lippmann Papers. For the views of another "realist," see Reinhold Niebuhr, "From Wilson to Roosevelt," *Christianity and Society*, VIII (Fall 1943), 3–5; and "Democratic Gods and World Order," *New Leader*, XXVII (September 23, 1944), 4–5.

11. Vera Dean, "Balances and Counter-Balances of Peace," *Saturday Review of Literature*, XXVII (July 8, 1944), 21. Speaking of Lippmann's plan, Senator Robert Taft declared, "It is in substance American imperialism." Speech, May 7, 1944, Taft Papers, Box 546, Library of Congress.

12. *U.S. War Aims*, pp. 33–40, 154, and quotation at p. 40.

13. *U.S. War Aims*, p. 52; Lippmann, *The Good Society* (Boston, 1943), pp. 344–351; and *The Public Philosophy* (Boston, 1955).

14. *U.S. War Aims*, pp. 132–142, 192–193, and quotation at p. 141. In 1943, Lippmann considered Wendell Willkie's *One World* and Joseph Davies' *Mission to Moscow* as the two finest analyses of the Soviet Union. See Paul Willen, "Who 'Collaborated' with Russia?," *Antioch Review*, XIV (Fall 1954), 272.

15. Walter Lippmann, "Today and Tomorrow," *Washington Post*, October 14, 1944; February 15 (quotation), and March 1 and 3, 1945. All columns are from the *Post* and hereafter are cited as "T&T," with the date of publication. Lippmann's columns, written for the *New York Herald-Tribune*, were widely syndicated and printed in the *Washington Post*, along with many other papers, on the same date they appeared in the *Herald-Tribune*.

16. "T&T," February 5, March 1 and 3, 1945. See Bernstein, "American Foreign Policy and the Origins of the Cold War," in Bernstein, ed., *Politics and Policies of the Truman Administration* (Chicago, 1970), pp. 21–32.

17. "T&T," April 28 (first quotation), May 3, 8, 12 (last quotation), 15, 1945. On Leahy, Leahy Diary, April 23, Leahy Papers, Library of Congress; on Stimson, paraphrase from Charles Bohlen's notes on meeting of April 23, Department of State, *Foreign Relations of the United States, 1945* (Washington, D.C., 1967), V, 254. See Bernstein, "Origins of the Cold War," pp. 25–31.

18. "T&T," May 8 (quotation), May 19, September 13, December 1, 1945.

19. "T&T," September 25 (quotations), September 27, and October 18, 1945.

20. "T&T," September 25, 1945. See also November 22 and 27, 1945.

21. "T&T," September 25, 1945.

22. Bernstein, "Origins of the Cold War," pp. 37–39.

23. *Ibid.*, pp. 18–39, 51–53, 58–60.

24. "T&T," October 30 and November 19 (quotation), 1945.

25. "T&T," November 27, 1945.

26. "T&T," December 29 and 18, and November 27, 1945.

27. "T&T," February 12 and 19, 1946. For Douglas, see Walter Millis, ed., *The Forrestal Diaries* (New York, 1955), p. 134. Stalin's speech is reprinted in J. P. Morray, *From Yalta to Disarmament: Cold War Debate* (New York, 1961), pp. 339–349.

28. "T&T," February 7, 14, and 26, 1946.

29. "T&T," February 26 and March 9, 1946 (quotations).

30. "T&T," March 9, 12 (first quotation), September 7, 1946 (second quotation).

31. "T&T," June 6, October 15, and November 21, 1946.

32. "T&T," December 1, February 17, and November 3, 1945; *U.S. War Aims,* pp. 115–120.

33. "T&T," June 6 and 8, February 19, May 18 and 23, and July 20, 1946 (quotation).

34. "T&T," June 8, 1946 (quotation); *U.S. War Aims,* p. 192.

35. "T&T," July 16 (first quotation), 8, and 20 (second quotation); Lippmann, *The Cold War: A Study in U.S. Foreign Policy* (New York, 1947), pp. 47–49.

36. "T&T," September 12, 14, 21, 1946; February 8, May 17, June 21, 1947; January 26, February 9, April 12, and May 11, 1948; *Cold War,* pp. 45–48. For another view, see Niebuhr, "The Fight for Germany," *Life,* XXI (October 21, 1946), 65–72. See also Lippmann to James Pollock, July 29, 1946, quoted in John Gimbel, *The American Occupation of Germany* (Stanford, 1968), p. 81. On Germany, see Gimbel, *American Occupation;* and Lloyd Gardner, "America and the German 'Problem,' 1945–1949," in Bernstein, ed., *Politics and Policies,* pp. 113–148. For Lippmann's later view, see *Isolation and Alliances,* pp. 51–54.

37. "T&T," October 2, November 1 and 17 (quotations). On Byrnes, see Stimson Diary, September 4, 1945; and Bernstein, "Origins of the Cold War," pp. 35–38.

38. "T&T," October 2, November 1 and 17, and December 11, 1945. On nuclear scientists, see Alice K. Smith, *A Peril and a Hope* (Chicago, 1965), pp. 253–342.

39. "T&T," June 18, 22, 25; Lippmann to Chester Barnard, June 28, 1946, Lilienthal Papers (quotation). See also Chester Barnard to Walter Lippmann, June 20 and 24, 1946, Lilienthal Papers. For earlier disagreements, see Bernard Baruch to Lippmann, November 8, 1945, and reply, November 10, 1945, Baruch Papers, Princeton University.

40. "T&T," July 6, September 28, and October 10, 1946. See also John McCloy to Lippmann, November 2, 1946, Stimson Papers; and Marshall MacDuffie, "Notes on a Discussion with Lippmann," December 23, 1946, MacDuffie Papers, Columbia University.

41. Estimates varied on when the Soviets would develop the weapon. Scientists believed four to five years, and Byrnes placed it at about seven years. (Franklin Lindsay to Bernard Baruch, September 12, 1946, Baruch Papers, Princeton University.) On difficulties with the GOP, see Richard Hewlett and Oscar E. Anderson, *The New World, 1939–1946* (University Park, Pa., 1962), pp. 475–477. For speculations on possibilities, see Lloyd Gardner, *Architects of Illusion: Men and Ideas in American Foreign Policy, 1941–1949* (Chicago, 1970), pp. 194–197; and Rosalind Navin Rosenberg, "Origins of American Foreign Policy on Atomic Energy" (unpublished manuscript, 1967).

42. "T&T," March 21, June 29 (quotation), October 2 and 10, 1946. See also P. M. S. Blackett, *Fear, War and the Bomb* (New York, 1949), pp. 80–83.

43. "T&T," September 19, November 30, and December 14, 1946; February 20, May 24 (quotation), December 4, 1947.

44. *Public Papers of the Presidents: Harry S. Truman, 1947* (Washington, D.C., 1963), pp. 178–179.

45. "T&T," March 6 (quotations) and 11, 1947. See also "T&T," January 1, 1948.

46. "T&T," March 15 (quotation), 18, 21, 25, and 29, 1947.

47. His columns of September 2–October 2, 1947, were reprinted in Lippmann, *The Cold War: A Study in U.S. Foreign Policy*. For Kennan, see "The Sources of Soviet Conduct," *Foreign Affairs*, XXV (July 1947), 566–582. In his *Memoirs, 1925–1950* (Boston, 1967), pp. 358–363, Kennan claims that he was not recommending military confrontations or alliances, but only economic assistance, when he used the term "counterforce." He also asserts that he was alarmed when he read Lippmann's critique of the X-article, for he realized that his own policy was being misunderstood and identified with the Truman Doctrine, which he had privately opposed on grounds similar to Lippmann's. For other views by Kennan on the impulse behind Soviet expansion, see *Memoirs*, pp. 531–582.

48. *Cold War*, pp. 9–20 and quotations at pp. 9 and 20.

49. *Ibid.*, pp. 20–31 and quotation at p. 23.

50. *Ibid.*, pp. 30–42; *U.S. War Aims*, p. 153; "T&T," November 22, 1945; June 4, 1946; February 2 and March 30, 1948.

51. *Cold War*, pp. 34–45 and quotations at p. 43. "T&T," March 20, 1947. David Horowitz, in *The Free World Colossus* (New York, 1965), pp. 243–258, is optimistic that Lippmann's proposal was a viable alternative to American policy and a likely route to a *modus vivendi*. On Kennan, see his *Russia, the Atom, and the West* (New York, 1957).

52. *Cold War*, pp. 44–59 and quotations at p. 59.

53. *Ibid.*, pp. 52–57 and quotation at p. 57; "T&T," March 20, April 5 and 17, May 1 and 13, January 21, November 11 and 13, 1947; June 6, 1946; February 16, 1948; Lippmann, "A Year of Peacemaking," *Atlantic Monthly*, CLXXVIII (December 1946), 38. For another view, see Lippmann, "The State of the World," *United Nations World* (May 1947), pp. 19, 80. For Lippmann's influence (and respect in Washington) on the formulation of the Marshall Plan, see Jones, *Fifteen Weeks*, pp. 227–232.

54. For policy-makers and the Marshall Plan, see Charles Bohlen, *The Transformation of American Foreign Policy* (New York, 1969), pp. 90–92; Thomas G. Paterson, "The Quest for Peace and Prosperity: International Trade, Communism, and the Marshall Plan," in Bernstein, ed., *Politics and Policies*, pp. 75–112. On Lippmann, see "T&T," June 3, 1947. Truman is quoted in Jones, *Fifteen Weeks*, p. 233.

55. "T&T," March 20, April 1 and 5, May 1, 10, and 29, June 10, 1947; March 15, 1948. *Cold War*, pp. 56–57; Bernstein, "Origins of the Cold War," pp. 52–53.

56. "T&T," May 23, 1946; April 19, 1945; November 25, December 23, 1947. In 1946 he granted the United States the right to "undisputed domination in Indonesia and Indo-China" (Lippmann, "Choice in the Pacific,"

Forum, CV [April 1946], 741–742). In early 1948 he opposed the plan that later developed into NATO, arguing that it "would divide and weaken, not strengthen and unify, Western Europe" ("T&T," January 22, 1948). For Lippmann's shifting views, see "T&T," March 22, April 15, May 4, and June 7, 1948; and *Isolation and Alliances,* pp. 45–46.

57. Most of his comments on economic policy were in reference to the British loan (October 4, November 6, December 8 and 15, 1945; February 12 and June 27, 1946); Lend-Lease (November 1, 1945); reciprocal trade (June 12, 1945); Bretton Woods (May 26, 1945); the Marshall Plan and the U.S. economy (May 13, March 20, June 12, and November 25, 1947); and aid to Russia and U.S. exports (May 12, 1945).

58. See Bernstein, "Origins of the Cold War," pp. 50–60.

59. Among "revisionist" historians of the Cold War, there is no agreement on whether this "ideology" was dysfunctional or an astute assessment of America's economic needs. See William Appleman Williams, *The Tragedy of American Diplomacy* (rev. ed., Cleveland, 1962); Gabriel Kolko, *The Politics of War* (New York, 1968) and *The Roots of American Foreign Policy* (Boston, 1969), ch. iii; Bernstein, "Origins of the Cold War," pp. 53–60, and "Our Empire's Roots," *Progressive,* XXXIV (June 1970), 45–48; Paterson, "Quest for Peace and Prosperity," pp. 1⌐2–104; and David Horowitz, ed., *Corporations and the Cold War* (Boston, 1969), pp. 9–24. Clearly the "ideology" was sufficiently supple, as in the case of dealing with Communist China, to allow policy-makers to cut off trade with a large state in an attempt to cause the collapse of the government and the political-economic system. Their aim ultimately was to use such tactics to defeat communism and restore the particular state to the world capitalist economy. See Bernstein, "Origins of the Cold War," n. 87.

60. On Eastern Europe and a *modus vivendi,* see Bernstein, "Origins of the Cold War," pp. 38–40; Gar Alperovitz, *Cold War Essays* (Garden City, 1970), pp. 43–47, 100–104; Gardner, *Architects of Illusion,* pp. 87–102; Horowitz, *Free World Colossus,* pp. 71–74, 243–262.

61. *Cold War,* p. 60 (quotation); "T&T," December 22, 1947; May 4, 1948; on Kennan, see "Sources of Soviet Conduct" and *Memoirs,* pp. 132–135, 255–258, 296–297, 355–367; on Acheson, see *Present at the Creation: My Years in the State Department* (New York, 1969), pp. 223, 374–381; and Coral Bell, *Negotiation from Strength* (London, 1962). For Kennan's later view on negotiations, see *Russia, the Atom, and the West,* p. 98.

by William C. Berman

James Paul Warburg: An Establishment Maverick Challenges Truman's Policy Toward Germany

Combining a successful career as a banker and investor with that of publicist for peace, the late James Warburg (1896–1969) emerged in the Truman years as one of a handful of thoughtful and perceptive critics of American foreign policy. The role of critic seemed odd for one who had been born into a great banking family, and whose father, Paul Warburg, was an architect of the Federal Reserve Act of 1913. James Warburg's family connections, his inherited wealth, his Harvard education and training had, after all, prepared him well for a career in the upper echelons of corporate society. After working in the banking business in the 1920's, Warburg joined the Roosevelt administration as an adviser to the American mission to the London Economic Conference of 1933. Afterward he returned to his investments, accumulating a sizable second fortune from his financial support of Edward Land's fledgling Polaroid Corporation. With the coming of World War II, he actively supported the Allied cause, contributing funds and ideas to William Allen White's Committee to Aid the Allies. And after Pearl Harbor, because of his intimate acquaintance with German banking and business elites and his mastery of the German language, Warburg was employed by the Office of War Information and served as a staff director of its London Bureau until 1944. Subsequently he was to fashion a new career as a critic of American foreign policy, largely because his character and conscience would not allow him to remain silent when a question of principle was at stake. Thus Warburg was motivated to question publicly the need for an American military escalation of the Cold War and the concomitant rehabilitation of Germany.[1]

He had acted in a like manner during the Roosevelt years, when in 1934–1935 he challenged in print the gold policies of a President for whom he had briefly worked, and for whom he still had the deepest respect and affection. With the onset of the Cold War and the freezing of American policy *vis-à-vis* the Soviet Union, Warburg chose to battle for a more flexible and ideologically restrained foreign policy. In time his views, which he articulated with increasing intellectual power and clarity, brought him into conflict with his old and trusted friend from New Deal days, Dean Acheson. It was a conflict that could not be avoided once Warburg had committed himself to educating the American people— through a series of books, pamphlets, and lectures—about the realities of world politics and the pressing need for Washington to develop a more constructive and realistic approach to international problems, especially with respect to Germany.[2]

Included among those realities which in Warburg's opinion Washington was ignoring, was the basic fact that a "world political crisis" had developed out of the turmoil of World War II and that this crisis was something more than a plot foisted on mankind by willful schemers in the Kremlin. By suggesting that the proper sources of the crisis could be found in the dissolution of the traditional balance of power, anti-colonial stirrings in Asia and Africa, the continuing revolution in science and technology, and the repudiation of the Atlantic Charter by all of the great powers, Warburg spoke on behalf of a more complex reality than that ostensibly perceived by American policy-makers. Surely, he contended, "the Kremlin had made dealing with a complicated world crisis infinitely more difficult," but he insisted that it had not precipitated that crisis, and was not solely responsible for its continuation, particularly in the context of a divided Germany.[3]

Complementing these core assumptions was Warburg's belief that the Soviet Union itself was not a military threat to the West in general or to the United States in particular. He simply refused to accept as credible the charge, so fashionable in the late 1940's and

1950's, that the Soviet Union was intent upon world domination, or that it was determined to establish at least a European hegemony based on the use of force. Writing in 1949, Warburg suggested "that Russian action to date *could* be explained on the basis of existing evidence as something quite different from a Hitlerian design for conquest. It *could* be explained as a gigantic disengagement operation in which the basic aim is to tighten ruthlessly every nut and bolt in the security belt around the Soviet Union and then retire into complete isolation." (Some twenty years later, Warburg's view of Soviet behavior and intentions would be shared by such a respectable scholar as Adam B. Ulam and, with ambivalence, by George Kennan.) [4]

Although Warburg did not believe in the inevitability of Soviet military aggression, he had no illusions about the nature and reality of the Soviet state, finding it morally and politically anathema. He was also extremely critical of Russian behavior in Eastern Europe, and he feared the ideological impact of Stalinism upon hungry and destitute peoples in postwar Europe and elsewhere. Consequently, he favored such programs as the Marshall Plan and supported even broader, more radically conceived development schemes, not for the purpose of furthering economic exploitation by the United States but, rather, as a means for promoting modernization and economic rehabilitation in the context of an interdependent world economy. In short, Warburg's answer to Stalinist political machinations, as well as to an increasingly militarized and status-quo-oriented American foreign policy, was some form of social democracy complemented by what he felt was the only viable political alternative to the suicidal policies of the nation state: world federalism. His ultimate goal of world government was chimerical, of course, and after a few years he muted his advocacy of this solution for man's political ills. Nevertheless, by calling for the transformation of the United Nations into a body that could resolve international conflict by means of adjudication, Warburg illuminated an essential point: that the contest between the United States and the Soviet Union was a power struggle that neither side could win— though, given the nature of the arms race after 1949, both sides could lose. [5]

The great prize in that power struggle, at least in the early years of the Cold War, was Germany, and on this subject Warburg wrote with knowledge and insight. Contending that the fate of Germany would determine for the foreseeable future the fate of Europe and, indeed, the world, Warburg took an early interest in developments affecting postwar Germany. In early 1944, upon the request of Assistant Secretary of War, John J. McCloy, an old banking friend, he was pleased to state his views regarding the future political, social, and economic organization of Germany. In his statement Warburg proposed that the Allied occupation of Germany be terminated quickly so that a genuine democratic revolution could take place for the purpose of cleansing the country of Nazism. Needless to say, the War Department rejected his recommendation, stating that "the government of the United States cannot undertake a policy designed to induce chaos." Evidently Warburg did not realize that official American policy in Europe in 1944, as recently shown by Gabriel Kolko, had already taken on a distinctly counter-revolutionary cast in an effort to thwart any left uprising, whether libertarian or communist. In any event, Warburg's memorandum to McCloy marked for him "the beginning of a period of years in which I was to be a frequent and outspoken dissenter from government policy, particularly with respect to Germany." [6]

The events of 1945 and 1946 strengthened Warburg's conviction that Germany was the pivotal issue on which postwar relations turned. As he phrased it: "The crux of the matter now lay in Germany. Nowhere else was four-power cooperation so explicitly on trial. If a workable agreement could be reached with regard to the future of Germany, the mounting East-West tensions might still abate." Those tensions to which Warburg referred had been generated in part by what he considered a faulty settlement negotiated at the Potsdam Conference of 1945. He criticized that agreement because it sanctioned: (1) the violation of pledges regarding self-determination contained in both the Atlantic Charter and the United Nations Declaration; (2) the granting to France of a zone of occupation and an equal voice on the Allied Control Commission amounting to a veto, without obtaining her signature on the Potsdam document; (3) the belief that "the four powers could impose what amounted to a complete political and economic revolution upon a defeated Germany without having first reached agreement among themselves as to what kind of Germany they desired to create." [7]

In specific terms, Warburg felt the Allies had opened a Pandora's box by allowing so much of what was formerly Eastern Germany to be annexed by Poland. This move, he felt, would fan the fires of revanchism; the French takeover of the Saar drew his disapproval for a similar reason. And Warburg's fears of a French veto over the workings of the Allied Control Commission proved justified. For reasons which they considered necessary and legitimate, mostly having to do with national security, the French in late 1945 and 1946 managed their zone literally as an entity separate from the rest of Germany, thereby weakening the authority of the Control Commission and obstructing its efforts to systematize the administration of Germany. (Their behavior in this case probably did as much, if not more, damage to the cause of Allied cooperation in Germany in the early postwar period as any action taken by the Soviet Union.) After the American and Russian argument in 1946 over the question of reparations, hopes for a uniform administration were permanently dashed.[8]

The reparations struggle surfaced after the United States, ignoring an earlier commitment made at Potsdam, decided to curtail shipments of a certain percentage of capital goods from its zone to the Soviet zone. This move was prompted by an American desire to utilize all available resources in order to establish a functionally viable zonal economy under direct American control and supervision. The Russians charged that the United States had repudiated through this action a wartime agreement reached at Yalta allowing for the extraction from Germany of $20 billion in reparations, of which $10 billion was to go to the Soviet Union. But Washington denied that these specific figures had ever been agreed upon. Because of this dispute over reparations, relations between Washington and Moscow were further strained and embittered.[9]

That the situation was polarizing in 1946 is not surprising, for the Allies shared no common frame of reference or common purpose with respect to Germany. Their joint failure to work out an accommodation there was a sad reflection of a more fundamental division first illuminated by the proceedings at Potsdam. At the conference, each side had sought to protect what seemed to be its most vital interests; each side had viewed the other with increasing suspicion and mistrust. From the very beginnings of the occupation, the United States and the Soviet Union became rivals for the affection and support of the German people. Perhaps sensing the potential danger in this development, Secretary of State James F. Byrnes said in his famous Stuttgart speech of September 6, 1946, that "it is not in the interest of the German people or in the interest of world peace that Germany should become a pawn or partner in a military struggle for power between East and West." [10]

Warburg had reached the same conclusion, but much earlier than Byrnes. So in the summer of 1946 he sought to examine the issues with the intent of offering a fresh focus for diplomatic action. After having been encouraged by Dean Acheson, then Assistant Secretary of State, and John J. McCloy, Assistant Secretary of War, to make an inspection trip to Germany, Warburg spent June of 1946 traveling in the four zones of occupation and interviewing important and influentially placed officials of the occupation powers. (His experience was later distilled in his first major book on the German question, *Germany—Bridge or Battleground.*) Upon returning to the United States he sent a memorandum to the State Department suggesting that the United States reopen the question of the German-Polish frontier, which the Potsdam participants had deferred for final settlement until the meeting of a European peace conference. Warburg took this tack because he favored restoring to Germany all territory east of the Oder-Neisse line, except Upper Silesia. Those lost eastern lands represented the agricultural base on which the future economic health of the country depended, and unless they were restored, Warburg argued, Germany would be reduced to a "charity patient." Thus he explicitly tied the revision of frontiers to the goal of a politically united and economically viable Germany. His other proposals included the raising of the ceiling on industrial production, which was then seriously restricted in the American zone, the settlement of the reparation claims, and, most interesting, the creation of an international police force to help prepare for a period of administrative transition, during which time other European powers would participate in the occupation of Germany, leading to the eventual termination of four-power military government and the creation of a united and pacified country. [11]

Of the several suggestions made by Warburg, State Department officials seriously considered only the one having to do with frontier revision. Hence they dispatched to Secretary Byrnes, then in Europe, the suggestion that he raise this point in future discussions with the Russians. On September 6, 1946, Byrnes included a reference to the frontier issue in his Stuttgart speech. But he failed to specify what he meant by frontier revision in the East, permitting the Russians and the Poles to assume "that he was advocating a return to Germany of the Upper Silesian industrial area, which would deprive Poland of its richest prize and run counter to the idea of a de-militarized German economy." Predictably, then, Russia and Poland rejected Byrnes's proposal, and Warburg's efforts to reopen that question seemed permanently blocked.[12]

With the publication of *Germany—Bridge or Battleground,* Warburg directed attention to another difficult problem, the Ruhr. He recommended the Europeanization of the Ruhr coal fields as a way of transcending French fears of German military use of that coal, and deflecting the desires of the United States to tie the Ruhr to a Cold War European economic complex. Washington found his proposal ideologically wanting. It went unheeded (though it would reappear several years later in a slightly different guise: the Schuman Plan), as did his warning about the danger involved in restoring to power those economic groups that helped to make Germany a "warrior nation." In *Germany—Bridge or Battleground* and in subsequent works Warburg expressed alarm over the fact that German industrial magnates, who had had Nazi associations, were making something of a comeback in the American zone. He attributed this development partly to an unwholesome influence exerted on policy-makers by American bankers and financiers who were determined to recartelize the German economy strictly for the sake of profit. Their opportunity had been enhanced by Washington's decision, made by 1946, to impose a private enterprise economy on its zone. Thus it is hardly surprising that capital eventually flowed from the United States into moribund German corporations to help create a viable or self-sustaining zonal economy, an economy that could then materially lower the costs of the American occupation. This potential was recognized by General Lucius Clay, the military commander of the American zone, who, from the start of the occupation, sought to revise the

Joint Chiefs of Staff directive No. 1067 which specified the original
stringent levels of industrial activity. Clay championed, instead, the
cause of industrial recovery consistent with American policy commitments and German needs.[13]

Warburg, too, favored the modification of JCS 1067, feeling
that it retained too much of the spirit of the Morgenthau Plan for
the pastoralization of Germany, for which he never had any sympathy. For him Germany remained "the hub" of a prosperous European economy. But believing this did not make him a supporter of
the free-enterprise model for Germany: on the basis of past experience he feared it would play havoc with efforts to establish more
democratic norms in German political and economic life. Warburg
advocated a "democratic socialist" alternative to American and
Russian goals and techniques, and articulated a radical idealism
which the Cold War climate would soon claim as a victim.[14]

The failure of the Moscow Conference of 1947, coming just after
the Truman Doctrine had been proclaimed on March 12, 1947,
confirmed that the great powers were deadlocked over the German
question. The chill winds of 1945–1946 had led ineluctably to the
deep diplomatic freeze of 1947 and after. Nevertheless, Warburg
praised the efforts of the new Secretary of State George C. Marshall to find a way out of the tangled German problem at the
Moscow Conference. Yet the issues were now so polarized that
no amount of good will, without an accompanying mutual desire for a compromise, could provide the means for a break-
through. Complicating the questions as to whether Germany should
have a centralized government or a decentralized one, a collecti-
vist economy or a private enterprise system, was the weighty
matter of reparations. So immediately divisive was this issue, for
reasons already mentioned, that by itself it was enough to produce the impasse that came out of the Moscow Conference. As
Warburg suggested, a generous concession by the United States
on the reparations question, coupled with a Marshall Plan type
of proposal to aid European recovery, might have produced a
diplomatic reconciliation:

Had we made some such proposal in March 1947 . . . , I believe that
recent history might have assumed a different aspect. We should then

have been in a position to demand political concessions, not only in Germany but in all of Europe, which might have ended the cold war before it involved East and West in a vicious circle of mutual provocation. It is true that such an approach might have also failed. Certainly it would not have provided an immediate solution for all the problems which had arisen. But it might well have opened the door to their gradual solution, whereas the Truman Doctrine and our uncompromising attitude on reparations wrote "finis" to the endeavor to find a basis for agreement.[15]

Apart from the Truman Doctrine, which Warburg attacked as dangerously simpleminded and crudely self-serving, the big news out of Washington in 1947 was the Marshall Plan. Warburg supported it because he believed it provided American foreign policy with a positive orientation. Any program designed to attack the causes of stagnation, misery, and chaos was not only intrinsically good but could serve America's interests by undercutting the appeal of the Soviet Union among the disadvantaged peoples of Europe. But while he applauded this realistic departure from the latent militarism of the Truman Doctrine, Warburg took issue with the way the United States construed Czechoslovakia's desire to be included in the proposed discussions about the Marshall Plan. By suggesting that Prague manifested an interest largely because it sought to rebuff the Soviets, Washington did the Czechs a real disservice, Warburg thought. They were engaged in a perilous political balancing act between East and West; and once their position had been compromised by words from Washington, they were left with no alternative but to withdraw from the program. They did so because of their feeling that, as it was officially stated, "Czechoslovakia's participation would be interpreted as an act directed against our friendship with the Soviet Union," a "friendship" predicated in part on Prague's genuine fear of Germany and Moscow's desire to establish a security belt in Eastern Europe. Thus, given Prague's need to retain Soviet good will, it is not surprising that she rejected Washington's proposal without being coerced by Moscow—or so Warburg was informed by his old friend Jan Masaryk, the Czech Foreign Minister, during a conversation in Prague in the summer of 1947. Upon his return to the United States, Warburg sent a memorandum to Under Secretary of State Robert Lovett suggesting that in the future the United States encourage Czech friendliness to both sides as a way of easing Cold War tensions in Central Europe. But, wrote Warburg, "the State Department . . . had apparently made up its mind that Czechoslovakia was lost—either that, or else it feared any friendly gesture toward that country would jeopardize congressional ratification of the whole Marshall Plan." [16]

Among the objectives of the Marshall Plan was the rehabilitation of the industrial complex that was situated in the Western zones of occupation in Germany. (In fact, the need for such action was part of the original impetus for the Marshall Plan.) Facilitating that rehabilitation at an earlier stage had been the merger of the Anglo-American zones of occupation into "Bizonia" in 1946. The next move—if it could be arranged—would require the merging of Bizonia with the French zone. At that point the embryo of a West German state would be formed. Warburg viewed this possibility with considerable alarm, for he feared that the political and economic future of Germany might be determined by the Russians since they could offer a West Germany something no longer in the power of the West to grant: the hope and promise of unification. He also found it difficult to see how West German economic life could thrive without a viable trade arrangement with the East, or, failing that, without becoming economically dependent on the United States. And there was the problem of Berlin, whose position, Warburg speculated, "might be undermined, if not totally abandoned," by the West if Russia made a separate peace with a nascent West German state.[17]

Although Warburg's fears were largely unfounded on all three counts, he was justified in thinking that a West German state would complicate, indeed exacerbate, Western relations with Moscow. Even without the existence of a West Germany, those relations were still full of friction, as the events of 1948 tragically confirmed. As Warburg suggested, "The first six months of the year 1948 were, in fact, noteworthy as a period of provocation and counter-provocation, as cold war preparation and deployment took place on both sides of the Iron Curtain." There is no need here to recapitulate in detail the events of that period except to mention that Warburg, unlike so many other Americans, believed that the Soviets in 1948 were responding to a European crisis, magnified by the incessant and deepening conflict over Germany, out of general fear of American intentions and a realization of their own basic economic and military weakness. In other words, their destruction of Czech democracy, their harsh and vindictive rule elsewhere in Eastern Europe, their placing the noose, albeit only temporarily, around the neck of Berlin, can be viewed as a systematic effort by the Soviets to consolidate their position of regional power in order to protect a sphere of influence from outside threat and penetration. If the sequence of events and cause-and-effect relationships are as Warburg suggests, then of course the United States bears a considerable responsibility for the Stalinization of Eastern Europe.[18]

Developments in Eastern Europe coincided with increased American vigilance in Western Europe. Thus the continent was split down the middle, with Germany remaining the center and chief focus of the conflict. Warburg's hope for the neutralization of Europe, from the Soviet frontier to the English Channel, was now doomed, for both sides saw little or no need for an accommodation except on terms which both could not accept. In short, diplomacy had become an instrument for promoting a stalemate, not a way of solving problems.

It was in this context, then, that Warburg began in 1948 to challenge openly the policies and practices of the Truman administration. Convinced that the issues now demanded public clarification and critical discussion, he began to lecture across the country to college audiences and Foreign Policy Association groups, and to write books and essays. Unlike President Truman, he eschewed a simple moralistic framework of good and evil in order to promote understanding, not blind support. In his private discussions with government officials, to whom he had access because of his high status and elitist background, Warburg found representatives from the military and the State Department who agreed with his analysis that the Soviet threat was not primarily a military one; but their power within the federal establishment was limited: the White House was immune to thoughts out of season.[19]

Nevertheless, at least for a brief period Warburg believed there was a prospect for a change of policy. Thanks to Truman's unexpected election victory in 1948, Dean Acheson was appointed Secretary of State. Warburg respected Acheson's cool intelligence and sophistication, and he hoped Acheson's presence in the councils of the administration would provide opportunities to alter the course and direction of American foreign policy. Given that prospect, Warburg went to see his old friend in January 1949. During their meeting Warburg spoke out against the possible creation of a separate German state, contending that such a move would force "the Russians to convert their zone into a satellite state and freeze the partition." Warburg also suggested to Acheson that the proposed NATO alliance consist only of the Brussels Treaty powers, plus the United States and Canada. He advised against including "Germany, or any part of Germany, in NATO since it would further provoke, not prevent conflict." This arrangement, Warburg believed, might make possible the neutralization of the rest of Europe, a neutralization that would require troop withdrawals from Germany by both the United States and the Soviet Union. Warburg also recommended that the Saar coal agreement of December 1948, which laid the foundation of a West European coal authority, be renegotiated in order to permit Russian participation in the administration of the Ruhr coal complex. Such a move, he felt, was one way of "ending the cold war." After having made his presentation to Acheson, Warburg waited to see what impact it would have.[20]

Before too many weeks had passed, Warburg was to discover:

that not only would the Administration's basic policy remain unchanged, but that its tactics would continue to be presented as an accomplished fact, submitted for ratification and approval—·but not for discussion; each step would be pictured as critically essential to save the world from communism; each step, once accepted, would make the next step inevitable.

The specific issue which prompted this shrewd assessment of the administration's *modus operandi* was the State Department's request for Senate approval of the signed NATO agreement. Sensing the manifold dangers in this latest administration maneuver to prevent the imagined Red hordes from engulfing Western Europe, Warburg was now prepared to challenge Secretary Acheson's defense of the treaty. On May 10, 1949, two weeks after the Secretary testified before the Senate Foreign Relations Committee, Warburg appeared before the same committee to call attention to what he believed were the shortcomings and deficiencies of the treaty. Warburg made it clear at the beginning of his prepared statement that he was not opposed to an Atlantic security pact as such. He did object to the move to tie the proposed NATO alliance to a rearmament program. Taking issue again with the proposition that the primary danger from the Soviet Union was military in character, Warburg thus rejected the underlying premise of containment as it had been spelled out by administration spokesmen. For him, the Soviet threat was largely subversive in character and could be handled by such programs as the Marshall Plan.[21]

After presenting his argument that Western Europe faced only a secondary danger from Moscow, Warburg asserted that those who claimed "a common heritage of ethical belief and democratic conviction" for the treaty's signatories ignored the fact that "large segments of the French, Dutch, Belgian, and Italian populations . . . willingly collaborated with and lived quite contentedly under Fascism." And what could one say about Portugal that would not mock the moral case for unity? In other words, the "free world" was really an oddly gerrymandered American sphere of influence.[22]

More important for the future were Warburg's speculations about Western military strategy against a Soviet attack. He suggested to the committee that if the NATO powers undertook to defend Western Europe at points contiguous with Soviet power, as had recently been indicated by remarks of General Omar Bradley, Chief of Staff, then such a commitment would require a much greater expenditure of manpower and material than anyone had publicly reckoned. In Warburg's view, the cost would be prohibitive. Why? As Secretary Acheson had already promised the committee that "there was absolutely no intention to send substantial numbers of American troops to Europe in any eventuality short of war," it seemed certain that Western Europe would be required to guard the ramparts against the Russian menace. But such a military buildup in Britain and France, Warburg suggested, would divert precious funds from the task of social reconstruction, thereby weakening the Western democracies at precisely that point where they were most vulnerable to Soviet pressure. And if for any reason Britain and France could not fulfill their prescribed military goals, then clearly the United States would have to assume the major responsibility for the active defense of the continent—unless of course a different defense strategy were devised.[23]

Warburg suggested to the committee that it clarify the nature of the American commitment to Europe so as to make it clear that the United States would consider an attack on Western Europe a *casus belli* requiring an immediate American response from outside the European continent. Such a clarification, Warburg believed, would make it possible for the United States to retain a maximum flexible response in all situations demanding American intervention, while obviating the need either to station troops in central Germany or to rearm the Germans, or both—actions which the Russians would surely consider provocative. On these terms, Warburg felt he could support the treaty in the belief that it had been "cured of its most dangerous defect." He concluded his statement to the committee by suggesting that "this [revised] program may well become a most useful stopgap device to buy time in which a positive, constructive American program for peace may be developed. Its ultimate effectiveness as such will then be determined by what we do . . . in Germany and in the southeastern rim of the Asiatic continent." [24]

As Warburg lacked powerful political allies, he could not persuade the administration to pursue a different course from the one it was following, namely, establishing the means whereby the United States could negotiate with Russia from a position of strength—or, more precisely, establishing the means to avoid negotiating with Russia at all. With that end in mind, President Truman sent his military assistance bill to Congress on July 25, 1949, providing for an appropriation of slightly more than a billion dollars to help Western Europe begin the task of rearming. After Truman acted, Warburg sent a statement to the Senate Foreign Relations Committee advocating that any Russian military aggression could best be contained through "the maintenance of adequate military power *uncommitted to any prearranged strategy of defense.*" He underscored this point because he feared that if the United States adhered to the policy adumbrated by Truman's remarks on military assistance, increased American troop participation in the defense of Europe was practically assured. And the next step would be a decision to rearm a West Germany that had by 1949 nearly achieved the status of a sovereign state.[25]

For reasons already mentioned, Warburg viewed the creation of a West German state with consternation. He also felt that it was "not the Germany that the majority of the German people wanted, not the Germany desired by the British people or the French people, but it was the Germany which Washington had wanted and which it hoped to use to good advantage." Konrad Adenauer, the head of that new regime, Warburg described as "a shrewdly calculating conservative leader of the Stresemann school." Nonetheless, West Germany was now a *fait accompli*. Soon, as Warburg had predicted, the Russians responded by creating the German Democratic Republic, an act which postponed indefinitely the prospects of German unification. Following these moves—which seemed so dialectically related—were "two actions which . . . Acheson had promised not to undertake: one was the rearming of Western Germany; the other was the stationing in Germany of additional American forces." [26]

Warburg, of course, was not privy to the great controversy which erupted within official Washington in 1949–1950 over the question of rearming the West Germans. The State and Defense Departments both had been involved in a prolonged altercation over the strategy and tactics of establishing a counterforce to the Russian military presence in Europe. The State Department initially balked at the Defense Department's recommendation calling for a German contribution to the defense of Europe, as it recognized the political and diplomatic repercussions of any move to remilitarize the German state. But the Korean War, coupled with a NATO report suggesting that any Western defense force would remain woefully understaffed without German help, resolved the controversy in favor of the Pentagon. In September 1950, with the cards no longer his to shuffle, Acheson formally announced in New York that a West German Army would be created, an announcement which promptly triggered an explosion that ripped through the foreign offices of Europe, especially in France and the Soviet Union. [27]

The announcement, though not unexpected, troubled Warburg for two reasons: first, it postponed action on the "brilliantly conceived Schuman Plan"; and second, it played directly into the hands of Konrad Adenauer by giving him the necessary leverage to obtain additional concessions from Washington that would further polarize Europe. The Schuman Plan, named after its leading public advocate, Robert Schuman, the French foreign minister, envisioned the integration and pooling of Western coal and steel production under a supranational authority. Warburg himself had advocated a similar scheme, particularly with respect to coal production, several years earlier, because he thought it might open the door to European-wide cooperation—a way of transcending the debilitating experience of the Cold War. It was Warburg's hope that the Schuman Plan would provide the same possibility, the same opportunity, but it too was lost because Washington insisted on "placing the military cart before the political and economic horses. . . ." (Later the Schuman Plan was implemented in such a way as to make possible the development and growth of the European Common Market.) [28]

The chief beneficiary of the Truman administration's decision to arm the Bonn regime was Konrad Adenauer, who cleverly used his newly acquired legitimacy to negotiate with the occupation powers a relaxation of their rule and administration over West Germany. Adenauer's success was such that it was only a question of time before he won complete sovereignty and internal autonomy for his country. As West Germany grew in strength, the United States ruled out the possibility of any serious negotiations about German unification except on its own terms, a position which suited Adenauer perfectly. According to Warburg, "Adenauer did not want talks on reunification. He was better off obtaining concessions and fighting for parity in the West. A four-power conference . . . would make Germany once more the object of negotiation instead of being one of the major participants." [29]

By the spring of 1951, then, the Bonn republic, "formerly the passing object of East-West negotiations, was rapidly becoming a co-maker of Western coalition policy." Concurrently, Secretary Acheson's European policy was evolving into "something like a sacrosanct fetish." In response to these interrelated developments, Warburg was prompted to write a letter to the *New York Times* on July 27, 1951, in which, like a voice crying in the wilderness, he once again called for the unification and neutralization of Germany. He also suggested that the American military buildup in Europe take place outside Germany so as not to provoke the Russians. A State Department official, perhaps Acheson himself, rejected Warburg's proposal on the grounds that "we have complete faith in the ability of Western Democracy to emerge victorious from any struggle with communism, when such a struggle is conducted on even terms. However, in the face of communist subversive tactics, with which we are not prepared to compete, a contest on even terms is impossible." In other words, the State Department was saying that Germany was really not a negotiable issue, and that neutralism in the German context was to be feared as an opening wedge for something more sinister and deadly—Russian-style communism.[30]

Even if the State Department had thought of reappraising its German position, the Korean War and the specter of McCarthyism made it impossible to generate any support for such a move. Vulnerable to right-wing hysteria, which it helped to create, and apprehensive about the Republican challenge in 1952, the Truman administration decided to shore up its European flank. The outlines of a frozen foreign policy were there for everyone to see, but those few Americans, like Warburg, who recognized that fact lacked the power to influence the necessary changes. The Cold War consensus hardened into a mid-century American dogma.

That the American position had become inflexible was never more strikingly illustrated than in 1952, the year of lost opportunity. The stage for developments that year was set at the NATO foreign ministers' meeting in Lisbon in late February. There it was decided, first, to push West Germany into the NATO alliance through the back door, by integrating the European Defense Community, with which West Germany was affiliated, with NATO; and second, to grant West Germany an early end to the occupation and the restoration of full rights of sovereignty, thus completing a remarkable metamorphosis for a country still occupied by troops of the greatest military alliance in world history. About the Federal Republic's accomplishment, Warburg commented:

. . . less than seven years after their unconditional surrender, the West Germans had not only achieved equality, a high degree of sovereign independence, and the right to rearm, but had actually become the major bulwark behind which the Western powers hoped to fortify themselves against a Soviet invasion. *The force to be contained had become the instrument of containment.*[31]

Once West Germany became America's chosen "instrument of containment," the Russians responded with unexpected alacrity and reasonableness to this perceived threat to their national interest. On March 10, 1952, Moscow dispatched a note to Washington on the subject of German unification that was extremely moderate in tone and full of diplomatic possibilities. The note unquestionably represented a major shift in Soviet tactics, and, presumably, in Soviet policy as well. For example, Moscow now indicated a willingness to unify Germany and allow it to maintain a national defense force on the condition that the country was neutralized. It was a tantalizing proposal, but did it mean that Moscow would permit free elections in her former zone of occupation? Only by engaging in serious negotiations with Moscow could Washington find out her true intentions about this and other matters. But at the moment the American government had no desire to hold talks other than on terms which would require Germany to remain within the NATO establishment. Thus Moscow's initiative was frustrated by American intractability. As Adam Ulam recently remarked about that lost opportunity, "the Americans overlooked the truth that patience and a sense of timing are major ingredients of the art of diplomacy." [32]

Warburg was less benign in his criticism of America's refusal to negotiate in the spirit of compromise. In testimony delivered to the Senate Foreign Relations Committee several days after the State Department publicly rebuffed Moscow's bid to open talks on Germany, Warburg challenged the conventional wisdom of the day by boldly suggesting that the United States was afraid to call the Soviet bluff for fear that it was not a bluff. The concept of a free, united, but neutral Germany frightened the State Department, Warburg argued, because it thought such an arrangement could be easily subverted by Moscow, as Czechoslovakia had been in 1948. But Warburg suggested the new situation would not be comparable to 1948: "Russia knew [then] that she could manipulate the Czechoslovak coup without the slightest risk of launching World War III; no such possibility would exist with regard to a free Germany." [33]

In his testimony Warburg also made it clear that he feared the new German republic, predicting that "once rearmed and fully sovereign, Germany will pursue one very simple objective: it will seek the reunification of East and West Germany and the recapture of its lost provinces." And in its attempt to achieve that goal, Warburg argued, Bonn could drag the Western alliance into a war with

Russia. Warburg's apprehension about West Germany's potential for mischief was by no means unique, as it was shared by some Englishmen, most Frenchmen, and all Russians. Many Americans, conditioned to think strictly of the Russian menace, simply failed to appreciate the European concern with a rearmed Germany. Fortunately for mankind, Warburg's worst fears about the Bonn regime were not realized and, hopefully, never will be. But this fact does not lessen the overall significance of his testimony: he was simply expressing an unpalatable truth when he informed the committee that the unresolved German question could endanger world peace and that the United States had done little or nothing to dampen this potential powder keg.[34]

In late May 1952 the Truman administration capped its work in Europe by signing an agreement with the Bonn government that gave it the autonomy which Chancellor Adenauer had sought since 1949. The very next day in Paris the European Defense Community was formally created. To commemorate the occasion Dean Acheson declared: "We are standing on the threshold of a New Europe and a New World." The work of the Truman administration in Europe was now finished.[35]

Warburg had resisted all along those developments which Acheson celebrated in Paris, for he realized how unnecessarily the Truman administration had militarized what was essentially a political and ideological struggle. Warburg knew the lost opportunities, the failure of historical imagination, and the lack of courage that characterized Washington's relations with the Soviet Union. It is not difficult to understand, then, why he judged Truman's policy in Europe as shortsighted, dangerous, and full of folly.[36]

Even after Truman left office, Warburg continued to press his campaign for a thorough revision of American policy. In 1953 he published his most important study, *Germany—Key to Peace,* a sadly neglected work which analyzed in depth the problems discussed in this essay. And in subsequent years, to his death in June 1969, Warburg continued to write and speak on behalf of a sane foreign policy based on a less politically interventionist and a non-militarized approach to world problems. His words had little or no impact on that first generation of Americans to experience the Cold War; now, because of the disaster of Vietnam and the spiraling domestic crisis, his general views have been incorporated into a liberal-left critique of American foreign policy which has been advanced in recent years by Senator J. William Fulbright and others. For students of American foreign policy who are concerned specifically with the origins of the malaise of the 1960's, Warburg's work remains a necessary point of departure for understanding the confusion and mistaken emphasis of the Truman administration's policy toward Germany.[37]

Notes

The author thanks Professor James Estes of the University of Toronto and Professor Thomas G. Paterson of the University of Connecticut for their help in the preparation of this essay, and the History Department of the University of Toronto for providing funds for clerical assistance.

1. James P. Warburg, *The Long Road Home: The Autobiography of a Maverick* (Garden City, 1964), pp. 110–240; James P. Warburg, *Germany —Key to Peace* (Cambridge, Mass., 1953), xi–xix; *New York Times,* June 4, 1969.

2. Warburg, *Long Road Home,* pp. 110–240.

3. James P. Warburg, *Last Call for Common Sense* (New York, 1949), pp. 30–32; James P. Warburg, *The United States in the Postwar World* (New York, 1966), p. 59.

4. Adam B. Ulam, *Expansion and Coexistence: The History of Soviet Foreign Policy, 1917–67* (New York, 1968), p. 404; Warburg, *Last Call for Common Sense,* pp. 27, 94; George F. Kennan, *Memoirs, 1925–1950* (Boston, 1967), p. 464.

5. James P. Warburg, *Put Yourself in Marshall's Place* (New York, 1948), pp. 41–55; Warburg, *Last Call for Common Sense,* pp. 32–65; James P. Warburg, *Faith, Purpose and Power* (New York, 1950), pp. 80–165; James P. Warburg, *How to Co-exist Without Playing the Kremlin's Game* (Boston, 1952), p. 35.

6. James P. Warburg, *Germany—Bridge or Battleground* (New York, 1947), pp. 1–10; Warburg, *Long Road Home,* pp. 207–210; Gabriel Kolko, *The Politics of War* (New York, 1968), pp. 31–42, 511–515; Warburg, *Long Road Home,* p. 208.

7. Warburg, *Long Road Home,* p. 225; Warburg, *United States in Postwar World,* pp. 16–18.

8. Warburg, *Last Call for Common Sense,* p. 64; John Gimbel, *The American Occupation of Germany: Politics and the Military, 1945–1949* (Stanford, 1968), pp. 16–18, 57–61; F. Roy Willis, *France, Germany and the New Europe, 1945–1967* (New York, 1968), pp. 15–19; Walter LaFe-

ber, *America, Russia and the Cold War, 1945–1966* (New York, 1967), p. 32.

9. Warburg, *Put Yourself in Marshall's Place*, pp. 20–22.

10. Kolko, *Politics of War*, pp. 568–575.

11. Warburg, *Long Road Home*, pp. 225–228; Warburg, *Germany—Bridge or Battleground*, pp. 10–20, 355–359.

12. Warburg, *Long Road Home*, p. 233; Warburg, *Germany—Key to Peace*, p. 32.

13. Warburg, *Germany—Bridge or Battleground*, pp. 231–232; Warburg, *Last Call for Common Sense*, pp. 12, 66; Kolko, *Politics of War*, pp. 503–512; Paul Hammond, "Directives for the Occupation of Germany: The Washington Controversy," in Harold Stein, ed., *American Civil-Military Decisions: A Book of Case Studies* (Birmingham, Ala., 1963), p. 439; Gimbel, *American Occupation of Germany*, pp. 19–34.

14. Warburg, *Germany—Key to Peace*, p. 23; Warburg, *Put Yourself in Marshall's Place*, p. 18; Warburg, *Last Call for Common Sense*, pp. 69, 93.

15. Howard K. Smith, *The State of Europe* (New York, 1949), p. 121; Warburg, *Germany—Key to Peace*, p. 44; Warburg, *Last Call for Common Sense*, p. 147; Warburg, *Put Yourself in Marshall's Place*, p. 23.

16. Warburg, *Put Yourself in Marshall's Place*, pp. 47–54; Warburg, *Long Road Home*, pp. 239–240; Warburg, *Last Call for Common Sense*, pp. 238–260. Thomas G. Paterson, "American Relations with Czechoslovakia, 1945–1948," unpublished manuscript in author's possession, 1969.

17. Gimbel, *American Occupation of Germany*, pp. 150–151, 164–169; Warburg, *Germany—Key to Peace*, pp. 53–58.

18. Warburg, *Germany—Key to Peace*, p. 58; Ulam, *Expansion and Coexistence*, p. 438; Warburg, *United States in Postwar World*, p. 60. See also Isaac Deutscher, "Myths of the Cold War," in David Horowitz, ed., *Containment and Revolution* (Boston, 1967), p. 18.

19. Warburg, *Long Road Home*, p. 249; Warburg, *Last Call for Common Sense*, pp. 23–200. See also Warburg, "The Defense of Western Europe: Deception or Blunder?," *Harper's*, June 1949, pp. 34–38; Warburg, "Bargain-Basement Diplomacy," *Harper's*, November 1949, pp. 50–54; Warburg, "An Alternative Proposal," *Nation*, March 19, 1949, pp. 331–333.

20. Warburg, *Germany—Key to Peace*, pp. 77–78; Warburg, *Faith, Purpose and Power*, pp. 72–89; Warburg, *Long Road Home*, pp. 255–256.

21. Warburg, *Germany—Key to Peace*, p. 80; Warburg, *Faith, Purpose and Power*, p. 37; Warburg, *Germany—Key to Peace*, pp. 93–101.

22. Warburg, *Germany—Key to Peace*, p. 95.

23. *Ibid.*, pp. 97–101.

24. *Ibid.*

25. David Horowitz, *The Free World Colossus* (New York, 1965), pp. 242–265; Warburg, *Germany—Key to Peace*, pp. 113–114, 317.

26. Warburg, *Germany—Key to Peace*, pp. 127–128.

27. Lawrence Martin, "American Decision to Rearm Germany," in Stein, *American Civil-Military Decisions*, pp. 645–660; Alexander Werth, *France 1940–1955* (New York, 1956), pp. 481–490; Willis, *France, Germany and the New Europe*, pp. 131–139; Ulam, *Expansion and Coexistence*, pp. 504–512.

28. James P. Warburg, *The United States in a Changing World* (New

York, 1954), pp. 444–450; Warburg, *Germany—Key to Peace*, p. 149; Willis, *France, Germany and the New Europe*, pp. 227–272.

29. Richard Hiscocks, *The Adenauer Era* (New York, 1966), pp. 29–40; Warburg, *Germany—Key to Peace*, p. 163.

30. Warburg, *Germany—Key to Peace*, pp. 153, 171–173.

31. *Ibid.*, p. 187.

32. Ulam, *Expansion and Coexistence*, pp. 535–537; Warburg, *Germany —Key to Peace*, pp. 190–192.

33. Warburg, *Germany—Key to Peace*, pp. 195–200.

34. *Ibid.*

35. Warburg, *United States in a Changing World*, p. 457.

36. Warburg, *United States in the Postwar World*, pp. 88–96; Warburg, *Long Road Home*, p. 263.

37. *New York Times*, June 4, 1969; J. William Fulbright, *The Arrogance of Power* (New York, 1966); *The Progressive*, June 1969. The James Paul Warburg papers are now in the possession of the John F. Kennedy Library; they were not available at the time this essay was written.

by Ronald Radosh
and
Leonard P. Liggio

Henry A. Wallace and
the Open Door

Many of his contemporaries considered Henry Agard Wallace an
arch New Dealer, a supporter of United States intervention in
World War II (before Pearl Harbor), and a radical exponent
of the "century of the common man." This reputation was seemingly vindicated after the war when Wallace emerged as one of the
nation's foremost critics of the Truman administration's Cold War
policies, winning him support among those American progressives
who were disenchanted with Truman. Wallace's stand, always
forcefully expressed, eventually led to his forlorn presidential campaign of 1948 on the Progressive party ticket. His defense of
"coexistence" with the Soviets in the late 1940's was an act of
heresy in that time, and produced a series of attacks which depicted
Wallace as a naive defender of Stalinist Russia.[1]

This abuse of Wallace's ideas, though paralleled in attacks from
the right, found its most forthright expression among the liberal
ideologues that Arthur M. Schlesinger, Jr., was later to dub the
"Vital Center." According to Schlesinger, Wallace generalized
from "his own sense of martyrdom" to a defense of "Soviet totalitarianism." Dwight Macdonald, then an anti-communist socialist,
saw Wallace as a simple tool of the Soviet government because he
supposedly refused to condemn Soviet actions. Wallace, Macdonald
argued, was opportunistic, captivated by a lust for power through
government. Yet the side to which Wallace committed himself,
Macdonald wrote, "is not that of his own country." Macdonald's
view has since become folklore: a recent interpretation by Alonzo

Hamby treats Wallace as a naive apologist who rationalized Soviet foreign policy and who failed to oppose Soviet expansion.[2]

In reality, Henry Wallace was an exponent of an American foreign policy that was traditional since 1898: economic expansion for American commerce through the Open Door abroad. Throughout his career Wallace was committed to the Open Door concepts of equal trade opportunity and multilateral internationalism. He arrived at this position during the 1920's, while editor of his grandfather's paper, *Wallace's Farmer*. In Iowa, Wallace adopted the concept of the Open Door for American exports. He also rejected competition and applauded large-unit economic institutions. These views were similar to those of Herbert Hoover, who served as Secretary of Commerce alongside Wallace's father, Henry C. Wallace, the Secretary of Agriculture during the Harding and Coolidge administrations. Henry A. Wallace implemented or elaborated his ideas when he became Secretary of Agriculture, 1933–1940, Vice-President of the United States (and chairman of the Board of Economic Warfare), 1941–1945, Secretary of Commerce, 1945–1946, editor of the *New Republic,* 1946–1947, and standard-bearer for the Progressive party, 1948.[3]

For Wallace, export markets were the saving mechanism of American capitalism. In 1934 he challenged the argument of the noted American historian Charles A. Beard that American capitalism could produce prosperity at home and peace abroad if only its leaders would abandon the expansionist ideology of Frederick Jackson Turner and develop new forms of allocating resources through a domestic Five Year Plan. Beard had set forth his own challenge to the expansionist tradition in his *Open Door at Home*. In *America Must Choose* (1934), Wallace insisted that the U.S. could not surrender its foreign markets without major internal readjustments that would make the domestic regulations of World War I appear trivial. Without an overseas frontier, he argued, the United States would move toward either fascism or socialism. Those in "the midst of business and political affairs," he advised Beard, could not afford the time or cost to institute the kinds of changes Beard favored.[4]

Business, labor, agriculture, and government, Wallace believed, formed a four-way partnership. One partner might for a time obtain a larger share of the national income, but this "pressure game" would explode unless all four partners united to produce a larger income to divide. The source of such an income was "large and expanding" foreign markets for business; the private enterprise system depended upon them "for its very survival." As the new Secretary of Commerce (January 1945), Wallace announced that one of his major goals would be the creation of a "revitalized foreign trade service," which he hoped would "play a more effective role" in promoting "vigorously a high level of foreign trade on a sustained basis." Full employment and 60 million jobs would be the result of government cooperating "with the export trade" to create "an aggressive sales campaign abroad." [5]

In Wallace's view, export markets were essential for the over-production of American industry which was sure to overtake domestic purchasing power after the war. Americans would again have to "look to foreign markets in order to exchange our surplus industrial and agricultural production." For this reason, Wallace, speaking for the Truman administration in 1945, joined Chamber of Commerce president Eric Johnston and John Abbink of the National Foreign Trade Council in advocating a large postwar loan to Great Britain. The purpose of such a loan was to preclude British tendencies to economic exclusiveness and Sterling-bloc restrictionism within the empire, and thus preserve open trade areas. The Labour party's victory in the elections of 1945 created additional pressures. "With a loan," Gabriel Kolko explains, "the United States might define the limits of British socialism as well, and neutralize it insofar as that were possible." Wallace understood this purpose. To those less sophisticated Americans who argued that a loan to the Labour government would further socialism in Europe, Wallace replied that "money is being loaned to Britain for the purpose of enabling her to do business in the way we are doing, rather than to pursue any further the path of socialization or nationalization." Private enterprise in foreign trade would permit other nations to "embrace [the American] system, which is not only in our best interests but in theirs also." [6]

As Secretary of Commerce, Wallace sought to apply these traditional views. His program of saving the economy by a search for large export markets owed a great deal to the approach first developed by an earlier Secretary of Commerce, Herbert Hoover. In fact, Wallace was frank to acknowledge his debt: "I have considerable sympathy with Herbert Hoover's problem as Secretary of Commerce right now," Wallace stated after his appointment, "because I can say that I am going to go all out to get the maximum use of whatever powers may reside in the bureau of Foreign and Domestic Commerce to foster and develop trade here and abroad." He predicted in 1945 an excess of exports over imports for at least ten years. And he admitted he "would be contributing perhaps as much as any single individual to producing a situation like that for which I criticized the Republican Party back in the decade of the twenties." America's traditional program of foreign expansion had seldom been questioned by liberals, who hoped that American influence abroad would create a liberal international structure as well as world peace. It was left to a conservative critic, Senator Robert A. Taft, to explain that while "dollar diplomacy is derided . . . it is exactly the policy of Government aid to our exporters which Mr. Wallace himself advocates to develop foreign trade, except that [previously] it did not involve our lending abroad the money to pay for all our exports." [7]

While Wallace subscribed to the need for foreign economic expansion, he did not follow those Cold War statesmen who believed that America should use its postwar economic and military power to shape the world in its own image, to force the Open Door on other nations, and to build a U.S.-dominated power bloc. The most militant Cold Warriors hoped to push Russia from Eastern Europe, thereby reducing Soviet political influence and opening up the Danube Valley to the goods and capital of the West. American economic objectives, as Kolko has shown, demanded a return to the prewar status quo in Eastern Europe. The United States called for multilateral trade patterns, equality of opportunity, and freedom to invest for American corporations. While the State Department gave lip service to Soviet fears for its own security, Washington wanted restoration of old trade patterns, so that Eastern Europe would maintain its semi-colonial status as breadbasket to the industrial West. Therefore the United States worked to prevent Russian dismantling of property for reparations, to keep oil from American-owned wells from being shipped to Russia, and to end all restrictions on the active return of American corporations to Eastern Europe. First priority was opposition to nationalization of Western companies, especially in oil. Eastern Europe was to be preserved as an area that would sell its raw materials primarily to Western Europe; Soviet security needs simply could not be permitted to interfere with American assets and trade.[8]

Henry Wallace opposed this aggressive postwar policy toward the Soviet Union. Conceding the Soviet sphere of influence in Eastern Europe to be an irreversible fact, Wallace chided the United States for attacking the Soviet sphere while maintaining its own sphere of influence in Latin America. To be sure, Wallace wanted Eastern European markets kept open to American commerce, but he preferred to "discuss with the Russians in a friendly way their long-range economic problems and the future of our cooperation in matters of trade." Soviet postwar reconstruction, he argued, offered a massive opportunity for the export of American commodities and personnel. The developing trade would not be one-sided. "Although the Soviet Union has been an excellent credit risk in the past," Wallace wrote President Truman in early 1946, "eventually the goods and services exported from this country must be paid for by the Russians by exporting to us." Moreover, Wallace viewed the Soviet Union as a natural billion-dollar market for American industrial surplus and as a source of necessary raw materials such as manganese ore. Mutually advantageous trade relations, Wallace hoped, would create a basis for negotiations and help end political misunderstanding. Problems relating to Eastern Europe might be solved if economic arrangements were worked out first. "Russian economic penetration of the Danube area might be countered," Wallace suggested, "by concrete proposals for economic collaboration in the development of the resources of this area, rather than by insisting that the Russians should cease their unilateral penetration and offering no solution to the present economic chaos there." Wallace believed that Soviet behavior was the "result of their dire economic needs and their disturbed sense of security," and he urged that "we can disabuse the Soviet mind . . . by proving to them that we want to trade with them and to cement our economic relations with them." [9]

Wallace's commitment to better trade relations with the Soviet government put him at odds with Cold War policy-makers. In January 1945 the Russians had issued a formal request for a $6 billion loan, but their hopes were destroyed as American leaders moved to use economic aid as an instrument of political and economic policy. A central figure in formulating a tough line toward the Soviets was Averell Harriman. As the main adviser on the loan question, Harriman argued that the Russians planned to triple their prewar steel output within fifteen years, and that the loan would help them achieve that goal. Rather than aid the Russians, he suggested that "our basic interest might be better served by increasing our trade with other parts of the world." If loans were granted, the United States ought to retain "the power to restrict or reduce them as we see fit." [10]

U.S. economic aid could be used as a lever for the attainment of political ends, "as a tool of diplomacy," to quote Herbert Feis' assessment of Harriman's views. Any loan to the Russians would depend upon their behavior in international relations. The Russians, as Thomas G. Paterson has explained, would have to "conduct their diplomatic affairs according to American wishes and standards." The State Department lined up behind Harriman; and when Truman became President he "adopted Harriman's view." The result was that the "American use of the loan as a diplomatic weapon, at the same time that Great Britain was granted a handsome loan at below two percent interest, fed exaggerated Soviet fears, but fears nevertheless, that the United States was creating an international bloc and repeating post-World War I experience." [11]

Wallace had first heard Harriman's view on the Russian loan in May 1945, during the first session of the United Nations Organization. At an off-the-record press conference, Harriman had argued that "Russia is in desperate need of economic rehabilitation." She wants a "$6 billion lend-lease credit from the United States. I would apportion that credit out piecemeal," Wallace reports Harriman saying, "demanding in return concessions in the political field." Chances for Russia's obtaining the loan were already slim, but Wallace believed that Truman could be won over to the position which Wallace shared with Treasury Secretary Morgenthau, Harry Dexter White of the Treasury Department, and Donald Nelson, and that a vigorous attack on the Harriman analysis would bear fruit.[12]

One month after hearing Harriman present his views, Wallace spoke out on the Russian loan for the first time. He was persistently to repeat the theme of his remarks until his forced resignation in September 1946. The enemies of peace, he told a meeting of *Churchman* readers, were exacerbating differences between Russia and the United States. They sought to wreck the United Nations before it was firmly established. Wallace urged Americans to follow the advice of Franklin D. Roosevelt, who had been "willing to give up a little sovereignty for a lot of peace." Because Russians and Americans held different ideologies was no reason for them to war against each other. And war would not occur, Wallace claimed, because President Truman was supporting Roosevelt's policy of peace with Russia "to the letter." [13]

Wallace had many opportunities during the remainder of 1945 to make his views known, and he took them all. But although he was keenly aware of the impact of Harriman's arguments, and the power of those who shared them, Wallace continually supported the administration and claimed that Truman was not following the path advocated by Harriman, Secretary of State James Byrnes, and Senator Arthur H. Vandenberg. Not until 1946, when he recognized that his views had been defeated, did Wallace sharpen the tone of his criticism.

Early in 1946 Wallace was able to challenge Harriman directly. At a testimonial dinner honoring Harriman's work on behalf of Russian war relief, Harriman asserted that Russia had not fulfilled its wartime agreements. Hinting that Russia had sabotaged the Yalta agreements on Poland, Harriman noted his pleasure that the United States was now taking a "clear position in opposition to those policies." Americans, Harriman insisted, could not "minimize differences that have arisen between our two governments."

Without attacking Harriman directly, Wallace followed him by making clear his own different perspective. The Soviet government, he told the audience, was aware of how capitalist nations had tried to destroy it between 1919 and 1921, and now detected new Western attitudes of hostility. The Soviets were simply "out to make every boundary secure. They fear capitalist encirclement. They are

hungry for science and machines and feel that time is short to prepare for a possible capitalist-provoked war." Even if Russia were
"wrong on every count," Wallace retorted, "I still say that the
United States has nothing to gain, but on the contrary, everything
to lose by beating the tom-toms against Russia." [14]

Wallace's growing sense of estrangement from the Cold Warriors was revealed explicitly during policy discussions on the postwar control of atomic energy. In an era when influential Americans
argued that the Soviets would never produce an atomic bomb, and
that the United States had to keep the bomb formula "secret" until
Russia agreed to be policed by the United Nations, Wallace argued
that it was illusory to base policy on the concept of an atomic
monopoly that could not possibly be maintained. His belief that
there was no such thing as an atomic bomb "secret" paralleled the
views of atomic scientists. He vigorously argued for an exchange
of scientific information with Soviet scholars. According to Secretary of Defense James Forrestal, Wallace was "completely, everlastingly and wholeheartedly in favor of giving [the bomb secret]
to the Russians." Forrestal claimed that at a September 1945
Cabinet meeting Wallace had argued that American failure to give
the Soviets "our knowledge would make an embittered and sour
people." Other cabinet members thought the bomb should be the
property of the United States alone. For Forrestal, the Russians
were orientals who could not be trusted. The United States would
have to "exercise a trusteeship over the atomic bomb on behalf of
the United Nations." [15]

Forrestal's account of Wallace's views was, however, highly
exaggerated. Wallace had merely supported the major comments
presented to the Cabinet by Secretary of War Henry L. Stimson.
In his private September 11 memorandum to the President, Stimson had argued that if the atomic bomb were to be considered an
instrument of power politics, the result would be a "secret armament race of a rather desperate character." Warning that Soviet-
American relations might be "perhaps irretrievably embittered by
the way in which we approach the solution of the bomb with
Russia," Stimson predicted that if we "fail to approach them now
and merely continue to negotiate with them, having this weapon
rather ostentatiously on our hip, their suspicions and their distrust

of our purposes and motives will increase." Wallace later recalled
that most major political leaders believed that Russia would not
have the bomb before 1955, and that the United States "had a
secret which we could use as a peacetime weapon in international
affairs. They did not ask," Wallace added, "what would happen to
our foreign policy when two countries had the bomb." [16]

In December 1945 Secretary Byrnes proposed an exchange of
scientific information with Russia as a first step toward a disarmament agreement. Senator Vandenberg, the Republican architect
of a bipartisan foreign policy, opposed the Byrnes plan and argued
that such exchanges would be "sheer appeasement" because "Russia had nothing to 'exchange.'" Before any scientific program
could be inaugurated, Vandenberg said, Russia had to be adequately policed through the United Nations. When Byrnes, Ernest
Bevin, and V. M. Molotov signed a joint statement on atomic
energy on December 27, Vandenberg called the announcement—
which included exchanges of basic information for peaceful purposes—"one more typical American 'give-away' on this subject."
By January 2, 1946, Truman had met Vandenberg's objections:
congressional legislation restricting the flow of atomic energy information was reinforced by executive decisions that no exchanges
would take place unless Russia first worked out methods of inspection and control. Complete and adequate "security" would be
part of each stage of disclosure. "In this manner," Vandenberg's
son later commented, "Vandenberg tied down the philosophy that
was to dominate the American proposal for atomic energy control." [17]

President Truman, to Wallace's dismay, had rejected Stimson's
call for a direct proposal to the Soviets. While he continued to
criticize the notion that the U.S. could enjoy a permanent monopoly on atomic weapons, Wallace emphasized a related issue: the
need for purely civilian control of the proposed Atomic Energy
Commission. Civilian control, Wallace argued, was needed to "assure a domestic program consistent with our international policy";
a "military clique" might use the commission to institute a new
imperialism. Ironically, Senator Vandenberg in mid-1946 also
supported the formation of a civilian commission, but on the
grounds that it would be the vehicle for accomplishing "a *totali-*

tarian control of atomic energy for the time being" (italics in original).[18]

Vandenberg knew that a civilian commission would be pledged to preserving the American atomic bomb monopoly, and that "international" policy proposed for the United Nations was now based on this concept. Vandenberg did amend the AEC bill to provide for a military liaison board to review commission decisions, and the amendment was passed by the Senate on March 12, 1946. Wallace called it the road to "military fascism," and urged the public to "rise up in their wrath" against the provisions for military review. But apparently Wallace still believed that the administration's policy on civilian control was different from Vandenberg's, and that President Truman was "everlastingly right on this subject." Vandenberg easily retorted that his military liaison group would be subordinate to civilians directly responsible to Truman himself. "It would not occur to me," he chided Wallace, "that we have gone Fascist when we rest the national defense in Mr. Truman's hands." Those who wanted civilian control, he commented privately, ignored the national-security factor altogether. They were supported in "this viewpoint by every Communist and every fellow traveller and every parlor pink in the country, because these latter groups would like to make our national security as insecure as possible." [19]

Vandenberg knew that the Truman administration was following his expressed policy on the atomic bomb. Yet Wallace continued to express his belief in the fundamental soundness of administration policy. He failed to realize that the bomb was adopted as an instrument of general diplomacy. Truman, Gar Alperovitz writes, "believed that the United States had sufficient power to force Soviet agreement to American economic and political plans for Eastern Europe," and its power "meant that there was no need to fear another German revival." It was years after the events before Wallace realized that his fight for civilian control had been irrelevant; that the victory he scored "was more apparent than real." The "major emphasis of the civilian members," of the Atomic Energy Commission, Wallace cogently put it, "has been on the making of bombs to be used by the State Department as a decisive element in diplomacy." [20]

The reality of Truman's atomic policy finally struck Wallace on June 6, 1946, when Bernard Baruch introduced the United States plan for control of atomic energy to the United Nations. Wallace realized it was based on the very assumption of permanent monopoly control which he had fought. In a letter addressed to the President on July 23, Wallace held that other nations should not be required to stop atomic research for military uses while the U.S. retained its right to withhold technical knowledge until an acceptable international control and inspection system existed. The United States was thereby notifying the Russians that if they were "good boys" America would eventually turn over to them its knowledge of atomic energy. But, Wallace noted, "there is no objective standard of what will qualify them as being 'good' nor any specified time for sharing our knowledge." Only after the Soviet Union had revealed its hand would the United States announce whether it would play out the game. An equitable agreement would be one in which the United States committed itself to disclose information and destroy its bomb stockpile at a specific time, not at its own discretion. The Russians, Wallace was convinced, would respond to such a proposal.[21]

A few weeks after this letter to the President, Wallace delivered the famous speech that led to his forced resignation from the Cabinet. On September 12, 1946, at Madison Square Garden in New York City, Wallace summarized and reiterated his critical theme. "Russian ideals of social-economic justice," he told his audience, "are going to govern nearly a third of the world. Our ideas of free enterprise democracy will govern much of the rest. . . . By mutual agreement this competition should be put on a friendly basis, and the Russians should stop conniving against us in certain areas just as we should stop scheming against them in other parts of the world." Wallace called for a sphere-of-influence concept. The United States, he insisted, "should recognize that we have no more business in the political affairs of Eastern Europe than Russia has in the political affairs of Latin-America." Each time the U.S. got tough with the Russians, Wallace emphasized, Russia would reciprocate. "I am neither anti-British nor pro-British, neither anti-Russian nor pro-Russian," Wallace claimed. Sections of his speech defending the Open Door concept and criticizing communism were met with vigorous boos from the New York left-wing audience, but Wallace insisted to the press that he was "following a straight American line." [22]

Wallace's speech was political dynamite to the developing bipartisan foreign policy. As he spoke in New York, Secretary of State Byrnes was in Paris negotiating with the Russians on European peace treaties. Wallace's speech threatened to disrupt Byrnes's "get-tough" approach, for Wallace stated that he had conferred with President Truman two days before delivering his remarks, and that the President had read the speech and told Wallace that it "represented the policy of his administration." Truman clumsily claimed on September 14 that he had approved only Wallace's right to make the speech, that he had not endorsed it as "a statement of the foreign policy of this country." But the President's denial did not satisfy Byrnes and Vandenberg. On September 18 Byrnes warned Truman that Wallace would have to be silenced on foreign affairs or Byrnes would not remain as Secretary of State even temporarily. Wallace had agreed to keep quiet until the Paris conference was over, but Byrnes was not satisfied. He insisted that Wallace threatened the entire bipartisan foreign policy. "You and I," Byrnes told Truman, "spent fifteen months building a bipartisan policy. We did a fine job convincing the world that it was a permanent policy upon which the world could rely. Wallace destroyed it in a day." On September 19 Truman asked Wallace to resign from the Cabinet, calling attention to the need of government to "stand as a unit in its relations with the rest of the world." [23]

The President, himself a leader of those who advocated a militant position toward Russia, appears to have been reluctant to ask Wallace to leave the Cabinet. "Wallace had a following," Truman noted; "his appeal had some effect." If he were kept in the Cabinet, "I might be able to put some check on his activities." Whether the President could have controlled Wallace is doubtful, for even after the furor over the Garden speech Wallace made it clear that he would continue to make his views known. But Truman did have good reason to fear Wallace's potential drawing power. As David A. Shannon has pointed out, "It was not until mid-1947 that Truman appeared as a champion of liberalism, after a Republican

Congress afforded him a conservative backdrop. The Democratic record on price control and inflation had been poor, housing was a mess, and Truman had even asked Congress for power to draft strikers. . . . In 1946, it seemed to the liberals that Truman would undo everything Roosevelt had gained." In this atmosphere the President may have hoped to prevent the emergence of a broad left opposition by keeping Wallace in the Cabinet. Even under pressure from Byrnes, Truman first asked only that Wallace refrain from criticism until the Paris negotiations were completed.[24]

Truman had good reason for avoiding a public break with his Secretary of Commerce. But this does not explain why Wallace stayed in the administration before September 1946. He might have led his supporters out at a time when doing so might have forced a shift of policy. Wallace, however, as the debate on atomic bomb policy revealed, did not blame the President for the militant turn in foreign policy. Instead, Wallace thought Truman shared his approach toward Soviet-American relations. He uncritically accepted Truman's statements at face value, and decided to try to influence policy from within the administration.

Some examples will indicate the effectiveness of the President's approach. On March 14, 1946, Truman had appointed General Walter Bedell Smith as Ambassador to Russia. Wallace wrote Truman expressing hope that Bedell Smith would be able to break the diplomatic deadlock in Soviet-American relations. He believed Smith's task would be made easier if the United States consented to discuss long-range economic problems with the Russians. America should prove its desire for peace, Wallace wrote, by trading with the Russians, and a delegation should be sent to Moscow to initiate talks on the subject.[25]

Truman wrote later that Bedell Smith had asked for Wallace's letter, along with Truman's initials, to indicate that the President approved of Wallace's view. Truman wrote: "I ignored this letter of Wallace's. I had expressed my policy to Bedell Smith and had suggested the approach he should take to the Kremlin. I could see little to be gained from the Wallace proposal." Clearly, Truman did not intend to see whether increased trade with Russia and a receptive attitude toward Soviet demands for security in Eastern Europe would promote better relations. Nor did he intend to grant the Soviets a loan. But he did not include in his *Memoirs* his answer to Wallace's letter. On March 20, he wrote Wallace:

I appreciated very much your letter in regard to the Russian situation which you handed me at the cabinet meeting last Friday. I have seen General Smith and have discussed conditions with him. I believe he is going to Russia with the right attitude in mind. I have great hope of his getting our relations on a better plane. He impressed me as being a capable person.

In the context of events, Wallace took this skillfully worded reply to mean that Truman agreed with his suggestions. Therefore, when Wallace appeared with the President at a dinner held on March 23, he praised Truman for carrying on FDR's fight for peace, claiming that the "people believe as you do, Mr. President" and that they "dislike all this talk of inevitable war." Wallace's analysis and endorsement brought forth no repudiation from the President.[26]

Another example of the effectiveness of Truman's approach was Wallace's debate with Cabinet members in March 1946 over the presence of American military bases in Iceland. On March 21, Reuben Karlstad, an Associated Press reporter in Sweden, told Wallace that Scandinavians were happy with the Russian withdrawal from the Danish island of Bornholm, and he asked Wallace when the United States would leave Iceland. Wallace responded that he thought Iceland wanted America's presence as a protection against Russia. That was not true, Karlstad said. Wallace then replied as a "private individual and not as a member of government, I thought it would be better for the peace of the world if the United States pulled out of Iceland." One day later, a report of this conversation appeared in the *New cork Times* and created havoc within the Cabinet. Secretary of State Byrnes felt that his efforts to get American air bases had been "aborted to a considerable degree by the statements and speeches of Secretary Wallace." James Forrestal backed Byrnes.[27]

The press also pictured Wallace's comments on Iceland as opposing a course of action favored both by the President and the Cabinet. Writing in *Life* in May 1946 Joseph and Stewart Alsop chided Wallace for supposedly believing that "Soviet realpolitik can be cured by loving kindness." Wallace had opposed "the agreed policy of the American government, approved by the President. . . . By an irresponsible intervention," the Alsops went on, "Wallace defeated his own government's policy." They then used the very argument the President himself would adopt when dismissing Wallace four months later. Wallace had a "right to his opinion," they wrote, but if it did not prevail he should "resign or . . . remain silent." Next in the line of attack was Washington columnist Bert Andrews, who reported for the *New York Herald Tribune* that President Truman himself believed Wallace should "go along with the policy . . . or keep quiet." [28]

This tempest over Iceland bases was a foreshadowing of the confrontation over the Madison Square Garden speech. Yet in June, Truman again indicated to Wallace that he was not dissatisfied with his Secretary. Wallace had sent the President a copy of his answer to *Life,* in which he claimed that the Alsops had distorted his real views and had based their argument on a purely personal talk with a Swedish reporter. Truman's answer to Wallace on June 7 indicated that the President agreed that the press was treating him unjustly. Truman wrote: "Your note of the 3rd enclosing my copy of your correspondence with Wilson Hicks of *Life* is all right. I was happy to receive it. It seems that *Life, Time* and *Fortune* magazines take particular delight in garbling anything that you or I have to say." By a judicious choice of language, Truman had linked distortions of the press against Wallace with those against himself. Wallace did not know of Byrne's attack upon him, since he had been absent from that particular Cabinet meeting. Thus his reaction to Truman's letter was to feel assured once again of the President's support in his fight for peace. Until his dismissal Wallace constantly argued that he and the President stood close on the question of Russian policy, and he believed that he was persuading, or could persuade, the President of his point of view.[29]

This belief led Wallace to reject the advice of those who sought to convince him to lead a national third-party effort in June 1946. He chose instead to fight within the administration "as long as blind acquiescence is not a condition of service in the Cabinet of the President." Indeed, Wallace was never acquiescent. Instead he intensified his critique. On July 23 he presented a memorandum to the President which summed up his entire approach toward foreign policy. It looked to the world, Wallace wrote, as if the United States were preparing for a war it held to be inevitable. Four-fifths of its budget was spent for warlike purposes; it had secured air bases around the world from which the rest of the earth could be bombed. Yet the United States criticized the Soviet Union's search for security along its immediate borders. Asking the President to consider reversing policy, Wallace inquired "how it would look to us if Russia had the ten-thousand-mile bombers and air bases within a thousand miles of our coast line and we did not?" The United States should "be prepared," he insisted, "to judge [Russia's] requirements against the background of what we ourselves and the British have insisted upon as essential to our respective security. We should be prepared, even at the expense of risking epithets of appeasement, to agree to reasonable Russian guarantees of security." [30]

As it turned out, "epithets of appeasement" was an unfortunate phrase which Truman used against Wallace. On September 18, the day before Truman announced Wallace's resignation, Wallace had told the President that the Soviet Union wanted peace but was afraid of America's intentions. After the conversation Truman decided that, "knowingly or not," Wallace "would lend himself to the more sinister ends of the Reds and those who served them." Referring to Wallace as "Mr. X," Truman wrote in his personal papers that X was not as "fundamentally sound" as he had thought. X was a "pacifist 100 per cent," who wanted to "disband our armed forces, give Russia our atomic secrets and trust a bunch of adventurers in the Kremlin Politburo. . . . The Reds, phonies and 'parlor pinks' seem to be banded together and are becoming a national danger. I am afraid they are a sabotage front for Uncle Joe Stalin." The President was able to evade Wallace's views by vulgarizing them. [31]

After his resignation as Secretary of Commerce in September 1946, Wallace was determined to pursue his public discussion of political issues. He accepted the editorship of the *New Republic* in December and looked forward to a program of major public speeches. On December 28–29, 1946, the National Citizens Po-

litical Action Committee and the Independent Citizens Committee
of the Arts, Sciences, and the Professions, which had jointly sponsored the September 12 Garden rally, met and merged to form
the Progressive Citizens of America. Addressing their meeting
Wallace declared:

> Those who put hatred of Russia first in all their feelings and actions do
> not believe in peace. Those who hold up Russian standards as a guide
> for us in the United States do not believe in freedom. As American
> progressives we are not interested in any fight between the Russia-haters
> and the Russophiles. We believe that such fighting is engineered by the
> enemy. We shall not allow the attacks of the enemy to stampede us into
> foolish red-baiting. Nor shall we allow those who owe their primary
> allegiance to some foreign power to determine our course.

Later Wallace described to a friend his objective at the time. Consistent with his attitude that both red-baiters and Russophiles were
ineffective in peace negotiations, Wallace said he hoped for an
agreement between the United States and the Soviet Union while
Russia was still economically and militarily weak and before it
was strong enough to challenge America's leading role.[32]

How this agreement was to be achieved in the context of the
United States' general objectives was indicated in the major articles
Wallace wrote for the *New Republic* and in his speeches. In them
he challenged the assumption of many American leaders that the
U.S. economic position was impregnable, and that they need only
sit back and reap the financial returns. Wallace advocated a positive policy to secure and improve this international position.

> . . . the United States must furnish its fair share of money for setting the
> backward areas of the world on their way toward expanded agricultural
> and industrial production. Money invested in this way will eventually
> be brought back to us many times over, provided we throw our influence
> on the side of lower tariffs and expanded world trade. Positive action
> in addition to the lowering of barriers to the freedom of trade, is needed.
> If the high volume of world trade necessary for American world pros-
> perity is to be sustained, this may involve not merely a TVA on the
> Danube but a series of them all over Europe.

From the realities of Europe's postwar situation, Wallace concluded that if all the countries of Europe, including the Soviet

Union, were to rebuild rapidly, they would have to rely almost entirely upon the United States for capital, technology, machinery, equipment, and semi-finished materials. Such a dependency would mean long-term American leadership in the European economy.[33]

Besides recommending temporary reconstruction measures, Wallace emphasized that American money be applied to the construction of transportation facilities and electric power resources, and the encouragement of East-West trade. This base was essential for the development of markets for advanced consumer and capital production:

There will soon be tremendous surpluses in the United States to match the great need in all of Eastern and Southern Europe. This year the [European Emergency Economic] Committee should put German, English, American, French and Russian technologists to work, under its direction. The one directive would be to lay out the railroads, the roads, the dams, the power plants and the factories, not from the standpoint of the next war but from the standpoint solely of self-liquidating projects which will service the expanding desires of these needy people.[34]

Wallace elaborated this general view in the case of Greece. "[Greece] needs modern agricultural machinery. Modern industry can be started in the cities. Dams could be built to develop the power possibilities of the rivers." The crisis in Greece had arisen in the winter of 1946–1947, exhausting the British postwar economy—until then the main prop for the Greek regime. As part of the Anglo-Soviet agreement of November 1944, Greece's internal politics were the sole affair of the British government, which attempted to eliminate the left-wing insurgent movement and establish a stable right-wing government. Britain's support of that government against left-wing guerrillas had become an unbearable strain on the British economy. Early in 1947 Britain asked the United States to take over the reconstruction of Greece.

Wallace welcomed this opportunity. Like other countries of Europe faced with economic reconstruction, he noted, "Greece cannot do this alone. . . . I don't believe in American imperialism, but as a stop-gap I believe that it is enlightened selfishness for the United States to step in now with a well-planned, efficiently administered loan." In August 1946 Secretary Wallace had sought a loan for Greece, but he had been opposed by the State and Treasury Departments and the Export-Import Bank. Greece, it was said, was politically unstable, corrupt, had a system of taxation which discriminated against the poor in favor of the wealthy, and was not a suitable country for viable development by American investment. Wallace shared these concerns, but he hoped to end political instability by bringing the insurgent left wing into a coalition government which would eliminate the economically disquieting system of repression and political imprisonment. To end corruption and insure that American money got to the people in need, Wallace suggested that a United States economic mission be established in Greece as a precondition for an American loan. "But our obligation goes much further than the mere giving of money. There is the further responsibility of seeing to it that the money we give is spent on the things for which we gave it." For the same reason Wallace hoped that United Nations agencies would oversee the efficient reconstruction of Greece.[35]

When President Truman presented the 80th Congress with his program for Greece and Turkey—the Truman Doctrine—he emphasized military aid rather than an economic program. Wallace reacted strongly:

March 12, 1947, marked a turning point in American history. On that day President Truman confronted the world with a crisis, not of the Greek economy, but of the American system. That which I feared when I wrote President Truman last July has come upon us.

Wallace called the Truman Doctrine "a military lend-lease program," a waste of $400 million. The money should have been devoted to the recovery of the Greek economy, which would also benefit the United States as a market for its capital and goods.[36]

On March 31, 1947, Wallace again spoke at Madison Square Garden to a "crisis meeting" on the Truman Doctrine. In detailing his opposition to it, Wallace summarized his view that positive American economic action was needed to maintain international economic stability. "The welfare of all peoples is our concern. Famine anywhere endangers plenty everywhere. Progress anywhere helps progress everywhere. Action to help the world must help America." He supported a United Nations Food and Agriculture

Organization plan for reconstruction in Greece and a $100 million International Bank loan.[37]

For Wallace, any international aid program would have to be long-term and regional in scope. He recommended that the International Bank fund a $600 million-a-year program for all countries of Eastern and Southern Europe. Responding to the Truman Doctrine, Wallace explained:

Of course I am not an isolationist. In opposing Truman's present program I do not want to see aid for reconstruction abroad discarded. In this climate of confusion the tired forces of isolation have been granted a second wind. The U. S. cannot flee from its world responsibilities any more than it can face up to them by ransoming wretched bureaucracies in the Near East. . . .

If a real job were to be done in Greece it would take $100 million a year for 10 years to fix up the roads and railroads, furnish agricultural tools and fertilizers, provide electricity and the beginnings of a modern industrial system. Many other countries have similar needs; some of them, including Bulgaria, Yugoslavia, Rumania, Poland and Hungary are within the Soviet sphere of influence. The United States is the only country that can come to their rescue; it should do so within the framework of a broad United Nations plan. There should be an economic 10-year plan to industrialize this entire area.[38]

Describing the tone which surrounded the debate over the Truman Doctrine, George Kennan has explained in his *Memoirs* how the imprecision of his writing in the "X" article in *Foreign Affairs* contributed to the universalization of his concept of containment. Kennan says he intended the concept of containment to have limited geographical application. Yet the strong expressions in his "X" article (which was written during December 1946–January 1947) were directed largely against critics of the Truman administration's foreign policy, such as Wallace. Among Kennan's reports from Moscow which had gained him the ears of decision-makers in Washington was a critique (March 20, 1946) of Wallace's position "that there is something our Government could and should do to persuade Stalin that we are not trying to form an anti-Soviet bloc." [39]

Lloyd Gardner has noted the importance Kennan attached to answering Wallace in his writing at this time:

Kennan interpreted Wallace's criticisms of the "get-tough" policy as a foolish desire to continue Rooseveltian personal diplomacy and, at Yale University, on October 1, 1946, indirectly criticized him in a lecture on the dangers of misunderstanding Soviet motives and policy. Unhappily, Kennan began, such bids for "trust" in international relations all too often had great appeal "to the Rotarian heart." . . . Here again, however, Kennan's overreaction to Rooseveltian foreign policy led him to draw militant images for instructional purposes rather than describe the reality of Soviet capabilities. He was chasing Roosevelt's ghost in Henry Wallace.[40]

By 1947 the general concept of a large-scale multi-national program of American aid for reconstruction had become common among American policy-makers. The basic State Department fear in the spring of that year—that a European economic crisis would threaten America's own economic stability—was expressed by Joseph Jones, a major drafter of the Truman Doctrine and Marshall Plan speeches. In a letter (February 26, 1947) to Assistant Secretary of State William Benton, Jones declared:

There are many signs that the world is approaching this year the greatest crisis since the turn in the tide of the war in November 1942. It is primarily an economic crisis centered in Britain and Empire, France, Greece, and China. . . . If these areas are allowed to spiral downwards into economic anarchy, then at best they will drop out of the United States orbit and try an independent nationalistic policy; at most they will swing into the Russian orbit. We will then face the world alone. What will be the cost in dollars and cents, of our armaments and of our economic isolation? I do not see how we could possibly avoid a depression far greater than that of 1929–32 and crushing taxes to pay for the direct commitments we would be forced to make around the world.[41]

Jones, in his book *The Fifteen Weeks,* describes the State Department's political and economic thinking which laid the foundation upon which the Marshall Plan was chartered. First, the United States sought to reduce trade barriers and end restrictions on currency convertibility. "The other pillar," Jones noted, "of United States foreign economic policy after the war was loans for reconstruction and development." In addition to the traditional financing by loans from the Export-Import Bank, the International Bank for Reconstruction and Development, and the International Monetary Fund, a new economic program would be based upon foreign aid.[42]

There was no telling what might be the effect on American economic expansion and on political stability in Europe if the European countries failed to recover soon. American exports during 1947 would be $16 billion, and imports only $8 billion. About $5 billion of this deficit would be financed by existing United States loans and the rest by payments of gold or currency. As Jones wrote:

The evidence overwhelmingly indicated that even the current volume and pattern of United States aid were not adequate to bring about world economic stability, support the liberal world-trading system desired by the United States, or attain the political objectives of the United States in certain critical countries. The President's Council of Economic Advisers expected a slight business recession within twelve months; if the expected export decline, due to foreign inability to pay, coincided with weakness in the domestic economy, the effect on production, prices, and employment in the United States might be serious.[43]

The theme of a large-scale multi-national program of American aid for reconstruction had been advocated by Wallace during a speaking tour in 1947 in Britain, Sweden, Norway, and France. He spelled out this aid program for Europe in a speech before the French Chamber of Deputies on April 23. His fundamental objective was reflected in a BBC speech: "The immense power and wealth of America is being used for strategic and military purposes rather than to raise the standard of living in countries which could become a great market for American exports." At Stockholm he stated: "I am not a Communist, I am not a Socialist. I am not only an American capitalist—or, as I told the House of Parliament in London—I am a progressive Tory who believes it is absolutely essential to have peace and understanding with Russia." [44]

Thus when Secretary Marshall presented the American foreign economic aid program in a speech at Harvard on June 5, Wallace received it favorably. Marshall's speech contained the clear warning that while it was not directed against "any other country or doctrine," any European country which refused to cooperate fully in the Marshall Plan's assigned role would not only not receive United States foreign aid but would "encounter the opposition of the United States." On June 12 Marshall specifically invited Soviet participation. Wallace praised Marshall for saying what Wallace had been saying, including that Russia be allowed to participate in the new foreign aid program. In a June 22 speech favoring the Marshall Plan, Wallace declared:

The Marshall doctrine looks toward an overall program which is what I have been advocating all along. . . . Marshall recognizes that the fundamental problem is one of economics, that Europe must share in the effort and that she must be aided as a whole and not country by country. He left the door open for Russia to participate in the plan.

The Soviets rejected the Marshall Plan because, they said, they disliked the idea of a supranational administration of economic aid, a concept which American policy-makers described as crucial for American dominance. Russia also feared that under the plan agricultural Eastern Europe would be subordinated to industrial Western Europe.[45]

On December 19, 1947, Truman presented to Congress his European recovery program. By then Wallace had lost much of his original enthusiasm for Marshall's proposals, for he felt that the economic objective of creating markets for American industrial and agricultural production was being subordinated to military purposes. Wallace responded to Truman's speech by announcing his own presidential candidacy on December 29, 1947:

I personally was for the humanitarian aspects of the Marshall Plan long before it was announced. . . . I pushed for help to Greece against the opposition of the Administration eight months before the Truman Doctrine was announced. But I have fought and shall continue to fight programs which give guns to people when they want plows. I fight the Truman Doctrine and the Marshall Plan as applied because they divide Europe into two warring camps.

The Marshall Plan was, Wallace said, American interference in the internal affairs of European countries with the aim of buying elections and creating an American-dominated military bloc. It had changed from the sound program for economic development which he had initially supported.[46]

Wallace elaborated his disappointment in testimony before the House Committee on Foreign Affairs, February 24, 1948. Describing his original favorable reaction to Marshall's proposal, he told how he had seen it as an extension of the lend-lease program. A new lend-lease program would be "a plan to help bring peace and prosperity to the world, with America again providing the moral, economic, and political leadership which it had under F.D.R."

Now the militarists and bankers, hiding behind the fine words spoken by Secretary Marshall last June, would have the American people repeat the Truman Doctrine on a European scale—with plans already announced for extension into Asia and the rest of the World. . . . These are the men in and out of Government who laid down the conditions for eligibility to the participating nations, who perverted the principles of self-aid and recovery into a program which in operation would subject the people of western Europe to the control of American finance at the endless expense to the American taxpayers.[47]

Wallace was especially critical of the Marshall Plan's requirement that recipient countries establish special funds of local currencies equal to the cost in dollars of the grants they received. "The administration makes it quite explicit that each participating country must agree to follow its principles in managing its currency." The "Administration's plea for the 'open door' means paving the way for restoration of monopoly power in the participating countries. It means driving small, independent businesses to the wall, restricting production, maintaining high monopoly prices." Opposing the possible re-emergence for European cartels, Wallace proposed a program which would assure a world market for American agricultural production and for steel, machinery, and equipment.

American benefits from this plan would not be limited to those flowing from assured employment and markets. We could expect from Europe and Asia a rich return flow of goods and services, endless supplies of raw materials to supplement our own large resources, new variety of our everyday living. . . .[48]

Although Wallace's analysis of the Marshall Plan and postwar U.S. economic policy included some fundamentally radical ideas, he did not object to the idea of foreign economic aid. His specific proposals represented a continuation of the New Deal's corporate liberalism which, through the utilization of political power, attained a stable, secure, and rational economy. His programs paralleled the economic aims of the Truman administration. But the administration's desire to dominate and coerce, as well as its search to broaden congressional support, caused it to avoid relying on an international agency. Wallace differed with Truman over these means, and proposed UN supervision. (This tactical difference was important but not basic, for Wallace knew that the United States had a dominant voice in the United Nations.)

In his exchanges with Representative Lawrence Smith (Republican, Wisconsin), the only member of the House Foreign Affairs Committee to oppose the Truman Doctrine, Wallace offered some clarification of the charge that he was a Soviet apologist. Smith questioned Wallace about the claim by supporters of the Marshall Plan that if it were not enacted the Soviet Union would have a free hand in Western as well as in Eastern Europe. Wallace responded:

I think our approach, with the intent of human freedom without compulsion, attracts human beings much more than the Russian approach, and the Russians would not penetrate into western Europe. . . . Hungry people reach out in desperation for very strong measures and usually totalitarian measures of some kind or another are there. However, with the situation as it now is, I do not see the danger of communism in western Europe. . . .

The Communist regime might come into power in one place or another but I do not see how it would satisfy the needs of the people very well if they were exceedingly short of goods. . . .

I have said for the past year that those countries on Russia's border were certain to have governments friendly to Russia; that it was in the cards, because Russia had been so often invaded by those countries, and the more vigorously we move in the United States, the more certain it has been that Russia would make certain in one way or another that those governments were friendly to her.

Wallace implied that the obvious division of spheres of influence between the Soviet Union and the Western allies should be respected. It had not been respected, he said, because of Western pressure in Eastern Europe, and Soviet counterpressure, as in the case of Greece. His recognition of spheres of influence was, for Wallace, simply a better means of achieving traditional American trade objectives. Wallace did go on to draw his own containment line beyond which Soviet encroachment could lead to strong United States military action.

England had an understanding with Russia in 1907 with regard to the Near East. It did not necessarily mean cooperation. I think we should have the same kind of understanding, covering a somewhat larger geographical area. As I say, Russia has every right to know just exactly the point beyond which, if she steps, there will be real trouble.

But Wallace wanted regional containment limits for the Soviet Union in place of the world-wide limits favored by Truman, Harriman, and Dulles—a distinction designed to reduce Soviet-American tension points and military preparations.[49]

Wallace fully developed his views of American international economic objectives in *Toward World Peace,* his major document in the 1948 presidential campaign. In the book he attacked those feudal and dictatorial governments around the world which failed to increase agricultural production and initiate industrialization through the introduction of modern machinery. "These native exploiters fear Russia and look to the United States as their only hope." Instead of supporting such exploitation, Wallace hoped the United States would show that it was better able than the Soviet Union to develop these economies.

I know that this is the only way of saving our own democratic capitalism. I know that increased efficiency on the part of the two-thirds of the people who live in the so-called backward areas will open up unlimited markets for the United States, Britain and Russia—not only markets we want in order to prosper, but markets that we must have in order to survive.

While Wallace supported the overall program of foreign economic aid, he criticized the historic methods of overseas investment as inefficient. They failed to contribute to the general economic needs of the American economy or other peoples:

In the backward countries the loans in the twenties were too often made for unproductive purposes and in some cases for outright graft. The interest rates were too high and there was no fundamentally sound program for increasing agricultural and industrial efficiency. Too often the primary purpose was to enable the underwriting banking house in the United States to unload its bonds on the unsuspecting public while the bank took a quick run for cover with its underwriter's profit.[50]

As for America's economic relations with the Soviet sphere, Wallace warned that U.S. trade objectives were undermined by the Truman administration's programs. The long-run aim in the Balkans of "the open door to trade and invest with safety" had been dangerously threatened. "Under the Truman Doctrine Anglo-American business operations in Eastern Europe will never be safe. Under the program I have described there can be a great expansion of business and markets for the benefit of the United States, Britain, and Russia as well as the Eastern European countries themselves." The Soviets, Wallace felt, could—at great internal cost—develop their postwar economy without American economic aid and credits. They had made rapid progress without American capital in the 1930's by extreme denial of consumer needs.

We can again force Russia and her satellite nations into a path involving severe discipline and the denial of the ordinary human rights. Or we can, with our capital and technology, greatly shorten the period required to make great progress in science, agriculture, and industrialization.[51]

If the Soviet Union and the United States clearly understood each other's expansive limits, it would serve as a basis for economic cooperation with the Soviets. Wallace spelled out his concepts of that limitation:

This will come in a realistic joint discussion of the logistics of geopolitical power. The Russians must know the points beyond which we cannot tolerate further Russian expansion—all of them. Conversely, they must be given the right to tell us the limits beyond which we cannot intervene without creating the danger of war at such time as they become strong enough to wage war. Both countries should speak frankly on these points as a preliminary to bargaining and settlement. . . . More than any other people Americans have been interested in raising the living standards of humanity everywhere. Therefore, in the peace conference with Russia we should make it clear that we are just as much interested in seeing the war damage repaired in Russia, and the standard of living raised in Yugoslavia, as in any other part of the world. Our ability to help in this is a trading counter that should match Russia's advantage deriving from the present misery of many peoples.

The political assurance the United States should require, therefore, is a pledge by Russia not to expand either by direct coercion or by Russian-directed communistic infiltration beyond the agreed-on boundaries.

This does not mean two worlds. It does mean a *modus vivendi* during a period of difficult postwar transition within one world. We should make it clear to Russia that we will not go outside the United Nations to give aid to or intervene in the affairs of any other country provided Russia will join the United States in agreeing to certain limitations on the use of veto power over United Nations decisions.[52]

Persistent in Wallace's thinking was the "official" U.S. concept that the United Nations was the center of America's postwar collective security system. It was part of the sophisticated program for America's world economic role which he had elaborated while Secretary of Agriculture and Vice-President. With United States economic leadership in the world an obvious fact, international organizations would operate on the basis of that fact to control the major areas of political friction which could impede international economic efficiency. Wallace noted this during his testimony against the North Atlantic Treaty Organization before the Senate Foreign Relations Committee on May 5, 1949:

The all-important thing . . . [is] above everything, the routing of international relief through a United Nations agency rather than the United States carrying it on directly. I believe that when the United States carries on international relief directly she is continually being suspected of interfering in the internal affairs of other nations, and she will be accused by one nation or another or one group or another within nations of having imperialistic designs. My program is to build up a strong United Nations, have such an understanding between Russia and the United States that both, without either one appeasing the other, will be happy to see a strong United Nations, and route these international matters through United Nations agencies instead of through either regional agencies or by one particular country carrying on the activity unilaterally.[53]

Wallace's testimony disputed the Truman administration's claim that NATO would strengthen the United Nations. A United Nations–based great-power unity would be more beneficial to the United States since it would mean a more productive world; competing great-power alliances, in Wallace's view, would retard American economic development. The unproductive drain on economic resources inherent in military expenditures was a constant theme in Wallace's testimony. NATO was, in his eyes, the ultimate failure of the Marshall Plan, which was supposed to preclude the need for a military program in Europe. Wallace therefore concluded:

. . . Any fair appraisal of [NATO's] consequences demonstrates that it can lead only to national insolvency, the surrender of our traditional freedoms, war, a possible military disaster, and the certain sacrifice not only of life and treasure but of the very system of government which it is supposed to preserve.[54]

Wallace's alternative to NATO was a U.S.-Soviet agreement based upon: a unified, demilitarized Germany; noninterference in the internal affairs of other nations; abandonment of military bases in all United Nations member countries and no export of weapons to other countries; unrestricted trade; general reduction of armaments; and "the establishment of a World Reconstruction and Development Agency within the UN to build a productive and economically unified Europe, without barriers between east and west, and to assist the free development of the industrially backward countries of Asia, Latin America, and Africa." [55]

Truman administration spokesmen and Republican leaders, such as Dulles and Vandenberg, Wallace noted, had emphasized that there was no threat of Soviet armed attack. In his prepared testimony, Wallace analyzed the major argument for NATO:

It is urged, however, that the Soviets are intransigent and uncompromising; that agreement with them is impossible of attainment, and that only a show of force can bring them to terms.

The first question to which I submit that your committee must find an answer is: What are our Nation's terms? What are the conditions on which we are prepared to end the undeclared war we are now waging and negotiate a settlement with Russia?

These terms have never been stated. Instead, the administration has persistently refused every invitation extended by the Russians to state them.

If it is unconditional surrender that we would exact from the Russians, then indeed we will have to wage a war to gain it. For unconditional surrender cannot be won from a strong and proud people. It can only be imposed on a defeated enemy.

If the demands are for something less, then why the hesitance to state our terms? Why the cold rejection—at least three times in the past year—of the Soviet offers to talk peace?

It is not my purpose here to review the difficult and tragic course of Soviet-American relations since the death of President Roosevelt in April 1945. But I say that no honest and objective student of the events of these 4 years can conclude that the failure of agreement can be laid wholly on the Russian doorstep.[56]

Wallace considered the American desire for international omnipotence to be conducive to war. But he continued to believe that America's objectives could be achieved in the natural course of the world economy through U.S. leadership in economic development and reconstruction. And the Soviet Union would not challenge America's position if the United States recognized the Soviet Union's sphere of influence and entered into sincere negotiations in which the political and geographical limits for each country were clearly stated.

Although he opposed most of the specific foreign policy decisions of the United States after World War II, Wallace did not develop a broadly critical or essentially radical analysis of American foreign policy. His shortcomings were evident in an exchange before the Foreign Relations Committee with Senator Tom Connally, who asked if current diplomatic moves to settle the Berlin crisis were not evidence of the peaceful intentions of the Truman administration. Wallace answered that while he had disagreed with the Truman administration's foreign policy, he found hope in the Berlin negotiations:

I will be glad to assume that when Secretary Acheson was appointed it meant a slow, certain, and gradual turn in the whole administration policy. It may be true. I hope it is. This may be the first sign of it. I hope it is.

(The Chairman) You think he is coming over to your view on everything?

(Wallace) It may be that the President himself is. I hope so. At any rate, I know the President at one time was quite completely in accord with my view.[57]

Thus, at the same time Wallace strongly opposed the ratification of NATO, and shortly after his sobering defeat in the 1948 elections, Wallace was prepared to judge positively the future policies of the same administration whose past policies he had criticized. This possibility was in fact realized when Truman decided to intervene in Korea in 1950. "When my country is at war and the United Nations sanctions that war, I am on the side of my country and the U.N. . . . I cannot agree with those who want to start a propaganda drive to pull the U.N. troops out of Korea." Instead Wallace proposed: "Truman and Stalin to meet to discuss a real Point Four program operating through the U.N. with money contributed by all the nations on the basis of one-third of the armaments expenditures." [58]

Despite his wavering line, Wallace made an important contribution to public awareness of American Cold War policies. He attacked the Truman administration's atomic diplomacy, its openness to influence by the military and by bankers and industrialists in foreign and defense policy-making, its heavy taxation and conscription necessary to fulfill those policies, and its creation of military alliances and construction of air bases around the Soviet Union. Unlike most administration figures, Wallace believed that peaceful accommodation was possible. He proposed alternate methods to achieve the Open Door objectives which he shared with the decision-makers in the White House and the State Department. Yet these shared common aims and his personal weaknesses (which, admittedly, were human strengths) made it difficult for Wallace to mount the kind of opposition that would effectively challenge administration policy.[59]

The policies pursued by the Truman administration were designed to gain the congressional support that Wallace's alternatives could not. But the problems raised by their application underline the value of Wallace's long-range perspective. The programs that Wallace proposed were more sophisticated, more likely to gain the full cooperation of the Soviet Union and other countries, than those which the Truman administration launched in its efforts to maintain American world economic hegemony. Wallace and Truman agreed on Open Door principles, but Wallace's alternate methods, his promotion of noncoercive international programs, and his restraint of the military, if followed, might have reduced Cold War friction and brought a largely liberal capitalist and partially communist world order based upon economic prosperity and stability.

Notes

1. President Truman said of Wallace that "knowingly or not," he "would lend himself to the more sinister ends of the Reds and those who serve them" (Harry S. Truman, *Memoirs*, 2 vols. [New York, 1955, 1956], I, 558). An interesting reflection of official thinking about Wallace after his resignation as Secretary of Commerce in September 1946 is the report of the United States chargé in the Soviet Union, Eldridge Durbrow, to the Secretary of State on Soviet attitudes (November 2, 1946): "Elimination of those 'malevolent forces' [Vandenberg, Baruch, Harriman, etc.] and their replacement by 'progressives,' Soviet press implies, would smooth the way for friendly co-existence. With regard to this group, too, names have been given: Wallace, Morgenthau, Pepper, and representatives De Lacy and Patterson. . . . An American 'progressive' administration could hope in the long run for scarcely more favorable attention than the present administration. . . . It consequently seems evident that it is not for love of mass of American 'progressives' that Kremlin has bestowed kind words upon them. It is simply that they can be currently useful to Kremlin." Department of State, *Foreign Relations of the United States, 1946* (Washington, D.C., 1969), VI, 798–799.

2. Arthur M. Schlesinger, Jr., *The Vital Center* (Boston, 1949), pp. 115–116; Dwight Macdonald, *Henry Wallace: The Man and the Myth* (New York, 1948), pp. 174–175; Alonzo Hamby, "Henry A. Wallace, The Liberals, and Soviet-American Relations," *Review of Politics*, XXX (April 1968), 153–169.

3. Russell Lord, *The Wallaces of Iowa* (Boston, 1947): Curtis D. MacDougall, *Gideon's Army*, 3 vols. (New York, 1965); Theodore Rosenof, "The Economic Ideas of Henry A. Wallace, 1933–1948," *Agricultural History*, XLI (April 1967), 143–153; Edward L. and Frederick H. Schapsmeier, *Henry A. Wallace of Iowa: The Agrarian Years, 1910–1940* (Ames, Iowa,

1968); Karl M. Schmidt, *Henry A. Wallace, Quixotic Crusade 1948* (Syracuse, 1960).

4. Lloyd C. Gardner, "From New Deal to New Frontiers: 1937–1941," *Studies on the Left,* I (Fall 1959), 30; William Appleman Williams, *The Contours of American History* (Cleveland, 1961), p. 454; Henry A. Wallace, "Beard: The Planner," *New Republic,* LXXXI (January 2, 1935), 225–226.

5. Henry A. Wallace, *The Century of the Common Man,* ed. by Russell Lord (New York, 1943), pp. 67–68; Henry A. Wallace, *Democracy Reborn,* ed. by Russell Lord (New York, 1944), p. 126; *ibid.,* p. 37, speech of February 9, 1944; *New York Times,* September 21, 1945; Henry A. Wallace, "How Much Planning?," *New York Times Magazine,* September 2, 1945, p. 45; Lloyd C. Gardner, "The New Deal, New Frontiers, and the Cold War: A Re-examination of American Expansion, 1933–45," in David Horowitz, ed., *Corporations and the Cold War* (New York, 1969), pp. 112–113, 126–130.

6. House of Representatives, Committee on Banking and Currency, *Anglo-American Financial Agreement,* 79th Cong., 2nd sess., Wallace testimony of May 27, 1946, pp. 402–403; Gabriel Kolko, *The Politics of War* (New York, 1968), pp. 491–492; House, *Anglo-American Financial Agreement,* Wallace testimony of March 12, 1946, p. 265; *New York Times,* November 13, 1945.

7. Lord, *Wallaces of Iowa,* p. 553. Lord quotes from Wallace before the Senate Commerce Committee, January 24–25, 1945; *New York Times Book Review,* September 9, 1945; Taft quoted in *Congressional Digest,* XXIV (October 1945), 235.

8. Kolko, *Politics of War,* pp. 314–340, 389–414; William Appleman Williams, *The Tragedy of American Diplomacy* (New York, 1962), pp. 220–243.

9. Wallace to Truman, March 14, 1946, in Truman, *Memoirs,* I, 555; Wallace to Truman, July 23, 1946, *New Republic,* CXV (September 30, 1946), 404.

10. Kolko, *Politics of War,* pp. 339–340; Thomas G. Paterson, "The Abortive American Loan to Russia and the Origins of the Cold War, 1943–1946," *Journal of American History,* LVI (June 1969), 70–92.

11. Paterson, "Abortive American Loan," pp. 76, 91; Kolko, *Politics of War,* pp. 500–501.

12. Henry A. Wallace, "Address to the Sixtieth Anniversary of the Prairie Club," April 29, 1950, Des Moines, Iowa (privately printed).

13. *New York Times,* June 5, 1945.

14. *New York Times,* March 20, 1946.

15. James Forrestal, *The Forrestal Diaries,* ed. by Walter Millis (New York, 1951), pp. 95–96; Gar Alperovitz, *Atomic Diplomacy: Hiroshima and Potsdam* (New York, 1965), pp. 223–230.

16. Henry L. Stimson and McGeorge Bundy, *On Active Service in Peace and War* (New York, 1947, 1948), pp. 642–646; Alperovitz, *Atomic Diplomacy,* pp. 276–279; Wallace, "Address . . . to the Prairie Club," p. 7; Wallace, *Toward World Peace* (New York, 1948), pp. 8–9.

17. Arthur H. Vandenberg, *The Private Papers of Senator Vandenberg,* ed. by Arthur H. Vandenberg, Jr., with Joe Alex Morris (Boston, 1952),

p. 227 (diary entries for December 10 and 27, 1945, and January 2, 1946, pp. 232–235).

18. Senate, Special Committee on Atomic Energy, *Atomic Energy Act of 1946,* 79th Cong., 2nd sess., Part II, 145, testimony of Wallace, January 31, 1946; Vandenberg, *Private Papers,* p. 253 (diary entry for July 20, 1946).

19. *New York Times,* March 13, 1946; Vandenberg, *Private Papers,* pp. 256–257 (diary entry for March 14, 1946).

20. *New York Times,* March 16, 1946; Alperovitz, *Atomic Diplomacy,* pp. 233–234; Alice K. Smith, *A Peril and a Hope: The Scientists' Movement in America, 1945–1947* (Chicago, 1965), pp. 75–200; Wallace, "Address . . . to the Prairie Club," p. 8.

21. Wallace to Truman, July 23, 1946, *New Republic,* CXV (September 30, 1946), 404; Walter LaFeber, *America, Russia and the Cold War* (New York, 1967), pp. 21–22, 34–35; John W. Spanier and Joseph L. Nogee, *The Politics of Disarmament* (New York, 1962), p. 58.

22. *U.S. News and World Report,* September 20, 1946, p. 65; text of Wallace speech of September 12, 1946, *New York Times,* September 13, 1946; U.S. chargé in the Soviet Union, Durbrow, reported, September 16, 1946, on the first reference to Wallace's speech in the Soviet press and indicated the somewhat negative Soviet first reaction: "While reproducing lengthy passages from Pepper's and Robeson's speeches at Madison Square Garden, Soviet press, September 15, carries only following brief allusion Wallace speech: "Wallace and Senator Pepper appealed for improvement in Soviet-U.S. relations and demanded return Roosevelt's foreign policy. Audience loudly applauded those portions of Wallace's speech in which he censured imperialism and speculation on threat of war, and it greeted with shouts of disapproval certain of his statements directed against USSR." *Foreign Relations of the United States, 1946,* VI, 782.

23. *U.S. News and World Report,* September 20, 1946, p. 65; Press Conference No. 82, Saturday, September 14, 1946, 2 PM, p. 2, Harry S. Truman Library (Independence, Missouri); James F. Byrnes, *Speaking Frankly* (New York, 1947), pp. 240–242; Press Conference No. 83, September 20, 1946, 10:46 AM, pp. 2–3, Truman Library. In his *Memoirs,* Truman wrote that he had not read the Garden speech and that Wallace had only "told me he was going to make a speech." But, the official record of the President's news conference of September 12 indicates that President Truman did approve the contents of Wallace's speech. In response to a question whether the speech represented administration policy, Truman replied, "That is correct." A few moments later he stressed and reiterated that "I approve the whole speech." Truman, *Memoirs,* I, 557; Press Conference No. 80, Thursday, September 12, 1946, 4 PM, pp. 4–5, Truman Library.

24. Truman, *Memoirs,* I, 558; David A. Shannon, *The Decline of American Communism* (New York, 1959), p. 128; *New York Times,* September 19, 1946. Truman's mild criticism of Wallace came one day after Wallace had released the text of his July 23 private letter to Truman, which had further infuriated Byrnes and Vandenberg. With the administration now taking a negative view of Wallace's speech, the Soviet press developed an interest in it. In a "Restricted, U.S. Urgent" message, the U.S. chargé Durbrow wrote to the Secretary of State, September 20, 1946: "Wallace speech

has received belated but extreme coverage in Soviet press. Its salient points on foreign policy were accorded column and half summary September 18. These were accompanied by dispatches affirming that President had given speech full approval as in line with Byrnes' policy, that he had later rectified his statement to indicate he meant approval only Wallace right to speak, and that President's prestige at home and abroad had suffered because Byrnes had compelled him to withdraw his original approval. Wallace issue was highlighted September 20 in all Moscow papers with three column spreads of July 23 letter to President. Also featured was Wallace press conference announcing friendly conversations with President as result of which Wallace proposed to make no more speeches until after Paris Conference." *Foreign Relations of the United States, 1946,* VI, 783–784.

25. Wallace to Truman, March 14, 1946, in Truman, *Memoirs,* I, 555.

26. Truman, *Memoirs,* I, 556; Truman to Wallace, March 20, 1946, quoted in Wallace to Ronald Radosh, March 24, 1960; *New York Times,* March 24, 1946.

27. Henry A. Wallace diary, notes of March 21, 1946, in Wallace to Ronald Radosh, March 24, 1960; *New York Times,* March 22, 1946; Millis, *Forrestal Diaries,* pp. 154–155, entry of April 19, 1946.

28. Joseph and Stewart Alsop, *Life* (May 20, 1946), 68; *New York Herald Tribune,* June 2, 1946.

29. Wallace to Wilson Hicks, May 21, 1946, in Wallace to Ronald Radosh, March 24, 1960; Truman to Wallace, June 7, 1946, in *ibid.*

30. Wallace to Political Action Committee of St. Louis, Missouri, June 14, 1946, in Lord, *Wallaces of Iowa,* pp. 572–574; *New Republic,* CXV (September 30, 1946), 404.

31. Truman, *Memoirs,* I, 558; William Hillman, *Mr. President* (New York, 1952), pp. 127–128; Lloyd C. Gardner, *Architects of Illusion* (Chicago, 1970), pp. 310–312.

32. MacDougall, *Gideon's Army,* I, 114–115.

33. Wallace, "The Opportunity for the GOP," *New Republic,* CXVI (February 10, 1947), 23. The concept of the TVA as a model for the central European countries' reconstruction had been proposed by President Truman at the time of the Potsdam conference, and *Business Week* (June 9, 1945), pp. 117–118, noted: "In an age of light metals, a TVA for the Danube and the harnessing of the area's hydroelectric power to an aluminum industry based on rich local bauxite deposits (in Yugoslavia and Hungary) could revolutionize the Balkans" (Gardner, *Architects of Illusion,* pp. 73–75). A month before Wallace's article, the TVA model for Europe had been presented in a major speech by John Foster Dulles on January 17, 1947 (the speech was approved in advance by Senator Arthur Vandenberg and Governor Thomas Dewey). See Joseph M. Jones, *The Fifteen Weeks* (New York, 1955), p. 220.

34. Wallace, "The Moscow Conference Can Succeed," *New Republic,* CXVI (March 10, 1947), 22.

35. Wallace, "The Way to Help Greece," *New Republic,* CXVI (March 17, 1947), 12–13.

36. Wallace, "The Fight for Peace Begins," *New Republic,* CXVI (March 24, 1947), 12–13.

37. Wallace, "Back to the United Nations" (address on March 31, 1947),

in the *Congressional Record,* 80th Cong., 1st sess., pp. A1572–A1573; Mac-Dougall, *Gideon's Army,* I, 128–129.

38. Wallace, "The Truman Doctrine—or a Strong UN," *New Republic,* CXVI (March 31, 1947), 12–13; cf. Wallace, "The State Department's Case," *ibid.,* (April 7, 1947), 12–13; Wallace summarized his attitude toward an international aid program in 1947 during his dictation of a retrospective statement of his political objectives previous to launching his presidential candidacy late in 1947 (August 1952): "Fundamental has been my approval of a steadily strong United Nations, looking toward full employment in one world of peace; expanded world trade; progressive capitalism in the United States—all three being realized to a considerable extent by the investment of surplus United States capital through the United Nations in so-called backward nations and using United States technical experts in backward nations of the world. Through that, expanded world trade to make progressive capitalism work in the United States and give the United Nations real meaning." MacDougall, *Gideon's Army,* I, 171.

39. George F. Kennan, *Memoirs* (Boston, 1967), pp. 373–387; Wallace, *Toward World Peace,* pp. 89–107; *Foreign Relations of the United States, 1946,* VI, 721.

40. Gardner, *Architects of Illusion,* pp. 292–294.

41. Jones to Benton, February 26, 1947, Joseph Jones Papers, Box 1, Truman Library, quoted in Henry W. Berger, "A Conservative Critique of Containment: Senator Taft on the Early Cold War Program," in David Horowitz, ed., *Containment and Revolution* (Boston, 1967), pp. 126–127.

42. Jones, *Fifteen Weeks,* pp. 94–95.

43. Jones, *Fifteen Weeks,* pp. 207, 228; on the economic reasons for the Marshall Plan, see Gunther Stein, *The World the Dollar Built* (New York, 1953), pp. 89–90, and David Horowitz, *Empire and Revolution* (New York, 1969), p. 84; on the political development of the Marshall Plan, see Jones, *Fifteen Weeks,* pp. 278–281, 252–253; Dean Acheson, *Present at the Creation* (New York, 1969), pp. 227–235; and Kennan, *Memoirs,* pp. 342–372.

44. Schmidt, *Wallace,* p. 30; MacDougall, *Gideon's Army,* I, 136, 139, 141; Rexford Tugwell suggests that it was Wallace's criticism of the Truman Doctrine which revealed to Marshall its dangers and caused the modification of foreign policy that led to the Marshall Plan. Rexford G. Tugwell, *A Chronicle of Jeopardy, 1945–55* (Chicago, 1955), pp. 74–79. Joseph Jones's *Fifteen Weeks,* also published in 1955, does not support Tugwell's suggestion in Jones's presentation of a detailed chronology of the development of the Marshall Plan.

45. Jones, *Fifteen Weeks,* pp. 249, 255, 283; Wallace, "Bevin Muddies the Waters," *New Republic,* CXVI (June 30, 1947), 11–12. Wallace's attitude toward U.S.-Soviet relations was summarized by him at this time: "I am convinced that the key to this relationship is not the contrast between Russia's military weakness and America's present military strength, but the contrast between her desperate need for capital resources and our increasing abundance of these resources. . . . America alone can provide it. Furthermore, it is in our immediate self-interest to provide it. A stable Russia is vital to peace." Wallace, "The Constructive Alternative," *New Republic,* CXVI (May 19, 1947), 11–12. Concerning Russia's response to the Marshall Plan, see Thomas G. Paterson, "The Quest for Peace and Prosperity: Inter-

national Trade, Communism, and the Marshall Plan," in Barton J. Bernstein, ed., *Politics and Policies of the Truman Administration* (Chicago, 1970), pp. 78–112, especially pp. 97–105.

46. Wallace, "I Shall Run in 1948," *Vital Speeches,* XIV, 172–174; Wallace, "My Alternative for the Marshall Plan," *New Republic,* CXVIII (January 12, 1948), 13–14; Wallace, "What We Must Do Now," *ibid.,* CXVII (July 14, 1947), 13–14.

47. House of Representatives, Committee on Foreign Affairs, *Hearings on United States Foreign Policy for a Post-war Recovery Program,* 80th Cong., 2nd sess., Part 2, 1581–1583, 1586; Schmidt, *Wallace,* pp. 84–85.

48. House, *Post-war Recovery Program,* pp. 1589–1591, 1603; Paterson, "The Quest for Peace and Prosperity," pp. 85–97; for the historical development of American corporate liberalism, see James Weinstein and David W. Eakins, eds., *For a New America* (New York, 1970), pp. 3–193.

49. Hamby, "Wallace . . . and Soviet-American Relations," p. 163; House, *Post-war Recovery Program,* 1610, 1623–1624; Kennan, *Memoirs,* pp. 378–379; Gardner, *Architects of Illusion,* pp. 281–282. A year later, during hearings on the North Atlantic Treaty, Wallace summarized for Senator Tom Connally of Texas, Foreign Relations Committee chairman, his concept of lines beyond which the United States should not accept expansion by the Soviet Union: "I have indicated very clearly that I think it would be a very serious matter indeed if Russia would take over the Dardanelles, for example. . . . In case Russia moved in to take over the Dardanelles, that would be a war matter. . . . But on the other hand, I think that when we move in with air bases in Turkey it becomes seriously close to being a war matter so far as Russia is concerned." Senate, Committee on Foreign Relations, *Hearings . . . North Atlantic Treaty,* 81st Cong., 1st sess., Part 2, p. 447.

50. Wallace, *Toward World Peace,* pp. 6–7, 44–45.

51. *Ibid.,* pp. 67, 40–41.

52. *Ibid.,* pp. 68–70, 91–92, 114–115.

53. Senate, *North Atlantic Treaty,* p. 437.

54. *Ibid.,* pp. 418–419, 424–425, 431.

55. *Ibid.,* p. 432; an example of Wallace's broader understanding of long-term dynamics in international relations occurred in an exchange with Senator Connally concerning Czechoslovakia's independence: "Well, 2 years ago you would have said that with regard to Yugoslavia. Now Yugoslavia is standing up very sternly, and you cannot tell when Czechoslovakia will do the same and when China will do the same." *Ibid.,* p. 449.

56. *Ibid.,* pp. 421–422.

57. *Ibid.,* p. 452.

58. *Time,* LVI (July 24, 1950), 13.

59. Lloyd Gardner has noted the common goals which Wallace shared with the decision-makers of the Truman administration, including Defense Secretary James Forrestal. To revive Far Eastern trade, Forrestal's recommendation was "to turn China over to American businessmen." "Forrestal's *bête noire,* Henry A. Wallace, pretty much agreed with this estimate. His statement before a congressional committee in 1951 revealed at once the chronological and ideological span of America's China policy. Within its wide boundaries, Forrestal and Wallace could agree upon goals even if they

divided sharply on methods. 'You see,' Wallace explained, 'I have had the view for many years, ever since 1909, in fact, that eventually the west coast would have as great a significance for this Nation as the east coast.' The basis for this development, Wallace added, was calculated upon 'the mounting percentage of our imports coming from the Far East and the possibility of our exports to the Far East mounting through the west coast ports.'" Gardner, *Architects of Illusion*, pp. 162–163.

by Thomas G. Paterson

The Dissent of
Senator Claude Pepper

In his successful bid in 1950 to unseat Florida's junior Senator Claude D. Pepper, George Smathers and his campaign organization invidiously published *The Red Record of Senator Claude Pepper*. Photographs of Pepper with Henry A. Wallace, 1948 Progressive party candidate for president, a list of Pepper's speaking engagements which included the American-Soviet Friendship Council, and some of the senator's statements isolated from context were arranged to suggest that he was a communist. This publication was the last chapter in the post–World War II story of the vociferous castigation of Pepper's foreign policy views. His opponents accused him of flirting with communism, befriending Joseph Stalin, and serving as a leading apologist for aggressive Soviet foreign relations. Presidential assistant Clark Clifford informed Harry S. Truman in 1947 that Pepper was "a devout if cynical follower of the Party line. . . ." And the *New York Times* fed the popular image of "Red" Pepper by reminding its readers that *Pravda* and Russian officials applauded some of Pepper's speeches and considered him a friend.[1]

Pepper's career in politics and the Senate was troubled, provocative, and somewhat lonesome, culminating in Smathers' campaign opening on January 12, 1950: "The leader of the radicals and extremists is now on trial in Florida. Arrayed against him will be loyal Americans. . . . Florida will not allow herself to become entangled in the spiraling web of the Red network. The people of our state will no longer tolerate advocates of treason." It was the era of anti-communist fervor in the United States; a few weeks after Smathers' strongly worded diatribe, Senator Joseph McCarthy of Wisconsin dramatically charged that the Department of State housed known Communists. Smathers facilely labeled Pepper a subversive, yet in 1948 the prestigious Senator Arthur Vandenberg of Michigan had stated that Pepper "is not an apologist for aggression by Soviet Russia, and that his plans for approaches to peace . . . are not uttered in terms of any sort of appeasement of Communist aggression." Pepper's stormy political career, his bluntly articulated positions on controversial issues, and his gradual shift—which Smathers ignored—to the Truman administration diplomatic line explain this divergence of opinion.[2]

Claude Pepper was only thirty-six years old when Floridians sent him to the Senate in 1936. Behind him were a rural Alabama childhood, jobs as a hat cleaner and steelworker in Birmingham, an active life of oratory and politics at the University of Alabama, years of insecurity at Harvard Law School among people of "family," and a one-year stint as instructor of law at the University of Arkansas, where J. William Fulbright sat as one of his students. In 1925 the young lawyer was attracted to Florida by a short-lived land boom. Pepper practiced law for a few years, and in 1928 he was elected to the Florida House of Representatives, where he cast a minority vote against a resolution censuring Mrs. Herbert Hoover for having tea in the White House with Mrs. Oscar dePriest, wife of a Chicago Negro congressman. Boldly in support of the New Deal, Pepper campaigned for Democratic tickets in the 1930's. "The cornerstone of the New Deal," Pepper declared in launching his 1934 senatorial campaign against incumbent Park Trammell, "is the welfare of the common man." Pepper lost to Trammell in a close primary runoff election, but the "common man" theme marked his voting record and his admiration for Henry Wallace thereafter. Trammell's death afforded Pepper another political opportunity in 1936, and his victory sent him to Washington as a New Deal senator ardently in support of Roosevelt's domestic and foreign policies. As the Second World War approached, Pepper incurred the wrath of isolationists for his advocacy of aid to Great Britain. He remarked in 1940 that he would be "ashamed to have posterity read the history of these days and find us relatively indifferent to civilization's collapse." [3]

In the postwar period, Pepper argued that the Truman administration had abandoned Roosevelt's foreign policy of international cooperation for a "get-tough" policy surfeited with a double standard, anti-communist hysteria, unquestioning consensus and bipartisanship, and American unilateralism. Disenchanted with Truman, Pepper thought of endorsing Secretary of Commerce Henry Wallace for President, even before the President fired Wallace from the Cabinet in September 1946. Pepper himself entertained the idea of running with Wallace as a vice-presidential candidate, and was in fact backed by the Minnesota Democratic Farmer Labor party for the position. In 1948, after unsuccessful efforts to persuade Dwight D. Eisenhower to seek the Democratic nomination, Pepper announced his own candidacy for the presidency. Pepper withdrew to support Truman because, like many other liberals, Pepper opposed the establishment of the Progressive party, and because all attempts to find a prominent opponent for Truman within the Democratic party had failed. The Florida senator, although a vigorous admirer of Wallace, feared that a third party would perpetuate the split among American liberals; yet he believed it good for the established parties "to be put upon the griddle by someone who is thinking only of the public and not the party interests." [4]

Pepper's political maneuvers and his criticisms of the Truman administration made him anathema to official Washington and its supporters. The leadership of the Department of State disliked him because he had questioned the appointment in 1944 of a number of assistant secretaries whom he considered to be representatives of wealthy interests. The President remembered that Pepper had favored Wallace over Truman for Vice-President in 1944, and that Pepper continuously chastised Truman for waylaying the New Deal. As Truman put it later, Pepper was an "agitator." Secretary of State James F. Byrnes told a Cabinet meeting that "his negotiations . . . were greatly embarrassed by the public utterances" of Pepper and Wallace, and Vandenberg recorded that both critics were "more or less constantly in his [Byrnes's] way." Pepper's party and Senate colleagues punished him for upsetting the foreign policy consensus by deliberately keeping him off the Senate Foreign Relations Committee for 1947–1948. After his vote against the Truman Doctrine, a publisher canceled his book contract.[5]

Too, many conservative voters in Florida were alarmed by Pepper's failure to participate in Southern filibusters, by his opposition to the poll tax, and by his advocacy of a national health insurance plan tied to social security. He called for an Equal Rights Amendment and sponsored minimum-wage legislation. When Truman startled Congress and the nation during the railroad strike of 1946 by asking for power to draft into the armed services striking workers of any industry taken over by the government, Pepper joined Republican Senator Robert Taft of Ohio as a strange bedfellow to argue against the "dangerous and highly improper" bill. Pepper voted against the Taft-Hartley Act, and constantly lambasted the National Association of Manufacturers for its lack of social responsibility. Often unresponsive to political pressure, Pepper demonstrated his independence when he voted for anti-lynching measures. By 1948 he probably agreed with a United States marshal who wrote from Florida that "you are in a Hell of a Spot. . . ." But Pepper was firm in his belief that "If a man really means his liberalism, he will make enemies." [6]

Pepper invited many enemies, but at times he stood with the majority in his party and in the Senate. He voted for Truman's domestic programs. In foreign policy, embracing the idea that international economic collaboration was essential to peace, Pepper supported the Reciprocal Trade Agreements Act, the Bretton Woods Agreements (World Bank and International Monetary Fund), and the $3.75 billion loan to Great Britain in 1946. He was an enthusiastic champion of the United Nations Organization. And he shared the pervasive American view of "peace and prosperity"; that is, that a healthy world economy and international trade were necessary foundations to pacific international relations, and that American foreign trade was vital to both American and international prosperity.[7]

It was Pepper's vigorous criticism of American foreign policy which distinguished him and consumed most of his time. He was convinced that a peaceful accommodation between the Soviet Union and the United States was possible in the critical 1945–1947 period, without sacrificing the national interest of either nation. His critics simplistically and wrongly belittled him as an advocate of appeasement. In depicting him as a mindless obstructionist, they besmeared his significant, articulate, and viable critique of American foreign policy, as well as his suggested policy alternatives. His opponents were annoyed by his persistent questioning, derived largely from his belief that Americans applied one set of standards to the international behavior of other countries and another set to that of the United States. Charles O. Lerche has described the "international double standard" as a tradition in American foreign relations:

Being different, and this difference being epitomized and most clearly demonstrated by moral preeminence, Americans had only a short step to take before arguing that [they] should be judged by a different set of standards than those applied to lesser states. In this way deeds wrong in themselves when done by other peoples became perfectly permissible when done by the United States. . . . It was not "imperialistic," for example, for the United States to annex overseas territories, since American purposes were high-minded and philanthropic; the United States was to rule colonial people for their own good.[8]

In rejecting the double standard, Pepper asked Americans to discover how other peoples looked upon them, to be candid enough to admit that the United States could not claim a celebrated first rank among nations without a contest, and that American actions taken under the notion of superiority and exceptionalism might in fact explain part of the escalating Cold War tension. The United States could not simply profess immunity and irrelevance when other governments criticized its foreign policy as aggressive, disruptive, and riddled with the double standard. "We must give up our double standard of international morality and cease to expect any nation to refrain from acting as we act to further our own security." In studying the Soviet insistence that governments on the Russian border be friendly, and the adamant American opposition, Pepper asked: "Have you heard Russia say anything about our relations with Mexico or Central and South America or Canada or even about our having bases in the Pacific?" In short, both Russia and America were maintaining postwar defenses, both had spheres of influence, and both were responsible for the developing crises in the early Cold War. As Pepper told the Senate in 1945: "We cannot exercise unlimited power and not expect other nations to make the same assertion." [9]

In early 1945 Senator Pepper commented that Stalin was "playing a cautious game." Historians are increasingly pointing out that Soviet foreign policy in the 1945–1947 period was indeed cautious, uncertain, halting, and perhaps defensive. Pepper suggested at that time what Ernest R. May has only recently written:

> The inner springs of Soviet foreign policy are, of course, mysteries. It is not inconceivable, however, that the Cold War was for the Soviets the mirror face of what it was for Americans. Suspicious, vulnerable, and weak from decades of revolution and war, the Soviet regime may have seen Anglo-American demands for representative governments and free elections in Eastern Europe as aimed at extending the empire of capitalism. The initial measures that so provoked President Truman may have been essentially defensive.

What appeared to Americans to be defensive American acts were actually seen as offensive by the Russians, and vice versa.[10]

Pepper outlined many times the history of Soviet-American relations and the long-standing tension fed in part by Soviet fears for its security and social system. He recalled American and Allied intervention against bolshevism in the Russian Revolution and the post–World War I economic blockade, both of which left diplomatic scars. Soviet Russia was excluded from the League of Nations, belatedly recognized in 1933 by the United States, and ostracized from the Munich Conference of 1938. Pepper concluded that America in the postwar period was inflaming old Soviet fears by denying the Soviets a sizable loan like that granted to the British, by constructing foreign military bases and increasing the military budget, by monopolistic control, stockpiling, and new explosions of the atomic bomb, by domestic anti-communist fervor, and by the tacit support of anti-Russian governments such as the London Polish exile group and Franco's Spain. And the Russians could not ignore, Pepper argued, America's bypassing of the United Nations, the rebuilding of Russia's vehement enemy Germany as a bulwark of the West, and the use of American economic power through loans, trade, and relief to mold an anti-Soviet bloc. Pepper recognized that Stalin's Russia was no international saint, but suggested that some of Russia's uncooperativeness was derived from its response to American actions and the American application of the double standard.[11]

The Soviet Union appears to have had two major postwar goals: economic reconstruction and territorial security. Stalin told Ambassador W. Averell Harriman that the Soviet Union would not tolerate another *cordon sanitaire* after World War II, and Harriman informed Washington as early as 1943 that the problem of "reconstruction is considered by the Soviet Union as, next to the war, the most important political as well as economic problem that confronts them." In response to the Anglo-American protest that the postwar Polish government was organized undemocratically to protect Soviet interests, Stalin replied that "the question of Poland . . . is a question of security. . . . Twice in the last thirty years our enemies, the Germans, have passed through this corridor." The Soviet Union never realized either of its goals, and the resulting insecurity further aggravated Russian-American friction. Pepper spoke frankly on the origins of the Cold War: "I think one of the things that contributed to the breach that is now giving us the cold war," he told a Chicago audience in 1948, "was the fact that they got the impression immediately after World War II that they were not going to have any aid from us, and they would have to make it on their own." Indeed, increasing evidence suggests that the American decision to deny postwar reconstruction aid to Russia led to an early diplomatic roadblock.[12]

Senator Pepper was closer to this subject than most of his colleagues, because he visited and discussed postwar aid with Stalin in Moscow during a European tour in the fall of 1945. Stalin catalogued Russia's massive war damage and appealed for heavy equipment and food from the United States. In return for American products, Russia would offer valuable manganese ore for steel production, chromium ore, timber, and gold. The Russian leader expressed "chagrin" that America had not opened negotiations on the Russian request for a loan, and stated that it would be "suicide" for the Soviets to use the funds for military purposes in the face of such economic dislocation.[13]

The history of the abortive American loan to Russia suggests that Pepper's advocacy of postwar aid to Russia was a viable alternative to American diplomacy in the 1943–1945 period. Secretary of State Edward R. Stettinius, Jr., later wrote that the loan issue was "one of the great 'if' questions of history." Ambassador Harriman himself cabled Washington in early 1945 that the Soviet Union placed "high importance on a large postwar credit as a basis for the development of 'Soviet-American relations.' I sensed from his [V. M. Molotov's] statement an implication that the development of our friendly relations depends upon a generous credit." [14]

The first pregnant discussion about a loan took place in 1943 among Harriman, Donald Nelson, chairman of the War Production Board, and A. I. Mikoyan, the Soviet Commissar for Foreign Trade. For Harriman, the loan was a "tool of diplomacy" which might allow the United States to influence Soviet foreign policy. It would also stimulate Russian orders for American goods which could "be of considerable value in easing dislocations to our employment problems. . . ." In early 1944 Mikoyan requested a loan of $1 billion. The Roosevelt administration, having no clear policy on the issue, delayed responding, and Harriman, eager to use the diplomatic leverage of a loan, berated the lethargy in Washington: ". . . the Soviets place great importance on knowing now our general attitude toward their reconstruction problems and if we push aside the consideration of their whole program doubts may be aroused as to our serious intents." [15]

There were advocates of a Russian loan who presaged Pepper's arguments. The president of the Chamber of Commerce, Eric Johnston, visited Russia in 1944, called for increased Soviet-American trade, and urged a loan which could serve as "the nub of our trade with the Soviet." Within the Roosevelt administration, Treasury Secretary Henry Morgenthau, Jr., and Harry D. White, an official in the Department, believed postwar aid to Russia would ease America's reconversion problem through expanded trade. A loan "would provide a sound basis for continued collaboration between the two governments in the postwar period," concluded White. When Morgenthau learned that the State Department had persuaded Roosevelt not to raise the loan question at the Yalta

conference, Morgenthau protested that "both the President and
Stettinius were wrong and that if they wanted to get the Russians
to do something they should . . . do it nice. . . . Don't drive such a
hard bargain that when they come through it does not taste
good." [16]

But the Truman administration soon developed a policy of
toughness which impeded any movement even toward negotiations.
Notes exchanged between the two governments did not bring them
to the conference table. The United States insisted that the Soviet
Union create an "open door" in Eastern Europe by disclosing its
trade treaties with the nations of that area. The Russians replied
that such treaties were not negotiable with the United States. Nor
would the Russians discuss membership in the World Bank, an
American-dominated institution from which they could derive little
benefit. The subject was further compounded by the bizarre State
Department announcement in March 1946 that the Russian loan
request filed in August 1945 had been "lost" since then. Claude
Pepper noted that this strange statement annoyed Russia, and
recently Arthur M. Schlesinger, Jr., has agreed that this episode
"only strengthened Soviet suspicion of American purposes." The
evidence is clear that the loan request was not lost. Yet whether
misplaced or not, the long delay and the American terms for an
agenda were too late for the loan to serve as an agent of amicable
Soviet-American relations. The Truman administration attempted
to use the loan as a diplomatic *weapon before* negotiations, rather
than as a diplomatic *tool during* discussions.[17]

The abortive loan issue raises some provocative questions.
Would the Soviet Union have sought such heavy reparations from
former Axis nations in Eastern Europe and would the issues aris-
ing from that region have been so tension-ridden had a loan been
granted? Harriman himself concluded in November 1945 that
American economic policy toward the USSR had "so far added to
our misunderstanding and increased the Soviets [sic] recent tendency to take unilateral action." In explanation he added: "This
has no doubt caused them to tighten their belts as regards improvement of the living conditions of their people and may have contributed to their avaricious policies in the countries occupied or
liberated by the Red Army." Secretary Morgenthau, according to

biographer John Blum, argued that a postwar loan would "soften the Soviet mood on all outstanding political questions." [18]

Would the Soviet Union have been so demanding *vis-à-vis* Germany had a loan been granted? Would the Soviets have eased their reparations demands and agreed early to unite the German zones, if the United States had acted with speed on the loan, as the Americans were to do with the British Loan? One scholar has written that a loan might have taken "the acrimony out of the Russian attitude on reparations." An assistant to Donald Nelson concluded that "It seems altogether probable that these two matters, an American credit and German reparations, were closely linked in Soviet political thinking, for our attitude toward both questions profoundly affected the rate of Russia's postwar recovery." And Gabriel Kolko has stated that "The Russians could not force the Americans to grant aid, but they had earned their rights to restitution from the Germans on the long and bloody battlefield from Stalingrad to the very borders of Germany." Indeed, American leaders were fully aware of the direct relationship between Russia's reparations demands and its postwar reconstruction crisis. Among others, Edwin Pauley, American Reparations Ambassador, wrote in 1947 that "It can be assumed . . . that Russia's intransigent position on unification and reparations is due to a desire to obtain the maximum amount of industrial and consumer goods from Germany, to meet internal political prestige needs and to rebuild the Soviet industrial machine." [19]

The commentary of critics like Pepper and Morgenthau that a postwar loan to Russia would facilitate the solution of divisive problems was ignored. Pepper was a lonely figure in the Senate on this question, reminding that body that the denial of a loan increased Soviet suspicion and fear, which Adam Ulam says "was built into the Soviet system." Senator Pepper could endorse the conclusion of Wallace in 1946:

From the Russian point of view . . . , the granting of a loan to Britain and the lack of tangible results on their request to borrow for rehabilitation purposes may be regarded as another evidence of strengthening of an anti-Soviet bloc.[20]

If the loan denial exacerbated Soviet-American conflict, so did some other crucial American decisions from which Pepper dissented, and to which he presented alternatives. The postwar trend of building an American military establishment abroad, the American monopoly of the atomic bomb, and the growing alliance system alarmed Pepper. The "get-tough" approach to diplomacy, Pepper warned, was a prostitution of Roosevelt's cooperation with Russia and his policy of holding out "the friendly hand of the good neighbor" abroad. Toughness in diplomacy would only encourage other powers to acquire "bigger sticks, and we begin that never ending vicious cycle of measure and counter-measure." The major powers, he wrote, "might as well recognize that they cannot indefinitely maintain the mastery of the strategic defense areas of the world without Russia striving for a comparable position." He called for the removal of Soviet troops from Hungary and Rumania, but also asked the United States to apply a consistent standard by rescinding its decision to construct an air base on Iceland, refraining from fleet demonstrations in the Mediterranean, and withdrawing the threat of American military forces in Latin America. Pepper's protestations against the 1946 negotiations with Iceland for permanent American bases angered the consensus officials in Washington. Senator Vandenberg complained that "everything was quite agreeable" until Pepper and Wallace questioned the Iceland deal, then "Hell immediately broke loose." Pepper also urged Truman to invite Britain to withdraw its troops from Greece, Iraq, Iran, and Jordan, and to give up its various colonies. "What I decry is the international hypocrisy, sham and pretense. If the British people want the Russians to get their troops out of Iran, let the British get their troops out of Iraq." Pepper feared that America would become a "guarantor of British imperialism." For this reason, he chastised Winston Churchill's "Iron Curtain" speech of March 1946, which Pepper read as an appeal for an Anglo-American military bloc "sharing bases the world over. . . ." Such action, concluded Pepper and his fellow Senators Glen Taylor of Idaho and Harley M. Kilgore of West Virginia, would "cut the throat of the United Nations" and launch an "anti-Soviet crusade." [21]

Shortly after Churchill's speech, Pepper suggested to Truman that rather than nurturing an Anglo-American alliance, which would freeze Big Three disunity, the President ought to hold a summit conference to end the "web of fear" gripping the world. Such a course would also reinforce the fledgling United Nations Organization, because after the Big Three "resolution of fears," the powers could lead fruitful discussions within that institution. But Truman rejected Pepper's suggestion, arguing lamely that the United Nations was supposed to be used for questions heretofore dealt with by heads of state. Truman's reply recommending the utilization of the United Nations, as we shall see, was not convincing in the presence of evidence which demonstrated that his administration actually sidestepped the international agency on a number of important questions. In 1948 Pepper urged the President to make a dramatic effort for peace by agreeing to meet with Stalin. Truman's only conference with the Russian leader was in July 1945 at Potsdam; an American President was not to meet a Russian Premier again until 1955.[22]

Senator Pepper, like many Americans, believed that fear could also be reduced by ending the "panicky atomic bomb race among the great powers." As long as America continued to stockpile, test, and maintain a monopoly of atomic weapons, Pepper concluded, it was to be expected that Russia would strive to develop the destructive instruments, too. Pepper applauded those atomic scientists who opposed continued stockpiling, and he, like the scientists, was proved correct when he stated that the bomb could not be kept a "secret" for long. He chastised those who "choose to think of atomic power not as a boon to mankind, but as a weapon America can hold over the rest of the world to force it to remake itself in our image and to our profit." Some American leaders, particularly Secretary of State James F. Byrnes, hoped indeed to use the bomb as a diplomatic weapon at the conference table. Although Adam B. Ulam does not think the American domination of the bomb caused "undue apprehension" within Russia, it seems clear that Russians viewed the bomb with fearful admiration and grave uncertainty, especially in the light of the "suspicion" Ulam concluded was endemic to Soviet Russia. As Louis Halle has written:

The United States, for a few years, had a unique atomic armament against which the Soviet Union was defenseless. Washington appeared to possess the means to destroy the Soviet state in one blow, and with impunity. In this moment, therefore, as never before, Russia stood naked to its enemies; and it must have been hard for its leaders to believe that those enemies would not take advantage of its nakedness.[23]

The Truman administration and Pepper clashed sharply over the means to achieve international control of the bomb and atomic energy. Pepper stated simply that the United States should "destroy every bomb we have, and smash every facility we possess which is capable of producing only destructive forms of atomic energy." With this action, Americans could enter international discussion "with the cleanest of hands. . . ." Knowledge of the bomb's construction should also be turned over to a military committee of the United Nations. Thus the United States would demonstrate to the Soviets that the bomb was not a threat to their security. Pepper did not offer a careful policy alternative, and his appeal for destruction of the bomb was naive and simplistic at the time; it was visionary to expect any nation to divest itself painlessly of a superior military weapon. But so too was the Baruch Plan of 1946 visionary. Proposed by the Truman administration, the plan would have established an International Atomic Development Authority empowered to control the use and sale of all fissionable materials. An inspection system would be set up, and America would relinquish its control of the bomb only after the entire system was functioning. The Russians responded negatively to this scheme, finding it too protective of the American monopoly and an infringement upon Russian sovereignty. Two scholars who believe that the Baruch Plan was largely presented for its propagandistic value have written:

. . . a plan that sought to ensure American safety was bound to be incompatible with Russian safety. American security could therefore be gained only at the cost of Russian security—which the Russians could hardly accept. In either case, however, the result was the same: The United States was permitted to pose as the champion of peace, and the Soviet Union was condemned as an aggressor and obstacle to peace.

Their assessment of the Baruch Plan generally agreed with an earlier criticism by Henry Wallace: ". . . we are telling the Russians that if they are 'good boys' we may eventually turn over our knowledge of atomic energy to them and to other nations." The

United States asked the Soviet Union to open its territory, its military secrets, and its resources to an international investigating team, to avoid producing or developing the bomb, and to accept an international commission where the veto was forbidden and a pro-American majority would sit—all before America gave up its exclusive control of the weapon. The Baruch Plan, whether well intentioned or not, was not conducive to atomic conciliation. Senator Pepper offered an unconvincing solution, but his diagnosis was accurate: America could not confine Russia behind a curtain of atomic weapons and retain mastery of such armaments without arousing Soviet resentment and alarm and encouraging an international arms race.[24]

One of Claude Pepper's most consistent and telling critiques of American foreign policy in the early Cold War was that the Truman administration professed eager support of international organizations but in fact acted unilaterally, as in its killing of the United Nations Relief and Rehabilitation Administration (UNRRA) by cutting off U.S. contributions, and in its bypassing of the United Nations in the Truman Doctrine and the Marshall Plan. Pepper was disturbed by the demise of UNRRA and the adoption of political relief by the United States. In December 1945 he commented, "I can bear testimony to the American people that not only is their money being well spent, but it is saving millions of lives . . . and keeping literally millions from starving." Fiorello LaGuardia, director of UNRRA, also defended the institution against congressional opponents who complained that UNRRA was being used by communists in Europe to further their ends, and that the large American contribution (almost 75 per cent) was thus a poor investment. evidence from the UNRRA records in the United Nations Library indicates that, although there were scattered incidents of abuse, the relief program saw a remarkably fair distribution of goods. "We have demonstrated to the world," LaGuardia told the UNRRA Council in 1946, "that forty-eight nations can work in harmony. . . . Let not that be lost to history." After American leaders decided to kill UNRRA and then vetoed LaGuardia's plan for a new United Nations relief operation, the former mayor of New York City protested: "Does the . . . United States intend to adopt a policy which will make innocent men and women suffer because

of the political situation which makes their Government unacceptable to the United States?" His allusion to the distribution of food
in war-torn Eastern Europe was anathema to American officials
who wanted ultimate control of distribution. So the Truman administration destroyed what appeared to be a viable international
institution in 1946. As the State Department's Dean Acheson explained to an inquisitive and prodding Pepper in the 1947 Truman
Doctrine hearings: "We took a very strong position that the future
relief, our future relief, should be granted in accordance with our
judgment and supervised with American personnel." It was the
postwar American position that international organizations had
to serve American interests, or at least not impede American international goals; if they failed American purposes, they could be
eliminated or ignored.[25]

This position was made evident in March 1947 when President
Truman requested large-scale direct American military and economic aid for Greece and Turkey. Pepper joined Senator Taylor,
who ran in 1948 as the Progressive candidate for Vice-President,
to offer a dissenting proposal in the form of a joint resolution.
They agreed with Truman that war-exhausted Greece needed relief and economic recovery; indeed, Pepper had urged aid to Greece
as early as March 1945. But he and Taylor argued against any
military aid to Turkey. Turkey was ruled by a dictatorship, hardly
fitting Truman's claim that America was preserving self-determination in the Near East, and had more often than not supported
Germany in World War II. Further, American military aid to the
Turkish army would in essence make it an appendage of the
American armed forces. As a result, Pepper declared, "the American army uniform will be the leverage by which reactionary and
perhaps corrupt governments may at least psychologically intimi-
date the opposition to their domestic policies." Russia was not
militarily assaulting Turkey; rather it was asking rather loudly for
joint control over the strategic Dardanelles—a traditional Russian
desire more than a communist one. Stalin stated at the Yalta conference that he could not "accept a situation in which Turkey had
a hand on Russia's throat." The United States refused to discuss
joint Soviet-Turkish control after World War II and encouraged
the Turks to be uncompromising. Pepper demanded that a double

standard not be applied. The Dardanelles were to Russia's defense what the Gulf of Mexico and the Panama Canal were to that of the United States. America, Pepper emphasized in the Senate, should not presume to determine the arrangement of control in the Dardanelles, unless it was willing to, invite Soviet consultation on the Caribbean and Panama. Pepper thus recognized the realities of international geopolitics and existing spheres of influence.[26]

Besides denying military aid to Turkey, the Pepper-Taylor alternative program suggested United Nations administration of an American contribution of $250 million for nonmilitary uses in Greece. It pointed out correctly that there were still UNRRA personnel in Greece who might be employed, and that a United Nations investigating team was already there. And the Food and Agriculture Organization (FAO) of the United Nations issued a report in 1946, advising a relief program of $100 million through the United Nations. The Truman administration ignored the FAO, a body not subject to veto authority by any of the major powers. The United States of course wanted to avoid a Soviet veto and the delay of discussions by working outside the international institution. Yet utilization of the FAO could have dodged a Soviet veto, and congressional debate and the establishment of the American program in Greece took probably at least as much time as what would have been required to create a United Nations project. Acheson admitted to Pepper that the United States at no time had consulted the United Nations or any of its members about the possibility of special sessions and a United Nations program. Not until two weeks after Truman's appeal to Congress did the administration formally notify the Security Council that an emergency and temporary Greek-Turkish program would be undertaken by the United States, with the hope that the United Nations would oversee any long-range plans. Indeed, Dean Rusk, director of the Office of Special Political Affairs which handled United Nations relations in the State Department, was not consulted during the development of the Truman Doctrine. Claude Pepper feared that this unilateral American action would weaken the United Nations severely, and Walter Lippmann agreed that bypassing the United Nations would "cut a hole in the Charter. . . ." Pepper and Taylor concluded their proposal by asking for a General Assembly investigation of the Greek civil war which was the cause of much of the economic chaos.[27]

Pepper noted in his critique of the Truman Doctrine, and most historians generally agree today, that the Greek monarchical regime was reactionary and hostile to social change, that the civil war began during the Second World War, that the British had tried desperately to shore up the faltering regime against the rebels, and that a large percentage of the revolutionaries were not Communists but rather Greek nationalists. Furthermore, the civil war was not engineered or carried out by the Soviet Union. Pepper stated in April 1947 that "I do not support the thesis that everywhere there is a Communist he was sent there by the Russians, and is directed and probably paid by the Russians." Winston Churchill himself has recorded that Russia honored a 1944 agreement and remained quiet during the initial British attempts to crush the anti-monarchical Greeks. Increasing evidence suggests that even through 1946 Stalin gave almost no aid or encouragement to Greek Communists, because he feared confrontation with the Anglo-American bloc. Stalin even urged Marshal Tito of Yugoslavia to cease his clandestine support of the Greek revolution. In fact, it was not only American military aid through the Truman Doctrine that ended the civil war in favor of the monarchy, but also the critical decision of the Yugoslavs to close their border to the rebels, who were then trapped by the American-equipped Greek army in 1949. Tito stopped his aid to the rebels because the Greek Communist party, gripped by factionalism, had turned pro-Stalin. In the United States, however, the popular and mistaken assumption was that Russia was manipulating the Greek revolution. As Richard Barnet has put it: "The fifth-column analogy from World War II dominated official thinking. The possibility that men had taken to the hills for reasons of their own and not as agents of a foreign power was never seriously considered." [28]

What American intervention meant, concluded Pepper, was a "stepping into empty British footprints in the imperial quicksands of the world." American military personnel in the Near East would be the "emissaries of a new imperialism," and the United States could not then "expect to carry conviction in our condemnation of the Russians for doing some of the same things." In short, the

Truman Doctrine would forfeit accommodation with Soviet Russia. But Truman disregarded the critique by Pepper and others. From a series of successful briefing sessions with key congressional leaders, the President perhaps knew even before he delivered his speech that Congress would accept his aid proposal. The hearings and debates were mere formalities. Few congressmen would challenge the President when it appeared that a major policy decision had already been formulated. And a crisis atmosphere had been stimulated by the administration with a rhetoric that suggested that to reject the Truman Doctrine would mean appeasement and the surrender of the Mediterranean and moral leadership of the world to the aggressive Soviets. "The rather shocking fact which emerges when considering the United States assumption of the British role in Greece and Turkey, and elsewhere," Bernard Weiner found, "is the lack of a discussion at the highest levels of meaningful policy alternatives." The Cabinet smacked of consensus, and probably only George F. Kennan in the Department of State questioned the open-ended universality of the policy and the extension of military aid. In the Senate the Truman Doctrine aid bill of $400 million passed 67 to 23, with Pepper, Taylor, and Edwin C. Johnson of Colorado dissenting from the policy, and others protesting the high monetary cost.[29]

Three months after the Truman Doctrine announcement, Secretary of State George C. Marshall introduced the idea of a European recovery plan. Pepper favored aid for European reconstruction but again advocated a United Nations program. Early in 1945 Pepper had told his colleagues that "If the economy of Europe shall collapse after the war, our economy will probably collapse with it." He understood the necessity for all segments of the interdependent world economy to be viable, and the prominent role of the American economy and foreign trade in the maintenance of international prosperity. Although he eventually voted for the Marshall Plan bill in March 1948, he earlier introduced a substitute plan utilizing the United Nations. Once again he denounced the policy of unilateral and political relief: "Will it be thought that those little children who will grow up in the so-called enemy countries will love America any better because their emaciated bodies attest the fact that their fathers were not in political accord with the dominant philosophy of the United States Government?" Pepper's proposal for a new United Nations fund was soundly defeated, 75 to 3, with only Taylor and William Langer of North Dakota joining him in the minority.[30]

Pepper was among a very few public figures who asked why the United States had bypassed the Economic Commission for Europe (ECE), a working United Nations agency. The invitation for a Marshall Plan conference was issued not by the ECE, which had Russia as a cooperative participating member, but rather by Britain and France after consultation with the United States. Pepper inquired why the Soviet Union had also been excluded from the French-British discussions which preceded the Paris meeting on a European recovery plan in July 1947. Indeed, the questions were meaningful and legitimate, for the manner of invitation, the by-passing of the ECE, and the obvious American domination of the plan certainly raised Soviet suspicions and doubts. The invitation had been sent to all European nations, including Russia and its Eastern European neighbors; but the evidence suggests that this was a diplomatic and propagandistic ploy to place the burden of exclusion on the Soviets themselves. Whether the invitation was serious or not, Congress would never have appropriated funds for a European recovery program which included Russia, especially after the anti-Soviet Truman Doctrine was launched. In short, the Marshall Plan was a weapon against Russia rather than a magnanimous, no-strings-attached undertaking to relieve destitute Europeans. Thus the ECE had to be skirted. George F. Kennan and Walt W. Rostow both saw the ECE as a viable enough agency to be used. But the United States chose to arrange an American-oriented institution and rejected the offer of the United Nations' Trygve Lie for a program through the ECE. Pepper deplored the American formulation of the plan, which in essence served as a "challenge" to the Soviet Union.[31]

During 1948 Pepper gradually shifted to support the Truman administration's foreign policy. He was shaken by the Communist *coup d'état* of February in Czechoslovakia. To him the event meant more than the elimination of an independent government; it meant also that his warnings that a unilateral "get-tough" American diplomatic stance would heighten world tension had been proven correct. Kennan, among others, agreed that the Czech *coup* was the Soviet reply to the Marshall Plan—the Soviet decision to secure its borders and neighbors tightly in a bloc. The collapse of Chiang Kai-shek further shocked Pepper, and the outbreak of the Korean War prompted him to issue a scathing attack upon the "Russian onslaught," and to applaud the action of the United States–United Nations effort in hurling back "aggression." He told a 1950 Labor Day audience: "Hell is not hot enough for those Red criminals who have thrust upon a world still groaning from one war, another war—who have betrayed not only their own revolution but the sacrifices of both the living and the dead over the earth for a peaceful world." [32]

Disturbed by events in Czechoslovakia, China, and Korea, aware of growing opposition to his re-election in Florida, and burdened by a sense of defeatism and helplessness, Pepper began to vote for such measures as the North Atlantic Treaty Organization (NATO), even though in mid-1948 he had introduced an amendment which would have removed all references to American military aid to Europe from the famous Vandenberg Resolution. NATO would stabilize the world, making it possible for the United Nations to work, argued Pepper, and it would hopefully bring "Russia to an awareness that they have got to make a case of good will before the world." Pepper voted for arms appropriations in 1948–1950, accepted a temporary selective service system, and warned Latin Americans to treat American business fairly or anticipate severance of American aid. But he still thought that economic aid to Russia would make their leaders more cooperative; he opposed the notion that "dissent becomes disloyalty" expressed in the Mundt-Nixon bill of 1948, and he hoped the Atlantic pact would be limited to a few years.[33]

The Cold War consensus had ultimately conquered and molded Senator Claude Pepper. He was despondent in 1949 when he recalled that in the first three years of the Cold War "I preferred another course. But my views did not prevail. . . ." The aggression and bellicosity that was absent from Soviet foreign policy in the period 1945–1947 was there in 1948–1950, Pepper concluded. Almost alone in the Senate in those early Cold War years, Pepper had appealed for a consistent standard, mutual cooperation, economic reconstruction, utilization of the United Nations, and international conferences. He believed that both Russia and the United States were responsible for the coming of the Cold War. After persistent setbacks and vituperative attacks upon his views and person, Pepper's spirit broke. In 1950 he paused to reflect that he had been "one of the last to give up hope that we could find some honorable basis of reconciliation. I was terribly penalized by certain critics when I was talking about peace and when I had in mind the terrible conflict that would become more and more probable if we did not stop it in its earlier inception." By the close of 1950, as biographer Alexander Stoesen has noted, "Pepper had lost nearly all his optimism. . . ." Pepper closed his troubled Senate tenure with words to a Senate chamber peopled, symbolically, with only three colleagues: "This is the darkest period of American history, if not human history." Overcome in 1950 by the Cold War, anti-communist hysteria, social and political conservatism, and white racism, Pepper in his defeat characteristically highlighted crucial American problems begging for neglected policy alternatives.[34]

Notes

I am grateful to Jack Muraskin, Les Adler, Alexander Stoesen, Nicholas Zangari, and Christopher Gozzo for their assistance in the preparation of this essay. The University of Connecticut and Harry S. Truman Institute provided valuable funds for research and typing, and Congressman Claude Pepper kindly allowed me access to his private papers.

1. Alexander R. Stoesen, "The Senatorial Career of Claude D. Pepper," unpublished Ph.D. dissertation, University of North Carolina, 1965, pp. 331–332; Clark Clifford to the President, November 19, 1947, Box 21, Clark Clifford Papers, Harry S. Truman Library; New York Times, March 9, April 10, 13, September 15, 1946, and May 1, 1947. See also Harry S. Truman, Memoirs (Garden City, 1955–1956, 2 vols.), II, 185; Marian D. Irish, "Foreign Policy and the South," Journal of Politics, X (May 1948), 310, 323, 324; Fred Rodell, "Senator Claude Pepper," American Mercury, LXIII (October 1946), 389–396.

2. Smathers quoted in Robert Sherrill, Gothic Politics in the Deep South: Stars of the New Confederacy (New York, 1968), pp. 148–149; Vanden-

berg in *Congressional Record,* 80th Cong., 2nd sess. (March 30, 1948), 3671.

3. Stoesen, "Senatorial Career," pp. 1–189. Pepper quoted in *ibid.,* p. 33, and Alexander R. Stoesen, "Spokesman or Seer? Claude Pepper and New Deal Foreign Policy," unpublished paper, 1968, p. 5.

4. *Washington Post,* August 14, 1946; *Minneapolis Tribune,* October 20, 1946; memorandum, n.d., Box 109, Claude Pepper Papers, Federal Records Center, Suitland, Md.; Stoesen, "Senatorial Career," pp. 275–294.

5. *Florida Times-Union* (Jacksonville), September 16, 1946; Truman, *Memoirs,* II, 185; H. Bradford Westerfield, *Foreign Policy and Party Politics: Pearl Harbor to Korea* (New Haven, 1955), pp. 112, 115; Stoesen, "Senatorial Career," pp. 215–216, 222. See also *Newsweek,* XXVIII (September 30, 1946), 29.

6. *New York Times,* July 19, 1946; Sherrill, *Gothic Politics,* p. 149; Stoesen, "Senatorial Career," pp. 235, 243–244, 246, 250–251, 258, 261; U.S. Marshal Chester S. Deshong to Pepper, April 2, 1948, Box 61, Pepper Papers; Pepper quoted in Stoesen, "Senatorial Career," p. 241.

7. For Pepper on the British Loan, which he considered "good business for America"; Bretton Woods, "without question absolutely essential for postwar international peace and prosperity"; and Reciprocal Trade, see Press Release, January 30, 1946, Box 44, Pepper Papers; *Congressional Record,* 79th Cong., 2nd sess., XCII (speech of January 31, 1946), A518 and 93 (January 27, 1947), 617; "Bretton Woods: Basis of Peace," February 2, 1945, Box 44, Pepper Papers; on the UN, Stoesen, "Senatorial Career," pp. 192–197. See also Thomas G. Paterson, "The Quest for Peace and Prosperity: International Trade, Communism, and the Marshall Plan," in Barton J. Bernstein, ed., *Politics and Policies of the Truman Administration* (Chicago, 1970), pp. 78–112.

8. Charles O. Lerche, *Foreign Policy of the American People* (Englewood Cliffs, 1967, 3rd ed.), p. 109. See also William G. Carleton, "The Southern Politician, 1900 and 1950" *Journal of Politics,* XIII (May 1951), 220, 225.

9. Claude Pepper, "America and the Peace Crisis," *Soviet Russia Today,* XV (June 1946), 9; Pepper, "Hands Across the Elbe," *ibid.,* XV (July 1945), 31; *Congressional Record,* 79th Cong., 1st sess., XCI (July 26, 1945), 8072. See also *New York Times,* April 5, 1946, and *New York Times Magazine,* November 3, 1946, p. 16.

10. Pepper quoted in Stoesen, "Senatorial Career," p. 199; Ernest R. May, "The Cold War," in C. Vann Woodward, ed., *The Comparative Approach to American History* (New York, 1968), p. 343. See also Urie Bronfenbrenner, "The Mirror Image in Soviet-American Relations: A Social Psychologist's Report," *Journal of Social Issues,* XVII (1961), 45–56. For recent literature on the hesitancy and uncertainty of Soviet foreign policy in the early years of the Cold War, see Fred W. Neal, *U.S. Foreign Policy and the Soviet Union* (Santa Barbara, 1961); Gar Alperovitz, "How Did the Cold War Begin?," *New York Review of Books,* March 23, 1967; John Bagguley, "The World War and the Cold War," in David Horowitz, ed., *Containment and Revolution* (London, 1967), pp. 76–124; Louis J. Halle, *The Cold War as History* (London, 1967); Isaac Deutscher, *Stalin: A Political Biography* (New York, 1960, 2d ed.), pp. 536–537; Fred W. Neal, "The

Cold War in Europe, 1945–1967," in N. D. Houghton, ed., *Struggle Against History* (New York, 1968), pp. 20–40; Adam B. Ulam, *Expansion and Co-existence: The History of Soviet Foreign Policy, 1917–67* (New York, 1968); Gabriel Kolko, *The Politics of War: The World and United States Foreign Policy, 1943–1945* (New York, 1968); Barton J. Bernstein, "American Foreign Policy and the Origins of the Cold War," in Bernstein, *Politics and Policies*, pp. 15–77; Manuel Gottlieb, *The German Peace Settlement and the Berlin Crisis* (New York, 1960), pp. 43–45; Robert D. Warth, "Stalin and the Cold War: A Second Look," *South Atlantic Quarterly*, LIX (Winter 1960), 1–12; Marshall D. Shulman, *Beyond the Cold War* (New Haven, 1966), pp. 6–7; Richard J. Barnet and Marcus G. Raskin, *After 20 Years: Alternatives to the Cold War in Europe* (New York, 1965), p. 13.

11. *Congressional Record*, 79th Cong., 2nd sess., XCII (March 20, 1946), 2465; *Southern Patriot* (Nashville), April 1945, Box 44, Pepper Papers; Claude Pepper, "A Program for Peace," *New Republic*, CXLIV (April 8, 1946), 470–473.

12. W. Averell Harriman, *Peace With Russia?* (New York, 1959), p. 12; Department of State, *Foreign Relations of the United States, Diplomatic Papers, 1943* (Washington, D.C., 1963–1965, 6 vols.), III, 788–789; Stalin quoted in James F. Byrnes, *Speaking Frankly* (New York, 1947), p. 31; Pepper speech, Executive Club of Chicago, February 20, 1948, Box 122, Pepper Papers. See also *Congressional Record*, 80th Cong., 2nd sess., XCIV (March 13, 1948), 2731. For a full discussion of the aid question, see Thomas G. Paterson, "The Abortive American Loan to Russia and the Origins of the Cold War, 1943–1946," *Journal of American History*, LVI (June 1969), 70–92.

13. "Conversation Between Stalin and Members of the House Special Committee on Post-war Economic Policy and Planning," September 14, 1945, Box 47, and "Conversation with Stalin," Box 46, Pepper Papers.

14. Edward R. Stettinius, Jr., *Roosevelt and the Russians: The Yalta Conference* (Garden City, 1949), p. 121; Department of State, *Foreign Relations of the United States, Diplomatic Papers: The Conferences at Malta and Yalta, 1945* (Washington, D.C., 1955), p. 313.

15. Herbert Feis, *Churchill, Roosevelt, Stalin: The War They Waged and the Peace They Sought* (Princeton, 1957), p. 643; Department of State, *Foreign Relations of the United States, 1944* (Washington, D.C., 1966–1967, 7 vols.), IV, 1034, 1049–1050.

16. *Nation's Business*, XXXII (October 1944), 21–22; Harry D. White to Henry Morgenthau, March 7, 1944, Part II: 23, Harry D. White Papers, Princeton University Library; Henry Morgenthau to President, January 1, 1945, *ibid.*; Henry Morgenthau to President, January 10, 1945, *ibid.*; John M. Blum, ed., *From the Morgenthau Diaries* (Boston, 1959–1967, 3 vols.), III, 305.

17. Paterson, "Abortive American Loan," pp. 85–89; Pepper in *Congressional Record*, 80th Cong., 2nd sess., XCIV (March 13, 1948), 2731; Arthur M. Schlesinger, Jr., "Origins of the Cold War," *Foreign Affairs*, XLVI (October 1967), 44.

18. "Certain Factors Underlaying Our Relations with the Soviet Union," November 14, 1945, W. Averell Harriman Papers (in his possession); Blum, *From Morgenthau Diaries*, III, 306.

19. J. P. Nettl, *The Eastern Zone and Soviet Policy in Germany, 1945–50* (London, 1951), p. 40; Albert Z. Carr, *Truman, Stalin, and Peace* (Garden City, 1950), p. 41; Kolko, *Politics of War*, p. 340; Edwin Pauley, "Paper on German Reparations, Revised, November 17, 1947," Edwin Pauley Papers (in his possession).

20. *Congressional Record*, 79th Cong., 2nd sess., XCII (March 20, 1946), 2465; Ulam, *Expansion and Coexistence*, p. 399; Wallace to Truman, July 23, 1946, reprinted in *New Republic*, CXV (September 30, 1946), 404.

21. Pepper quoted, respectively, in speech to Democratic Club of Baltimore, August 21, 1946, Box 44, Pepper Papers; Pepper, "Program for Peace," p. 470; *Churchman*, June 1, 1946, p. 14; *Congressional Record*, 80th Cong., 2nd sess., XCII (April 4, 1946), 3087; Press Release, March 6, 1946, Box 44, Pepper Papers; Vandenberg in Arthur H. Vandenberg, Jr., *The Private Papers of Senator Vandenberg* (Boston, 1952), p. 266. See also "FDR Believed in Democracy," March 23, 1946, Box 44, Pepper Papers; *Congressional Record*, 79th Cong., 2nd sess., XCII (April 4, 1946), 3089–3090; (July 9, 1946), A3984; (July 16, 1946), A4181, and 80th Cong., 1st sess., XCIII (April 17, 1947), 3601; Stoesen, "Senatorial Career," p. 213; Senate, Committee on Foreign Relations, *Assistance to Greece and Turkey* (Hearings), 80th Cong., 1st sess., March 24, 1947, p. 62; Millis, *Forrestal Diaries*, p. 154; *New York Times*, March 6, 17, 1946.

22. *Congressional Record*, 79th Cong., 2nd sess., XCII (March 20, 1946), 2463–2465; *Public Papers of the Presidents of the United States: Harry S. Truman, 1946* (Washington, D.C., 1962) pp. 164–165; *New York Times*, March 22, 1946; March 29, 1948; *Congressional Record*, 80th Cong., 2nd sess., XCIV (March 30, 1948), A1997.

23. *Congressional Record*, 79th Cong., 2nd sess., XCII (March 20, 1946), 2465; *Churchman*, June 1, 1946, p. 14; "Soviet Agriculture," n.d., Box 44, Pepper Papers; Gar Alperovitz, *Atomic Diplomacy: Hiroshima and Potsdam: The Use of the Atomic Bomb and the American Confrontation with Soviet Power* (New York, 1965); Ulam, *Expansion and Coexistence*, p. 414; Halle, *Cold War as History*, p. 147.

24. Pepper in *Congressional Record*, 79th Cong., 2nd sess., XCII (March 20, 1946), 2466; *Churchman*, June 1, 1946, p. 14; *New York Times*, September 4, 1945; John W. Spanier and Joseph L. Nogee, *The Politics of Disarmament: A Study in Soviet-American Gamesmanship* (New York, 1962), p. 66; Wallace to President, July 23, 1946, in *New Republic*, CXV (September 30, 1946), 402. For the Baruch Plan, see Walter LaFeber, *America, Russia, and the Cold War, 1945–1946* (New York, 1967), pp. 35–36; Richard J. Barnet, *Who Wants Disarmament?* (Boston, 1960), pp. 7–21.

25. Pepper in *New York Times*, December 14, 1945; LaGuardia in George Woodbridge, *et al.*, *The History of the United Nations Relief and Rehabilitation Administration* (New York, 1950, 3 vols.), I, 50, and David Horowitz, *The Free World Colossus* (New York, 1965), p. 70; Acheson in Senate, *Assistance to Greece and Turkey*, March 24, 1947, p. 37.

26. Pepper in *Congressional Record*, 80th Cong., 1st sess., XCIII (April 10, 1947), 3281; Stalin in *Foreign Relations: Yalta*, p. 903. See also *New York Times*, March 25, 1945; *Congressional Record*, 80th Cong., 1st sess., XCIII (March 25, 1947), 2525–2526; (April 10, 1947), 3282–3283; (April 17, 1947), 3606–3608; Bernard Weiner, "The Truman Doctrine: Background

and Presentation," unpublished Ph.D. dissertation, Claremont Graduate School, 1967, p. 209.

27. *Congressional Record,* 80th Cong., 1st sess., XCIII (March 25, 1947) 2525–2526; Claude Pepper, "Aid to Greece—But Through the U.N.," *Soviet Russia Today,* XVI (May 1947), 9; Weiner, "Truman Doctrine," p. 256; Senate, *Assistance to Greece and Turkey,* March 24, 1947, pp. 45–46; Richard J. Barnet, *Intervention and Revolution: America's Confrontation with Insurgent Movements Around the World* (New York, 1968), p. 120; Lippmann in LaFeber, *America, Russia, and Cold War,* p. 45. See also Walter Lippmann, *The Cold War: A Study in U.S. Foreign Policy* (New York, 1947).

28. Pepper in *Congressional Record,* 80th Cong., 1st sess., XCIII (April 17, 1947), 3603; Barnet, *Intervention and Revolution,* p. 121. See also Weiner, "Truman Doctrine," pp. 43–70, 89–117; Winston Churchill, *Triumph and Tragedy* (Boston, 1953), p. 293.

29. Pepper in *Congressional Record,* 80th Cong., 1st sess., XCIII (April 10, 1947), 3283, 3287; Joseph M. Jones, *The Fifteen Weeks* (New York, 1955), pp. 138–142; Weiner, "Truman Doctrine," pp. 248–251 (quoted from p. 255); George F. Kennan, *Memoirs, 1925–1950* (Boston, 1967), pp. 313–324; *Congressional Record,* 80th Cong., 1st sess., XCIII (April 22, 1947), 3793. See also Pepper's persistent questioning of Acheson in Senate, *Assistance to Greece and Turkey,* March 24, 1947, pp. 36–47.

30. *Congressional Record,* 79th Cong., 1st sess., XCI (July 26, 1945), 8073, and 80th Cong., 1st sess., XCIII (December 1, 1947), 10972. See also "McNaughton Report," March 13, 1948, Box 13, Frank McNaughton Papers, Truman Library; *Washington Post,* September 9, 1945; *New York Times,* December 2, 1947; "The New Frontiers in Exports," June 13, 1946, Box 44, Pepper Papers.

31. *Congressional Record,* 80th Cong., 2nd sess., XCIV (March 13, 1948), 2735; *New York Times,* October 13, 1947; March 14, 1948; Kennan, *Memoirs,* pp. 338–341; Walt W. Rostow, "Machinery for Rebuilding the European Economy, I: The Economic Commission for Europe," *International Organization,* III (May 1949), 254–268; N.K., "East-West Trade in Europe: Economic Advantages and Political Drawbacks," *World Today: Chatham House Review,* V (March 1949), 103; Paterson, "Quest for Peace and Prosperity," pp. 97–102. See also David Wightman, *Economic Co-Operation in Europe: A Study of the United Nations Economic Commission for Europe* (London, 1956).

32. *Congressional Record,* 80th Cong., 2nd sess., XCIV (March 13, 1948), 2724, 2729–2730; Kennan, *Memoirs,* p. 401; "Radio Report No. 34," September 12, 1949, Box 124, Pepper Papers; "Labor Day Speech, Jacksonville," September 4, 1950, Box 124, Pepper Papers; *New York Times,* November 5, 1950.

33. Stoesen, "Senatorial Career," pp. 225–228; *New York Times,* February 28, July 16, 1949; Pepper quoted from "Radio Speech No. 21," July 13, 1949, Box 124, Pepper Papers; Vandenberg, *Private Papers,* p. 411; *Congressional Record,* 80th Cong., 2nd sess., XCIV (March 30, 1948), A1996; (February 17, 1949), 1352–1354; "Radio Report No. 29," August 8, 1949, Box 124, Pepper Papers; Radio Interview, June 15, 1948, Box 109, Pepper Papers.

34. Pepper quoted in Stoesen, "Senatorial Career," pp. 227, 230 (quoted from p. 230); *Congressional Record,* 80th Cong., 2nd sess., XCIV (March 13, 1948), 2724, 2729–2730; *Miami News,* March 31, 1963. In 1958 Pepper made an unsuccessful attempt to secure a Senate nomination; but in 1962 he was elected to the House of Representatives, and re-elected in 1964, 1966, 1968, and 1970, representing Dade County (Miami).

by William C. Pratt

Senator Glen H. Taylor:
Questioning American Unilateralism

A March 1950 issue of *Time* magazine featured an article entitled "The Senate's Most Expendable." Included among the "most expendable" was Idaho's Glen H. Taylor, a persistent liberal critic of Truman's foreign policy. Said *Time:* "Glen H. Taylor, 45, Democrat from Idaho, the banjo-twanging playboy of the Senate. An easy mark for far-left propaganda, he ran as Henry Wallace's vice presidential candidate on the 1948 Progressive Party ticket, has since tried to be a good boy to get Democratic help in his re-election campaign."

By 1950 the rest of the news media shared this view of Taylor, and, after his defeat in the Democratic primary that year, publications such as *Newsweek* and the *Saturday Evening Post* could not conceal their pleasure. Few people remember Taylor today, and fewer remember his contributions to the foreign policy debates in the 1946–1949 period. Yet a re-examination of Taylor's record suggests that he may have been one of the Senate's *least* expendable. His persistent opposition to the Truman foreign policy and his proposed alternatives to it were frequently based on reasonable grounds and were much more consistent with professed American ideals of internationalism and democracy.[1]

President Truman's speech before a joint session of Congress on March 12, 1947, when he requested an emergency appropriation of $400 million in military and economic aid to bail out the Greek and Turkish governments, was the first public announcement of what became the Truman Doctrine. In the course of his remarks,

Truman proclaimed: "I believe that it must be the policy of the United States to support free peoples who are resisting attempted subjugation by armed minorities or by outside pressures." Although liberals may flinch at these words today, they have readily accepted the rationale of the Truman Doctrine. It was in the national interest, according to this view, to support anti-communism universally, and to construct and maintain a *cordon sanitaire* around the communist world. The implementation of the Truman Doctrine and its corollaries, the Marshall Plan and the North Atlantic Treaty Organization, was the product of a bipartisan foreign policy consensus. Yet large numbers of liberals opposed the Truman Doctrine when it first appeared. Henry Wallace, Claude Pepper, Vito Marcantonio, and Glen Taylor were the most prominent political figures who spoke out against the new interventionist direction in American policy, and all of them had a considerable public following until the outbreak of the Korean War. Taylor's political career is, in itself, a case study of a liberal opponent of the Cold War and the price paid for that opposition.[2]

Before Taylor was elected in 1944, he seemed unlikely material for the United States Senate. Adverse family finances compelled him to quit school at the age of thirteen, and after a brief stint as a sheepherded in Idaho's Bitterroot Mountains, he entered vaudeville and continued in the entertainment field until 1940. "The Crooning Cowboy," as he was then billed, became interested in politics in the thirties and attempted unsuccessfully to organize a farmer-labor party in Nevada and Montana. In 1938 Taylor entered Democratic politics in Idaho, seeking the party's congressional nomination. Relying heavily on his entertainment background, he campaigned in what was to be typical Taylor fashion. He and his troupe would strike up the music, attract a crowd, and then intersperse "Stuart Chase–Franklin Roosevelt economics with cowboy ballads." Taylor was defeated in his 1938 bid but won the party's senatorial nomination in 1940 and again in 1942. Both times, however, he lost in the general election. In 1944, after again winning the Democratic senatorial nomination, Taylor was finally elected to the Senate by 4,723 votes out of more than 200,000 cast. This time he had conducted a more sedate campaign and had received some support from a reluctant party organization.[3]

During the early part of his term, though the general press referred to him disparagingly as the "Cowboy Senator," Taylor received favorable coverage from some liberal journalists. Richard Neuberger, later a Democratic senator from Oregon, wrote two complimentary articles about Taylor, saying as early as May 1945: "Glen Taylor has proved one of the outstanding liberals to arrive in Washington in recent years." *Collier's* ran a sympathetic article in mid-1945 which stressed Taylor's seriousness. He was also praised in the *Nation,* and in 1947 John Gunther felt justified in writing that "he has already proved himself one of the most useful senators the country has." [4]

The chief explanation for Taylor's high standing in these liberal circles was his domestic voting record in the 1945–1947 period. Taylor rose for the first time in the Senate to urge the confirmation of Henry Wallace as Secretary of Commerce. On this occasion, as he did throughout his Senate career, he displayed his sympathy for the small businessman and his corresponding antipathy toward big corporations. Taylor associated himself from the start with other liberal Democrats of similar mind, such as Florida's Claude Pepper and West Virginia's Harley Kilgore. (Later, he would join them in an unsuccessful effort to prevent the Senate from overriding Truman's veto of the Taft-Hartley Act of 1947.) As early as July 31, 1945, a cadre of liberal Democrats caucused to plan postwar legislation. Pepper and Kilgore had invited ten other senators, including Taylor, to a luncheon meeting. Rumors circulated in Washington that the meeting had been called because its participants believed that Truman had given up the New Deal and was traveling "too far to the right." Later, meetings of this nature were sponsored by Calvin "Beanie" Baldwin of the National Citizens Political Action Committee. Given little or no publicity, these sessions were attended by Senator Elbert D. Thomas of Utah, Wallace, Pepper, and Taylor, as well as by some liberal congressmen, including Helen Gahagan Douglas of California. According to Pepper, both domestic and foreign policy were discussed at such meetings.[5]

Taylor and Pepper developed a close political relationship from the beginning of Taylor's term. They found themselves on the same side of almost all political issues until mid-1948, and their Senate careers had several parallels. Both were in the left wing of the party and were unwilling to follow the Truman leadership down the line. Fearful of a revival of German militarism, they took a flexible and perhaps realistic stand on Russian political activity in Eastern and Central Europe, and received occasional favorable publicity in the *Daily Worker*. Later both of them were to fall victim to red-baiting in their unsuccessful 1950 campaigns for renomination.

Taylor's break with Truman's foreign policy was a gradual development which was not complete until the debate on the Truman Doctrine in March 1947. As early as 1945, however, he began to question the administration's willingness to reach an accommodation with the Soviet Union. In February of that year, Taylor inserted into the *Congressional Record* an article by Eugene Cox, an attorney from Lewiston, Idaho, entitled "Germany's Place in a Post-War World." The United States, Cox argued, should guard against the rebuilding of the German war machine. At the same time, the capitalist powers should recognize that Russia had justifiable fears concerning her security. World War II had devastated Russia; because it was guided by its national interests, it was now more concerned with world stability than with the spread of communism. Cox implied that world peace would be threatened more by the capitalist powers' failure to recognize Russian border security problems than by Russian ambitions of expansion.

Throughout the 1945–1949 period, Taylor argued along these lines and asked his colleagues to imagine how the world situation looked through Russian eyes. But his appeal fell on deaf ears. Several recent scholars have also stressed Russian security fears as an important factor in the causation of the Cold War. For example, Ernest May suggests: "Suspicious, vulnerable, and weak from decades of revolution and war, the Soviet regime may have seen Anglo-American demands for representative governments and free elections in eastern Europe as aimed at extending the empire of capitalism. The initial measures that so provoked President Truman may have been essentially defensive." Russian security fears, however, were not an important concern of American policy-makers in the Truman administration.[6]

On October 23, 1945, Truman appeared before a joint session of Congress and requested legislation for Universal Military Training. Taylor, already an opponent of peacetime conscription, responded the next day with a resolution calling for a world republic. It was Taylor's first resolution and, in his eyes, the most important one he introduced during his entire tenure in the Senate. He urged world-wide disarmament and a UN monopoly of weapons. Arguments against a world republic in 1945 were no better, according to the Idaho senator, than those used against the Constitution in 1787. Taylor also asserted that the postwar world situation was like that of the American states during the Confederation period, and that unless international tensions were quickly reduced, a third world war was inevitable.

Although the world republic idea was not new to him, Taylor revealed, the atomic bomb had accelerated his thinking on the matter. He clearly anticipated that the Russians would soon develop their own bomb. Throughout his Senate career, he demonstrated that he feared nuclear war more than anything else, and it provoked him to argue continually for international cooperation. Of course, to create a world republic the United States had to give up some of its sovereignty; but it was worth the price. "Preservation of world peace cannot be left to the whims of sovereign states, or to conferences of foreign ministers, or to security councils."

The response to Taylor's world republic resolution was predict-able: no one in the Senate spoke to the measure when it was introduced, and it received almost no coverage in the press. The *New York Times* commented that Taylor "made an oration in the solemn tones of a preacher, predicting a 'ghastly orgy of death and destruction' . . . if the world did not form a world union." Despite the general news blackout, however, a considerable num-ber of people did hear about the resolution, and Taylor ultimately mailed approximately 180,000 copies of it. His continued support of this utopian scheme throughout his Senate career, though it was obviously an impractical political position in the 1940's, demon-strated Taylor's commitment to internationalism as well as his be-lief that nationalism must be reduced if world war was to be avoided.[7]

As Taylor feared, relations between the great powers continued to deteriorate in late 1945 and early 1946. After Winston Church-ill's Conservative government had been repudiated by the English electorate, the former Prime Minister visited the United States in

February and March 1946, seeking support for an Anglo-American military alliance. It was in the course of this visit that Churchill made his famous "iron curtain" speech, criticizing Russian repression in Eastern Europe. At the time, Truman disclaimed any special knowledge about the content of Churchill's speech, but later acknowledged "that he had sponsored . . . [it] as a trial balloon." As the President had traveled over a thousand miles to participate in the ceremony at Fulton, Missouri, in the midst of an international crisis over Iran, many people assumed that Churchill was speaking for Truman.[8]

The response to Churchill's address was mixed. Truman coyly refused to commit himself publicly to Churchill's analysis, but many supporters of his foreign policy were enthusiastic about it. Large numbers of liberals, however, denounced the speech, and some participated in demonstrations against it. On March 14, 1946, at a dinner of the Independent Citizens Committee of the Arts, Sciences, and Professions, several speakers attacked the Churchill speech. Harold Ickes expressed grave concern over the anti-Russian direction of American policy and warned that a third party might be necessary to counteract this drift. FDR's eldest son, James Roosevelt, was also critical of Churchill's remarks.[9]

Immediately following Churchill's speech, Taylor, Pepper, and Kilgore deplored it in a joint statement: "Mr. Churchill's proposal [an Anglo-American alliance against the USSR] would cut the throat of the United Nations Organization. It would destroy the unity of the Big Three, without which the war could not have been won and without which the peace cannot be saved." These three dissenters were convinced that the proposal, despite Churchill's protests to the contrary, was incompatible with the UN and would further polarize the world. Later, in 1948, Taylor said that the "iron curtain" speech "did more to undermine our relations with Russia than any one thing that had occurred up to that time." At the Independent Citizens Committee dinner on March 14, 1946, Taylor stated that Churchill had joined the "tough-talk boys" and that his "proposal would in effect serve notice on Russia that the two English speaking peoples had banded together to perpetuate the age-old game of European power politics which has

started the two world wars of our time." Three months later, in an
NBC radio forum on July 6, 1946, Taylor and Senator George
Aiken of Vermont agreed that American foreign policy followed
"the British lead entirely too often." Aiken also said: "Britain and
Russia have been opposed to each other for two hundred years.
We should steer clear of this conflict, and work instead to bring
the two nations together." [10]

Liberals who protested against Churchill's speech feared that
Truman was gradually repudiating FDR's foreign policy. Many of
them thought Truman could be won back to the fold if he could
be warned against his own advisers. In the case of the Churchill
address, they believed Churchill was trying to bring the United
States into an anti-Russian sphere to protect Britain's colonial
empire. Later, however, many liberals came to realize that Truman
was not a *tabula rasa* upon which his advisers pressed their interpretations of the world, but that he was frequently the author of
his own foreign policy. Truman had been a hard-liner on Soviet
relations from the beginning of his presidency, and he surrounded
himself with those who shared similar views. But in May 1946
Taylor was still willing to blame the President's advisers for the
anti-Russian direction of American foreign policy. In the same
speech, Taylor denounced the two components of what in later
years came to be called the industrial-military complex: ". . . Our
Army and Navy officers, seeing their great prestige evaporating
and coming face to face with the possibility of being demoted, of
losing their rank, are very anxious to start a war with somebody,
and Russia seems to be the handy country with which to start the
war." Other advisers with Wall Street backgrounds, Taylor thought,
were persuaded that American prosperity was contingent on war,
and this conviction was playing an important role in American
foreign policy. As early as July 1945, Taylor had demonstrated
concern over the appointment of Edward Stettinius as United
States representative on the UN Security Council: "I have been a
little worried over the fact that we have appointed as our representative to the Security Council a man whose background has
been associated with United States Steel. We know, of course, that
United States Steel has a great interest in armaments, and war
naturally means prosperity for a concern of that kind." Taylor

soon became less critical of Stettinius, but he continued to nurture doubts about the economic background of American foreign policy-makers, and he came to speak particularly of them more and more as he became disillusioned with American foreign policy.[11]

From time to time, Taylor lapsed into a conspiratorial view of history which detracted from his criticism of Truman foreign policy. This was especially true during his campaign as Wallace's running mate, but it had also been present in Taylor's speeches in 1946 and 1947. Although he saw the government dominated by Wall Street and the military, Taylor usually emphasized the Wall Street influence. Sometimes, however, he talked as though Truman himself was the source of American foreign policy difficulties, while on other occasions he asserted: "Truman does not control his administration but his administration is controlled by the military men and Wall Streeters." Secretary of the Navy James Forrestal and John Foster Dulles assumed especially sinister roles in Taylor's eyes, and, during the 1948 campaign, he claimed that they had "helped to finance Hitler in his rise to power, with the understanding that he would fight Russia." Taylor's denunciation of "Wall Streeters" frequently reached demagogic proportions. For example, at Madison, Wisconsin, on September 20, 1948, Taylor attacked Forrestal, Dulles, and Under Secretary of the Army William Draper (another frequent Taylor target): "Nazis are running our government, so why should Russia make peace with them?" This side of Taylor should not be ignored, but it does not negate the more reasonable arguments with which he opposed the Truman foreign policy.[12]

The occasion for Taylor's final break with the administration was Truman's March 12, 1947, request for aid to Greece and Turkey. Civil war between royalist and anti-royalist forces had plagued Greece intermittently since late 1944. Due to Churchill's timely military intervention, the royalist forces had controlled the Greek government since the Germans left the country. At the Moscow conference in October 1944, Stalin had acknowledged that Greece was within the British sphere of influence, and the evidence suggests that the Russians gave no aid to the anti-royalists in the 1944–1945 period. After a temporary lull, the civil war resumed in the fall of 1946. The British had maintained approximately forty thousand troops in Greece as military advisers, and had pumped in large amounts of economic and military aid to buttress the shaky royalist regime. Postwar Britain, however, could not afford to underwrite the royalists indefinitely, and on February 21, 1947, the British ambassador informed the State Department that his nation would have to suspend aid to Greece at the end of March. The administration had known for some time that the British government wanted to be relieved of its Greek obligations by shifting the burden to the United States, and the State Department had been planning for this development.[13]

Since the early days of his administration, Truman and his advisers had been viewing the world simplistically in terms of communism and anti-communism. Knowing that the Greek guerrilla army was under communist leadership, they quickly concluded, in Truman's words, that "the rebels were masterminded from the satellite countries." Actually, there was considerable doubt about this in the minds of many independent observers. Yugoslavia, Bulgaria, and Albania extended the Greek guerrillas aid and sanctuary, but the rebel army, the EAM, was directed by indigenous Greek leadership and supported by many noncommunist Greeks. Equally significant was the fact that Stalin did not aid the Greek insurgency. But Greece had become an important part of the United States' overall anti-communist strategy of containment, and by February 1947 the administration was convinced that American intervention in Greece was necessary if this entire strategy was not to be jeopardized.[14]

The administration was successful in persuading Congress to approve its intervention plans, and what has become known as the Truman Doctrine was implemented. Congress appropriated $400 million for aid—largely military—to the Greek and Turkish governments for the next fiscal year, and it authorized the President to send military and civilian advisers to these countries. Before the Truman Doctrine was approved, however, it precipitated the most important foreign policy debate since the advent of World War II.[15]

Among Senate liberals, Taylor and Pepper opposed the Greek-Turkish aid bill. First, they rejected the initial premise of the proposal—that the United States would be defending freedom in

Greece and Turkey by bailing out the existing governments there. Taylor was convinced "that the Greek and Turkish governments were corrupt, fascist tyrannies that did not deserve our support. . . ." Many students of the Truman Doctrine have avoided this subject entirely, but at least one friend of the proposal, Joseph Marion Jones, has since acknowledged "that the Greek government was corrupt, reactionary, inefficient, and indulged in extremist practices was well known and incontestable. . . ." Taylor cited articles from a variety of publications, which painted a much more complex picture of the issues at stake than did Truman's address. According to Taylor's sources, large numbers of royalist officials had collaborated with the Nazis during the German occupation, and the parliamentary elections of 1946 were hardly the free elections that Truman described. After these "free" elections, a *New York Times* reporter wrote: "Greece is beginning to take on some aspects of a police state. . . ." One article that Taylor relished was from the *New York Post*. Once the royalists won the 1946 elections, it stated, "they set about obliterating their opponents as a political force, pursuing the 'Communists,' which became a generic term covering any democrat who was against the king." [16]

Greece, Taylor pointed out, had had "exactly the same pattern of preelection violence" that "our press complains so bitterly about in Poland," yet the administration wanted to aid the Greek government. Attacking the double standard, Taylor asserted that American policy was self-defeating: "Surely we will create more Communists if we represent to the people of Greece and to the oppressed peoples of the world that the only alternative to fascism and Royalist oppression is communism." He wanted the United States to pressure the existing Greek government into liberalizing itself before any aid was given. Unless truly free elections were held in Greece, Taylor asserted, American aid would be "used to promote fascism," and this would be done "in the name of democracy." [17]

Taylor himself was quite sympathetic with the Greek guerrillas and cited *New York Times* articles which maintained that the vast majority of them were not communists. The guerrillas, in his view, were a group "whose membership is overwhelmingly non-Communist and in many cases anti-Communist, and whose real solidarity lies in opposition to Greece's imported Danish king. . . ." [18]

Taylor later returned to American policy in Greece in his attack on the Marshall Plan in 1948, believing that this new program demonstrated the administration's hypocrisy. Aid to Greece had served to further destroy Greek democracy, despite Truman's high-sounding rhetoric, and Taylor pronounced: "I cannot and I will not vote to inflict on other people the sad fate that has overtaken the Greeks since we set out to teach them about democracy." A recent study on the Greek civil war in fact corroborates Taylor's criticism on this matter. Edgar O'Ballance, in *The Greek Civil War,* maintains:

The Americans took a much tougher line than had the British, who had been cautious and reluctant to interfere in Greek domestic politics. . . . In December [1947], the right to strike was abolished, and then there was a purge of all Government employees who were Communists, suspected of Communist sympathies or had been engaged in disseminating Communist propaganda. The Americans said that all this should have been done months before.[19]

An even more important objection to the Truman Doctrine was that it bypassed the United Nations and would thus seriously weaken that body. Taylor and Pepper had opposed Churchill's "iron curtain" speech the year before for the same reason. This time, however, it was the United States that was initiating a unilateral program which could very easily lead to war with the Soviet Union. Taylor compared the Greek situation with the Japanese invasion of Manchuria: "We stand at a crossroads in history. This is the most portentous moment since Japan was allowed to invade Manchuria in 1931." Pointing out that the Manchurian invasion signified the end of the League of Nations, Taylor urged the Senate not to destroy the UN through similar action.[20]

Taylor also resented the bipartisan effort to push the Greek Turkish bill through the Senate with a minimum of debate. Believing that the Truman Doctrine would set the nation on "a course from which there is no turning back," he urged his colleagues not to act in haste: "We must not be driven to rash action by the false urgency that has been injected into this question." In his view, the administration had created an "artificial" crisis in order to rush through a program which neither was in the national interest nor desired by the American people. He also turned his guns on the bipartisan foreign policy, saying at one point: "Simply because a proposition is bipartisan does not make it a wise policy. Many suicide pacts are bipartisan." [21]

Behind the "crisis" talk, Taylor asserted, was the real reason for the administration's request—Middle East oil. In early April he said on a radio program: "It becomes unmistakably clear that the objective is not so much food for the Greek people as oil for the American monopolies—the oil that lies in the great underground resources in the lands just east of Greece and Turkey." Taylor continually discounted or ignored the role that ideological factors played in foreign policy. To him, ideology was simply a smoke screen for economic motives, and he frequently lapsed into a simplistic economic determinism as "the" explanation for American foreign policy. Apparently he had been greatly impressed by a pamphlet on this subject prepared by the Office of Naval Intelligence, and he was much given to quoting one passage from it: "Realistically, all wars have been for economic reasons. To make them politically and socially palatable, ideological issues have always been involved." [22]

Taylor had no difficulty finding articles in business publications such as the *Wall Street Journal* and *Business Week* to support his arguments that economic considerations were behind the Truman proposals. Anticipating new markets for American goods, commentators in these media also pointed out that the new policy would protect American oil investment in the Middle East. Although Taylor sometimes greatly oversimplified the administration's motives, there was some truth to his rhetorical question: "Can we not detect a rather oily smell here?" At the beginning of 1947, American oil investment in the Middle East amounted to approximately $360 million, but three years later, *Fortune* estimated that the American oil investors' stake in the Middle East had reached $850 million. [23]

Taylor and Pepper had no delusions about their chances of stopping the Greek-Turkish aid bill. They did, however, offer a substitute resolution which embodied their alternative to the Truman Doctrine. Under this proposal, all aid was to be channeled through a fund administered by the UN, and American contributions to this fund were to be contingent on the pledge of the Greek government not to discriminate in its distribution of relief on the basis of race, creed, or political belief. Neither Taylor nor Pepper thought Turkey deserved aid, Taylor saying: "All the things that we object to so strongly in Poland and Bulgaria, have been going on for years in Turkey." For this reason, all aid in the Taylor-Pepper proposal was restricted to Greece. The resolution also "specifically excluded" all military aid. As expected, the Senate overwhelmingly rejected it and passed the Greek-Turkish aid bill 67 to 23.[24]

The Greek-Turkish aid bill was only one of a series of actions in foreign policy which led dissenting liberals to form a third-party movement for the 1948 election. In late December 1947, Henry Wallace announced his candidacy for the presidency of the United States on a third-party ticket. After being fired from the Truman Cabinet in September 1946, Wallace continued to be fancied by many liberals as the legitimate heir to FDR. Truman's bungling on such domestic issues as price controls, his threat to draft strikers, and his uncompromising foreign policy alienated large segments of the old Roosevelt coalition and made his election prospects in 1948 seem dim. By early 1947 a liberal alternative to Truman either within the Democratic party or on a third ticket was a real possibility. Anti-Truman liberals, however, were unable to coalesce, and they exhausted themselves in counterproductive efforts. The behavior of Taylor and Pepper in this regard is illustrative of the plight of left-wing liberals in the 1948 election. Pepper, a firm believer in the two-party system, floundered within the Democratic party along with ADA liberals, seeking an alternative to Truman but reluctantly supporting the President.[25]

Taylor, on the other hand, decided to bolt the Democrats and accept the second slot on the Wallace ticket. He pondered this decision for almost two months. Friends and family argued vigorously against Taylor's defection, and a six-week survey of his Idaho constituency suggested that it would amount to political suicide. Taylor finally announced his decision to stand with Wallace on February 23, 1948. In the end, it was his "conviction that the Truman Administration's foreign policy was imperialistic and certain to lead to war [that] caused him to disregard the advice of his wife and others, and join what he considered a crusade for peace." [26]

Taylor made his announcement over a CBS radio broadcast in the presence of Wallace. Here he asserted: "I am not leaving the Democratic Party. It left me. Wall Street and the military have taken over." He seemed relieved of a great burden, saying, "Now I will be free to fight this bipartisan coalition and all its works: Taft-Hartley, universal military training, the drive toward war, high prices and racial discrimination and suppressed civil liberties." During the press conference which followed the broadcast, Taylor claimed that Truman's foreign policy was destroying all that FDR had built. A few days later he said:

I believe the big issue in the 1948 campaign will be the necessity of having peace in the world. . . . I feel that our present get-tough-with-Russia foreign policy will inevitably end in war. I believe that Henry Wallace is the only American who could reach an understanding with Russia because he has not spent his time in denouncing the Soviet Union week after week.[27]

The timing of Taylor's announcement proved unfortunate, for at the very time of his broadcast the Communists were seizing power in Czechoslovakia. Wallace had long been labeled a fellow traveler by both Republicans and pro-administration Democrats, as well as by some ADA liberals. Stewart Alsop's comment was typical: "The Wallace third party movement has been indecently exposed for what it is: an instrument of Soviet foreign policy." The Czechoslovakian *coup* further served to impress the "red" label on the Progressives. Urging a more conciliatory policy toward Russia, Wallace and Taylor were severely disadvantaged when the communists in Eastern Europe assumed a more rigid stance.[28]

Both before and after the 1948 election, many observers felt that Wallace's refusal to repudiate Communist support accounted for his poor showing. On November 1, 1948, the *New York Times* reported that earlier in the campaign Wallace had been expected to receive seven or eight million votes, but that now it was thought that his total might "drop to half that number. . . . Growing belief that Communists dominate the Progressive party appears to be the reason for a decline in the Wallace strength." (On

election day, his vote actually was a mere 1,157,140.) But Wallace
and Taylor refused to repudiate Communist support for reasons
of principle: they did not care to contribute to further red-baiting.
Taylor felt that if the Communists wanted to vote for his ticket,
which stood for a progressive capitalist program, that was all right
with him. Later he said that he welcomed "the vote of any
qualified voter. . . . It's hypocrisy to say that you don't want certain votes." Taylor and other Progressives maintained that even
Communists could be on the right side of some issues. In Taylor's
view, the Progressives sought to *reform* the American system,
"making our economy work so well and our way of life so attractive . . . that Communism will never interest more than the infin-
itesimal fraction of our citizens who adhere to it now." [29]

But Taylor's rationale received little attention in the daily press
or the weekly news magazines. *Newsweek's* treatment of his announcement speech was typical of the coverage. Pointing out that
he had received favorable publicity in the *Daily Worker* over the
past two years, *Newsweek* declared: "In that time he has out-
stripped Claude Pepper of Florida to become the most popular
senator so far as the Communists are concerned." Taylor also
found such once-friendly liberal journalists as Richard Neuberger
rivaling the daily press in their efforts to discredit him. Fearful of
a Republican victory, liberals were being won back to the Democratic party and eventually even "swallowed" Truman to avoid
that possibility. The *Nation* denounced the third-party movement
at its inception primarily for the effect that it had on Democratic
chances. Although the *New Republic* featured articles both pro
and con on the Wallace movement, T.R.B. criticized it from the
beginning for splitting the liberal vote. Both the *Nation* and T.R.B.
pointed out that the Wallace-Taylor ticket received strong backing
from the Communists, the *Nation* saying that "the speeches of Mr.
Wallace and Senator Taylor echoed the party line closely. . . ."
Neuberger took a different approach in a piece in the *American
Mercury*. Earlier, the Oregon journalist had interpreted Taylor as
an "outstanding liberal," but in 1948 he dismissed him as an op-
portunist "determined to get into the headlines, no matter what the
cost." To be sure, Neuberger was a Democratic candidate for the
Oregon state senate in 1948. He wrote two other articles that year

•

which referred to Taylor, but nowhere did he mention the Idaho Senator's overall voting record. Between 1945 and 1947 Taylor had supported the Democratic administration measures 94 per cent of the time. Senate Majority Leader Alben Barkley, in comparison, scored only 88 per cent.[30]

Soon after his break with the Democrats, Taylor made a long speech against the Marshall Plan and introduced a substitute proposal. Basically, his argument against the Marshall Plan was the same as that against the Truman Doctrine—it bypassed the UN and further polarized Europe into two armed camps. Taylor had long urged his colleagues to put themselves in the Russians' position and look at American foreign policy from their point of view. Suppose, suggested Taylor, that the Russians had intervened with arms and advisers in Mexico as the United States had done in Iran? What would be the American response? Would not Russian intervention mean war? "I would be one of the first to insist that such unfriendly action should cease immediately," Taylor said. Such intervention in Latin America would be provocation, yet the United States had been making similar provocations along the Russian borders. War had not occurred between the United States and Russia, Taylor maintained, only because the Russians were still weak from World War II.[31]

In order to preserve world peace, the United States must recognize the Russian sphere of influence as the Russians had recognized that of the United States. Taylor pointed out, citing both Cordell Hull's and James Byrnes's memoirs, that Churchill and Stalin had divided the Balkans between them in 1944. He did not deny "that the Russians have now included several other nations in their sphere of influence, not by direct military action, perhaps, but by techniques of ideological infiltration. . . ." Russian expansion, according to Taylor, was accomplished "in much the same way that we use dollar diplomacy." Neither Wallace nor Taylor ever seemed comfortable about the Czechoslovakian *coup,* but Taylor reminded his colleagues that Czechoslovakia "was in the Russian sphere before the change of government." In his eyes, *both* of the major powers had expanded their spheres of influence after the war. "At any rate the Russians are not alone in their expansion of their spheres of influence." Taylor pointed to the American presence in

Western Europe, Greece, Turkey, Arabia, North Africa, Greenland, Japan, Okinawa, South Korea, and China, concluding "that
we are at least equally guilty in the matter of expansion." [32]

Taylor ridiculed the humanitarian arguments advanced in favor
of the Marshall Plan, saying that they were used only to persuade
humanitarians to support the policy. The real reason for the Marshall Plan was economic. According to Taylor, the proposal was
really a scheme to capture new markets for American goods. He
cited articles in business journals and *U.S. News,* as well as remarks of other senators, to support his thesis of economic imperialism: "It seems to me . . . that we are simply trying to find ways and
means of dumping our excess production abroad in the hope that
by so doing we will get foreign nations accustomed to our products,
and . . . find markets for the day when home consumption can no
longer take up the slack." [33]

If the motivation for the Marshall Plan really was humanitarian,
Taylor suggested, then all aid should be given through the UN
with no political strings attached. In keeping with this belief, Taylor offered a substitute amendment to the Marshall Plan bill. This
amendment repudiated the Truman Doctrine, saying it "has bypassed the United Nations and provoked international suspicion
and tension which, if unchecked, can lead only to war." Taylor's
proposal provided that the United States contribute $5 billion a
year for five years to a UN-administered program. Priority for
these recovery funds was to "be given to those nations which suffered most severely from Axis aggression." (Taylor was especially
irked that Germany was to be so well treated under the Marshall
Plan. He rejected the Morgenthau Plan, but believed that Germany's victims deserved more aid than Germany.) Doubting the
sincerity of the administration's offer to include Russia and her
satellites within its recovery program, Taylor provided that all
funds under his substitute plan would be distributed "without regard to the character of the political and social institutions of the
recipient nation and without the imposition of any political conditions or any economic conditions. . . ." No recovery funds could
be spent on armaments or military programs; and the United States
must declare itself in favor of universal disarmament and work
toward a world-wide 10 per cent annual reduction in military
budgets.

Immediately after the introduction of the Taylor amendment, the Senate's bipartisan leadership arranged a vote on it, and it was defeated 74 to 3. Only Taylor, Pepper, and North Dakota's William Langer supported it. Four days later, on March 13, 1948, the Senate approved the Marshall Plan 69 to 17, Taylor being the only liberal to vote against the measure, and it became law in early April. Later, in 1949, Taylor acknowledged that the Marshall Plan had done "some good," but he still opposed it because it was a unilateral program which bypassed the UN.[34]

The Marshall Plan is one of the few truly successful American programs of the postwar period. It restored Western Europe's economy, helped America prosper, and "immunized" Western Europe against serious internal threats of communism. This success cannot be overlooked, but it came at a steep price. Once again the UN had been weakened. More important, however, was the fact that the Marshall Plan further polarized Europe and, in the eyes of the Russian leaders, threatened Russian control in Eastern Europe. Marshall Shulman has written in *Stalin's Foreign Policy Reappraised*: "Assessing the Marshall Plan as a threat to its tenuously established position in Eastern Europe and as a device to secure American hegemony in Western Europe, the Soviet Union defined a policy in the fall of 1947 which called for speeding up the consolidation of its controls in Eastern Europe. . . ." At the time of the Czechoslovakian *coup,* Taylor and other critics of administration foreign policy interpreted it as a response to American provocation. But few influential Americans believed that the Russians were pursuing a defensive policy by 1948, and they were not at all receptive to the idea that the Czechoslovakian *coup* was the result of a Russian sense of insecurity.[35]

The Marshall Plan was much more palatable to liberals than had been the Truman Doctrine. When Marshall first made his proposal in mid-1947, he extended an invitation to participate to Russia and the Eastern European countries within its sphere of influence. Friends of the Marshall Plan insist that this offer was sincere, but it is more likely that it was a scheme to embarrass the Russians, knowing that they would refuse. The administration had taken no steps to convince Congress of the desirability of Russian participation in the Plan. After the implementation of the Truman Doctrine, it is highly unlikely that Congress ever could have been persuaded to accept a Russian aid program. Even if the administration was sincere in this offer, the Russian leadership thought the conditions of the program unacceptable. As Taylor and Pepper had long maintained, the Russians were greatly weakened, and they did not care to have the Western world realize how precarious their economic position was. According to Isaac Deutscher in his revised biography of Stalin: "It turned out that to obtain aid the Soviet Union was required . . . to draw up a balance sheet of its economic resources; and, according to the Soviet experts, the Americans attached to the aid conditions that would hamper the U.S.S.R. in its economic planning, and the governments of eastern Europe in nationalizing their industries."

Such terms were unacceptable to Stalin, maintains Deutscher, who points out that Stalin was not willing to let even the Russian people know of the "appalling exhaustion and frightful gap in her manpower" which Russia had suffered as a result of World War II. Deutscher suggests that Stalin feared that participation in the Marshall Plan would lead to "American economic penetration into eastern Europe and even into Russia. . . ." Taylor and the Progressives had not been aware of all the implications of the Marshall Plan, but they did demonstrate that it could further divide Europe into communist and anti-communist blocs, and that it was another important source of antagonism in the Cold War. Adam Ulam writes: "The beginning of the Marshall Plan constitutes a watershed in the cold war. . . . With the Marshall Plan the cold war assumes the character of position warfare. Both sides become frozen in mutual unfriendliness." [36]

With the poor November 1948 showing of the Wallace-Taylor ticket, Taylor quietly dropped out of the Progressive party and tried to mend his fences with the Democrats in 1949. With no regret for his 1948 apostasy, however, he continued to defend the Progressive platform and suggested that the Wallace-Taylor campaign had caused Truman to pursue a more liberal domestic policy in 1948. He also opposed the Russian blockade of Berlin, denied that he favored unilateral disarmament, and deplored the 1948 Czechoslovakian *coup*. Taylor explained why he did not constantly criticize Russian actions: "the main reason is that I can't run Russian foreign policy. . . . I do have some voice in our foreign policy. . . ." [37]

Taylor had continued to exert this voice in vain. On July 20, 1949, he had argued against the North Atlantic Treaty in a long speech. Now his opposition was somewhat toned down and not directed at Truman personally. Claiming that he had tried to support NATO, Taylor said, "I do not like to be pictured as a maverick. Even including my votes on foreign policy, my record of party regularity is excelled by few. . . ." Despite his desire for party regularity, however, Taylor could not conscientiously support the treaty. The United States was again undercutting the UN, and in his eyes that was not internationalism:

I, myself, think isolationism is very bad—that we all must live together in this shrinking world. But . . . seeking to bypass, undermine, and destroy the United Nations is not internationalism. That is not thinking in world terms. And opposition to alliances of a military nature, or any arrangements outside the United Nations, which tend to weaken that organization certainly is not isolationism.

As he had done in previous debates, Taylor asserted that the Russians had assumed a defensive posture in Eastern Europe and were no threat to legitimate American interests. The proposed treaty, however, "needlessly provoking the Russians by setting up bases on their very frontier," increased the possibility of war. He again pointed out that the American monopoly of the atomic bomb would not continue, and suggested that the Russians might already have that weapon (Truman announced the first explosion of a Russian atomic bomb on September 22, 1949). This possibility made it imperative that the United States reach an accommodation with the Russians.[38]

Taylor had often complained that the administration created artificial "crises calculated to affect the outcome of legislation before the Senate. . . ." In the case of the North Atlantic Treaty, Taylor charged, the administration was reverting to its old tricks: senators not on the Foreign Relations Committee were not privy to all the information they needed to make decisions in foreign policy, and the executive departments withheld important data from them. Taylor urged the Senate to "be jealous of its rights and prerogatives which are bestowed upon us by the Constitution," and announced: "We should call a halt here and now to the practice of presenting grave and important matters to the Senate in the nature of a fait accompli." [39]

Taylor's July 20, 1949, remarks against the North Atlantic Treaty was his last major speech on foreign policy. Looking ahead to the 1950 campaign, he began to limit his remarks almost entirely to domestic topics. In the fall of 1949 *Time* reported that Taylor "paid a sheepish and belated visit to the White House." And on May 5, 1950, Taylor announced that he would no longer oppose appropriations for the Economic Cooperation Administration. Reminding his colleagues that he never had been opposed to the principle of foreign aid, Taylor repeated his objection that this aid had been administered outside the UN. As there was "no possibility of changing it at this late date," he would begin to vote for the existing program.[40]

But it was too late for Taylor to rebuild a political constituency. After his 1948 apostasy, Democratic leaders in Idaho pledged to retire him in the 1950 primary. Communism became a major issue in the campaign, and the outbreak of the Korean War at the end of June hurt him seriously, despite his immediate endorsement of Truman's Korean policy. As had Pepper in the Florida primary, Taylor found himself the target of a massive red-baiting campaign. The anti-Taylor forces borrowed directly from the Florida campaign: the *Idaho Daily Statesman* serialized *The Red Record of Claude Pepper* under the headline, "A Man Is Known by the Company He Keeps." This same paper reprinted an article from a back issue of the *Daily Worker* which referred to Taylor as one of the Eightieth Congress' "heroes." These tactics, along with a split in the labor vote between Taylor and another pro-labor candidate, resulted in Taylor's defeat by 949 votes. He was never again elected to office.[41]

Glen Taylor was not an astute politician. Unlike that breed, he did not have a well-developed sense of survival. Without a strong political base in Idaho, Taylor ruined his career by joining Henry Wallace's 1948 campaign. Taylor and a few others in Congress sought to strengthen the UN and to discourage American unilateralism, believing that the bitterness of the Cold War was avoidable. Perhaps naive on occasion, the one-term Idaho Senator was no match for the vast congressional majority which had become convinced after the war that conflict with Russia was inevitable. Taylor protested in vain that American foreign policy often served to provoke the Russians into aggressive action, and his warnings that the United States would soon lose its monopoly of the atomic bomb received little attention. By the time of his defeat in 1950, the United States no longer had the options that Taylor had urged. His involuntary retirement, as well as those of Pepper and Vito Marcantonio, also marked the end of an era of American liberalism. In postwar America, liberalism had polarized over the issue of foreign policy. The "hard line" approach of the Truman administration was challenged by the Peppers, the Taylors, and the Marcantonios, but these dissenters were vanquished as American liberalism came to demand orthodoxy in foreign policy—an orthodoxy of anti-communism.

Notes

1. *Time,* LV (March 20, 1950), 18; *Newsweek,* XXXVI (August 21, 1950), 32; *Saturday Evening Post,* CCXXIII (October 28, 1950), 10–12. For a short study of the contrast between Taylor's public image and his record, see William C. Pratt, "Glen H. Taylor: Public Image and Reality," *Pacific Northwest Quarterly,* LX (January 1969), 10–16. A recent dissertation treats Taylor's political career; see Frank Ross Peterson, "Liberal from Idaho: The Public Career of Senator Glen H. Taylor" (unpublished Ph.D. dissertation, Washington State University, 1968). See also Peterson, "Fighting the Drive Toward War: Glen H. Taylor, the 1948 Progressives, and the Draft," *Pacific Northwest Quarterly,* LXI (January 1970). Peterson is now completing a biography of Taylor.
2. *Congressional Record,* 80th Cong., 1st sess., XCIII (March 12, 1947), 1981.
3. Pratt, "Glen H. Taylor," p. 10; Richard L. Neuberger, "Cowboy on Our Side," *Nation,* CLXIII (August 24, 1946), 210. For short biographical sketches of Taylor, see "Taylor, Glen H.," in Anna Rothe, ed., *Current Biography 1947* (New York, 1948), pp. 628–630, and Frank Gervasi, "Low Man on the Wallace Poll," *Collier's,* CXXI (May 8, 1948), 16–17, 72–74. For a detailed account of Taylor's life before he entered the Senate, see Peterson, "Liberal from Idaho," pp. 1–48.
4. Neuberger, "From 'Singing Cowboy' to United States Senator," *Progressive* (May 7, 1945) in *Congressional Record,* 79th Cong., 1st sess., XCI (May 7, 1945), A2137; Kyle Crichton, "Idaho's Hot Potato," *Collier's,* CXV (June 30, 1945), 21, 64; John Gunther, *Inside U.S.A.* (New York, 1947), p. 108.

5. *Congressional Record,* 79th Cong., 1st sess., XCI (March 1, 1945), 1609; Curtis D. MacDougall, *Gideon's Army* (New York, 1965), I, 173; *New York Times,* August 1, 1945; MacDougall, *Gideon's Army,* I, 53; personal interview with Claude Pepper, October 9, 1969. For Taylor's domestic record in the Senate, see Peterson, "Liberal from Idaho," pp. 50–112.

6. Eugene A. Cox, "Germany's Place in a Post-War World," *Congressional Record,* 79th Cong., 1st sess., XCI (February 12, 1945), A582; Ernest R. May, "The Cold War," in C. Vann Woodward, ed., *The Comparative Approach to American History* (New York, 1968), p. 343.

7. *Congressional Record,* 79th Cong., 1st sess., XCI (October 24, 1945), 9987–9989. Taylor still believes that this resolution was his most important act in the Senate. Peterson, "Liberal from Idaho," p. 113. *Congressional Record,* 79th Cong., 1st sess., XCI (November 8, 1945), 10497. Taylor repeated his arguments for a world republic in Glen H. Taylor, "Why a World Republic?," *Free World,* X (December 1945), 27–31; *New York Times,* October 25, 1945; *Congressional Record,* 81st Cong., 1st sess., XCV (July 20, 1949), 9780.

8. Eric Goldman, *The Crucial Decade—And After* (New York, 1960), pp. 37–38. James Byrnes, then Truman's Secretary of State, reveals that both he and Truman were familiar with the contents of the speech before it was given. James Byrnes, *All in One Lifetime* (New York, 1958), p. 349.

9. Goldman, *Crucial Decade,* p. 38; *New York Times,* March 7, 13, 15, 1946. The *Times* reported: "Members of Congress today generally agreed with Winston Churchill's remarks about Russia, but were cool to his alliance proposal. . . ." *Ibid.,* March 7, 1946. See also MacDougall, *Gideon's Army,* I, 30–31.

10. *New York Times,* March 7, 1946. Secretary of Commerce Henry Wallace labeled Churchill's speech "shocking" and endorsed the Pepper-Kilgore-Taylor statement. *Ibid.,* March 8, 1946; *Congressional Record,* 80th Cong., 2nd sess., XCIV (March 10, 1948), 2448; *New York Times,* March 15, July 7, 1946. Pepper, Kilgore, and Taylor were joined by Washington Senator Hugh B. Mitchell in a second statement occasioned by a Churchill speech in New York City: "Mr. Churchill's proposal is simply a call for the preserving and rebuilding of British imperialism, with the aid of the United States, regardless of the consequences to the peace." *Ibid.,* March 17, 1946.

11. As early as April 23, 1945, Truman had declared "that he felt our agreements with the Soviet Union so far had been a one-way street and that he could not continue; it was now or never. He intended to go on with the plan for San Francisco and if the Russians did not wish to join us they could go to hell. . . ." Bohlen notes in Walter Millis, ed., *The Forrestal Diaries* (New York, 1951), p. 50. Later the same day, Truman told Molotov that he expected the Russians to adhere to his interpretations of the Yalta accords. Molotov responded to his lecture by saying: "I have never been talked to like that in my life." To which Truman said: "Carry out your agreements and you won't get talked to like that." Harry S. Truman, *Memoirs* (Garden City, 1955–1956), I, 82. See also D. F. Fleming, *The Cold War and Its Origins* (Garden City, 1961), I, 268; Gar Alperovitz, *Atomic Diplomacy: Hiroshima and Potsdam* (New York, 1965), pp. 19–20, 28–29. *Congressional Record,* 79th Cong., 2nd sess., XCII (May 16, 1946), 5094; XCI (July 28, 1945), 8168.

12. In May 1946, Taylor talked of a "great conspiracy of the Fascists all

over the world to fight Russia now while we have a bomb which they do not have." *Congressional Record,* 79th Cong., 2nd sess., XCII (May 16, 1946), 5094; Taylor speech, Grand Rapids, Mich., *ibid.,* 80th Cong., 2nd sess., XCIV (August 7, 1948), A5102. He also referred to Admiral Leahy as "a Fascist sympathizer." *Ibid.* (June 18, 1948), 8796; MacDougall, *Gideon's Army,* III, 688; *New York Times,* September 21, 1948. Earlier Taylor had said: "We have moved into Hitler's shoes and are determined to conduct a war against Russia and then to exploit the world. That is part of the scheme to enable our businessmen to infiltrate and gain control of the industries of other countries." *Congressional Record,* 80th Cong., 2nd sess., XCIV (May 12, 1948), 5683. See also Peterson, "Liberal from Idaho," pp. 175–177, 226.

13. Two recent works on the Greek civil war are Edgar O'Ballance, *The Greek Civil War, 1944–1949* (London, 1966) and D. George Kousoulas, *Revolution and Defeat: The Story of the Greek Communist Party* (London, 1965). See also Todd Gitlin, "Counter-Insurgency: Myth and Reality in Greece," in David Horowitz, ed., *Containment and Revolution* (Boston, 1967). Winston S. Churchill, *Triumph and Tragedy* (Cambridge, Mass., 1953), pp. 227–228; James F. Byrnes, *Speaking Frankly* (New York, 1947), p. 53; Isaac Deutscher, *Stalin: A Political Biography* (New York, 1967), pp. 515–517. Churchill points out: "Stalin . . . adhered strictly and faithfully to our agreement of October, and during all the long weeks of fighting the Communists in the streets of Athens not one word of reproach came from *Pravda* or *Isvestia.*" Churchill, *Triumph,* p. 293; Walter LaFeber, *America, Russia, and the Cold War, 1945–1966* (New York, 1968), p. 18; O'Ballance, *Greek Civil War,* pp. 125–130; Truman, *Memoirs,* II, 98–100.

14. *Ibid.,* 108; O'Ballance, *Greek Civil War,* pp. 121–126, 131; Kousoulas, *Revolution and Defeat,* pp. 237, 244–245, 289–291; Richard J. Barnet, *Intervention and Revolution: The United States in the Third World* (New York, 1968), pp. 110–113, 121. O'Ballance, Kousoulas, and Barnet believe that Stalin encouraged the guerrillas at first, but agree that he gave them no aid. See also Milovan Djilas, *Conversations with Stalin* (New York, 1962), pp. 131–132, 181–183. Gitlin maintains that "the earliest armed bands sprang up before the Communists made their decision to opt for armed resistance." Gitlin, "Counter-Insurgency," p. 163.

15. For a State Department insider's account of the Truman Doctrine, see Joseph Marion Jones, *The Fifteen Weeks* (New York, 1964). See also LaFeber, *America, Russia, and the Cold War,* pp. 44–46.

16. *Congressional Record,* 80th Cong., 1st sess., XCIII (April 15, 1947), 3386; Jones, *Fifteen Weeks,* p. 185. See also Barnet, *Intervention and Revolution,* pp. 99–101. *Congressional Record,* 80th Cong., 1st sess., XCIII (April 15, 1947), 3390; (April 18, 1947), 3695; (April 15, 1947), 3392.

17. *Ibid.,* pp. 3390, 3406, 3394, 3407, 3388.

18. *Ibid.,* pp. 3391, 3389. Taylor overemphasized the ecumenicism of the guerrillas, but Fleming agrees that most of them were non-communist. Fleming, *Cold War,* I, 439. McNeill discusses the appeal that the guerrilla movement had to Greeks in 1946–1947. See William Hardy McNeill, *Greece: American Aid in Action, 1947–1956* (New York, 1957), pp. 23, 26–27. Gitlin points out that the administration did not claim that all the guerrillas were Communists, quoting Acheson: "There are among them

many persons who honestly, but in our opinion mistakenly, support the Communist-led forces because they do not like the present Greek government." Years later, Senator Gaylord McGee of Wyoming, a historian by training, stated: "We had to back not the good guys but the bad guys in Greece. . . . We did not back the people. We backed the monarchy; we backed those who happened to be in the driver's seat at that moment." Gitlin, "Counter-Insurgency," pp. 168, 140.

19. *Congressional Record*, 80th Cong., 2nd sess., XCIV (March 10, 1948), 2456–2457; O'Ballance, *Greek Civil War*, p. 155.

20. *Congressional Record*, 80th Cong., 1st sess., XCIII (April 15, 1947), 3387, 3406.

21. *Ibid.*, (March 31, 1947), 2870; (April 15, 1947), 3387.

22. MacDougall, *Gideon's Army*, I, 145; *Congressional Record*, 80th Cong., 1st sess., XCIII (April 15, 1947), 3387; (April 22, 1947), 3788.

23. *Ibid.* (April 15, 1947), pp. 3405–3407, 3387; Charles Issawi and Mohammed Yeganeh, *The Economics of Middle Eastern Oil* (New York, 1962), p. 59; "World Oil in Turmoil," *Fortune*, XLI (February 1950), 110.

24. *Congressional Record*, 80th Cong., 1st sess., XCIII (April 15, 1947), 3407, 3394; (April 22, 1947), 3793.

25. Alonzo L. Hamby, "Henry A. Wallace, the Liberals, and Soviet-American Relations," *Review of Politics*, XXX (April 1968), 160–161. For liberal disenchantment with the Truman administration, see MacDougall, *Gideon's Army*, I; Karl M. Schmidt, *Henry A. Wallace: Quixotic Crusade 1948* (Syracuse, 1960), pp. 15–40. A remark that Pepper recently made in reference to Taylor is perhaps illuminating about his own decision. Pepper stated that Taylor had made one mistake: he left the Democratic party and ran with Wallace. Personal interview with Claude Pepper, October 9, 1969.

26. MacDougall, *Gideon's Army*, II, 307–310. See also Peterson, "Liberal from Idaho," pp. 140–146. Peterson reveals that Taylor even discussed this matter with Truman before he bolted. *Ibid.*, p. 144.

27. *New York Times*, February 24, 26, 1948.

28. MacDougall, *Gideon's Army*, I, 248. Wallace's handling of the Czechoslovakian issue was especially inept. *Ibid.*, II, 334–335; Schmidt, *Henry A. Wallace*, p. 247; Hamby, "Henry A. Wallace," p. 168.

29. *New York Times*, November 1, 1948. Vito Marcantonio said later: "Wallace should have made a strong statement that he was not a Communist, that the Progressive party was not communistic nor even socialistic, and that even if the Communists wanted to come in, they were not welcome." MacDougall, *Gideon's Army*, II, p. 434; Schmidt, *Henry A. Wallace*, p. 335 (vote table). For statements of Wallace on this matter, see MacDougall, *Gideon's Army*, I, 157–158; II, 426–427, 434, 496. *New York Times*, February 26, 1948; "Senator Glen Taylor Meets the Press," *American Mercury*, LXIX (October 1949), 431. In this interview he stated: "Simply because Communists happen to be for something that's good is not going to make me turn away from it. You'd have to be against an awful lot of good things if you opposed everything the Communists are for." Schmidt, *Henry A. Wallace*, p. 248. See also *Congressional Record*, 80th Cong., 2nd sess., XCIV (June 18, 1948), 8787.

30. *Newsweek*, XXXI (March 8, 1948), 20; *Nation*, CLXV (December

27, 1947), 693. See also Freda Kirchwey, "Wallace: Prophet or Politician?," *ibid.*, CLXVI (January 10, 1948), 29–31; Robert Bendiner, "Politics and People," *ibid.* (February 28, 1948), 229–230; and *ibid.*, (March 1, 1948), 261–262. Howard K. Smith, however, wrote a sympathetic article on the Progressive convention; see "The Wallace Party," *ibid.*, CLXVII (August 7, 1948), 145–147; T.R.B., "Washington Wire," *New Republic,* CXVIII (January 26, 1948), 3–4; *ibid.*, CXIX (August 9, 1948), 4; *Nation,* CLXVII (July 31, 1948), 113; Neuberger, "Glen Taylor: Crooner on the Left," *American Mercury,* LXVII (October 1948), 266. See also "Glen Taylor: Leftwing Minstrel," *Progressive,* XII (April 1948), 18–21, and "Slow-Bell Campaign in the Northwest," *Nation,* CLXVII (October 16, 1948), 422–423. Taylor's voting record is discussed in Schmidt, *Henry A. Wallace,* p. 59, and MacDougall, *Gideon's Army,* II, 308.

31. Taylor gave a very general statement opposing the Marshall Plan in *Fraternal Outlook.* Glen H. Taylor, "Fraternal Outlook Interviews Congressmen on High Prices and Marshall Plan," *Fraternal Outlook,* IX (December 1947), 6. *Congressional Record,* 80th Cong., 2nd sess., XCIV (March 10, 1948), 2449.

32. *Ibid.* (March 9, 1948), p. 2394; (March 10, 1948), p. 2453.

33. *Ibid.* (March 9, 1948), pp. 2386–2388; (March 10, 1948), p. 2448.

34. *Ibid.*, pp. 2458–2459; (March 9, 1948), p. 2398; (March 10, 1948), pp. 2459, 2460; (March 13, 1948), p. 2793; 81st Cong., 1st sess., XCV (April 8, 1949), 4141.

35. Marshall D. Shulman, *Stalin's Foreign Policy Reappraised* (Cambridge, Mass., 1963), pp. 14–15; *New York Times,* February 29, 1948. Kennan maintains that both the Czechoslovakian coup and the Berlin blockade "were defensive reactions on the Soviet side to the initial success of the Marshall Plan initiative. . . ." George F. Kennan, *Memoirs, 1925–1950* (Boston, 1967), p. 401.

36. Hamby, "Henry A. Wallace," pp. 165, 168; Millis, *Forrestal Diaries,* p. 279; Arthur H. Vandenberg, Jr., ed., *The Private Papers of Senator Vandenberg* (Boston, 1952), p. 377; Kennan, *Memoirs,* p. 343; Jones, *Fifteen Weeks,* p. 253; LaFeber, *America, Russia, and the Cold War,* pp. 48–49; David A. Shannon, *The Decline of American Communism* (New York, 1959), pp. 29–30; Deutscher, *Stalin,* p. 583; Adam B. Ulam, *Expansion and Coexistence: The History of Soviet Foreign Policy, 1917–67* (New York, 1968), p. 437. See also Fleming, *Cold War,* I, 481.

37. Schmidt, *Henry A. Wallace,* p. 282; Boyd A. Martin, "The 1950 Elections in Idaho," *Western Political Quarterly,* IV (March 1951), 76; "Senator Glen Taylor Meets The Press," pp. 429–432, 436–437; Peterson, "Liberal from Idaho," pp. 188–189.

38. *Congressional Record,* 81st Cong., 1st sess., XCV (July 20, 1949), 9787, 9783, 9787; LaFeber, *America, Russia, and the Cold War,* p. 79.

39. *Congressional Record,* 81st Cong., 1st sess., XCV (July 20, 1949), 9779. Vandenberg had complained privately along the same lines at the time of the Truman Doctrine debate. Vandenberg, *Private Papers,* pp. 340, 342.

40. *Time,* LIV (October 3, 1949), 10; *Congressional Record,* 81st Cong., 2nd sess., XCVI (May 5, 1950), 6439.

41. *New York Times,* July 16, 1950; *New Republic,* CXXIII (August 21,

1950), 7. The *New Republic* commented: "The same tactics that were used against Senators Claude Pepper of Florida and Frank Graham of North Carolina have been employed to add Glen Taylor's name to the list of liberal casualties in the Senate this year." Martin, however, believes that the split in the labor vote was the single most important factor in Taylor's defeat. Martin, "The 1950 Elections," p. 77. For a detailed account of the 1950 primary election, see Peterson, "Liberal from Idaho," pp. 200–216. Taylor made two more attempts to win back his seat. In 1954 he again won the Democratic nomination but was swamped in a bitter red-baiting campaign in the November election. Two years later Taylor came within two hundred votes of again winning the primary. See Merrill D. Beale, "The 1954 Election in Idaho," *Western Political Quarterly,* VII (December 1954), 606–610; Martin, "The 1956 Election in Idaho," *ibid.,* X (March 1957), 122–126; Peterson, "Liberal from Idaho," pp. 217–221. Today Taylor is the president of his own wig company, Taylor Topper, Inc., in Millbrae, California. *Newsweek,* LXXII (September 9, 1968), 16.

by Henry W. Berger

Senator Robert A. Taft Dissents from Military Escalation

In a suggestive article published on the eve of the 1964 Republican convention's nomination of Senator Barry Goldwater, Professor Murray Rothbard attempted to distinguish the foreign policy of present conservatives from that of conservatives of World War II and the early years of the Cold War. Rothbard contended that while many conservatives today are dedicated to the goal of military annihilation of communism and thus support any and all efforts to achieve that end, the "prevailing trend, certainly among the intellectuals of the old Right, was a principled and trenchant opposition to war and to its concomitant destruction of life and liberty and of all human values." [1]

This distinction is particularly relevant to the ideas and ideals of Senator Robert A. Taft of Ohio. Acknowledged by admirers and critics alike as the most prominent and influential Republican politician in Congress after World War II, Taft was a persistent conservative critic of American foreign policy.[2] His terse and frequent disclaimers against the overseas programs of the Truman era came at a time when the essential features of America's contemporary international posture were developed. Senator Taft's skepticism and disapproval of many official policies, and the influence which his views commanded in the Republican party and among a sizable group of voters, reveals that American foreign policy during those years was subject to criticism from conservatives as well as from radicals and disaffected liberals. An analysis of Taft's views also illustrates the generally ignored significance of Professor Rothbard's argument and at the same time demonstrates the contradictions and limitations of the conservative critique of American foreign policy.

Two conclusions from such a study emerge at the outset. Taft was no isolationist, as was so often charged during his career and by some writers after his death in 1953.[3] Some scholarly critics have tried to refine this description with new labels, as for example when Arthur Schlesinger, Jr., called Taft a representative of "the New Isolationism." [4] On the other hand, Professor John P. Armstrong, whose 1955 monograph remains the most fair-minded study of Taft, concluded that because he was "against practically everything," Taft "had no foreign policy." [5] Further investigation suggests that these evaluations fail to do adequate justice to the Senator's position.

To be sure, Taft was fiercely partisan and frequently hostile to the way in which the United States conducted its globally oriented foreign affairs. And he occasionally changed his mind, though such shifts occurred far more as the result of altered circumstances than from revisions of his own principles.[6] But at no time did Taft quarrel with the central axiom of postwar American foreign policy —anti-communism. Indeed, he repeatedly complained that the Truman administration had not been vigorous enough in combatting communism, especially in Asia, and he insisted that this weakness was inconsistent with America's anti-communism elsewhere in the world.[7]

Senator Taft *did,* however, question and challenge the strategy and tactics of American policy-makers as they pursued their objectives overseas. He feared that many of their actions could limit America's freedom of choice abroad and involve the United States in war, and might compromise or destroy the traditional roots of American society. An understanding of these concerns discloses the second important point about Taft's outlook on foreign affairs: he was dedicated to the preservation of American democracy and private enterprise, two ideals he associated together and preferred to call "political and economic liberty." [8] Taft was convinced that these twin principles had been responsible for the nation's greatness in the past and that they must be maintained and perfected in the future. Foreign policy, he said, should be tied to this objective. "I believe," he declared in the only book he ever wrote, that "the ultimate purpose of our foreign policy must be to protect the liberty of the people of the United States." [9]

This simple assertion was the clue to Taft's thinking about the strategy and goals of foreign policy. On the one hand he wanted to be sure that America's involvement in foreign affairs did not undermine liberty at home; on the other hand he favored domestic policies that would strengthen America's hand abroad. The importance of maintaining domestic political and economic liberty with a minimum of government controls was the touchstone of his political philosophy, and he regarded such a policy as the most essential principle of America's relationship with the rest of the world. "The United States," he insisted, "should set an example of living so well at home that all other nations will wonder, envy and decide to emulate us." [10]

The association which Taft made between domestic issues and foreign policy was, of course, not unique, and his perception of the connection grew out of his own experiences. The son of William Howard Taft, President and Chief Justice of the Supreme Court of the United States, Taft grew up in traditional Republican surroundings. He was educated for the most part in New England and spent some time in the Philippine Islands, where his father served as the first American civil governor from 1900 to 1904. During World War I, Taft was an assistant counsel to Herbert Hoover, then United States Food Administrator, and traveled to France with Hoover in 1918 as counsel for the American Relief Administration. Like his father, Taft also declared himself a supporter of the League of the Nations with the understanding that American membership in the League ought not commit the United States in advance to any specific course of action.[11]

Armed with a wide range of experiences and a famous name, Taft returned to Ohio after the war and resumed the law practice he had started in 1913. He quickly entered politics and successfully won election to the Ohio legislature in 1920. This event inaugurated his active career in the Republican party, which he considered the "party of American principles." [12] An expert in financial and tax matters and an astute politician, Taft soon earned a distinguished record in the legislature and gained ascendancy in the state Republican party. The depression and the Democratic sweep of 1932 momentarily retired him from public office, but in 1938 he won election to the United States Senate and thus reached national prominence.[13]

Both before and after his election to the Senate, Taft was a vigorous opponent of the New Deal. He firmly believed that Roosevelt's policies would lead to socialism and tyranny, and declared that such a result would be "absolutely contrary to the whole American theory on which this country was founded." [14] Taft attacked the National Industrial Recovery Act, the Agricultural Adjustment Act, and the Tennessee Valley Authority as dangerous to the survival of capitalism. A strong critic of corporate monopoly in business, he accused the New Deal of fostering public monopolies and of centralizing power in the executive branch of government through vast expenditures of funds and artificial price and wage controls. Such policies, he emphasized, would also limit personal freedoms and erode democratic liberties.[15]

Yet Taft also believed that society as a whole had a responsibility to remove poverty, guarantee economic opportunity to all its citizens, and prevent depressions. He warned that failure to fulfill these obligations could mean the "end of the whole system." He approved those sections of the National Recovery Act that regulated child labor and established minimum-wage scales, and he endorsed the principle of social security. Originally opposed to aid to education, Taft changed his mind during World War II and sponsored legislation to give educational assistance to the states, in proportion to need. He also supported voluntary medical insurance, and one student of the subject has written that Taft's leadership was most responsible for the passage of the Public Housing Act of 1949.[16]

Although he was roundly condemned at the time as anti-labor because of his authorship of the restrictive Taft-Hartley Act of 1947, Taft's record on labor matters was actually more complex. He had opposed wage controls in 1942 and cautioned against prohibiting the strike weapon. He worked closely with liberals in 1946, for example, to defeat President Truman's request for power to conscript striking railroad workers into the armed forces. He objected to the power such a proposal would have conveyed to the

President, the serious attack upon the Constitution which it represented, and the threat which it posed to labor unions.[17]

Taft was often ambiguous as to the exact point at which government activity intruded upon liberty, but it is clear that he protested much of the domestic program of Roosevelt and Truman because he believed the result would destroy "the substantial freedom of private enterprise" and would prevent the realization of "political and economic liberty" he valued so much. "As I see it," he claimed in his famous statement supporting Dwight Eisenhower for President in 1952, "there is and has been one fundamental issue between the Republican Party, and the New Deal or Fair Deal or Stevenson Deal. It is the issue of liberty against creeping socialism in every domestic field." Liberty, he reiterated, "is the foundation of our government, the reason for our growth, the basis of our happiness, and the hope of our future." [18]

As in the field of domestic issues, Robert Taft's response to foreign policy questions was based on the relationship of such matters to his notions about the preservation of economic and political liberty. His election to the Senate in 1938 coincided with America's drift to war, and he regarded those events with apprehension and opposition. Taft argued that the United States should remain neutral, that American territory and freedom were not threatened by the Axis powers, however repugnant their political system might be. Most of all he claimed that "war would destroy democratic government in the United States." [19]

Taft was confronted almost at once by the dilemma that actions by the Axis powers *and* the Roosevelt administration brought the country closer to the war he dreaded. He continued to oppose specific measures in Congress which he believed amounted to intervention, such as Lend-Lease and repeal of the cash-and-carry provisions of the Neutrality Act. At the same time, he supported legislation to increase defense appropriations (especially for air and sea power), to establish a reserve of strategic materials, and to repeal the Arms Embargo Act "on the condition that arms be exported on a cash and carry basis, and American ships be kept out of the war zone." He did not believe any of these actions violated American neutrality.[20] In place of Lend-Lease, which he considered an excessive delegation of power to the President besides

virtually involving the country in war, Taft proposed a direct loan
of $2 billion to Britain, Canada, and Greece. He felt this idea was
fundamentally sound, would avoid war, would prevent usurpation
of legislative power by the President, and yet would provide aid to
those allies whom he personally favored. Even so, Taft's alternative
suggestion (hardly an isolationist proposal) also would have been
a form of intervention into the conflict. It was defeated, and Lend-
Lease was enacted in March 1941.[21] Nine months later the United
States was at war. In the meantime, Taft had opposed various actions by the Roosevelt administration leading to greater involvement; but once the Japanese attacked Pearl Harbor and Germany
and Italy declared war on the United States, Taft supported America's entrance into the struggle.[22]

Senator Taft's devotion to liberty and peace remained central to
his ideas about foreign policy during the war years and the postwar
Truman administration. As such, his concern for domestic security
dictated his response to the Cold War, the central crisis of American foreign policy after 1945. One of Taft's major fears was that
American foreign policy might become associated with moral and
economic imperialism and that this might in turn lead again to
war—an ever more destructive threat, given the power of nuclear
weapons. He thought it a mistake, for instance, to think of America's participation in World War II as a crusade "to impose our
ideas of freedom on the rest of the world." To force "any special
brand of freedom and democracy on a people," he later recalled,
"whether they want it or not, by the brute force of war will be a
denial of those very democratic principles which we are striving to
advance." [23] Taft warned in 1944 that "it is important that the
President make it perfectly clear that when this war ends it really
does end; and that we give up any idea of ruling the world, or
telling other countries how to manage their own affairs." [24]

Taft preferred that the United States exercise its influence
through example. But he agreed to the need for some framework
to prevent future aggressions, and to some means of controlling
the devastating energy of the atomic bomb, once its existence became known in 1945. Thus he voted for the United Nations Charter in July 1945, but hedged his support and weakened his case by
insisting that the international organization remain loosely struc-

tured and not infringe on the freedom of the United States to act unilaterally in foreign affairs. Taft also wanted Congress to withhold authority from the President to delegate any power over war to America's representatives at the United Nations. Because he incorrectly concluded that Congress was yielding part of its power to *make* war to the United Nations, Taft voted in December 1945 against the appointment of delegates to the various agencies of the world body. The force of his argument, however, implied that Taft's greatest concern was concentration of more power in the hands of the President, which the appointment of delegates did in fact represent.

In any event, Taft certainly did not oppose United Nations initiatives to prevent war. At the time of the December vote he introduced an unsuccessful amendment urging the Security Council to "take immediate action [toward the] limitation of armaments and the prohibition of weapons such as the atomic bomb and poison gas." Taft added that the veto power, which he felt weakened the UN's power to halt conflicts, should not be applied in this matter. Senator Arthur H. Vandenberg, a key Republican colleague and later chairman of the Senate Foreign Relations Committee, opposed Taft's amendment and objected "to laying down any rules" about atomic energy. "I am not so sure," Vandenberg said, "that we in America are prepared to discuss, as yet, such a development." [25]

Beyond his genuine fears about war as the result of moral imperialism and the threat of larger and more dangerous weapons, Senator Taft was further disturbed by the possibilities of conflict brought on by American economic expansion overseas, especially under government auspices. He had earlier ridiculed the idea that the United States should enter World War II to protect its foreign trade, asserting that such trade was negligible, that the home market was the key to American prosperity, and that excessive exports and investments abroad would produce an unstable domestic economy, would lead to American political control over other countries and ill will against the United States, and would increase the chances for war.[26] Confronted after World War II by proposed measures to increase private and public investment overseas, including foreign aid, Taft criticized the efforts, fought back when he could, and reluctantly accepted some of the programs.[27]

Large economic investments abroad, Taft contended, would "soon likely . . . be resented and involve us in disputes that constitute a threat to peace. . . . It is easy," he wrote in 1949, "to slip into an attitude of imperialism and to entertain the idea that we know what is good for other people better than they know themselves. From there it is an easy step to the point where war becomes an instrument of public policy rather than the last resort to maintain our liberty." [28] Added to his fears of an unbalanced domestic economy and expanding government power still further, Taft's arguments were the most forceful of those mustered by conservative opponents of postwar American economic foreign policy.[29]

When, for example, Assistant Secretary of the Treasury Harry Dexter White testified in June 1945 before the Senate Committee on Banking and Currency in support of United States ratification of the International Monetary Fund and the International Bank for Reconstruction and Development, Taft, who served on the committee, clashed head on with the Truman administration. White argued that ratification of these instruments, designed to promote postwar reconstruction, private economic development, and increased world trade, would contribute to peace *and* American prosperity. Taft denied it and answered "baloney." Later in the hearings Taft asserted that these programs would not meet postwar economic emergencies and would probably create anti-American sentiments in other countries, particularly in underdeveloped nations. "I am a little troubled," he pondered, "by this theory of exporting capital so that we own billions of dollars of property all over the world—haven't we experienced that this has created hard feelings. We have been absentee landlords and they are always accusing us of exploiting people. In Cuba, the fact that we have invested large sums of money . . . is the principal argument of the tremendously growing communist movement there today." [30]

There was, however, a contradiction in Taft's position. Forecasting accurately that the Bank and Fund would be financed mostly by American capital and that this would create foreign resentment, Taft nevertheless argued that the United States would still have only minority representation and power on the boards of these agencies, without any effective controls over expenditures. Taft failed to acknowledge that overwhelming United States influence would dominate the Fund and Bank through the formal structure of organization and personnel and through the informal power of American political leadership and capital.[31] Moreover, while Taft strenuously opposed "government guarantee of private investment overseas," he was less apprehensive about American private concerns going into foreign countries on their own, and he frequently endorsed such efforts over government involvement. He minimized the risks of private investments and loans, especially the dangers of political and economic imperialism which he had exposed in the case of government activity of this sort. So while Taft was unenthusiastic about either private or public economic expansion abroad, when confronted with a choice he preferred private enterprise. He also emphasized that any government-sponsored programs should be under exclusive American control.[32]

Taft therefore approved the Export-Import Bank (though seeking to limit its appropriations) over other government institutions in this field. It was entirely American in character, its operations were under greater private control, and Taft thought its activities more nearly represented sound economic policies.[33] On the other hand he denounced President Truman's "Point Four" program for United States technical assistance to underdeveloped countries, even though it was an entirely American effort. Taft argued that the country could not afford such a commitment (the appropriation was $35 million, $10 million less than the President had requested), and that it was another way the United States "can go around the world and interfere with the affairs of other people and try to improve the standards of living of other people." The United States was not "so capable of giving out advice to other countries" about health, education, and so forth, particularly when "we have not done too well in our own country." [34] Beyond this, Taft declared, these efforts supplied a cause for Americans to go to war to defend the results of foreign aid, and this was precisely what Taft opposed most. Significantly, he also thought that this kind of government aid would allow the Russians and their allies to charge American "imperialism." [35] Taft did not think the risk of private assistance on either of these counts was nearly so great.

Senator Taft did not consider such questions in the context of the Cold War until after 1946. While many congressmen, for example, responded to administration appeals to approve the 1946 loan to Britain as an anti-Soviet measure, Taft's opposition to the bill was unwavering. The loan, he argued, was too expensive; it was a means to force multilateral trade agreements upon the British Empire. Taft later observed that the British paid a price for the loan when the United States "insisted upon sterling being made convertible into dollars. We have created the impression that we are desirous of forcing American control over the entire world and particularly imposing the Hull-Clayton theory of free trade. This has come about," he charged, "from an itching desire on the part of the Administration to tell the rest of the world how it shall run its affairs." [36] Taft proposed as an alternative to the loan an outright gift to Britain, provided the British spent the funds in the United States. He also wanted to cut the aid authorization from $3.75 billion to $1.25 billion, a figure he thought the United States could afford. When his amendments failed, Taft cast a minority vote against the final measure which appropriated the larger figure. [37]

Taft's refusal to be rushed into support of the British loan as part of an anti-Soviet program does not mean that he was not a vigorous opponent of communism. He saw communism as a world force, and he regarded Russia as a growing threat primarily because of its radical and contagious social system and its increasing power. Taft considered the contest between the Soviet Union and the United States to be world-wide and primarily ideological rather than military. He wished to avoid a military confrontation, and did not believe the Russians wanted war. Indeed, he rather feared that various *American* actions might well provoke the Russians to a military response and thus precipitate a world war.

As early as May 1945, just after V-E Day, Taft admonished that the United States "cannot and should not go to war with Russia," and he resisted specific measures he thought would contribute to war. [38] When, in late July 1946, an administration bill came to the Senate floor authorizing the President to send military advisers to nations requesting them, Taft opposed the bill and declared that he felt "very strongly that we should not send military missions all over the world to be teaching how to fight the American way." The dispatch of such missions, he argued, undercut the United Nations and constituted preparations for war. The bill was

pigeonholed by the Senate Foreign Relations Committee but rein-
troduced the next year. The Truman administration partly justified
its second request by invoking an alleged Soviet military threat to
the Western Hemisphere. Taft was unconvinced and said the proposal was tantamount to "interference and promoted war." He
doubted that Latin America was "really threatened by communist
attack," and said he had been impressed by a letter from a close
Republican political associate in Texas who wrote that to "arm,
equip, and train armies in these countries" would mean "promoting
bigger and better wars in Latin America." The Senator's arguments
carried weight in the new, Republican-controlled 80th Congress,
and again the measure was shelved.³⁹

Taft's objections to the Latin American military missions were
reflected in his early reactions to the Truman Doctrine of March
12, 1947. By then the Cold War had greatly intensified. In Greece
a civil war, in which communists played a prominent role, was underway against an authoritarian regime of the right supported by
Great Britain. On February 21 the British informed Washington
that they could no longer defend the area. Then, in a historic
effort to extend American power abroad, the Truman administration moved to supplant the British in Greece, to extend aid to
Turkey, and to fashion a broad program of action on behalf of an
international status quo.⁴⁰

After the President's address, Senator Taft reacted cautiously,
but critically, to the proposed Greek-Turkish aid request. He indicated approval for limited relief loans to Greece and Turkey but
raised important questions about the President's wish to send armaments and military missions to those nations. He remarked that this
might be an attempt to "secure a special domination over the affairs
of these countries," a judgment in which Taft proved to be substantially correct. Such action, he remarked, was "similar to Russia's
demands for domination in her sphere of influence. If we assume a
special position in Greece and Turkey," he warned, "we can hardly
. . . object to the Russians continuing their domination in Poland,
Yugoslavia, Rumania, and Bulgaria." ⁴¹

Taft then asked whether the policy might not provoke a war
with the Soviet Union. "I do not want war with Russia," he asserted. "Whether our intervention in Greece tends to make such a
war more probable or less probable depends upon many circum-

stances regarding which I am not yet fully advised and, therefore, I do not care to make a decision at the present time. I want to know," he inquired, "what our top military people think of the possibility that Russia will go to war if we carry out this program, just as we might be prompted to go to war if Russia tried to force a communist government on Cuba." [42]

When the aid bill came to the Senate for a vote a month later, however, Taft announced he would support the program in its entirety. He offered no amendments or alternatives, and explained that he was going to vote for Truman's proposals because he believed the national interest was at stake, because he hoped the measure would be a limited, temporary action, because he was satisfied war could be avoided, and because he believed President Truman had virtually committed the country to the program before Congress had even acted on it. Indeed, Truman had magnified the crisis in order to obtain quick congressional approval and had called in leaders of both parties in Congress only after the policy had been formulated. Even at that, Senator Vandenberg had to remind the President that he had omitted Taft from the first White House meeting on the crisis. [43]

On April 11, 1947, Taft revealed what he would do about the President's aid requests. "I intend to vote for the Greek and Turkish loans," he affirmed, "for the reason that the President's announcements have committed the United States to this policy in the eyes of the world, and to repudiate it now would destroy his prestige in the negotiations with the Russian Government, on the success of which ultimate peace depends." Taft did not confront the obvious point that the aid program might make those negotiations more difficult, but he did make it clear that he saw the program as temporary, quickly separated the economic loans from the military assistance (which constituted 75 per cent of the authorization), and indicated his approval of both as a contribution to peace. "In so far as the loans are for reconstruction and rehabilitation," he remarked, "we are only doing what we have done elsewhere. In so far as they help preserve order, I think they must be justified as a means of maintaining the status quo during the period while the basis for peace is being worked out." [44]

In giving his qualified support to the Truman Doctrine, Taft was not acting under any illusions about the nature of the Greek government which Washington was helping. "In Greece," he wrote later, "we moved in with overwhelming support for the Greek Government, even though it at first had strong reactionary tendencies." [45] Recognizing this fact, and believing that the Truman proposals should not constitute permanent involvement, Taft advised that "the United States withdraw whenever a Government representing the majority of the people requests us to do so, and whenever the United Nations finds that action taken or assistance furnished by it makes the continuance of our assistance undesirable." [46] This was the essence of an amendment to the bill which Senator Vandenberg sponsored in answer to the many criticisms that the administration's request to Congress bypassed the United Nations. With this understanding, Taft then voted to authorize the program.[47]

But Senator Taft's conception of the legislation was never realized. The Truman Doctrine was not a limited, temporary effort but became the basis of American foreign policy for a generation thereafter and set a precedent for American military intervention elsewhere in the world, including the present involvement in Vietnam. George Frost Kennan, then on the staff of the National War College and author of the 1947 containment policy against the Soviet Union, recognized "the sweeping nature" of the Doctrine at the time and objected to the language of Truman's message, though not its specific application to Greece.[48] Taft was also wrong in assuming that the United Nations would exercise any control over American actions in Greece and Turkey. The United States acted unilaterally in the crisis, and American dominance in the area was never challenged by the international organization. Finally, democratic order and stability in the region were never attained.[49]

It was anti-communism, however, which clearly and increasingly influenced Senator Taft's foreign policy. Such was the case with the Marshall Plan, which Taft eventually supported after criticizing it. The proposal for a large-scale economic recovery program for Western Europe came swiftly on the heels of the Greek-Turkish aid action. Suggested at first in a little-noticed speech by Under Secretary of State Dean Acheson on May 8, 1947, at Cleveland, Mississippi, the idea was dramatized by Secretary of State George C. Marshall in his celebrated commencement speech at Harvard University on June 5, 1947.[50]

During the remainder of 1947 the Western European governments and the Truman administration worked out the details of the plan. The administration proposal to Congress would have authorized $17 billion for the four and one-fourth years' program, $6.8 billion for the first fifteen months. The recipient countries would be obliged under these agreements to increase production, guarantee American private investments, restore monetary stability, reduce barriers to trade, procure certain American surplus commodities, especially agricultural goods, and make efficient use of resources including supplies furnished under the aid program. The United States could veto the expenditures of local currency obtained by European governments in selling to their own people the goods supplied by the United States. Funds would have to be placed in a special account in each country to be held or used only for purposes agreed upon by that country and the United States. This would give the United States considerable influence over financial policies and sometimes over political decisions in the recipient countries. This was certainly one reason why the Soviet Union refused to participate or to allow her Eastern European satellites to subscribe to the plan. At the same time, Washington considered the program as vital to American security as to the economic recovery of Western Europe. In submitting the specifics to Congress for approval, the administration forwarded a State Department memorandum which declared that "the principal reason for wanting an economically stable Europe is that it is a prerequisite to the maintenance of the civilization in which the American way of life is rooted." [51]

Senator Taft raised storm warnings about the Marshall Plan even before the bill reached the Senate floor on March 1, 1948. In an address to the World Affairs Council at Tacoma, Washington, on September 25, 1947, he stated his initial objections: "I have always felt that we should help the nations whose economy was destroyed by the war to get on their own feet. . . . Certainly we wish to help, but an international WPA would fail to solve the problem. . . . I do not believe that America can save the world with money." [52]

When the argument was raised that the Marshall Plan was necessary to prevent the spread of communism, Taft did not deny it. "But," he cautioned, "in the long run, the people of France, for

instance, are going to decide for themselves whether they go communist or not." Then Taft raised again the spectre of imperialism
as a danger in the program. "We are too much inclined to over-
estimate the effect of American dollars. A credit of American dollars encouraging unsound policies and giving the basis for the
charge that we are trying to dominate their country," he warned,
"may easily assist communism rather than prevent it." [53]

The Marshall Plan measure was debated in the Senate for thirteen days, from March 1 to 13. A new note of urgency and necessity was introduced by the communist *coup* in Czechoslovakia on
February 25. This event, combined with fears of a Communist
victory in the Italian elections and a general war hysteria, considerably strengthened the anti-Soviet arguments of Senator Vandenberg and others who sought to win support for the Marshall Plan.[54]

On March 12, Taft introduced an amendment to reduce the
authorization for the European Recovery Plan from $5.3 billion
for the first year as recommended by the Senate Foreign Relations
Committee, to $4 billion. As he presented his alternative, Taft de-
livered his major Senate speech on the entire bill. Arguing that he
was "in favor of giving aid," he stated that he was "strongly opposed to committing ourselves to any overall global plan to make
up some theoretical deficiency in exports" (as strongly suggested
by leading administration officials in congressional testimony) "and
to making any moral commitment beyond the amount authorized
for the first year."

Then, in spite of his own earlier warnings, Taft stated the primary reason for supporting the program. "I am in favor of extending further aid to the countries of Western Europe beyond the
demands of charity," he announced, "only because of the effect our
aid may have in the battle against communism." The nature of the
struggle against communism, Taft insisted, was one of "ideologies,
a battle of the philosophy of justice and equality against the
philosophy of a totalitarian state." Taft denied that the communist
threat was military, and in this denial he was perceptive. "This program," he protested, "is not aimed at opposing any communistic
military attack." And then he offered a few ideas on his conception
of the political state of Europe. "I know of no indication," he said,
"of Russian intention to undertake military aggression beyond the

sphere of influence which was originally assigned to them. The situation in Czechoslovakia was indeed a tragic one, but Russian influence has predominated there since the end of the war." [55]

Taft repeated these observations in comments made to the press after the Senate debate, the defeat of his amendment (by a vote of 56 to 31), and the favorable vote on the Marshall Plan. He attacked the hysterical American military response to the communist *coup* in Czechoslovakia. Disagreeing with former Secretary of State James F. Byrnes, who viewed developments in Europe as a portent of Russian military aggression, Taft described the events in Czechoslovakia as a Russian "consolidation step" and said, "There's no sense in our having voted the Marshall Plan if there is going to be a war. All this was based on the assumption of peace." The real contest with Russia, he asserted, was an ideological one. "That's why I supported the Marshall Plan." George F. Kennan has since written that "the consolidation of communist power in Czechoslovakia" (and the Berlin blockade crisis) "were defensive reactions on the Soviet side to the initial success of the Marshall Plan initiative," and that Soviet planning did not contemplate military action against Western Europe and the United States. In his own assessment of the situation at the time, Taft thus displayed an acute sense of reality and a refusal to panic. Indeed, war, possibly provoked by American actions, would have serious consequences for Taft's conception of the American way of life.[56] Such a posture set the stage for the Senator's greatest disagreement with the Truman administration's foreign policy—the North Atlantic Treaty Organization pact (NATO) of 1949 and the American rearmament program which followed.

Several events marked the emergence of NATO, including the Brussels Pact of March 1948 (a fifty-year alliance between Britain, France, the Netherlands, Belgium, and Luxembourg, which was strongly backed by the United States). The Czech *coup* and the Berlin blockade no doubt also hastened the creation of NATO, as did extreme fears and official characterization of the Soviet Union as a militarily aggressive nation. On the same date the Brussels Treaty was signed, March 17, President Truman delivered to Congress an emotionally laden message in which he not only called for speedy passage of the Marshall Plan by the House of Representatives but virtually proclaimed the need for a national rearmament policy to match the political and economic aspects of America's Cold War program. The President called for quick enactment of the selective service military draft and universal military training. And he declared, "The United States must remain strong enough to support those countries of Europe which are threatened with communist control and police-state rule." [57]

The administration clearly believed it was necessary to promote a program of military alliances and armaments buildup in order to deter the Soviet Union—despite lack of evidence of a Soviet military threat. Groundwork for congressional approval of an American role in a European military alliance was established by Senator Vandenberg in June 1948. He worked out the essentials of a Senate resolution with Under Secretary of State Robert A. Lovett, a close personal friend, in a series of private meetings in late March and April. [58]

The resolution, which passed the Senate on June 11, 1948, by a 64 to 4 vote, affirmed that the United States ought to seek "regional collective arrangements for self defense." Ironically, Taft was inexplicably absent from the single day of debate and vote on the resolution. Senator Claude Pepper, a strong liberal critic of the Truman foreign policy, anticipated future Taft objections to NATO, however, when he offered an amendment to delete sections of the statement concerning collective security arrangements on the grounds they had been drafted to prepare the nation for a military alliance with Western Europe. Vandenberg denied this, and Pepper's amendment lost on a vote of 61 to 6. [59]

But Pepper was correct in his charge. Top-secret negotiations with the Brussels pact nations and Canada began within a week of Senate passage of the Vandenberg resolution, and on April 4, 1949, the North Atlantic Treaty was signed in Washington. [60] Sixteen days of Senate hearings on the treaty followed, in which the Truman administration pursued the none too successful political tactic of separating the treaty from the arms aid measure. The latter was embodied in the Mutual Defense Assistance Bill of 1949, but the administration realized that military assistance was much more controversial in an economy-minded Congress and chose to defer that aspect of the program. Truman and Secretary of State Acheson simply denied that the treaty contained any obligation by the United States to extend military assistance to any of the signatories. But Articles 3 and 5 of the treaty implied the opposite. Senators Kenneth Wherry (Republican of Nebraska), Forrest C. Donnell (Republican of Missouri), and Taft quoted a May 1949 State Department publication which showed quite conclusively that military aid was a "vital corollary" of the North Atlantic Treaty.[61]

This issue formed the outlines of the Senate debate on the treaty which began on July 5 and lasted until July 21. On July 11 Taft made his most important speech on NATO. He began by insisting that "the pact carries with it an obligation to assist in arming, at our expense, the nations of Western Europe. . . . I believe it will promote war in the world rather than peace. . . . I would vote for the pact if a reservation were adopted denying any legal or moral obligation to provide arms."

To arguments that the pact was a defense mechanism, Taft replied: "Every good defense includes elements of offense. We cannot have an adequate armament for defense which cannot be converted overnight into a weapon of offense. We talked of defense for years before entering World War II, while our preparations were really for offense. The result is, no matter how defensive an alliance may be, if it carries the obligation to arm it means the building up of competitive offensive armaments. This treaty, therefore, means inevitably an armament race, and armament races in the past led to wars." Taft drew a distinction between arms to Greece and Turkey in 1947 (and to Nationalist China in 1948) and "building up a tremendous armament for eleven different nations for a long-term commitment and with no immediate specific crisis to face."

He denied again that Russia was bent on military aggression against the West, and charged policy-makers with inflating the danger of such a threat. On the contrary, he maintained, the treaty would lessen the chances for peace. The Soviet Union might be inclined to view the entire scheme as provocative. "We have chosen to give economic assistance," he explained in a reference to the Marshall Plan. "That assistance is given on the theory that the Russians do not contemplate aggressive war, but intend to fight their battle by propaganda and a production of chaotic economic conditions. I believe we will have to choose whether we give economic assistance or arms. I believe the undertaking of both types of assistance is beyond the economic capacity of the United States. The first, I believe, has contributed and will contribute to peace. The second, I think, will make war more likely. We are undertaking to arm half the world against the other half. We are inevitably starting an armament race. The more the pact signatories arm, the more the Russians are going to arm." [62]

Furthermore, Taft pointed out, the arms might be used by European countries in dealing with colonial possessions outside the scope of the pact. In a remarkable forecast of American assistance in this way to French military efforts in Indo-China, Taft declared: "Surely anyone can see that all the armed forces possessed by any country are in one pool and that the bigger that pool is, the more easily they can find arms to undertake action which may be considered aggression in the colonies." [63]

It was obvious, too, that Taft's concern for the economic wellbeing of the United States was an element in his opposition to the kinds of military obligations he envisioned as implicit in the Atlantic Pact. He argued that "our economic health is essential to the battle against communism and . . . arms should be sent only to a country really threatened by Russian military aggression." If nations invested heavily in arms they would decrease their standard of living. Countries "must choose between guns and butter," he said.[64]

Taft proposed as an alternative a unilateral declaration by the United States stating that *if* Russia attacked the countries of Western Europe, America would come to their assistance. To this end he and Senator Ralph Flanders (Republican of Vermont) offered a resolution which would have "extended the Monroe Doctrine to Western Europe." The chairman of the Senate Foreign Relations Committee, Democrat Tom Connally of Texas, called Taft's idea illogical because it "would leave the United States solely responsible for the defense of Western Europe without allies or bases," but Connally's criticism did not answer any of Taft's fundamental objections to NATO.[65] The Taft-Flanders proposal was buried in committee, and Senator Kenneth Wherry's amendment prohibiting American military assistance to NATO members was defeated on the floor of the Senate. Taft supported the Wherry amendment, then voted against the final treaty ratification.[66] Only two days after the ratification vote came the administration request for arms. The bill proposed to authorize $1.45 billion to provide military assistance to "nations which have joined with the United States in collective defense . . . and other nations whose increased ability to defend themselves against aggression is important to the national interest of the United States." [67]

Taft castigated this request. "The program presented by the President and the bill to carry it out," he declared, "demands that Congress substantially abdicate all functions relating to foreign policy, and authorize the State and Defense Departments to make alliances throughout the world and involve us in any and all wars, civil or internal, going on anywhere in the world. Arms aid may be given to any nation or any government within a nation selected in the arbitrary discretion of the President, whether it be in Europe, Asia, Africa, or America." [68]

Clearly, Taft was objecting not merely to the arms assistance feature of the bill per se, but also to the wide authority which the measure conveyed upon the Executive. Seeking to weaken the bill in whatever way he could, while recognizing it would pass, Taft voted in favor of several efforts to cut the amounts authorized by the proposed act. All of these amendments failed, and Taft offered none of his own. But he voted against the final measure, which passed the Senate 55 to 24 on September 22.

The next day President Truman disclosed that America's four-year security under the atomic bomb had ended with the detonation of a nuclear device by the Soviets.[69] This event, coupled with the collapse of China to the Communists in October 1949, sparked a full-scale, intensive, and secret review of American foreign policy, which by the early spring of 1950 resulted in the formulation of a document known as NSC-68 (National Security Council Paper No. 68). Among other things, this position paper sought to redesign American tactics in order better to fight the Cold War. The successful Soviet atomic explosion called into question certain aspects of the Kennan containment policy, in particular its assumption of a continued American nuclear monopoly. The 1950 study now urged "the United States to take the lead in a rapid and substantial build-up in the defensive power of the West, beginning 'at the center' and radiating outward. This means virtual abandonment by the United States of trying to distinguish between national and global security. It also means the end of subordinating security needs to the traditional budgetary restrictions; of asking, 'How much security can we afford?' In other words, security must henceforth become the dominant element in the national budget, and other elements must be accommodated to it." [70]

The Korean War turned what was a theoretical statement of planning into accelerated reality as America's military budget for fiscal year 1951 soared from $13 billion to $48.2 billion. (Truman had originally requested $13.5 billion for fiscal year 1951.) Paul Hammond has astutely written that "undoubtedly, much of what was done in the Korean military build-up would have been done anyway. Yet the existence of NSC-68 at the outset of the war contributed a particular quality to that build-up. From its beginning, and through its most frantic phases, the Korean War remained only a part of the larger picture of the national strategy. For most people who knew anything about it, NSC-68 represented that larger picture." [71]

Part of the scenario included the dispatch of American troops to Europe, a plan announced by President Truman in late 1950. There were already occupation troops in Germany, but Truman's proposal constituted a larger American commitment to NATO, with four additional divisions of men to be sent as an initial step. The President's plan stimulated a great debate in which prominent public figures such as General Dwight D. Eisenhower (the man Truman wished to designate as NATO commander), Herbert Hoover, and Taft participated.

Taft began his attack on Truman's decision first in the Senate on January 5, 1951. He insisted the action contemplated by the President was beyond his authority and the terms of the Atlantic Pact. "The Atlantic Pact may have committed us to send arms to the other members of the pact, but no one ever maintained that it committed us to send many American troops to Europe," he declared. Taft believed that to allow the President to transfer armed forces to Europe would grant him the sole power to determine war and peace and the economic prosperity of the country. Taft produced figures designed to show that an air and naval system of defense would at once give the nation the protective power it required and also enable it to retain its economic solvency.[72]

Taft had long favored primary reliance upon air and sea power to defend the United States. He believed the next war would be fought predominantly in the air and cited America's control of the skies over Germany toward the end of World War II as evidence to support his contention. He also thought that in order to be consistent in guaranteeing the defense of the nation while preserving its fundamental domestic liberties, military projects had to be "reasonable and selective in order to meet the Russian threat." He believed that air and sea power would meet that test and also serve other purposes of foreign policy. "A superiority in air and sea forces throughout the world can achieve other purposes than mere defense," he wrote later. "It can protect all island countries, furnish effective assistance to all those nations which desire to maintain their freedom on the continent. It can achieve a balance of power under which more peaceful relations throughout the world can constantly be developed." [73]

The argument for air power was also linked to Taft's belief that as a defensive measure it would be less likely to provoke war than massed armies. "In the field of military operations our strongest position is in the air and on the sea, and we should not be a power on the land. We should not be a military aggressor," he said, "or give the impression of military aggression or incite a war which might otherwise never occur." Beyond this, Taft argued, the disposition of American land armies to Europe would "wreck the internal economy of this country and commit us to obligations we are utterly unable to perform. The course which we are pursuing will make war more likely. I think," he reflected in somber tones, "that the Atlantic Pact was a tremendous mistake. In my opinion, it could at least be interpreted as an aggressive move." [74]

Taft sought to make clear his position during joint Senate committee hearings on the dispatch of troops in February 1951. Reiterating his earlier arguments, the Senator also disputed the deterrent value of an army buildup in Europe. He thought the Russians might consider such a military measure a "very definite incitement . . . to begin a war before the army reached that point, assuming that they have the intention of making a military attack on Western Europe." Taft considered the Russian military threat "overestimated," and then went on to warn against American overcommitment abroad. He believed it might very well turn the country into a garrison state and destroy "all the freedoms which have made America what it is today." [75]

These ideas explain Taft's reluctance to allow the President to permit the United States to participate in an overseas armed force. He denied that he opposed an international army in principle, "though I am doubtful about the wisdom of it"; rather, he was against sending troops to any area without congressional approval or when such action might provoke war. Taft stipulated that in any land army in Europe the European nations themselves should provide the bulk of the military forces needed. He again noted American superiority on air power and suggested it would be decisive in deterring Soviet attack. Finally, he wanted three basic restrictions on American participation in any European army: (1) no American troops should be sent to Europe until other participating countries agreed to put up sufficient troops for the endeavor; (2) the Joint Chiefs of Staff should "certify the number of armed forces necessary to do that"; and (3) any presidential commitment of American troops to Europe should state the character and number of men to be assigned and "be subject to the approval of Congress." [76] These reservations suggest that a very substantial part of Taft's argument concerning the dispatch of American troops to Europe stemmed from his traditional fear of executive usurpation of congressional authority. Indeed, the fact that he achieved apparent satisfaction on this point explains more than anything else his ultimate acceptance of the President's action.[77]

Taft's testimony before the congressional committee, however, revealed some contradictory points of view. In the first place, his indication that he would support the program if it were limited, temporary, and under congressional control did not answer his own criticism that the dispatch of American troops to Europe might itself provoke the Soviet Union to hostilities. Then too, Taft never satisfactorily answered the obvious objection to his preference for air and naval superiority: Was this not as potentially provocative to the Soviets as a land force in Western Europe? Taft said no, but never made clear why.[78] Finally, he did not explain why, if he doubted there was a danger of a Russian invasion of Western Europe, he was willing to see a multi-national land army of European nations established in the first place, especially when he understood that it alone could not prevent Soviet attack.

The resolution favoring the assignment of American ground forces to Europe came to a vote on April 4, 1951, when the Senate endorsed President Truman's immediate program, 69 to 21, confirming the dispatch of four divisions and approving the President's action in designating General Eisenhower as NATO commander. But an important amendment was attached to the resolution by Senator John McClellan. Approved by a close vote, 49 to 43, the amendment stated that it was "the sense of the Senate that no ground forces beyond the four divisions planned should be sent to Europe without Congressional approval." This seemed to satisfy Taft, for he supported the final vote in favor of the resolution.[79]

If Senator Taft opposed a larger American military commitment in Europe and feared war as a result, he was much more prepared to risk a conflict in Asia. He took this position because he considered Asia an area vital to the security of the United States as a consequence of the region's economic resources and strategic importance. Moreover, he thought communism in the Far East could exploit unstable conditions which were ripe for revolution. Japan's defeat and the collapse of Chiang Kai-shek's regime in China had destroyed the balance of power which had previously existed, Taft thought, and had strengthened the Soviet Union in the area. He held the Roosevelt and Truman administrations largely responsible for the growth of communism in Asia—the result of decisions made at the conferences of Allied leaders during World War II, especially the Yalta and Potsdam agreements. He charged the American leaders had made concessions which built up Soviet power and influence in the Far East and undermined Chiang Kai-shek's government in favor of the Russians and the Chinese Communists.[80]

In this judgment Taft grossly oversimplified the truth and ignored certain key issues, including the fundamental fact that neither the Soviet Union nor the United States had very much to do with Chiang's defeat. By the end of the war Chiang's corrupt government had simply ceased to command the support of the Chinese people. Taft, however, berated the Truman administration for not coming to Chiang's assistance in a more vigorous way, despite American assistance of over two billion dollars in all types of aid to China from V-J Day to the end of 1948, a figure which far exceeded any aid ever given the Chinese Communists by the Soviet Union during the civil war.[81]

After the final collapse of the mainland to the Communists in 1949, Taft said the United States should protect Formosa from the Chinese Communists, even if it meant dispatching the Navy there, an action President Truman eventually took after the Korean War began in June 1950. Taft attacked Truman's statement of January 5, 1950, that the United States would not "provide military aid or advice to Chinese forces on Formosa," but stopped short of advocating the intervention of American ground forces in the area.[82] Indeed, Taft made it clear that he thought the introduction of American troops was a dangerous action which might unduly incite the Russians to war, just as he believed such action would in Europe. Moreover, though he wished to deny Formosa to the Communists, he did not envision it as a rival Chinese state. Rather, he wanted to see an independent republic of Formosa and thought the Chinese Nationalists should accept this solution.[83]

With the outbreak of the Korean War, Taft became more militant in his views about Asia. He supported the principle of American intervention in Korea but criticized the Truman administration for its quick action in sending troops there without consulting Congress or the United Nations. This, he asserted, "was a usurpation of authority in the making of war"—a criticism Truman ignored. In the same speech, delivered three days after hostilities began, Taft accused the administration, especially Secretary of State Acheson (whose resignation he demanded), of appeasement policies which led to the war, and for not making it clear in advance that an attack on Korea would mean retaliation by the United States.[84]

Taft particularly had in mind Acheson's speech of January 12, 1950, to the National Press Club in Washington, in which the Secretary of State had omitted Korea from American military defensive strategy in the Pacific. This omission, Taft claimed, encouraged the North Korean attack on South Korea. But in fact the strategic decision had been made by the Joint Chiefs of Staff, with General Douglas MacArthur's approval, as early as 1947, and American troops were withdrawn from Korea in 1949 according to plan. As Acheson wrote later and scholars have noted, Republican members of the House of Representatives had opposed and defeated a proposed administration extension of economic aid to Korea early in 1950.[85]

As American military efforts in Korea became stalemated, Senator Taft's attacks upon administration strategy intensified and his own proposals for victory turned bolder. The extent to which Taft was willing to risk all-out war in Asia in order to defeat communism was clearest in his approval of American air attacks on Manchuria and South China and the use of Chinese Nationalist troops to raid the mainland. These recommendations, also advanced by General MacArthur, came in the wake of Chinese Communist entry into the Korean War in late November 1950. Taft was fully aware that bombing Manchuria and China "might bring Russia into the war. But it's a risk to take if we're to bring the war to a close in Korea." In any event, he insisted, the United States had already made commitments in Europe—such as the Atlantic Pact and the rearming of Germany—"which the Russians may regard as threatening security. I cannot see that any bombing of China without invasion [by the United States] can be regarded in any way by Russia as an aggressive move against Russia itself, or a reason for war." Taft joined these remarks to a scathing denunciation of President Truman's dismissal, in April 1951, of General MacArthur as commander of American troops in the Far East and of United Nations forces in Korea. Truman defended his removal of MacArthur and charged that the bombing proposals by the general and the senator would risk a third world war.[86]

To be sure, Taft's rancorous attacks on Truman and the Democrats were in part politically inspired, especially in view of the approaching presidential election of 1952.[87] But most of Taft's views about Asia and American foreign policy as a whole continued into the Eisenhower administration and stemmed from long-held ideas. In the last year of his life he reiterated his position that there should be no American troops involved in a land war in Europe or Asia, that American military and economic commitments abroad ought to be limited, and "that the consideration which ought to determine almost every decision of policy today is the necessity of preserving, maintaining, and increasing the liberty of the people of our country as fundamental to every other progressive purpose." [88]

Taft also repeated his conviction that America have a free hand in the conduct of foreign relations if it was to realize a successful foreign policy. In his last, famous speech to the National Conference of Christians and Jews, delivered for the ailing senator by his son Robert Taft, Jr., he extended the principle to the Korean War and the United Nations. Because of the veto power, Taft had always been skeptical of the UN's effectiveness, especially in combatting aggression. Now, he argued, the world organization was unable to pursue the Korean conflict to a satisfactory conclusion. The United States, he said, should "forget the United Nations as far as the Korean War is concerned" and should "reserve to [itself] a completely free hand. No one," he declared, "should be shocked at my suggestion about the United Nations in Korea, because in Europe we have practically abandoned it entirely." He recalled American commitments to Greece and Turkey in 1947 and the North Atlantic Treaty of 1949 as examples of what he meant. No matter how one disagreed with Taft's views about current policy, he was correct in pointing out that the United States had bypassed the United Nations before.[89]

Of course, Taft was on difficult grounds, since he did not wish to see the "free hand" in foreign policy abused by the executive branch of government or used for policies of which he disapproved. Nor did he believe the conflict against communism should be primarily military in nature. The communist threat, he said again and again, was mainly ideological and must be countered by a positive program of American ideological warfare. He elaborated upon the details of such a program in his book, *A Foreign Policy For Americans*, published in 1951.

As he believed so firmly in the righteousness of the principles underlying American society, Taft's first recommendation was that Americans set an example of conduct at home that would be attractive to peoples abroad. Second, he advocated the extensive use of propaganda overseas to popularize Americanism. The purpose of such a campaign, as he had said earlier, was "to arouse the same religious fervor for the American doctrine of liberty and free government as the communists have for communism." [90] Then, in a departure for him, Taft endorsed a program of subversion within the communist camp through the infiltrating of secret agents. He acknowledged that such activity was "not in accordance with American tradition and is no part of a permanent foreign policy." Though he emphasized the temporary nature of this tactic and justified it as a response to Soviet methods of a similar character, Taft overlooked the role subversion might play in increasing tensions and the chances for war, and did not succeed in resolving the doubts he himself raised concerning the morality of such an effort.[91]

Finally, Taft urged support for "those forces in friendly countries or neutral countries which believe in liberty and are prepared to battle against communism"—though he failed to make clear just what he meant by "support." "In short," he concluded, "a war against communism must finally be won in the minds of men. The hope for ultimate peace lies far more in the full exploitation of the methods I have suggested than in a third world war, which may destroy civilization itself." [92]

Taft died believing that "communism [could] be defeated by an affirmative philosophy of individual liberty," a philosophy he was sure had been the strength of the nation since its earliest days.[93] It was precisely that faith which now entered its most profound era of crisis at home and abroad, and Taft seemed in many ways to represent the great anxiety that had come to engulf America after 1945. He voiced the apprehensive attitudes, the hopes and fears, and the perplexities of many Americans. But this was not the reaction of an isolationist. It was the doubt of one who wished to preserve the essential tenets of a threatened tradition. Taft had been negative more often than positive in his views in an effort to block those measures which he felt would destroy the very system he wanted to maintain.

In spite of inconsistencies and contradictions, Taft did subscribe to a set of ideas about foreign policy, and his critique of the Truman foreign policy was often quite perceptive. The most outstanding features of this critique were his warnings about the overcommitment of American military and economic power abroad; his understanding of the imperialist implications of American economic investment in the underdeveloped world; his resistance to the expansion of executive power in foreign relations; his skepticism of an aggressive Soviet military threat after World War II; his refusal to abandon criticism of foreign policy in the name of officially proclaimed national interest when he thought the policy injured the national interest as he understood it; and, above all else, his genuine concern about the dangers and effects of war. Taft's dissent from the foreign policies of the Truman period represented the viewpoint of a conservative nationalist at odds with the struggling attempts of liberal American policy-makers to fashion a program in the postwar years. Many who had shared Taft's general outlook became more frustrated, doctrinaire, and extreme in their views in the decade that followed the senator's death in 1953.[94] Their movement paralleled the deepening crises and failures of American foreign policy, produced in good measure by some of the very policies of which Robert A. Taft had been so critical.

Notes

1. Murray N. Rothbard, "The Transformation of the American Right," *Continuum,* II (Summer 1964), 221.

2. For extensive evaluations of Taft's foreign policy, see William S. White, *The Taft Story* (New York, 1954); Russell Kirk and James McClellan, *The Political Principles of Robert A. Taft* (New York, 1967); John P. Armstrong, "The Enigma of Senator Taft and American Foreign Policy," *Review of Politics,* XVII (April 1955), 206–231; Vernon Van Dyke and Edward L. Davis, "Senator Taft and American Security," *Journal of Politics,* XIV (May 1952), 177–202; H. Reed West, "Senator Taft's Foreign Policy," *Atlantic,* CLXXXIX (June 1952), 50–52; John A. Sylvester, "Robert A. Taft and World Strategy, 1951" (unpublished M.A. thesis, University of Wisconsin, 1958); Henry W. Berger, "Senator Robert A. Taft and American Foreign Policy" (unpublished M.S. thesis, University of Wisconsin, 1961). Taft's most comprehensive statement on foreign policy was a book which served in part as a platform statement during his bid for the Republican presidential nomination in 1952: *A Foreign Policy For Americans* (New York, 1951).

3. The association of Taft with isolationism or neo-isolationism during his lifetime was most frequently made by liberal journalists. See, for example, the numerous references in the *Nation* by Willard Shelton, CLXXII (1951), and Carroll Kirkpatrick, "Taft: 20 Degrees Cooler Inside," *New Republic,* CXV (December 23, 1946), 868–871. Examples of these de-

scriptions of Taft in later, more scholarly works include the following: Selig Adler, *The Isolationist Impulse* (New York, 1957), pp. 401–405; Cecil Crabb, Jr., *Bipartisan Foreign Policy: Myth or Reality* (Evanston, Ill., 1957), p. 94; Norman Graebner, *The New Isolationism* (New York, 1956), pp. 24–31; Lawrence S. Kaplan, *Recent American Foreign Policy: Conflicting Interpretations* (Homewood, Ill., 1968), pp. 73, 82, 147–148; Hugh Ross, *The Cold War: Containment and Its Critics* (Chicago, 1963), pp. 15–16; Thomas A. Bailey, *A Diplomatic History of the American People* (New York, 1969), pp. 772, 810, 818, 824–825. More balanced references to Taft are the following: Richard W. Leopold, *The Growth of American Foreign Policy* (New York, 1962), p. 551; Herbert Agar, *The Price of Power: America Since 1945* (Chicago, 1957), p. 67; Eric Goldman, *The Crucial Decade: America, 1945–1955* (New York, 1956), pp. 54–56; Foster Rhea Dulles, *America's Rise to World Power, 1898–1954* (New York, 1955), pp. 212, 244, 263; Walter LaFeber, *America, Russia, and the Cold War* (New York, 1967), pp. 129–131.

4. For Schlesinger, the Ohio Republican was "a man in transition, an Old Isolationist trying hard to come to terms with the modern world." Arthur Schlesinger, Jr., "The New Isolationism," *Atlantic*, CLXXXIX (May 1952), 34. Contrast Schlesinger's characterization of Taft in this article, written at the height of the 1952 Republican presidential nominating contest, in which Taft was then the leading contender, with Schlesinger's earlier views of Taft in *Collier's*, CXIX (February 22, 1947), 12–40. Others who accepted Schlesinger's 1952 analysis of Taft were Graebner, *New Isolationism* and Adler, *Isolationist Impulse*.

5. Armstrong, "Enigma of Senator Taft," p. 231. Armstrong's article was based on his unpublished Ph.D. dissertation, "Senator Taft and American Foreign Policy: The Period of Opposition" (University of Chicago, 1953).

6. And this, it might be added, was the real meaning of the oft-quoted statement attributed to Taft: "I am charged with moving in on foreign policy; the truth is that foreign policy has moved in on me." See, for instance, Goldman, *Crucial Decade*, p. 28.

7. Taft, *Foreign Policy*, pp. 103–113.

8. Taft, "The American Way of Life," in T. V. Smith and Robert A. Taft, *Foundations of Democracy: A Series of Debates* (New York, 1939), p. 12; Taft, "The Case Against President Truman," *Saturday Evening Post*, CCXXI (September 25, 1948), 18–19; "Speech to the American Medical Association at Los Angeles, California, December 5, 1951," quoted in Caroline Harnsberger, *A Man of Courage: Robert A. Taft* (Chicago, 1952), p. 281; "The Republican Party," *Fortune*, XXXIX (April 1949), 110.

9. Taft, *Foreign Policy*, p. 11.

10. Taft quoted in Harnsberger, *Man of Courage*, p. 68; "Speech to World Affairs Council at Tacoma, Washington, September 25, 1947," in *New York Times*, September 26, 1947; Taft, *Foreign Policy*, pp. 17–20.

11. Berger, "Senator Robert A. Taft," pp. 3–6; Henry F. Pringle, *The Life and Times of William H. Taft* (New York, 1939, 2 vols.), II, 906, 941. A useful description of the American Relief Administration, in which Taft is mentioned but his role is not discussed, is Suda L. Bane and Ralph H. Lutz, *Organization of American Relief in Europe, 1918–1919* (Stanford, 1943), *passim*.

12. Taft, "The Republican Party," p. 118.

13. White, *Taft Story*, pp. 3–40; Kirk and McClellan, *Political Principles*, pp. 7–22. Even while out of office, Taft did not disappear from GOP politics but was quite active. He was the "favorite son" candidate of his party to the 1936 Republican national convention.

14. Taft, "The New Deal: Recovery, Reform, and Revolution," speech delivered before the Warren, Ohio, Chamber of Commerce, April 1935, in Robert A. Taft Papers, Library of Congress, quoted in *ibid.*, p. 13. At the moment, the Taft Papers are not generally open for inspection by researchers. Kirk and McClellan obtained special permission; now James Patterson of Indiana University has exclusive access to the papers for seven years during which time he is preparing a full-length biography of Taft.

15. Taft, "Speech at Gettysburg National Cemetery, May 30, 1945," *Vital Speeches*, XI (July 1, 1945), 554–557, "Police State Methods Are Wrong," *ibid.*, XIV (December 1, 1947), 104–107.

16. Richard O. Davies, " 'Mr. Republican' Turns 'Socialist': Robert A. Taft and Public Housing," *Ohio History*, LXXIII (Summer 1964), 135–143; Oscar T. Barck, Jr., *History of the United States Since 1945* (New York, 1965), p. 92; Joseph and Stewart Alsop, "Taft and Vandenberg," *Life*, XXI (October 7, 1946), 104; Schlesinger, "His Eyes Have Seen the Glory," *Collier's*, CXIX (February 22, 1947), 36.

17. Taft in *Congressional Record*, 80th Cong., 1st sess., XCIII (May 9, 1947), 4885–4886; Senate, Committee on Labor and Public Welfare, *Taft-Hartley Revisions* (Hearings), 83rd Cong., 1st sess., April 7, 1953, pp. 716–717.

18. Taft, "What Is Liberalism?," *New York Times Magazine*, April 18, 1948, p. 10; *Statement in Support of the Candidacy of General Dwight D. Eisenhower: The Issues of the Campaign* (Washington, D.C., 1952), p. 1.

19. Taft, "Let Us Stay Out of War," *Vital Speeches*, V (February 1, 1939), 254–256; "Let's Mind Our Own Business," *Current History*, L (June 1939), 32–33; "Should Congress Amend the Present Neutrality Law?," *Congressional Digest*, XVIII (October 1939), 244–246. The best volumes on American neutrality in the 1930's and which deal extensively with the noninterventionists in Congress, of whom Taft was a conservative member, are Robert A. Divine, *The Illusion of Neutrality* (Chicago, 1962) and Manfred Jonas, *Isolationism in America, 1935–1941* (Ithaca, N.Y., 1966).

20. Armstrong, "Enigma of Senator Taft," p. 210; Jonas, *Isolationism*, p. 200; Divine, *Illusion*, pp. 310, 317; Taft to AFL convention, in *American Federationist*, XLVI (November 1939), 1197–1202; Taft to George F. Stanley, September 8, 1944, in Taft, *Foreign Policy*, p. 125, Appendix.

21. *Congressional Record*, 77th Cong., 1st sess., LXXXVII (January 29, 1941), A297–A298; (March 8, 1941), 2080–2082.

22. Taft, "Shall the United States Enter the European War?," in *New York Times*, May 18, 1941. Among the measures Taft opposed after passage of Lend-Lease were the dispatch of troops to Iceland in July 1941 and the repeal of the neutrality act in November 1941. Taft, *Foreign Policy*, pp. 30–31, 126.

23. *Congressional Record*, 78th Cong., 1st sess., LXXXIX (March 30, 1943), A1511; Taft, *Foreign Policy*, p. 16.

24. Taft, "A Post-War Peace Organization of Nations," *Vital Speeches,*
X (June 1, 1944), 495.
25. *Congressional Record,* 79th Cong., 1st sess., XCI (December· 4,
1945), 11401–11409.
26. Taft, "Let's Mind Our Own Business," pp. 32–33. Little attention has
been given to this aspect of Taft's career despite the fact that he served on
the Senate committees on appropriations (later finance) and banking and
currency. For Taft's views before 1945, see, for example, Senate, Committee
on Banking and Currency, *To Continue Operations of the Commodity
Credit Corporation, the Export-Import Bank, and the Reconstruction Finance Corporation* (Hearings), 76th Cong., 1st sess., February 14–21, 1939,
esp. pp. 12–13, 29–44; Senate, Committee on Banking and Currency, *Increasing the Lending Authority of the Export-Import Bank of Washington,
D.C.* (Hearings), 76th Cong., 3rd sess., July 30, 1940, esp. pp. 12–13;
Congressional Record, 76th Cong., 3rd sess., LXXXVI (September 10,
1940), 11833–11848.
27. Total American investment overseas, public and private, climbed
from $16.8 billion in 1945 to $39.5 billion in 1953, the year of Taft's death.
United States military and economic aid abroad from 1945 to 1954 was
nearly $50 billion. Total American exports of goods and services rose from
$5.26 billion in 1940 to $20.6 billion in 1955. U.S. Bureau of the Census,
Historical Statistics of the United States, Colonial Times to 1957 (Washington, D.C., 1960), p. 565; *Statistical Abstract of the United States, 1954*
(Washington, D.C., 1954), p. 898; *Statistical Abstract of the United States,
1965* (Washington, D.C., 1965), p. 856.
28. Taft, "The Republican Party," p. 118.
29. *Congressional Record,* 79th Cong., 1st sess., XCI (January 22, 1945),
A220, and 80th Cong., 1st sess., XCIII (December 15, 1947), A4735.
30. Senate, Committee on Banking and Currency, *Bretton Woods Agreements Act* (Hearings), 79th Cong., 1st sess., June 13 and 15, 1945, pp. 37,
98.
31. Studies of the Bank and the Fund indicate that many of Taft's criticisms were valid, but also that the United States did exercise decisive power
over the decisions of these institutions, especially in promoting the cause of
private capital investments and in using the Bank and Fund as political instruments against communism and communist states in the Cold War. See,
for example, Jack N. Behrman, "Political Factors in United States International Financial Cooperation, 1945–1950," *American Political Science
Review,* XLVII (June 1953), 431–460; Raymond Mikesell, *United States
Economic Policy and International Relations* (New York, 1952), pp. 168–
170 and 199–206; Lloyd C. Gardner, *Economic Aspects of New Deal Diplomacy* (Madison, Wisc., 1964), pp. 285–291; Gabriel Kolko, *The Politics of
War: The World and United States Foreign Policy, 1943–1945* (New York,
1968), pp. 255–258; Richard N. Gardner, *Sterling-Dollar Diplomacy* (Ox-
ford, 1956), esp. pp. 110–144, 257–268, 287–305 (still the best book on the
origins of the Fund and the Bank); David A. Baldwin, *Economic Development and American Foreign Policy, 1943–1962* (Chicago, 1966), an excellent study.
32. See, for example, Taft's remarks on the Fund and World Bank:
Congressional Record, 79th Cong., 1st sess., XCI (July 12, 1945), 7439–

7446, (July 17, 1945), 7617–7625, (July 18, 1945), 7669–7670, (July 19, 1945), 7753–7754, 7772–7774; Taft, "Government Guarantee of Private Investments Abroad," *Vital Speeches,* XI (August 1, 1945), 634–638.

33. Senate, Committee on Banking and Currency, *Export Bank Act of 1945* (Hearings), 79th Cong., 1st sess., July 17, 1945, pp. 4–14; *Congressional Record,* 79th Cong., 1st sess., XCI (July 20, 1945), 7834. Taft supported the loan to Brazil in the early 1940's to develop the Volta Redonda steel complex and, more interestingly, announced in July 1945 that he was willing to see Russia obtain up to $1 billion through a loan from the Export-Import Bank. The loan was never given. Taft, *Foreign Policy,* p. 16; *New York Times,* July 16, 1945.

34. *Congressional Record,* 81st Cong., 2nd sess., XCVI (May 5, 1950), 6478–6481, 6479.

35. Taft, "Address Before a Group of Businessmen at St. Paul, Minnesota, September 20, 1951," *Congressional Digest,* XXXII (January 1, 1952), 17–19. Truman's later explanation of the purposes of Point Four illustrates that the criticisms offered by Taft were quite relevant. Truman wrote: "It seemed to me that if we could encourage stabilized governments in underdeveloped countries in Africa, South America, and Asia, we could encourage the use for the development of those areas some of the capital which had accumulated in the United States. If the investment of capital from the United States could be protected and not confiscated, and if we could persuade the capitalists that they were not working in foreign countries to exploit them but to develop them, it would be to the mutual benefit of everybody concerned." Harry S. Truman, *Memoirs* (New York, 1955–1956, 2 vols.), II, 268–269.

36. Taft, "The British Loan," *Vital Speeches,* XII (June 1, 1946), 501–502. Hull was Secretary of State in the Roosevelt administration; Clayton was Assistant Secretary of State for Economic Affairs from 1944 to 1946 and Under Secretary of State for Economic Affairs from 1946 to 1947. Taft, "Speech to the World Affairs Council, September 25, 1947." Richard N. Gardner's analysis of the British loan suggests that Taft's assessment of the motives of American policy-makers in recommending the loan was very close to the truth and confirms that Taft was not, as were other legislators, pushed into supporting the measure by anti-Soviet arguments. Gardner, *Sterling-Dollar Diplomacy,* pp. 208–254. On the Soviet factor, see also David S. McClellan and John W. Reuss, "Foreign and Military Policies," in Richard S. Kirkendall, ed., *The Truman Period as a Research Field* (Columbia, Mo., 1967), pp. 54–55.

37. Taft, "The British Loan," pp. 500–508; *New York Times,* April 11, 1946.

38. *Congressional Record,* 79th Cong., 1st sess., XCI (May 21, 1945), A3413; Taft, *Foreign Policy,* pp. 18–20.

39. *Congressional Record,* 79th Cong., 2nd sess., XCII (July 29, 1946), 10336; *New York Times,* July 30, 1946, and June 8, 1947; John C. Campbell, *The United States in World Affairs, 1945–1947* (New York, 1947), pp. 227–229; *The United States in World Affairs, 1947–1948* (New York, 1948), pp. 109–120. President Truman finally achieved the desired result through a provision of the Mutual Security Act of 1951, which authorized military assistance to Latin American countries. Edwin Lieuwen, *Arms and Politics*

in Latin America (New York, 1961), pp. 196–202. Taft voted for the omnibus bill, but by then the United States was involved in the Korean War. Even so, he continued to oppose arms for Latin America and asserted correctly that the danger of a communist military threat to the United States in the area was "nonsense."

40. On the Greek-Turkish crisis, see especially Stephen Xydis, *Greece and the Great Powers* (Thessaloniki, 1963); Joseph M. Jones, *The Fifteen Weeks* (New York, 1964); and Richard J. Barnet, *Intervention and Revolution* (Cleveland, 1968), pp. 97–131. Truman's message to Congress of March 12, 1947, is found conveniently in Barton J. Bernstein and Allen J. Matusow, eds., *The Truman Administration: A Documentary History* (New York, 1968), pp. 251–256.

41. *New York Times,* March 13, 1947. Most of this section on Taft's response to the Truman Doctrine is drawn from Henry W. Berger, "A Conservative Critique of Containment: Senator Taft on the Early Cold War Program," in David Horowitz, ed., *Containment and Revolution* (Boston, 1967), pp. 125–139. For a discussion of the fulfillment of Taft's criticism concerning an American "special position" in Greece, see Maurice Goldbloom, "What Happened in Greece," *Commentary,* XLIV (December 1967), 68–74; Barnet, *Intervention,* pp. 127–128; and Center of Planning and Economic Research, *Analysis and Assessment of the Economic Effects of the United States Public Law 480 Program in Greece* (Athens, 1965).

42. *New York Times,* March 16, 1947.

43. Arthur Vandenberg to Harry Truman, February 1947, in Arthur H. Vandenberg, Jr., *The Private Papers of Senator Vandenberg* (Boston, 1952), p. 319; Crabb, *Bipartisan Foreign Policy,* pp. 60–61. Taft was included in a second conference on the Greek-Turkish situation.

44. *New York Times,* April 11, 1947.

45. Taft, *Foreign Policy,* p. 112.

46. *Congressional Record,* 80th Cong., 1st sess., XCIII (April 22, 1947), 3786.

47. Vandenberg, *Private Papers,* pp. 346–350. The vote on the Greek-Turkish program is in *Congressional Record,* 80th Cong., 1st sess., XCIII (April 22, 1947), 3793. Among critics of the Truman Doctrine because of its unilateral character was Walter Lippmann, who summarized his views in *The Cold War: A Study in U.S. Foreign Policy* (New York, 1947).

48. George F. Kennan, *Memoirs, 1925–1950* (Boston, 1967), pp. 313–324.

49. Goldbloom, "What Happened in Greece"; Barnet, *Intervention.*

50. "Address by the Undersecretary of State [Dean] Acheson on the Requirements of Reconstruction, Cleveland, Mississippi, May 8, 1947," in Raymond Dennett and Robert K. Turner, eds., *Documents on American Foreign Relations, 1947* (Princeton, 1949), pp. 162–163; "Address by Secretary of State George C. Marshall at Harvard University, June 5, 1947," in Bernstein and Matusow, *Truman Administration,* pp. 256–259.

51. Quoted in Campbell, *U.S. in World Affairs, 1947–48,* pp. 484–486. On the Marshall Plan, see Seymour Harris, *The European Recovery Program* (Cambridge, Mass., 1948); Harry B. Price, *The Marshall Plan and Its Meaning* (Ithaca, N.Y., 1955); Robert H. Ferrell, *George C. Marshall,* Vol. XV of *The American Secretaries of State and Their Diplomacy* (New

York, 1966), pp. 99–134; Mikesell, *U.S. Economic Policy*, pp. 250–252, 262–268; Thomas G. Paterson, "The Quest for Peace and Prosperity: International Trade, Communism, and the Marshall Plan," in Barton J. Bernstein, ed., *Politics and Policies of the Truman Administration* (Chicago, 1970), pp. 78–112.

52. *New York Times*, September 26, 1947.

53. *Congressional Record*, 80th Cong., 1st sess., XCIII (November 20, 1947), A4253.

54. H. Bradford Westerfield, *Foreign Policy and Party Politics: Pearl Harbor to Korea* (New Haven, 1955), pp. 269–270, 285–290.

55. *Congressional Record*, 80th Cong., 2nd sess., XCIV (March 12, 1948), 2641–2643, 2708. Taft's reference to the sphere of influence "originally assigned to them" implied recognition of the wartime arrangements, including the Churchill-Stalin agreements of October 1944.

56. For Taft's comments to the press, see *New York Times*, March 15, 1948. Kennan's views are summarized in his *Memoirs*, pp. 379, 399–402. Taft's favorable vote on the Marshall Plan can further be explained by Vandenberg's deft legislative tactic in limiting the term for the initial authorization of the program to twelve months instead of keeping the original fifteen-month plan, thereby reducing the cost of the legislation without any actual loss of funds. In addition, Taft was pleased that the administration of the Marshall Plan was to be placed in the hands of a separate agency, the Economic Cooperation Administration, more directly responsible to Congress, rather than under the direction of the State Department. Malcom Jewell, *Senatorial Politics and Foreign Policy* (Lexington, Ky., 1962), p. 122.

57. The war scare was intensified by a telegram to Washington officials from the American military commander in Berlin, General Lucius Clay, on March 5, 1948, in which he wrote that war might "come with dramatic suddenness." Walter Millis, *The Forrestal Diaries* (New York, 1951), p. 387. Kennan has commented that what resulted was extreme hysteria and overreaction which he believed was unwarranted. *Memoirs*, p. 400. Truman's speech to Congress of March 17, 1948, can be found in part in Bernstein and Matusow, *Truman Administration*, pp. 269–271. Taft, it should be noted, had voted against the Selective Service Act of 1940. He had always opposed Universal Military Training and did so again in 1948. He voted for extending the Selective Service Act of that year "with reluctance" and in part to prevent enactment of Universal Military Training. *New York Times*, June 11, 1948.

58. Vandenberg, *Private Papers*, pp. 404–405. On the question of the danger of a Soviet military attack and how policy-makers inflated the threat, see, for example, Kennan, *Memoirs*, pp. 397–414; William A. Williams, *The Tragedy of American Diplomacy* (New York, 1962), esp. pp. 273–276; and John Lukacs, *A History of the Cold War* (Garden City, 1962), pp. 75–77; Lloyd C. Gardner, "America and the German 'Problem,' 1945–1949," in Bernstein, *Politics and Policies*, pp. 113–148.

59. The text of the resolution can be found in Bernstein and Matusow, *Truman Administration*, pp. 274–275. The Senate vote is in the *Congressional Record*, 80th Cong., 2nd sess., XCIV (June 11, 1948), 7846.

60. Truman, *Memoirs*, II, 277–289.

61. "The U.S. Military Assistance Program," *Department of State Bulletin*, XX (May 22, 1949), 643–650; *New York Times*, July 9, 1949; Edward A. Kolodziej, *The Uncommon Defense and Congress* (Columbus, Ohio, 1966), pp. 60–65. Article 3 of the North Atlantic Treaty enjoined the signatories to a policy of individual and collective assistance to resist armed attack. Article 5 stipulated that an armed attack "against one or more" of the signatories "shall be considered an attack against them all" and would constitute grounds for action, "including the use of armed force." Ruhl Bartlett, ed., *The Record of American Diplomacy* (New York, 1964), p. 734. The way in which the Truman administration linked military aid to NATO paralleled the connection that was made between NATO, the Marshall Plan, and the Brussels Pact. Historian Lawrence Kaplan has written: "There was no genuine alternative to an alliance in which the United States was fully joined to Western Europe if the purposes of both the Marshall Plan and the Brussels Pact were to be served." Kaplan, "The United States and the Origins of NATO, 1946–1949," *Review of Politics*, XXXI (April 1969), 219.

62. *Congressional Record*, 81st Cong., 1st sess., XCV (July 11, 1949), 9205–9209; (July 21, 1949), 9887. It so happened, of course, that NATO's military power never matched the hopes of its designers and, as NATO historian Robert Osgood has written, it is doubtful that NATO could have stopped a Soviet invasion of Western Europe if one had been contemplated. Osgood argued that NATO was "intended to provide political and psychological reinforcement in the continuing political warfare of the cold war. There was no significant fear of a massive Russian invasion." Osgood, *NATO: The Entangling Alliance* (Chicago, 1962), p. 30. See also Richard J. Barnet and Marcus G. Raskin, *After Twenty Years: The Decline of NATO and the Search for a New Policy in Europe* (New York, 1965).

63. *Congressional Record*, 81st Cong., 1st sess., XCV (July 11, 1949), 9209–9210.

64. Taft, "The Washington Report," August 3, 1949, and November 2, 1949, in Harnsberger, *Man of Courage*, pp. 237–238, 330.

65. *New York Times*, July 15, 22, 1949. The Democrats had regained control of Congress in the presidential election of 1948.

66. *Congressional Record*, 81st Cong., 1st sess., XCV (July 21, 1949), 9886, 9916; *New York Times*, July 22, 1949. The vote was 82 to 13. All but two of the dissenting votes were cast by Republicans. The two rebel Democrats were Glen Taylor of Idaho (Henry Wallace's running mate on the Progressive party ticket in 1948) and Edwin C. Johnson of Colorado.

67. Quoted in Cabell Phillips, *The Truman Presidency* (New York, 1966), p. 269.

68. *New York Times*, July 26, 1949.

69. Congressional Record, 81st Cong., 1st sess., XCV (September 22, 1949), 13165–13168. Truman's announcement is in Bernstein and Matusow, *Truman Administration*, pp. 286–287.

70. The best discussion of NSC-68, from which this material is drawn, is Paul Y. Hammond, "NSC-68: Prologue to Rearmament," in Walter Schilling, Paul Y. Hammond, and Glenn H. Snyder, *Strategy, Politics, and Defense Budgets* (New York, 1962), pp. 271–378 and especially 304–307. Other paraphrases of NSC-68 are in Phillips, *Truman Presidency*, pp. 305–308, and more recently in Walter LaFeber's documentary collection, *Ameri-*

ca in the Cold War: 20 Years of Revolution and Response, 1947–1967 (New York, 1969), pp. 74–77.

71. Hammond, "NSC-68," pp. 351, 362.

72. *Congressional Record,* 82nd Cong., 1st sess., XCVII (January 5, 1951), 55.

73. Taft, "Speech Before Lincoln Club of Denver, Colorado," *New York Times,* February 15, 1948; Taft, *Foreign Policy,* pp. 74, 77.

74. *Congressional Record,* 82nd Cong., 1st sess., XCVII (January 5, 1951), 55–62.

75. Senate, Committee on Foreign Relations and Committee on Armed Services, *Assignment of Ground Forces of the United States to Duty in the European Area* (Hearings), 82nd Cong., 1st sess., February 26, 1951, pp. 610–613.

76. *Ibid.,* pp. 621, 656–657. On American superiority in the air and on sea, see, for example, Louis J. Halle, *The Cold War as History* (New York, 1967), pp. 263–264.

77. Malcom Jewell has pointed out that only two members of the Senate Republican Policy Committee, of which Taft was chairman, opposed the dispatch of *any* troops to Europe under any conditions. They were Senators Wherry of Nebraska and Homer J. Ferguson of Michigan. Jewell, *Senatorial Politics,* p. 91.

78. Senate, *Assignment of Ground Forces,* pp. 620–624, 632.

79. *Congressional Record,* 82nd Cong., 1st sess., XCVII (April 4, 1951), 3282–3283, 3293–3294. The resolution was not endorsed by the House of Representatives.

80. See, for example, *Congressional Record,* 80th Cong., 2nd sess., XCIV (February 24, 1948), A1073, and Taft, *Foreign Policy,* pp. 47–63.

81. O. Edmund Clubb, *Twentieth-Century China* (New York, 1964), pp. 273–284, 288; memo from Secretary Acheson to Senator Connally, March 15, 1949, in Dean Acheson, *Present at the Creation* (New York, 1969), pp. 749–750. On American policy in China, see also the excellent study by Tsang Tsou, *America's Failure in China, 1941–1950* (Chicago, 1963).

82. *Congressional Record,* 81st Cong., 2nd sess., XCVI (January 11, 1950), 298–300; 82nd Cong., 1st sess., XCVII (May 22, 1951), A2931–2934; Tsou, *America's Failure,* pp. 530–534, 560–561. Truman's statement on Formosa is in Bernstein and Matusow, *Truman Administration,* pp. 346–347.

83. *Congressional Record,* 81st Cong., 2nd sess., XCVI (January 11, 1950), 300.

84. *Ibid.* (June 28, 1950), 9319–9323; Taft, *Foreign Policy,* pp. 32–33, 103–113.

85. Acheson, *A Citizen Looks at Congress* (New York, 1957), pp. 83–84; LaFeber, *America, Russia, and the Cold War,* pp. 86–89; Tsou, *America's Failure,* pp. 537–538. Acheson's "perimeter" speech is in Bartlett, *American Diplomacy,* pp. 760–764.

86. *Congressional Record,* 82nd Cong., 1st sess., XCVII (April 13, 1951), A2031. Truman's speech of April 11, 1951, is in Bernstein and Matusow, *Truman Administration,* pp. 455–461.

87. The political side of things was also revealed in Taft's refusal to publicly disapprove Senator Joseph McCarthy's reckless campaign of "soft-

on-communism" charges, and worse, against the Democrats. That this action was clearly political on Taft's part and that Taft did not really share McCarthy's views has been judiciously suggested by Richard Rovere's unmatched account, *Senator Joe McCarthy* (New York, 1959), pp. 179, 187–190.

88. Taft, "Speech at Chicago, Illinois, February 21, 1953," in Frederick L. Burdette, ed., *Readings For Republicans* (New York, 1960), pp. 18–19.

89. Taft, "Address Before the National Council of Christians and Jews, Cincinnati, Ohio, May 26, 1953," in Peter V. Curl, ed., *Documents on American Foreign Relations, 1953* (New York, 1954), pp. 110–114.

90. Taft, "Russia and Communism, September, 1949," quoted in Harnsberger, *Man of Courage,* p. 298; Taft, *Foreign Policy,* pp. 114–118.

91. *Ibid.,* pp. 118–120.

92. *Ibid.,* pp. 120–121.

93. *Ibid.,* p. 121.

94. For an especially perceptive view of this development as well as of Taft, see the fascinating piece by Karl Hess, principal author of the 1960 Republican party platform, co-author of the 1964 platform, and Barry Goldwater's chief speech writer in 1964. "An Open Letter to Barry Goldwater," *Ramparts,* VIII (October 1969), pp. 28–31.

by Mark Solomon

Black Critics of Colonialism and the Cold War

By the end of World War II, black American intellectuals were united in believing that the battle against white racism in their own country could not be won without a larger international battle against colonial imperialism in Africa. The fate of black Africa would be the fate of black America: so argued such diverse organizations as the NAACP, the National Urban League, and the Council on African Affairs (CAA), and such politically diverse individuals as W. E. B. DuBois, George Padmore, Horace Cayton, Paul Robeson, and Rayford Logan. Along with the weekly commentators in the *Pittsburgh Courier,* these men and organizations pleaded simultaneously with the black public and the postwar government to support the liberation of colonial Africa (and, as time and imperialism went on, colonial Asia). It was that, they said, or watch colored people everywhere go under.[1]

American Negro awareness of Africa had been growing throughout the twentieth century. As the guiding spirit and founder of Pan-Africanism—the conviction that all persons of African descent are commonly oppressed by a common enemy—W. E. B. DuBois was one of its earliest and strongest proponents. Considering the rise of modern imperialism, the deepening of American race prejudice, the first uprisings among the colonial masses, and the publication of Lenin's Colonial Theses of 1920, which welded the struggles for colonial freedom to the proletarian movements of the industrial nations, DuBois' famous declaration that "the problem of the twentieth century is the problem of the color line" appeared to be truly prophetic.[2]

Subsequent events proved DuBois' declaration valid. As modern imperialism internationalized racism, the racial consciousness of black Americans was gradually internationalized. The extensive redistribution of colonial empires following World War I was matched by an intensification of racial strife within the United States. As the urban ghettos of the 1920's grew, nurturing among their citizens characteristically ambivalent feelings of optimism (in numbers) and despair (in oppression) Marcus Garvey conceived and spread his vision of a black grandeur rooted in Africa. The American Negro, he stated, could grow strong only by the rediscovery of his African roots.[3]

With the onset of the Great Depression, DuBois continued to expound (and expand) his concept of Pan-Africanism. Wracked with doubt about the survival of blacks in depression America, he called upon all the colored peoples of the world to forge their salvation together. After all, he declared, the American Negro shared more with the dark people of the world than he did with white Americans; with his dark brothers in Asia, Africa, and Latin America, he shared "color caste, discrimination, exploitation for the sake of profit, public insult and oppression." [4]

Other developments in the thirties served further to internationalize racial consciousness. *Opportunity,* the normally subdued journal of the Urban League, commented with bitter irony on the dispatch of Marines to Haiti to bring the "blessings of democracy" to "the lesser breeds" at the very time that the national press carried ghastly photos of the bludgeoning and lynching of blacks in Sherman, Texas. The Negro press was quick to sense that this violation of Haiti's sovereignty was cut from the same cloth as the American brutalization of black people. "If the marines must fight," the *Baltimore Afro-American* declared, "we suggest that President Hoover order them to Mississippi, Alabama, Texas and Georgia," where white mob uprisings bent on lynching and burning had gone unchecked. Walter White, secretary of the NAACP, charged that the Haitian drive for independence was actually inflamed by the "swaggering dictatorial attitude of the American . . . imbued by race prejudice." [5]

Relying upon generations of experience in white America, Negro commentators were quick to note the irony and sham in their government's attitude toward colored nations. Ironic themselves, these commentators asked if Japan's "crime" in China might not be her temerity in horning in on the white imperialist game. What mind-boggling, hypocritical racism, *Opportunity* proclaimed, to excoriate Japanese actions while the United States government "stabilized" Haiti through "the extermination of three thousand peasants with aeroplanes and machine guns." The moral inconsistencies of the great Western nations were nauseating: if Japan were to withdraw from Manchuria, would Britain withdraw from India and Africa? Would the United States withdraw from Haiti and Nicaragua? No. Thus, "Japan has learned her lessons well. She has taken a leaf from the book of Christian civilization." [6]

Events of the Second World War served only to increase black American awareness of Africa. Mussolini's rehearsal for war in the attack on Ethiopia (which proved that "black people in their native land of Africa have no rights that whites are bound to respect" [7]), the prominence of the African war theater and the participation of dark peoples in those battles, the anti-fascist, anti-colonialist slogans of the allied powers, and the rise of colonial liberation movements, including those in the Far East—all these events raised the possibility (if not the necessity) of an intensified and world-wide drive for black freedom. The unshackling of oppressed Africans and Asians would bring new pride and dignity to black Americans; since no Negro could really be free while his brothers were in chains, those chains would be broken. Indeed, these thoughts, uttered in the Negro press soon after the war, were verified by a leading youth activist of the 1960's:

When most of [the young black students who were born during World War II] were finishing high school, Nkrumah was walking in the United States—tall, black and proud. Sékou Touré, with his penetrating eyes, had said "hell no" to Charles De Gaulle. Images of black men in flowing African robes, sitting at the United Nations and carrying on the business of their governments, had a profound effect on the consciousness of these black babies born during World War II. These new African realities disproved the old Hollywood images of black people as servants of Tarzan and rifle carriers for the Europeans. A new generation of blacks was emerging.[8]

Of the black American organizations operating during the Cold War, the Council on African Affairs was engaged exclusively in disseminating information and organizing programs and petitions designed to win mass American support for African anti-colonial struggles.[9] Founded by Paul Robeson, the renowned black singer, and Dr. Max Yergan, a black YMCA worker based in South Africa, the Council was the result of the two men's associations during the 1930's with London's African community, particularly with such revolutionaries as Kwame Nkrumah, Nnamdi Azikiwe, and Jomo Kenyatta. The Council thus took root in the United States at a point when the moral authority of the Soviet Union and communism in general was appealing in the black community—indeed throughout the country and the world. Barely a year had passed since the founding of the (American) National Negro Congress which included federated black organizations ranging from left to moderate and accepted Marxist thought as a legitimate force in black life.

During the middle 1930's, the CAA welded the anti-colonialist with the pro-Soviet impulse. Robeson believed that the Soviets had turned a society formerly a tsarist prison-house of subject nations into a land of equality. By constitutionally banning racism, they were also the leading international force opposing colonialism. The emergence of Soviet world power, so Robeson and the Council maintained, would generate new power balances, allying subject peoples with a strong socialist ally. In fact, the Council believed that Soviet policy was identical with the interests of such peoples; thus, during World War II, they confidently expected American-Soviet cooperation to usher in an era of colonial independence.[10]

It was in 1943, when thousands of American troops helped defeat the fascist armies in Africa, that the CAA anticipated "the greatest possibility for a new day for Africa." Not only was the American government sending soldiers and supplies in abundance, but lend-lease officials, economic commissions, and other agencies were also stationed throughout the continent. American influence in the French, Belgian, and Portuguese possessions was, according to the Council, "far greater than ever before." They therefore hoped that the United States, unencumbered by any long-term history of colonialist activity in Africa, would "bring about the application of the Atlantic Charter [which endorsed the national right of self-determination] to the life of the African people." The CAA's Executive Director Max Yergan pointed out that the goals of international cooperation and amity expressed in the Charter absolutely negated the continued existence of colonies and/or their concomitant state of economic underdevelopment. In an argument characteristic of contemporary black faith in free enterprise as a stabilizing force, Yergan insisted that "avoidance of an economic slump" in Europe and the United States required building the purchasing power of the "so-called 'backward' areas." [11]

This was essentially black radical belief; moderates, on the other hand, were not so sanguine that liaison with the Soviets would produce postwar colonial freedom. Writing in the moderate NAACP journal *Crisis* in the summer of 1943, L. D. Reddick suffused his hopes with skepticism: "What happens in Africa in the immediate future will reveal to the submerged masses everywhere, and to ourselves, whether our stirring declarations have meaning or whether this is just one more indecent war." He pointed out correctly that postwar planning for Africa and the world would proceed in a new environment in which American economic and military power was expanding and British imperialism declining. Yet this development alone did not constitute any guarantee that the colonies would attain independence.[12]

George Padmore, a former Communist currently an ardent Pan-Africanist and propagandist of African liberation, made Reddick's suspicion conviction. In a scathing 1944 analysis of postwar Anglo-American intentions, Padmore claimed that any such collaboration, in which the United States would undoubtedly act as senior partner, would clothe neo-colonialist objectives in a "democratic camouflage" of formal disavowals of colonialism. By supporting the victorious colonial powers on the one hand and mildly appeasing colonial aspirations for self-determination on the other, the United States, Padmore insisted, would "emerge from this war as the dominant imperialist power, whose needs for new markets, sources of raw materials, air and sea bases, etc., will have to be satisfied." While America would not attempt to acquire outright political control of African colonies, her dollar diplomacy would guarantee commercial and strategic advantages—and without the burden of policing colonial territories. Although some American leaders argued that an end to European colonial domination would benefit the country by forcing the colonies to seek machinery and financial assistance from America, Padmore believed that the American leadership would achieve this goal not by freeing the colonies but by forming an alliance with Great Britain in which regional organizations developed by Great Britain and the other victorious colonial powers would invite American financial investment. Thus Padmore perceived the outlines of postwar colonial settlements to be: (1) United States accommodation of British colonial interests in exchange for Anglo-American political and military alliances; (2) American acceptance of white-settler hegemony in South Africa in exchange for an Open Door investment policy; and (3) betrayal of the aspirations of colonial peoples through absorption of the native-educated elite into minor roles in "regional councils" controlled by the great powers.[13]

Despite Padmore's pessimism, the CAA continued to be sanguine about the development of postwar Africa, and mainly because they pinned their hopes not on Anglo-American but on American-Soviet cooperation. A CAA-sponsored conference in the spring of 1944 adopted a resolution asking the United States to promote international agreements "establishing effective machinery for securing the social, economic and political advancement of the African and other colonial peoples. . . ." Max Yergan urged elimination of "land alienation, labor exploitation, social coercion and restrictions which have followed from the economic penetration of the European into Africa. . . ." For the postwar era Yergan envisioned international agreements to "establish in cooperation with the representatives of the peoples affected, labor, social and civic standards and rights for the indigenous population of every dependent territory. . . ." Such agreements, enforced by the great powers, "would guard against monopolistic restrictions and controls and would encourage public, cooperative, and collective enterprise among the indigenous population. . . ." Yergan also stressed the urgent need to resolve the problems of the former Italian empire in Africa, the World War I mandates, and the projected regional groupings of African territories, through commitment by the great powers to advancing "the right of self-determination to the people of any dependent area and [to promote] development of all such people towards self-government according to a specific time schedule." Thus the Council's postwar expectations were deeply pro-African, pro-labor, and pro-international—which, in CAA terms, meant pro-Soviet. The delegations, petitions, and rallies launched by the CAA in the late war and early postwar years consistently reflected this outlook.[14]

The wartime government was reluctant to respond to CAA pressure. A petition presented to President Roosevelt and the Secretary of State, Edward R. Stettinius, Jr., in December 1944, and endorsed by, among others, Mary McLeod Bethune, Harry Emerson Fosdick, Horace Mann Bond, Dorothy Height, and Theodore Dreiser, asked the government to take the lead in promoting the rapid industrialization of Africa "with due regard that the Africans themselves shall be principal beneficiaries. . . ." Stettinius replied vaguely and blandly that "the Department of State recognizes the importance in world affairs of the problems of dependent peoples, in Africa and elsewhere. It is the intent of the Government that the proposed United Nations Organization should protect and promote the welfare of all peace-loving peoples." In public statements the Secretary of State endorsed the goal of independence for colonial peoples, provided these peoples were "prepared" for it.[15]

Despite its evasive responses, the government in the waning days of the war could still count on the support of the Council. In fact, the CAA chose to defend the Dumbarton Oaks Conference—which met in the fall of 1944 to hammer out a draft charter for the United Nations Organization—against skeptics and detractors in the black community. The editors of *The Crisis,* for example, criticized the conference for rejecting a proposed clause in the charter which would have established national and racial equality as basic principles of international relations. They perceived in this rejection the start of a new cycle of betrayal of colored peoples, similar to the rejection by the Versailles negotiators of demands for racial justice. While the CAA immediately condemned these charges as "partisan and baseless," they could not help but wonder at the Dumbarton Oaks failure either to condemn racism or even mention the representation of colonial peoples in the UN.[16]

As late as mid-1946 the CAA could argue that the corporate and political interests of the United States were not inconsistent with pro-labor and pro-independence policies in Africa. By that point, a large proportion of Africa's trade had been diverted to the United States. American tin plate was boiled in African palm oil, and cobalt from the Congo was used in forging high speed American machine tools. In fact, in 1944 United States import-export trade with the Belgian Congo alone amounted to $100 million, thereby equaling the total value of American exports to all of Africa in 1938. Nonetheless, the CAA did warn the government that "its important political and economic stakes in Africa" were being undermined by continuing European control of colonial administrations. "The question now," the Council insisted, "is whether these war-time gains in United States–African trade will be cancelled out by the return of the former economic restrictions which are an integral part of the colonial imperialist system." [17]

This effort to turn growing American involvement in Africa into a foundation for anti-colonialist policies got nowhere. In the sub-dued observation of the political scientist and African specialist Rupert Emerson, "official American policy was discreetly re-strained in its advocacy of an overhauling of the African colonial structure." A key reason for this restraint was the Cold War. The American-Soviet cooperation on which the CAA had largely predicated its wartime hopes for African salvation had become the postwar American-Soviet antagonism before which all other inter-national issues languished—except insofar as they related to or served to advance the cause of Soviet containment. Thus American policy-makers placed primary importance on cementing alliances with European colonial powers. As for Africa, in Emerson's words, "since [her] stability and security were obviously products of colonial rule, it was evident that the United States rated the ab-sence of a crisis more highly than an attack upon the European colonialism which served in fact as a welcome bulwark against the allegedly greater evil of Communism." [18]

For the CAA, the critical test of American intentions in Africa was the development of the United Nations trusteeship system. The system was to be established on the principle that colonial territories wrested from defeated armies should not be annexed by any victorious nation but should instead be administered by a mandatory or trust power under international supervision until such time as the territories were able to determine their own future status. The CAA greeted trusteeship as a path to liberation for the whole colored world, but on this provision: that the great powers, acting in concert under the principles of the Atlantic Charter, would eventually apply the trusteeship principle to *all* colonial possessions, not just to those which were spoils of war. In 1945 the Council also called for specific schedules for the realization of self-government and independence, and for a program of economic assistance for the colonies based primarily upon the needs of indigenous labor.[19]

At the 1945 San Francisco UN conference the United States introduced eleven proposals for the establishment of a trusteeship system. But instead of projecting trusteeship as a definite means to colonial liberation, the American draft proposed only a vague "progressive development toward self-government." Trusteeship was to be limited to old League of Nations mandates, territories taken from the Axis powers, and territories voluntarily placed under the system by "States responsible for their administration." Specific trusteeship arrangements would be agreed upon only by "the States directly concerned." The Council interpreted this last proposal virtually to exclude the Soviet Union from participation in the system.[20]

Naturally enough, the CAA's reaction to these proposals was uneasiness quickly replaced by dismay. What about Indonesia, Malaya, Indo-China, the Philippines, India, Kenya, Algeria—all those great portions of the underdeveloped world held by victorious powers? Were they to continue as colonies? The implication in the American draft that they could be transferred to UN administration by a "voluntary" principle the CAA considered an absurd and groundless fancy. The Council was also greatly disappointed in the apparent effort to isolate the Soviet Union from the trusteeship system. A strong Soviet role in Africa, the Council maintained, would stimulate a healthy competition among the great powers, each to demonstrate that he had the strongest commitment to indigenous African interests. The American government did not share this view. When the Russians proposed an alternate trusteeship goal of "self-government and self-determination with the active participation of the peoples of these territories . . . [and] the aim of expediting the achievement by them of full national inde-

pendence," and then attempted to put this goal into effect by ac-
quiring a share of trusteeship over Libya, an American State
Department official dismissed the action as a threatened "extension
of the Soviet Union's sphere of influence into Africa." [21]

By the summer of 1945 the CAA noted with increased alarm
that American naval authorities were calling for exclusive and
permanent United States control of the Marshalls, the Carolines,
and other Pacific islands; the Navy wanted them for strategic bases.
Warhawks and opponents of postwar Anglo-American-Soviet cooperation quickly championed this move; to them, "security" took
precedence over either colonial liberation or international amity.
It was becoming clear to the Council that these pressures on the
government to construct hostile military and political blocs could
effectively scuttle the cause of colonial freedom.[22]

But by far the most galling element in the whole colonial situation was the fact that the United States actually initiated and
fought for an inadequate trusteeship system, one which set no
limits on the length of supervision (which in any case was not
compatible with self-determination) and granted no representation
to colonial peoples in trusteeship administrations. Despite President Truman's pious declarations in support of self-government,
the United States was in fact doing very little to oppose colonialism. In its journal *New Africa,* the CAA imagined a moment of
absolute candor among the great powers in which the Europeans
told the Americans: ". . . We are reassured by the evidence that
you are doing nothing to prevent the restoration of European
imperialism. . . . As long as you are content simply to *talk* about
self-government for the colonies, we don't mind very much. . . ."
Thus, in the uneasy early Truman years, the American failure
forcefully to support effective trusteeships, the growing tendency
toward militarization of vast areas of the globe, including Africa,
and the corroding effects of the Cold War on every aspect of
international relations, altered and shaped anew the critical assumptions of both left-wing and moderate black leaders.[23]

As the Cold War deepened, members of the black community
beyond the Council on African Affairs perceived that United States
policies were riveting the nation to anti-communist European al-

liances. In turn, these alliances obviated any direct action on behalf of either black Africa or black America. Anti-communist priorities in fact required that the United States aid those now-crippled European powers which traditionally had been the colonial masters of Africa and Asia. In a particularly angry editorial on Cold War priorities, the NAACP stated that ". . . there are other 'enslaved peoples' about whom no one in high places [has] ever raised a voice. These 'enslaved peoples' are colored, not white; they are Africans and Asians, not Europeans." [24]

Writing from the 1945 London Peace Conference the black historian and political commentator Rayford Logan insisted that the liberal principles of the Atlantic Charter were being trampled by white-supremacist power politics. He reported that Ethiopia was given only the right to represent in writing to the conference her request for a port facility, while the Union of South Africa was to be permanently represented in discussions over the disposition of Italian colonies. Logan was convinced that the Western colonial powers, backed by the United States, were maneuvering to turn over only marginal mandates to UN trusteeship, while they themselves retained the more vital colonies.

In much the same vein, the black political commentator A. J. Siggins, writing in the moderate *Pittsburgh Courier* in the fall of 1946, argued that a world front of dark colonial peoples, supported by the Soviet Union, was in conflict with the white imperialist powers over the future of the colonies and, indirectly, over world power balances. The imperialist states, Siggins wrote, were attempting to fortify a chain of islands extending from Singapore to Western Samoa across the Indian Ocean to East Africa, as well as construct a dominating cordon of states "from North America to Great Britain with the West Indies and the Azores as Atlantic 'bastions,' across Africa . . . to Australia and Sumatra." Siggins also perceived an anti-Soviet, pro-colonialist scheme to allow South Africa to annex Southwest Africa, Bechuanaland, and adjacent territories; thus, between them, Rhodesia and South Africa would control most key southern African resources. Siggins concluded that "the greatest menace to world peace and world relief and reconstruction is white imperialism." [25]

The black American hope for an extensive trusteeship system

of territories resolutely moving toward self-determination and peaceful development under the cooperative leadership of the United States and the Soviet Union was quickly diminishing in face of the construction by America of a span of anti-Soviet military bases and strategic alliances. Ultimately, only eleven territories (such regions as Togoland and Western Samoa), comprising less than one million square miles and relatively small populations, came under trusteeship. South Africa was able to withhold Southwest Africa from international control, while the goal of freeing the labor of other dependent areas from excessive exploitation was generally subordinated to the task of "efficient administration." The strategic and economic concerns of American foreign policy spawned support for France's vast colonial system in Indo-China and North Africa, for the British colonies in Malaya and for the Belgian colonies in the Congo—and this at the very time that the hope for freedom among those dependent peoples had reached new heights. Black critics correctly saw in the anti-colonial trends of postwar American foreign policy the seeds of United States involvement in future colonial wars and, in the larger context of Cold War, the possibility of American-Soviet confrontations in the underdeveloped world.[26]

To all these early postwar developments, Negro writers and critics reacted with a deeply rooted skepticism born of a forcibly detached, outcast position. Estranged from the government by the great-power conflicts of the Cold War, their responses to American foreign policy were striking in the depth of their mistrustful variance from the apologies of white Establishment commentators. This continued black estrangement, a prime feature of Negro thought throughout the twentieth century, was apparent in the early Cold War to those whites who dared or cared to listen. Few in the Truman administration did.

In 1946 George Padmore, drawing upon an ideology built from years of battle against imperialist politics, insisted that the Soviet Union at the Paris Peace Conference (convened to settle the fate of Italy, Hungary, Rumania, and Bulgaria) was engaged in "a fundamental conflict over the right of Anglo-American capitalists to enjoy the trade of eastern and central Europe. . . . The great Capitalist Colossus, America . . . is trying hard to resuscitate capitalist regimes. . . ." Thus, Padmore argued, Soviet Foreign Minister Molotov was justified in wishing to protect territories within the Soviet sphere from Anglo-American exploitation. To revive those societies slowly and painfully re-emerging from devastation, the Russians had instituted planned economies reinforced by agrarian reforms. Thus, Padmore claimed, they had to encroach on the resources of American and British interests (especially Rumanian oil). But hoped-for recovery of the rights of trusts and cartels impelled American Secretary of State James F. Byrnes, "a mouthpiece of Wall Street," to claim passionately the "open door" in the Danubian region.[27]

Perhaps the sharpest attack on the Anglo-American allegiance, one prosecuted by a cross-section of black critics, occurred after Winston Churchill's "iron curtain" speech at Fulton, Missouri, in early 1946. These critics considered Churchill's speech a blatant attempt to persuade the United States to save the British Empire by brandishing the Soviet menace. The Council on African Affairs protested President Truman's silence in the face of what they deemed a call to an Anglo-American alliance against a wartime ally. The *Pittsburgh Courier* called the Churchill speech an "invitation to imperialism," one which confirmed the fact that old-fashioned cynical power alliances and spheres of influence still ruled world politics. Noting that a major portion of Churchill's speech called for a military alliance, the *Courier* declared that such a pact would commit American money and men to fight subject peoples. "If England cannot defend her empire alone," the *Courier* asserted, "let her lose it."

Expanding on this point of view, the sociologist Horace Cayton accused Churchill of playing "a master race game" by advocating "the white hope of the dying cause of imperialism" and attempting to goad the United States into reinforcement of the status quo all the way from India to Hong Kong to Palestine. On the other hand, Cayton insisted, the United States had no irreconcilable differences with Russia; thus the danger was that America might be dragged into an unwanted and unjust war simply to protect Britain's imperial interests. In a related development, Walter White, in a telegram to President Truman concerning the British Loan of 1946, questioned the reported use of British troops armed with American weapons to crush the anti-colonial Indonesian rebellion. He wired that "none of the money [should] be used to perpetuate imperialism or to deny any colonials of the British Empire full freedom and justice. Reported use of American war materials by British against Indonesian people constitutes one of the greatest scandals and tragedies of contemporary history." It was left to the acerbic J. A. Rogers to hurl the final epithet. Speaking of Churchill, Rogers said, ". . . though he spouts democracy, he is a fascist at heart. Imperialism and jim crow are fascism." [28]

The outrage over the tightening Anglo-American alliance inspired P. L. Prattis, political writer for the *Pittsburgh Courier,* to offer his own interpretation of the origins of the Cold War. First he went back to the eve of the San Francisco Conference of the United Nations, on April 24, 1945, when the Hearst Press was beating its drums against the "Russian bogey" and the United States and Britain were assiduously cultivating votes to defeat the Soviets. Prattis then argued that the United States had showed contempt for Russia in admitting Argentina over Soviet objections. He accused American foreign policy-makers of drawing Monroe Doctrine lines from Greenland to far below the Falkland Islands, and charged that

at distances five to ten thousand miles from our western shores we have grabbed and garrisoned Pacific islands, tied in Japan and as much of Korea as we can. . . . We are mesmerized by the oil in Iran, Trans-Jordan, Saudi Arabia, Palestine. We tell the Turks what to do and what not to do where Russia is involved. We help the British elect a non-wanted king in Greece. Our warships ply the Mediterranean threateningly. . . . We scheme to force our brand of democracy upon the so-called Russian satellite nations, even Poland right next door to Russia.

Prattis next argued that American political leadership maintained a double standard, tacitly backing Dutch imperialism in Indonesia and British intrigues between Jews and Arabs in Palestine, but viewing Russia as a dangerous ogre when she tried to deal for friends, oil, and the protection of her shipping routes on the Black Sea. "Votes for the Bulgarians" the United States yelled, "but not [Prattis maintained] for black South Carolinians." Prattis then concluded with the anti-imperialist, anti-McCarthy view that "the people of the United States . . . are actually not interested in polishing off Russia quickly so that the plutocrats of plunderland can maintain their system which they euphemistically call democracy. The people want and need peace." [29]

The Greek crisis of 1947 brought into sharp relief black resentment against increasing American involvement with British interests and her easy willingness to pour billions into foreign regimes while black Americans continued to suffer from poverty and discrimination. Columnist Marjorie McKenzie stated simply that the government could do far better spending $400 million to promote democracy in the South than to maintain a decadent Greek monarchy. More dramatically, Joseph D. Bibb, a Chicago newspaper editor, cried that it was a "hollow mockery and withering irony in using taxpayer money to bolster Britain's puppet Greek government. . . . Would it not be asinine and ridiculous for colored Americans to advocate funds for democracy in Greece—funds derived from their taxes—when there is terror, autocracy, exploitation and feudalism in their own bastions and bailiwicks?" Nor, Bibb maintained, would the supposed red scare turn blacks into supine anti-communists: "No! We do not sustain the Marxist philosophy. . . . But we do not hate nor revile [Marxism] as bitterly as we do the imperialistic concepts of Smuts and Churchill. . . . We tremble no more from conceptions of concentration camps under Russian control than we do from visions of the lyncher's rope and the reign of Talmadge." Commenting on the Greek crisis, Prattis stated, "The United States today is definitely an aggressor nation, sending its money and force far beyond the confines of its true national interest." But as Britain withdrew from center stage, "the strong wine of world leadership . . . will go to the head of America and it will discover that instead of fighting for the world it is fighting against it." [30]

The eminent black educator Mordecai Johnson echoed Prattis' criticism of the expanding American role of world policeman. Arguing that the Truman Doctrine had set the limits to Communist expansion very close to Soviet borders, Johnson charged that if Russia had instead tried to expand into Mexico, the United States would have gone to war. But Russia, Johnson said, had enhanced its moral power because it did not seek war. Thus President Truman had no justification in throwing money into Greece and Turkey—money never used to meet the challenge to democracy in the American South. Benjamin Mays, president of Morehouse College, was troubled by Truman's justification that he did not want to see a free people coerced: "I wish," Mays said, "I could believe that we were really concerned about establishing freedom in these countries. I am troubled at this point because there are so many areas in the United States where democracy doesn't work." For Horace Cayton, the Greek episode was a fiasco in which the United States was goaded by British and its own communist phobias into supporting "scandalously fascist" executioners of Greek patriots who were themselves not necessarily communists. Now the British were walking out, and the United States was being called upon to take over support of a government whose principles were completely antithetical to the Four Freedoms.[31]

Far Eastern involvement prompted yet more black criticism of American foreign policy, and it was the same anti-imperialist argument used against Greek policy. J. A. Rogers insisted that the Chinese Communists were national patriots struggling against the corrupt regime of Chiang Kai-shek, while Prattis characterized Chiang's Kuomintang as a bunch of "venal crooks." He hoped that "Negroes will make it clear that they are against their government's taking their money and transforming it into boodle for the leeches of China." With the impending collapse of the "corrupt" Kuomintang in 1949, Horace Cayton announced that China was lost to exploitation by the white West. Nonetheless, the American government immediately pledged support for Chiang's government-in-exile on Formosa. Although the colonial peoples of China had become united, "the west," Cayton pointed out, "apparently had not learned that democracy can mean anything but white supremacy." Cayton did suggest an alternative Asian policy, however, one which could yet balance the accumulating ruin of China disaster. The United States could support Jawaharlal Nehru's Indian government; America might yet demonstrate a willingness to free the orient from Anglo-American domination. For this, Cayton speculated, the imperial powers would damn us, but we would win the respect and gratitude of oppressed peoples everywhere.[32]

Negro reaction to both the Atlantic Pact and Soviet acquisition of the atomic bomb demonstrated a stubborn critical integrity in the face of rising McCarthyism. Marjorie McKenzie characterized the Atlantic Pact as a consolidation of the "old concept of Anglo-Saxon power," an expression of "the arrogance of whiteness and bigness" in which the twelve-nation Atlantic community would attempt to run world politics and to dominate the policies of "small dark nations," particularly the latter's dealings with the communist bloc. Miss McKenzie was especially distressed by an arrangement made in the spring of 1950 between Secretary of State Dean Acheson and French Foreign Minister Maurice Schuman by which the United States would send assistance to Vietnam and the associated states of Indo-China. When the two foreign secretaries reported a "satisfactory" agreement to encourage a "healthy nationalism," Miss McKenzie correctly interpreted it as support for the French client regime of Bao Dai. The United Nations, she charged, was only being weakened by such lily-white coteries formed outside the world body to dominate the internal life of colored nations: "The Atlantic Council has gotten rid, not only of the Russian veto, but also of everybody of the sizes and colors that do not traditionally run the world." [33]

As for black reaction to the Soviet bomb, in at least one instance it took the form of ill-repressed glee. Not averse to stretching credulity in order to twit the lily-white establishment—the seriously embarrassed lily-white establishment—Joseph Bibb viewed Soviet development of the bomb as the doom of white supremacy, the end of the truculence and strut of "white imperialism." After all, the Russians were not Anglo-Saxon but a peculiar mixture of oriental breeds. Thus, he went on, the Soviet achievement signalled that China, India—even the African nations— would soon split the atom. Yes, Bibb said, it was a "great day when the Anglo-Saxons lost their monopoly over the instruments of war and terror. . . ." Out of the shattering of pompous conceit, he speculated—and now with dead seriousness—could come a better understanding between colored and white peoples.[34]

At the outset of the Korean War, the venerable labor leader A. Philip Randolph called upon black Americans to close ranks in support of the war. Negroes, he declared, had a vital stake in stopping the unjust aggression of North Korea. Still in his stridently anti-communist phase, Randolph justified this support, "not only because [American intervention] gives strength and upholds the integrity of the United Nations, but [because it] reinforces and fortifies the bastions of democracy throughout the world. . . ." Thus he concluded, it also aided the cause of the Negro.[35]

Despite Randolph's plea, American Negroes continued to judge international events from the standpoint of racial self-interest. Such judgments were—and remain—the core of their political and social survival. Thus their brief initial enthusiasm over the exploits of black soldiers and airmen disappeared before subsequent reports of mistreatment of black GI's (who were fighting in segregated units) and the disturbing record of Negro courts-martial. These developments, combined with traditional Negro skepticism and estrangement from foreign policy, the absence of objective evidence that black self-interest would be served by the conflict, and, significantly, the fact that the Korean War was essentially an American war against colored people, made Randolph's clarion call a jingoistic whisper.

Realizing the threat which the war posed to black existence, black critics began hardheadedly to sort out the controversial origins of the conflict. J. A. Rogers insisted that the division of Korea into competing puppet regimes by the United States and the Soviet Union had been a bad bargain for all Koreans, one which, by generating strong pressures for reunification on both sides of the thirty-eighth parallel, retroactively laid the blame for the war on white imperialistic oppression. Thus the critical significance of the conflict for Rogers was that his own country, trapped in a political swamp in Europe, was also becoming mired in Asia. "And Asia, Communist or not, intends to be free of white dominance." [36]

While Walter White of the NAACP was quite willing to admit that, in the characteristic rhetoric of the day, the Korean conflict was one between dictatorship and democracy, he could not dismiss the disquieting fact that the war was also one between "those who have been robbed and scorned because of color and place of birth and those who have done the robbing." Like it or not, he said, the peoples of Asia were determining that "their lot would be better served under Soviet instead of democratic control." This decision (or process of decision) was largely due to the "racial arrogance" of white America; moreover, Western plundering of underdeveloped areas had engendered among all colored peoples a deep and tragic distrust of American motives. Our greatest error, White declared to the second convention of the International Union of Electrical Workers, has been our blindness to and contempt of what the dark world thinks of us.[37]

Stimulated by reports of inter-army black GI mistreatment, the uneasy mood of the black community was then deepened by reports of contemptuous and brutal American troop behavior toward Koreans. Racist contempt was rife in Korea. The Chinese and Koreans had become collectively "the Asiatic hordes," the adversary himself "the gooks." The cheapness with which Americans regarded Asian lives was revealed in U.S. soldier remarks that "We're here to kill Koreans," and "We can beat those gooks at anything." What bitter hypocrisy to fight to bring the fruits of democracy to people one contemptuously called "gooks," a term, for Cayton, which had the same hateful, dehumanizing effect (and intention) as "nigger." *Crisis* insisted that ". . . We will never win the political war in Asia as long as Koreans and Asiatics are 'gooks' in the eyes of our fighting men. Whether we know it or not, Asia is in revolution. Her people fight for nationhood. Here is America's opportunity to live up to her own revolutionary past by helping the struggling masses of Asia to economic security and political independence." [38]

Faced with the prospect of full United States mobilization, the *Pittsburgh Courier* finally asked: Is the nation to prosecute such a perilous undertaking when no young American agreed, by ballot or by congressman, to die for the "democratic" prerogatives of South Korea? Other inescapable questions which the *Courier* posed: "Why are we in Asia? Do [the Asians] think we are their friends? Would they defend us? Do they enjoy the spectacle of our defending them by waging war in their countries? Are they willing to be the victims of such defense?" The answers for the *Courier* were apparent: Asia does not want our "assistance." Asia looks to our record of "arrogance and exploitation" and despises us. The only tenable choice was to get out.[39]

Finally, all roads led back to Africa. Behind every national and international criticism made by Negroes during the early postwar years lay an anguished response to United States policy in Africa—policy which, to them, appeared never firmly to support independence. This conclusion was only made more binding by the Marshall Plan and the Point Four Assistance programs—those cornerstones of American Cold War policy.

In an editorial on the Marshall Plan on May 21, 1949, the *Pittsburgh Courier* declared that "it is one of the curiosities of international politics that American Negroes, overwhelmingly opposed as they are to colonialism as represented by the Imperialistic rule of subject colored people by France, Italy, Belgium and Holland, are committed nevertheless through the Marshall Plan to the support of these nefarious enterprises." Of course, the *Courier* admitted, the plan was formulated not to encourage imperialism, but to stabilize the economies of "free world" nations against the Soviet threat. But these "free world" nations were showing "increased reliance . . . on the African colonies for raw materials and the stepped-up exploitation which that will impose." Blacks thus saw themselves victims of a crowning irony: while their votes had played a decisive role in maintaining in power an administration publicly committed to civil rights, that administration was doing next to nothing to protect those rights. On the other hand, the Truman administration did require Negroes to pay heavy taxes for a European aid program which supported international colonialism at the price of national social reform. Thus, the *Courier* noted, Negroes were betrayed on two continents at once: under the "beneficence" of the Marshall Plan, the colonialist members of the Atlantic pact were receiving taxpayers' money which came in part "from people who have been spit upon . . . and denied the civil rights that are heralded as evidence of the democratic principle [which the Marshall Plan purported to maintain]." [40]

Although Walter White and the NAACP did support Cold War policies, they traditionally used that support to drive home their view that independence of the colored nations would directly benefit the anti-communist struggle. Testifying in 1948 before the Senate Foreign Relations Committee, White urged that the European Recovery Program be extended to Africa, Asia, and

Latin America: "I want to remind the United States Senate that hunger is as painful to brown, yellow and black stomachs as it is to white ones." He also expressed fears that possible domestic inflation produced by ERP would fall hardest on American Negroes. Finally, speaking for the NAACP, he stated that the United States has "a moral obligation to require that these countries [receiving foreign aid] adopt programs under which people currently subjected to their rule shall speedily be given a chance for freedom which these nations ask for themselves." [41]

To William Worthy, foreign correspondent of the *Baltimore Afro-American,* White was speaking after the fact. Worthy claimed that loans to Africa made under the Marshall Plan's Economic Cooperation Administration had "no other purpose than to facilitate the extraction of raw materials for foreign profit." Like British capital in the past, the loans only supported the high-profit combination of white supremacy and cheap labor against which the Africans continued to rebel. W. Alphaeus Hunton, who became CAA's executive director in 1948, stated that the American taxpayer paid for "direct ECA colonial grants and loans (actually payments for colonial raw materials) or for the Marshall Plan aid to Europe, [both of] which directly or indirectly made possible at least part of the contributions of the colonial powers toward expanding their colonies' production." [42]

By this point, the late 1940's, the Council on African Affairs had abandoned all faith in America's economic and political policies in Africa. As far as the CAA was concerned, the United States had joined, if not helped to form, the ranks of neo-colonialism —a new form of the old in which direct political and administrative rule of colonies was replaced by foreign control of major portions of the economic life of underdeveloped nations. In exchange for Yankee dollars, an impoverished Europe had allowed America a wedge in Africa. As the Council argued, "In this day of the Marshall Plan, it is hardly likely that Britain, France and Belgium can oppose America's access to the wealth of their respective African empires. They have little choice in the matter if they accept American dollars on American terms. The best they can hope for is that Wall Street and Washington will agree to some joint international scheme so that Africa may not be completely con-

verted from a European appendage into an American colony."
Nonetheless, American colonialism seemed the rule. The priorities
of ECA and the Organization for European Economic Cooperation (OEEC), allowed the building of a vast extractive enterprise
(including military-related "strategic materials") to the detriment
of indigenous economic development or the immediate material
needs of the African people. The Marshall Plan went even further
to provide the funds and mechanisms for the perpetuation of empire. As a joint congressional committee had itself pointed out, the
enabling act of the Marshall Plan directly guaranteed Americans
"suitable protection for the right of access" to African resources.[43]
Figures for the period reveal the enormous American profits
made in Africa. Between 1943 and 1953 private American investments rose from $50 million to $212 million in South Africa, $27
million to $77 million in the British colonies, and $13 million to $37
million in the French colonies. In the rest of Africa (mainly the
Belgian Congo) the rise was from $6 million to $26 million. From
1938 to 1955 African exports to the United States leaped from
$55 million to $619 million, more than eleven times greater in
1955 than in 1938 and 56 per cent greater than in 1948. In the
same period (1938–1955) African imports from the United States
rose from $118 million to $623 million and leveled off after 1950
to approximately 10 per cent of all of the continent's imports.
While United States–African economic dealings during the postwar years remained relatively marginal in terms of America's
world-wide involvements, the figures do show a significant increase
in American competition with European interests in Africa, particularly with Britain for dominance in the South African market
and for second place after Belgium in the Congo market. By 1950
American investments on the continent totaled over $352 million
or 3 per cent of the total private overseas investment of the United
States. Moreover, these investments were marked by a high rate
of profit. In 1951, the zenith of profit-taking, United States earn-
ings on the African continent reached 25 per cent, compared to
a rate of 17 per cent on the total of world-wide American investments the same year. As of today, Africa supplies the bulk of
American diamond (industrial and gem), columbium, and cobalt
consumption, and around a quarter of American consumption of
antimony, chrome, graphite, and manganese.[44]

In contrast to the Marshall Plan, the Point Four Program was one of supposedly disinterested assistance to underdeveloped nations; to the extent it failed to fulfill this goal it encountered sharp criticism from black commentators. Rather sardonically, William Worthy pointed out that President Truman had declared Point Four to hold "the nucleus of unprecedented U.S. prosperity because it can create massive demands for American goods." Indeed, W. Alphaeus Hunton of the CAA replied; but the program was of relatively minor significance for Africa herself. Similar to the technical assistance given under ECA, much of the Point Four appropriation was geared to providing expert surveys of transport facilities and resources which in turn expedited American investments. The humanitarian motives of the Point Four program disappeared before its profitable (American) effect. Horace Cayton called the program "a new form of imperialism" geared to enhance such developments as the "perhaps controlling [American] interest in a Belgian company called Union Minière du Haut Katanga," and other investments in Rhodesia and South Africa. While analysis of Point Four aid does show that its original appropriation was considerably less than ECA's ($27 million as compared with $2.25 billion for ECA and $342 million for occupied Germany alone), the application of those funds did not in fact implement the program's intentions. In the Middle East, Point Four investments generally flowed into oil-rich areas, not to hungry people. Under Point Four, United States investments in India increased from $38 million in 1950 to $113 million in 1957. But Canada received a $5 billion increase in American investments during the same period. Thus investments under Point Four tended to support established areas or projects of potential profit maximization, rather than to supply food and economic improvement for underdeveloped areas.[45]

To Negro critics, American involvement in South Africa followed an even more sinister pattern. The CAA contended that the American Anglo-Transvaal Corporation established in 1946 had "acquired control of vast mining areas throughout South Africa and substantial interest in over 100 industrial companies." In addition, Goodyear, Firestone, General Motors, and Ford were expanding manufacturing and assembly operations in South Africa. By 1946 American South African imports ($66 million before the war) had risen to $230 million. An independent nation, South Africa consistently held approximately one-third of the United States' African trade, mostly because the European colonial powers still resisted large-scale American economic penetration of their colonies. The CAA considered these expanding economic ties with South Africa the key factors behind America's failure vigorously to combat South Africa's moves to solidify control of Southwest Africa.[46]

But by far the greatest source of postwar black anxiety in the late 1940's was the location of American military bases in North Africa. As part of the strategic ring around the Soviet Union, they brought Negroes into direct confrontation with the fundamentals of Cold War philosophy. In the first place, protection of bases such as Wheelus Air Force Base near Tripoli seemed to influence the way America voted in the UN. In supporting France's blunt rejection of any advice or assistance from the world organization during crises in Morocco and Algeria, the United States simultaneously defended its military autonomy and France's colonial autonomy. Moreover, the establishment of the bases seemed to produce *de facto* American neo-colonialism. Wherever a base was constructed, oil concessions followed. The host government extended the concessions and also permitted the bases, which then became insurance against expropriation of U.S. interests.[47]

Thus, to blacks the world over, America had become a triple threat: she was militaristic, capitalistic, and neo-colonialist. Nowhere were these characteristics more evident than in the United Nations, where the United States continually gave verbal support to self-determination but her vote continually to the European colonial powers. A tally of American votes on African issues provided a depressing pattern: on a series of eight UN votes involving efforts to force South Africa to submit the Southwest African mandate to a UN trusteeship, motions dealing with education and health conditions in the colonies, and proposals to strengthen the voice of colonial peoples in the UN, the United States voted consistently "no." [48]

On the other hand, the Soviet Union voted consistently "yes." As early as 1946 Rayford Logan pointed out the anomalies of this power-bloc voting: "The Soviet Union has, of course, fired the heaviest guns in the battle to make the trusteeship an effective method for promoting the welfare and the ultimate independence or self-government of colonial subjects. . . . The student of world affairs cannot fail to be impressed by this regular aligning of the Soviet Union, her satellites, and [the] dark peoples against the white colonial powers and their satellites." Six years later, the pattern remained the same. Horace Cayton found it "tragic" that Soviet Russia, not the United States, had become the champion and spokesman for the independence of Africa.[49]

As the African independence movement gathered force throughout the fifties and sixties, much of the old colonialism was consigned to the ashes of history. Black criticism of American policies continued to play a vital part in that consignment. In 1954 William Worthy charged that the United States, in the face not only of a world-wide revolutionary tide but of the growing recognition that gross international inequalities would always threaten peace, nevertheless continued to pursue its narrow pro-colonial interests. Had not President Eisenhower declared that "foreign policy should be based on the need for America to obtain profitable foreign markets and raw materials to sustain her economy"? Worthy went on to bemoan the international American military and economic presence; it represented only present American aggrandizement and potential American aggression. In April 1954 he stated that Washington had learned nothing from its painful involvement in Korea; now "our current recession is likely to be 'solved' by direct intervention in the Indo-China war. . . ." Where would it end? For Worthy the unremitting impulse to play international watchdog would inevitably militarize American life, tear its society apart, and pave the way for a domestic garrison state.[50]

Although the Council on African Affairs had formally ceased to function in 1955, its former leaders continued to criticize American neo-colonialism. In 1957 W. A. Hunton wrote:

Even though Europe yet has much larger stakes in Africa than the United States . . . it is still nevertheless true that the United States holds the decisive responsibility for either blocking or promoting the rapid and peaceful liberation of Africa. . . . The question is whether America's authority will make itself felt in the United Nations on the African's side, or whether it will continue to be directed toward serving American strategic and profit-making prerogatives in the continent, utilizing and supporting the European systems of control or shifting to a go-it-alone policy in areas where Europeans are no longer in the saddle.[51]

In light of this statement, as well as their record over the years, it is difficult to deny that the Council's pleas for United States support of African independence, for economic policies that would guarantee African control of African wealth, and for a new American-Soviet cooperation based on the resolution of these African problems, would have resulted in a more tenable American foreign policy and a more viable world. Against the often blind anti-communism of United States African policy, and despite the Council's rigid faith in Soviet beneficence, the CAA did offer an alternative worth consideration. One can only wonder at the testimony of Joseph C. Satterthwaite, Assistant Secretary of State for African Affairs, before the Senate Foreign Relations Committee in 1960. Satterthwaite conceded the State Department's reluctance to criticize South Africa's racism when that nation "strongly supports the United States in the overriding issues of our times." The Sharpeville massacre followed shortly thereafter.[52]

At the opposite political pole from the CAA, the NAACP did accept the basic rationalizations of Cold War policy. Nonetheless its criticism of American neo-colonialism remained pungent. In 1949 the NAACP urged that Marshall Plan aid be discontinued to countries which suppressed movements for colonial freedom. In 1950 it resolved that "the United States in French Indo-China and elsewhere in South and Southeast Asia give support only to genuine freedom movements which aim to set the people free from domination by America, West European countries or Russia." In 1951 it urged the government to control private investment in underdeveloped areas in order to "prevent imperialistic exploitation," and it demanded that Point Four aid be utilized to strengthen the potential for economic self-reliance of colonial peoples. In 1952 the NAACP called for a total end of American support for South Africa. In fact, throughout the Cold War the Association challenged every major United States vote in the United Nations against the cause of colonial liberation.[53]

Thus the oppressed condition of Negroes in the postwar United

States infused blacks of all political outlooks with a deep and abiding understanding of the yearning for freedom among similarly oppressed peoples. Better than any other significant group in American life, American Negroes were able to grasp the spirit behind the revolutionary mood sweeping the underdeveloped world. While the tenability of their proposals can be challenged in some cases, their underlying plea for the awesome powers of America not to be turned against the tide of colonial revolution offered, in balance, a path of enlightened self-interest for America. Had the country taken this path, had it understood and sympathized with the dynamics of revolutionary change, had it tried to adapt its international involvements to movements of freedom, socialism, social mobility, and indigenous economic development, it might have been able to accept the possibility of a different system of relations with the Soviet Union and the communist world.

It might also have realized its own internal failure fully to liberate its black citizens. The fates of black Africa and black America are as closely tied today as they were during the Cold War. And the final chapter has not yet been written. In concert with all the world's oppressed, black America's continuing drive for liberation may in the end hold nothing less than the key to the liberation of the whole of America's potential and spirit.

Notes

1. For a general discussion of historical relationships between Africa and black Americans, and Afro-American sentiments toward Africa, see Earl E. Thorpe, *The Mind of the Negro: An Intellectual History of Afro-Americans* (Baton Rouge, 1961), Ch. 12; Harold R. Isaacs, *The New World of Negro Americans* (New York, 1963); W. E. B. DuBois, *The World and Africa* (rev. ed., New York, 1965), pp. 265–268, 334–338; E. Franklin Frazier, *The Negro in the United States* (New York, 1949), Ch. 1; St. Clair Drake, "Negro Americans and the 'Africa Interest,' " in J. P. Davis, ed., *The American Negro Reference Book* (Englewood Cliffs, 1966), pp. 662–705; Rupert Emerson and Martin Kilson, "The American Dilemma in a Changing World: The Rise of Africa and the Negro American," *Daedalus*, XCIV (Fall 1965), 1055–1084; John A. Davis, ed., *Africa as Seen by American Negro Scholars* (New York, 1960); C. A. Chick, Sr., "American Negroes' Changing Attitude Toward Africa," *Journal of Negro Education*, XXXI

(Fall 1962), 531–535; John A. Davis, "The American Negro and Africa," *Jewish Frontier,* XXXI (March 1964), 11–15; St. Clair Drake, "The American Negro's Relation to Africa," *Africa Today,* XIV (December–January 1967–1968), 12–14. For a thorough anthology of the attitudes of individuals and organizations, see Adelaide C. Hill and Martin Kilson, *Apropos of Africa: Sentiments of Negro Leaders on Africa from the 1800's to the 1950's* (London, 1969). For an expression of literary and cultural evocations of the African past, see Alain Locke, ed., *The New Negro* (New York, 1925) pp. 231–267. For an exhaustive analysis of surveys of black public opinion on Africa and a variety of foreign policy issues, see Alfred O. Hero, Jr., "American Negroes and U.S. Foreign Policy: 1937–1967," *Journal of Conflict Resolution,* VIII (June 1969), 220–251. See also R. Weisbord, "Africa, Africans and Afro-American: Images and Identities in Transition," *Race,* X (January 1969), 305–321.

2. For some major antecedents of contemporary Pan-Africanism, see selections from the writings of Martin R. Delany, Edward W. Blyden, James T. Holly, and Alexander Crummel in Howard Brotz, ed., *Negro Social and Political Thought, 1850–1920* (New York, 1966), pp. 37–190; Edwin Redkey, *Black Exodus: Black Nationalist and Back-to-Africa Movements, 1890–1910* (New Haven, 1969). E. U. Essien-Udom's *Black Nationalism: A Search for an Identity in America* (Chicago, 1962), deals with Pan-Africanism from the standpoint of an emerging nationalist consciousness. DuBois' *Dusk of Dawn* (New York, 1940) and the *Autobiography of W. E. B. DuBois* (New York, 1968) give occasional insights into Pan-Africanism as an expression of international solidarity of peoples of African descent. For a more detailed exposition of DuBois' views, see his articles "The Pan-African Movement," in George Padmore, ed., *Colonial and Coloured Unity, a Program of Action: History of the Pan-African Congress* (Manchester, England, 1947), pp. 13–26, and "Pan-Africa: A Mission in my Life," *United Asia,* VII (April 1955), 65–70. Colin Legum's *Pan-Africanism* (rev. ed., New York, 1965) is a recent study of the subject. On the relationship between imperialism and racist ideology, see Richard Hofstadter's *Social Darwinism in American Thought* (rev. ed., Boston, 1955), pp. 170–200, and Ralph J. Bunche, "Race and Imperialism," from *A World View of Race* in Hill and Kilson, *Apropos of Africa,* pp. 337–343. Afro-American responses to imperialism can be sampled in Herbert Aptheker, ed., *A Documentary History of the Negro People in the United States* (New York, 1951), pp. 750–826. DuBois' quotation is from *Souls of Black Folk* (Chicago, 1903), p. vii.

3. There is as yet no thorough study of the impact of twentieth-century imperialism upon racism as a world-wide phenomenon. C. Vann Woodward's classic *Origins of the New South, 1877–1913* (Baton Rouge, 1951) contains some suggestive material on the role of world-trade-oriented Northern monopolies in shaping postbellum Southern racial practices. The relationship between racist ideology, caste, and semi-colonial status is dealt with in Gunnar Myrdal's *An American Dilemma: The Negro Problem and Modern Democracy* (New York, 1944), pp. 221–229. Frantz Fanon has written fairly extensively on modern colonialism and racism in *The Wretched of the Earth* (New York, 1963), *Toward the African Revolution* (New York, 1967), *Studies in a Dying Colonialism* (New York, 1965), and *Black Skins, White Masks* (New York, 1968). Negro expectations as a re-

sult of World War I are summarized in John Hope Franklin's *From Slavery to Freedom* (3rd ed., New York, 1967), pp. 452–493. The redivision of Africa by the victorious powers is reviewed by W. Alphaeus Hunton, *Decision in Africa* (rev. ed., New York, 1960), pp. 16–39. St. Clair Drake and Horace Cayton's *Black Metropolis* (New York, 1945) is the classic study of the political and cultural impact of the great Negro migrations between the two wars. Recent discoveries of hitherto unknown materials on the Garvey movement will undoubtedly inspire reassessments of the great nationalist movement of the 1920's. E. David Cronon's *Black Moses: The Story of Marcus Garvey and the U.N.I.A.* (Madison, Wisc., 1955) remains the standard work on the subject.

4. A series of scholarly essays and an extensive bibliography on the Afro-American experience during the Great Depression has been collected by Bernard Sternsher, ed., *The Negro in Depression and War: Prelude to Revolution, 1930–1945* (Chicago, 1969). The quotation is from DuBois, "Pan-Africa and New Racial Philosophy," *Crisis,* XL (November 1933), 247.

5. Quotations respectively from editorial, *Opportunity,* VIII (June 1930), 168; editorial, *Baltimore Afro-American,* December 19, 1929, p. 1; Walter White, "Danger in Haiti," *Crisis,* XXXVIII (July 1931), 231.

6. Quotations respectively from the *Baltimore Afro-American,* February 6, 1932, p. 6, and *Opportunity,* X (March 1932), 71.

7. The quotation is from William N. Jones, "The Significance of Abyssinia," *Baltimore Afro-American,* February 23, 1935, p. 4. Jones wrote a regular weekly column throughout the thirties and forties, mainly on foreign affairs. He was consistently challenging and perceptive in his analyses, yet he remains, among others, an unjustly neglected figure in Negro intellectual and political life. DuBois' views are summarized from the *Baltimore Afro-American,* November 16, 1935, p. 2. For some examples of black American sentiments on Ethiopia see Charles H. Wesley's "The Significance of the Italo-Abyssinian Question," *Opportunity,* XIII (May 1935), 148–151; editorial, "And Ethiopia Shall Stretch Forth Her Arms," *ibid.,* XIII (August 1935), 230; George Padmore, "Ethiopia and World Politics," *Crisis,* XLII (May 1935), 138; editorial, "The Golden Calf," *Chicago Defender,* November 2, 1935, p. 16.

8. The first quotation and the general sentiment expressed is from Hugh Weston in the *Pittsburgh Courier,* April 27, 1946, p. 13. Earl E. Thorpe, in *The Mind of the Negro: An Intellectual History of Afro-Americans,* p. 43, discusses the postwar mood among blacks. The last quotation is from James Forman, *1967: High Tide of Black Resistance* (Student Non-Violent Coordinating Committee, [n.d.], New York), p. 4.

9. While there is no detailed account of the background and activities of the CAA, a brief but pointed description of its work is contained in an appendix by W. Alphaeus Hunton to Paul Robeson's *Here I Stand* (New York, 1958), pp. 126–128. In Hunton's words, the prime objective of the CAA was to "provide a sound basis of accurate information so that the American people might play their proper part in the struggle for African freedom." The organization serviced the press with African news and background information, and circulated pamphlets and reports. It also maintained an extensive African library and research facilities, and organized conferences, rallies and demonstrations to enlist public support for its programs. But the CAA was never structured as a mass membership organiza-

234 Cold War Critics

tion. Paul Robeson served as chairman, Dr. William J. Schieffelin and (from 1948) DuBois as vice-chairmen, Max Yergan as executive secretary, and Hunton as educational director. In 1948 the Council was placed on the Attorney-General's list of "subversive organizations." In retaliatory defense, Yergan issued a newspaper release attacking "communists." DuBois recalls that "Robeson protested. His position was that the Council was not a Communist organization even if some of the supporters were Communists. It was doing a specific and needed work; that the political or religious opinions of its members or officials were their own business, so long as the actions of the organization as such were legal." Subsequently Yergan was charged with frustrating the objectives of the Council and mishandling finances, and was replaced as executive secretary by Hunton. At the high point of its activity in 1947, the Council listed an interracial body of "members" which included Herbert Aptheker, Mrs. Carlotta Bass, Judge Hubert T. Delany, Earl B. Dickerson, Dean Dixon, Roscoe Dunjee, Rabbi Max Felshin, E. Franklin Frazier, Belford V. Lawson, Jr., Alain Locke, Rayford W. Logan, Rep. Vito Marcantonio, Rep. Adam Clayton Powell, Jr., Dr. Gene Weltfish, J. Finley Wilson, and Bishop R. R. Wright, Jr. Despite this interracial character, however, the organizational and political functions of the group appeared to be entirely run by Negroes. The Council was finally dissolved in 1955 under ferocious McCarthyite attacks.

10. The leftward political mood in the black community in the mid-1930's is expressed in John P. Davis, *Let Us Build a National Negro Congress* (Washington, D.C., 1935) and in the *Official Proceedings of The National Negro Congress* (Washington, D.C., 1936). Robeson's views on the USSR are summarized in *The Negro People and the Soviet Union* (New York, 1950) and *Here I Stand*. His speech lauding the Soviet Union, upon his receiving the Spingarn Medal from the NAACP, is quoted in the *Pittsburgh Courier*, October 27, 1945, p. 7. DuBois expresses his attitude toward the Soviet Union in his *Autobiography*, pp. 29–43. Dr. Mordecai Johnson of Howard University continually needled the racial policies of the United States by favorably commenting on Soviet practices. For an example, see *Chicago Defender*, June 10, 1933, p. 2. For other examples of efforts to utilize the USSR in this fashion, see I. D. W. Talmadge, "Mother Emma," *Opportunity*, XI (August 1933), 245–247 (report on matriarch of Moscow's small community of expatriate American blacks); Langston Hughes, "Going South in Russia," *Crisis*, XLI (June 1934), 162–163; Henry Lee Moon, "Woman Under the Soviets," *ibid.*, XLI (April 1934), 108; editorial, *ibid.*, XXXVII (October 1930), 343; editorial, *Pittsburgh Courier*, August 9, 1930, p. 10; editorial, *Chicago Defender*, July 11, 1931, p. 4. Positive views of the impact of the Soviet Union on the struggle against colonialism are represented in Leonard Barnes, *Soviet Light on the Colonies* (London, 1944); George Padmore, *How Russia Transformed Her Colonial Empire* (London, 1946); Leonard Barnes, "How the U.S.S.R. Aids its Backward Peoples," *New Africa*, II (November 1943).

11. Editorial, *ibid.*, II (August 1943). The Yergan quotation is from *ibid.*, III (February 1944).

12. L. D. Reddick, "Africa: Test of the Atlantic Charter," *Crisis*, L (July 1943), 20ff. For skeptical views of the potential of Great Power cooperation in behalf of colonial independence, see Ernest E. Johnson, "A Voice at the Peace Table," *ibid.*, LI (November 1944), 345; P. L. Prattis, "Far

East to See a New Era of Plunder," *Pittsburgh Courier,* September 1, 1945, p. 7; editorial, "A Declaration by Negro Voters," *Crisis,* LI (January 1944), 16.

13. George Padmore, "Anglo-American Plan for Control of Colonies," *ibid.,* LI (November 1944), 355–357. For an account of the political and ideological development of Padmore, see James R. Hooker, *Black Revolutionary: George Padmore's Path from Communism to Pan Africanism* (London, 1967).

14. *New Africa,* III (May 1944); the Yergan quotation is from Hill and Kilson, *Apropos of Africa,* pp. 210–211. Among co-sponsors of the conference were the African Students Association, the National Council of Negro Women, the National Maritime Union, the Club Employees Union of the American Federation of Labor, and the African Methodist Episcopal Church.

15. The petition "Africa and Post-War Security Plans" is in *New Africa,* III (December 1944). Also among the original signers were James E. Allen, DuBois, Countee Cullen, Langston Hughes, Benjamin Mays, William L. Patterson, Michael J. Quill, Judge Charles E. Toney, Harry F. Ward, Gene Weltfish, and Charles H. Wesley. Stettinius' reply to the petition is in *ibid.,* IV (February 1945). His qualification on independence is in *New York Times,* May 19, 1945, p. 1.

16. For examples of CAA support for the government's policies, see *New Africa,* III (September 1944), III (October 1944), and III (November 1944). The critical view is from the editorial "Race Equality in the Peace," *Crisis,* LI (October 1944), 312.

17. *New Africa,* V (June 1946).

18. Rupert Emerson, *Africa and United States Policy* (Englewood Cliffs, 1967), p. 22.

19. For general studies of postwar trusteeship, see H. Duncan Hall, *Mandates, Dependencies and Trusteeship* (Washington, D.C., 1948) and Charmian Edwards Toussaint, *The Trusteeship System of the United Nations* (London, 1956). The Council's views on proposed Trusteeships are in *New Africa,* IV (January 1945) and IV (February 1945).

20. The American proposal is in *Department of State Bulletin,* XII (May 6, 1945), 854.

21. Editorial, *New Africa,* IV (May 1945). Soviet efforts to make self-determination the stated goal of trusteeship are detailed in *New York Times,* May 30, 1945, p. 14. The State Department official who reportedly made the comment was identified as James C. Dunn in *New Africa,* IV (October 1945). The diverging views of the Soviets and Americans are reviewed in *New York Times,* June 1, 1945, p. 11, and September 15, 1945, p. 15.

22. Columnist Arthur Krock reported an intense dispute between the armed forces and the State Department, with the former resisting trusteeships over military base areas. See *New York Times,* May 1, 1945, p. 22. Later President Truman stated the United States would acquire military bases under the trusteeship plan. See *New York Times,* August 10, 1945, p. 12. CAA reactions are expressed in "United Nations Colonial Policy Must be Strengthened," *New Africa,* IV (June 1945), and editorial, *ibid.*

23. In a Navy Day address on October 27, 1945, Truman stated: "We believe that all peoples who are prepared for self-government should be

permitted to choose their own form of government by their own freely expressed choice, without interference from any foreign source." *Public Papers of the Presidents of the United States: Harry S. Truman, 1945* (Washington, D.C., 1961), p. 434. The CAA quotation is from an editorial, *New Africa,* IV (November 1945).

24. Editorial, "Liberating 'Enslaved Peoples,' " *Crisis,* LX (April 1953), 228. The NAACP consistently attempted to extract kernels of self-interest for black Americans when allying itself with government foreign policies. It regularly reminded the political leadership that efforts to extend American influence and credibility in the struggle against communism, particularly among dark peoples, required a powerful commitment to wipe out racial injustice at home. Yet the Association often walked a tightrope between affirmations of loyalty and bitter criticism of unfolding United States global policies. For examples of these tendencies, see Roy Wilkins, "Undergirding the Democratic Ideal," *ibid.,* LVIII (December 1951), 647–651; editorial, "Answer to Vishinsky," *ibid.,* LVIII (December 1951), 666–667; editorial, "Foreign Policy and FEPC," *ibid.,* LIV (May 1947), 137; editorial, "Foreigners React to American Prejudice," *ibid.,* LVIII (February 1951), 103; James W. Ivy, "American Negro Problem in the European Press," *ibid.,* LVII (July 1950), 413–418; John E. Owen, "U.S. Race Relations—A World Issue," *ibid.,* LXI (January 1954), 19–22.

25. Rayford Logan, "Colonial 'Spectres' Haunt London Peace Conference," *Pittsburgh Courier,* September 22, 1945, p. 1. A. J. Siggins, "Russia Backs Colonials in War Against Imperialist Countries," *ibid.,* September 21, 1946, p. 13.

26. Some American statements of determination to retain bases in dependent areas are detailed in *New York Times,* January 16, 1946, p. 1; February 1, 1946, p. 4; and October 22, 1946, p. 5. Under pressure from its navy, the United States got a "strategic area" trusteeship of over 1,500 mandated islands seized from Japan which gave America sole trustee status and placed the islands under the Security Council, where the United States had a veto, rather than under the Trusteeship Council. See D. F. Fleming, *The Cold War and Its Origins, 1917–1950* (2 vols., London, 1961) I, 427. The objectives of trusteeship were finally compromised to read ". . . to promote . . . progressive development towards self-government or independence as may be appropriate to the particular circumstances of each territory. . . ." For the final text of the UN charter on trusteeship articles, see *Department of State Bulletin,* XII (July 24, 1945), 1129ff. For a complete list of trusteeships and their political status in 1961, see Eighth National Conference, United States National Commission for UNESCO, *Africa and the United States: Images and Realities* (Boston, 1961), pp. 9–12.

27. George Padmore, "Review of the Paris Peace Conference," *Crisis,* LIII (November 1946), 331–333, 347–348. For a summary of American positions at the conference, see Department of State, *Paris Peace Conference, 1946: Selected Documents* (Washington, D.C., 1949).

28. The CAA's reaction is in *New Africa,* V (April 1946). Representatives of the Council participated in a picket line against Churchill in New York on March 15, 1946. The *Courier* quotation is from an editorial, "Invitation to Imperialism," *Pittsburgh Courier,* March 16, 1946, p. 7. Cayton's comment is in *ibid.,* March 16, 1946, p. 8. White's comment is quoted from a telegram to Harry S. Truman, December 13, 1945, OF 212-A, Harry S.

Truman Papers, Truman Library. The Rogers quotation is from the *Pittsburgh Courier*, March 16, 1946, p. 8.

29. The quotations are from *ibid.*, October 12, 1946, p. 13, and October 19, 1946, p. 12. Prattis added that "they started out after Russia again when sixteen Poles from the exile nucleus in England were arrested by the Russians. Anthony Eden shrieked. Our newspapers blared. Suddenly everybody receded from that hot issue. Yet the Russians had taken the exact action against known spies and provocateurs which England had been known to take in specific, not forgotten instances."

30. Marjorie McKenzie, *ibid.*, March 22, 1947, p. 7; Joseph D. Bibb, *ibid.*, March 22, 1947, p. 8; P. L. Prattis, *ibid.*, March 15, 1947, p. 8.

31. Johnson is quoted in *ibid.*, March 29, 1947, p. 2; Benjamin Mays, *ibid.*, April 16, 1947, p. 8. Horace Cayton, *ibid.*, March 15, 1947, p. 8.

32. J. A. Rogers, *ibid.*, December 4, 1948, p. 18; P. L. Prattis, *ibid.*, December 11, 1948, p. 18. Cayton's statements are from *ibid.*, December 11, 1948, p. 19, and February 5, 1949, p. 18. Black writers were also infuriated by the reported statements of Madame Chiang, who, traveling in the United States in 1948 searching for American support, had been confronted by reporters on American racial issues. At one point she reportedly reminded the press that she was herself "a southerner." On another occasion Madame Chiang was quoted as saying that she would have to know how Negroes would vote before offering an opinion on the poll tax. See J. A. Rogers, *ibid.*, December 4, 1948, p. 18, and Cayton, *ibid.*, December 11, 1948, p. 19.

33. Marjorie McKenzie, *ibid.*, June 10, 1950, p. 13.

34. Joseph D. Bibb, *ibid.*, October 8, 1949, p. 14.

35. *Ibid.*, July 8, 1950, p. 2.

36. For an example of heavy coverage of Negro GI's in combat, see *ibid.*, July 19, 1950, p. 1, and August 19, 1950, p. 1. On discrimination against black troops, see Thurgood Marshall, "Summary Justice—The Negro GI in Korea," *Crisis*, LVIII (May 1951), 297ff., and Walter White, "Report on Civil Rights in 1951," *ibid.*, LIX (February 1952), 97–98. Rogers' comments are in the *Pittsburgh Courier*, July 15, 1950, p. 13, and July 22, 1950, p. 14. He claimed that in the wake of widespread arrests of dissidents and significant uprisings in South Korea after President Syngman Rhee refused in 1949 to get rid of a corrupt cabinet as demanded by the legislative assembly, the North Koreans interpreted the great unrest and Rhee's defeat in a 1950 election as "a green light to come in and be welcomed."

37. White's comments reported in *ibid.*, December 16, 1950, p. 2.

38. Editorial, "Is This White Chauvinism?," *Crisis*, LVIII (February 1951), 103; Horace Cayton, *Pittsburgh Courier*, August 12, 1950, p. 13. The final quotation is from an editorial, *Crisis*, LVII (August-September 1950), 511.

39. Editorial, *Pittsburgh Courier*, December 23, 1950, p. 7.

40. Editorial, "The Marshall Plan and the Colonies," *ibid.*, May 21, 1949, p. 14. For a discussion of the failures of the Truman administration in civil rights, see Barton J. Bernstein, "The Ambiguous Legacy: The Truman Administration and Civil Rights," in Bernstein, ed., *Politics and Policies of the Truman Administration* (Chicago, 1970), pp. 269–304. On Negro aspirations leading into the postwar years, see Richard M. Dalfiume, "The 'Forgotten Years' of the Negro Revolution," *Journal of American History*, LV (June 1968), 90–106. Symbolic of the profound disappointment among

Negroes in postwar America was a dramatic petition, under the editorship of DuBois, presented by the NAACP to the United Nations on October 23, 1947, protesting discrimination against black Americans. It was later reprinted for mass distribution under the title *Appeal to the World* (New York, 1947). Also see Hugh H. Smythe, "The N.A.A.C.P. Protest to U.N.," *Phylon,* VIII (Fourth Quarter 1947), 355–358, and DuBois, "Three Centuries of Discrimination," *Crisis,* LIV (December 1947), 362ff. The final quotation is from Joseph D. Bibb, *Pittsburgh Courier,* April 23, 1949, p. 13. For Bibb, imperialism was still in pursuit of rubber in Indonesia and Malaya; gold, iron, and diamonds in Africa; and cheap labor in all underdeveloped countries.

41. *Ibid.,* February 7, 1948, p. 3. The official NAACP position on the Marshall Plan voted at its Los Angeles convention in July 1949 urged "that similar aid be extended as needed to peoples in Asia, the Middle East, the Near East, Africa, the Caribbean and Latin America." See "NAACP Stand on Colonialism and U.S. Foreign Policy," *Crisis,* LXII (January 1955), 24.

42. William Worthy, "Of Global Bondage," *Crisis,* LXI (October 1954), 464–474, 512. Hunton discusses ECA in *Decision in Africa,* pp. 74–79.

43. Neo-colonialism is defined and probed in Kwame Nkrumah's *Neo-Colonialism: The Last Stage of Capitalism* (New York, 1966). The CAA quote is from *New Africa,* VI (December 1947). Hunton's comments are from *Decision in Africa,* pp. 84–85.

44. The information on American shares of African import-export trade are drawn from United Nations, *Statistical Yearbook* (New York, 1953), pp. 386–389; United Nations, *Review of Economic Conditions in Africa* (New York, 1951), p. 92; United Nations, *Economic Development in Africa, 1954–55* (New York, 1956), p. 84. Figures on direct private investments and profits in Africa are from U.S. Treasury Department, *Census of American-Owned Assets in Foreign Countries* (Washington, D.C., 1947) and statistical reports in *Survey of Current Business,* December 1952, August 1955, and August 1956. The information on American consumption of African mineral resources is provided by Andrew M. Kamarck in "The African Economy and International Trade," in Walter Goldschmidt, ed., *The United States and Africa* (rev. ed., New York, 1963), p. 157.

45. Worthy is quoted from "Of Global Bondage," *Crisis,* LXI (October 1954), 469. Hunton discusses Point Four in *Decision in Africa,* pp. 81–83. The UN's program is summarized in the article "U.N. Economic Aid Program Points Way to End Cold War," *New Africa,* VIII (November 1949). Cayton is quoted from the *Pittsburgh Courier,* September 20, 1952, p. 7. The statistics on Point Four are drawn from Department of Commerce, *Foreign Aid, 1940–51* (Washington, D.C., 1952) and Department of Commerce, *United States Business Investments in Foreign Countries* (Washington, D.C., 1960).

46. The quotation is from *New Africa,* VI (December 1947). CAA's deep concern about conditions among blacks in South Africa is detailed in the pamphlet *Seeing Is Believing—Here Is the Truth About South Africa* (New York, 1947). For specific demands before the UN by the Council, see *New Africa,* V (October 1946) and VI (July-August 1947). The discussion of American economic activity in South Africa is from Emerson, *Africa and United States Policy,* pp. 33–34.

47. The relationship between bases and oil is discussed by Hunton in *Decision in Africa*, pp. 91–99. Hans J. Morgenthau discusses American activity in Africa from the standpoint of military contingencies in "United States Policy Toward Africa," in Calvin W. Stillman, ed., *Africa in the Modern World* (Chicago, 1955), p. 323.

48. *New Africa*, VI (November 1947). The eight votes were: an Indian resolution requesting submission of a trusteeship agreement for Southwest Africa; an Assembly vote on whether a resolution on Southwest Africa should be approved by a simple majority or a two-thirds majority; two Trusteeship Committee votes urging "all or some" territories of colonial powers be brought under UN trusteeship; a Trusteeship Committee vote asking for statistics on educational and health needs of territories; two Assembly votes on whether a simple majority or a two-thirds majority should be required to establish a special committee to make recommendations regarding information on colonial territories; an Assembly vote on a Soviet-sponsored resolution providing for the participation, without vote, of non-self-governing territories of Asia and the Far East in the UN Economic Commission for those areas.

49. Rayford Logan, *Pittsburgh Courier*, December 7, 1946, pp. 1, 12; Horace Cayton, *ibid.*, July 12, 1952, p. 7.

50. For examples of growing interest in colonial liberation movements, see George Padmore, "Facts Behind the Gold Coast Riots," *Crisis*, LV (July 1948), 206–207; Padmore, "Bloodless Revolution in the Gold Coast," *ibid.*, LIX (March 1952), 172–177, 197–199; Ndukwe Eghonu, "Nigeria in Transition," *ibid.*, LX (May 1953), 265–272, 317–319; Padmore, "British Parliamentary Delegation Reports on Kenya," *ibid.*, LXI (May 1954), 273–277, 314. Padmore's book, *The Gold Coast Revolution: The Struggle of an African People from Slavery to Freedom* (London, 1953) was banned by the colonial government in Kenya. See also Padmore's "A Review of the Gold Coast—Final Stage to Independence," *Crisis*, LXII (January 1955), 11–14. Also published during this period was Jomo Kenyatta's *Facing Mount Kenya* (London, 1953). By 1950 the Council on African Affairs was emphasizing the increasing waves of strikes, demonstrations, and political organization for independence sweeping across Africa. See *New Africa*, IX (February-March 1950). See also Padmore's "The Vietnamese Struggle for Independence," *Crisis*, LV (March 1948), 78–79, 91–92. For expressions of support for Iranian attempts to end foreign control of its resources, see P. L. Prattis, *Pittsburgh Courier*, March 31, 1951, p. 6; Horace Cayton, *ibid.*, June 30, 1951, p. 6. For concern over Algeria and Tunisia, see "French Imperialism," *Crisis*, LXII (October 1955), 482–489. In addition, Negro press opinion generally interpreted the 1948 Jewish struggle in Palestine as anti-British and anti-imperialist in content and thus greeted it warmly. See editorial, *Pittsburgh Courier*, March 13, 1948, p. 7. Worthy is quoted from "Of Global Bondage," *Crisis*, 467ff.

51. Hunton, *Decision in Africa*, p. 237.

52. Satterthwaite testimony discussed in Emerson, *Africa and United States Policy*, p. 100.

53. "NAACP Stand on Colonialism and U.S. Foreign Policy," *Crisis*, LXII (January 1955), 23–26.

by Norman Kaner

I. F. Stone and the Korean War

According to Henry Steele Commager, I. F. Stone is "a modern Tom Paine, celebrating Common Sense and the Rights of Man, hammering away at tyranny, injustice, exploitation, deception and chicanery. . . . He is the last of that long succession of radical pamphleteers which includes Paine and Garrison and Theodore Parker, Henry George and E. A. Ross and Henry Demerest Lloyd, Upton Sinclair and Lincoln Steffens and the Rev. A. J. Muste— crusaders all . . . never more effective than when the causes they championed were desperate." [1]

This long overdue accolade from one of America's leading intellectual historians is a testament to a man whose journalistic career began in his boyhood home of Haddonfield, New Jersey, where at the age of fourteen he began publishing an independent paper entitled *Progress*. The paper had a strong Wilsonian flavor and championed the cause of American entry into the League of Nations. One year later, in 1923, Stone joined the staff of the *Camden Courier Post* on a part-time basis. He continued this work until his third year at the University of Pennsylvania, when he decided to embark on a full-time career in journalism. In his own words: "I always loved learning and hated school. . . . I looked down on college degrees and felt that a man should do only what was sincere and true without thought of mundane advancement. . . . I majored in philosophy with the vague thought of teaching it, but though I revered two of my professors, I disliked the smell of a college faculty. I dropped out in my third year to go back to newspaper work." [2]

After leaving college in 1927, Stone joined the staff of the *Phil-*

240

adelphia Record. The *Record,* or "that paper" as it was known among Philadelphia's conservative upper crust, was the only Democratic paper in the city. I. F. Stone was named its chief editorial writer at the age of twenty-six. In December 1933 he left to join the *New York Post* in a similar capacity. The *Post's* editorial positions in the 1930's reflected an impatience with some of the more "conservative" of FDR's reforms, although the paper was decidedly pro–New Deal. To this day Stone maintains that despite all the shortcomings of the New Deal (and he agrees that there were many), Franklin Roosevelt was a truly great President.[3]

In 1937 Stone's first book, *The Court Disposes,* appeared. Claiming in the introduction that "the power of the Supreme Court has become so great, the views that dominate it so backward," Stone maintained that it was essential to social progress that the "power of the Court be curbed." In addition to supporting the President's "court-packing" scheme, Stone suggested that legislation might be enacted to limit the appellate jurisdiction of the Court, and an amendment passed to make "amendment of the Constitution easier." [4] The President ultimately abandoned his efforts to restructure the Court, but because the justices became more receptive to New Deal legislation, the ends sought by both Stone and FDR were achieved.

International affairs replaced domestic concerns in the late 1930's, and Stone's writings reflected this change. In a 1937 *Nation* article he deplored the tendency among "most workers, liberals and radicals" to equate the menace posed by Nazism with that posed by Kaiserism. Claiming that much of the opposition to American participation in collective-security efforts was sustained by this false parallel, Stone cogently refuted the arguments of the isolationists. At the same time he called for the democratic nations to cooperate with the Soviet Union in preventing the spread of fascism. Stone emphasized that he was not advocating "war against the fascist powers," though the article seems to imply that war might be necessary.[5]

Stone steadfastly held to this position before Pearl Harbor. While not advocating direct American entry into the war, in both the *Nation* and *PM* he assailed the complacent pace of American mobilization. These columns formed the basis for Stone's second book,

Business as Usual (1941), which claimed that after the first year
of our $40 billion defense program only about 25 per cent of this
figure had actually been spent "for armaments and munitions."
After an exhaustive analysis of the woes confronting the nation's
defense industries, Stone concluded that only a "democratic reorganization of the economy" would reduce the power of the profit-
minded monopolists and insure a "successful struggle against
Hitlerism abroad." [6] While Stone was perhaps vague about how
such a change could be brought about, his indictment of our
mobilization efforts was certainly persuasive.

By mid-1944, when it became apparent that the Axis were to
suffer defeat, Stone turned his attention to the shape of the postwar
world. He contended that "the job of preserving world peace begins
at home, with the job of creating full employment." In order to
implement this goal, which was in Stone's words "a governmental
responsibility," it would be necessary to introduce a "large measure
of national planning." [7]

Although the jubilation of the Allied victory was momentarily
silenced by the death of President Roosevelt, Stone remained
optimistic about the chances for a lasting and durable peace. In
commenting on President Harry S. Truman's first nation-wide
address, he claimed that Truman "had made a good and whole-
some start," and he loudly applauded the president's intentions to
build "a strong and lasting United Nations organization" as well
as his desire to implement the Bretton Woods agreement and renew
reciprocal trade agreements. "I think Mr. Truman will carry on Mr.
Roosevelt's work," Stone declared, "and carry it forward to that
stable peace Mr. Roosevelt so deeply desired." [8]

These were probably the last kind words Stone ever wrote or
uttered about Harry Truman. In covering the San Francisco conference of the United Nations for both *PM* and the *Nation,* Stone
sensed a pervasive undercurrent of anti-Soviet feeling within the
American delegation. Rather than seeing the conference as laying
the cornerstone for cooperation between the two nations, Stone
reported, American officials viewed the meeting as a vehicle to
organize an anti-Soviet bloc, a move which could "lay the foundation for a third world war." Stone in fact asked whether these
attitudes reflected the thinking of those at the very highest level of
the government.[9]

Stone's fears would be borne out tragically in the next few years as relations between the United States and the Soviet Union steadily deteriorated. Many of his writings during the early years of the Cold War dealt with both the internal and external manifestations of American anti-communism. While recognizing the existence of real problems between the two nations (problems that he contended exist at the conclusion of all wars in which the balance of power is upset), Stone maintained that the ideological gulf tended to replace logic with cant, rationality with paranoia, and balance with overreaction.

After Winston Churchill's "iron curtain" speech on March 5, 1946, Stone judiciously demonstrated that the Russian desire for security on her European borders was a result more of the enormous suffering wrought by World War II than of any Marxist categorical imperative. The American monopoly on atomic weapons was no more reassuring to the Russians than it would have been to America had the situation been reversed. In Stone's judgment, the creation of a durable peace was not served in the least by Churchill's "call for an Anglo-American alliance against the Soviet Union in defense of the status quo," and by the former Prime Minister's assumption "that war must come sooner or later." [10]

Stone continued to argue the need for international compromise, but none was forthcoming. The enunciation of the Truman Doctrine added a touch of finality to the division of the world into "good guys" and "bad guys," a prospect Stone abhorred. During the 1948 campaign he reluctantly cast his lot with Henry Wallace and the Progressive party, hoping that a big vote for Wallace would be interpreted as "a protest vote against cold war, high prices and hysteria. . . . A big vote for peace in November might have its effect. . . . More effect, anyway, than staying home and playing charades." [11]

By this time Stone had severed his connection with the *Nation* and had become the featured columnist for the short-lived *New York Star* and, beginning in May 1949, the *Daily Compass,* a paper founded by Ted O. Thackrey, former editor of the *New York Post.* The *Daily Compass* was intensely critical of the growing stridency of American policy *vis-à-vis* the Soviet Union, and provided Stone with one of the few forums available to a

non-cold warrior during the late forties and early fifties. Tabloid
in format and occasionally sensationalistic, the *Compass* brought
together a talented coterie of journalists which included military
affairs expert Max Werner, political columnist Jennings Perry, and
former radio commentator Johannes Steele. The paper, in the
words of Thackrey, reflected "a protest against reliance on arms as
opposed to negotiation for peace" in relations between the two
great powers.[12]

In the pages of the *Compass* I. F. Stone continued to plead
the cause of reconciliation between America and Russia, fearing
a great conflagration if misunderstanding persisted. Commenting
on President Truman's 1949 inaugural address which reiterated
much of the Truman Doctrine, he maintained, "The only conclusion one can draw is that Mr. Truman believes other people
should be 'free to govern themselves as they see fit'—so long as
they see fit to see as we see fit." Not only was Truman's narrow
view devoid of historical perspective, but, according to Stone, the
United States "has too many motes in its own eye to preach a
dubious freedom in Eastern Europe and China." Stone referred to
"bypassing the U.N., currying favor with Perón, doing business
with Latin military dictators, dealing with Franco, interfering in
Italian elections, and supporting reactionaries in Greece." He
concluded that Truman's words meant "that we set ourselves up
to police the world . . . [and act] with malice toward none except
half of mankind (Russia and China), and with charity toward
all willing to give us military bases." [13]

When hostilities erupted in Korea in late June 1950, President
Truman's decision to send American troops to aid the South
Koreans was almost universally approved. This action, taken in
conjunction with two United Nations resolutions, was designed to
thwart the North Korean invasion across the 38th parallel. Stone,
who within six months would be asking the administration em-
barrassing and for the most part still unanswered questions about
the Korean situation, tried to see the Korean problem as the
prelude to a genuine understanding between the United States and
the communist powers. He accepted the premise of North Korean
aggression, though with considerable reservations, pointing out that
President Syngman Rhee had made numerous threats in the past to

unify Korea by force. It was not impossible to conceive of deliberate provocations by Rhee's troops to win needed American support for his own invasion plans. Nevertheless, Stone admitted that this hypothesis was "weakened by the sweep of the Northern invasion which would seem to be too well planned for a mere counterattack." [14]

The White House announcement of June 27, 1950, that President Truman had made a direct appeal to Moscow for aid in effecting a cease-fire was warmly endorsed by Stone, who perhaps naively hoped that Russia would seize this opportunity to usher in "the beginning of the end of the cold war." Somewhat caught up in his own optimism, Stone claimed that "it does not matter whether Mr. Truman was 'right' or 'wrong.' This is not a time for leftist demagogy but for focusing attention on the real political factors which will determine war or peace." [15]

Moscow's rebuff and the rapid disintegration of the South Korean army led to Truman's decision to employ large-scale American ground troops in defense of South Korea, in compliance with the Security Council resolution of June 30. As the war in Korea accelerated and as American commitments brought the nation closer to the cataclysm that Stone so dreaded, on behalf of the *Daily Compass* he issued an appeal for mediation by Prime Minister Jawaharlal Nehru of India in the "hope of preventing World War III." Claiming that Nehru was a man of stature, respected by both sides, and the spiritual heir to Gandhi, Stone singled him out to help end the Korean conflict before it engulfed the globe. "It is not possible," he wrote, "to exaggerate what may lie ahead if conflict spreads. Hundreds of millions may die, great cities become smoky ruins, men prowl like sub-human beasts in the lonely debris of a planet wrecked by atomic war." [16]

On July 13, Prime Minister Nehru, though not necessarily in response to Stone and the *Compass'* appeal, sent notes to both the United States and the USSR. Nehru issued broad proposals aimed at initiating discussions for a peaceful solution to the conflict. He called for the immediate seating of the People's Government of China in the UN General Assembly and Security Council. Russia had walked out of the Security Council in January 1950 over the Council's failure to seat the Chinese Communists; Nehru claimed that his suggestion, if accepted, would not only bring the Russians back but would pave the way for fruitful diplomatic contacts as well. In fact, on July 9 Stone had cogently argued himself that the seating of the New China on the Security Council "may be the last and only hope for peace." While the Russians welcomed Nehru's initiative, Secretary of State Dean Acheson, much to Stone's dismay, refused even to consider the Indian proposal, claiming subsequently that this would merely "transfer the center of attention and discussion from the aggression in Korea to who should represent China on the Security Council." [17]

The Russians finally did return to the Security Council in late July 1950. Ambassador Jacob Malik arrived with little besides vituperation, while American delegate Warren Austin, somewhat more polite, seemed more interested in scoring debating points than in resolving the conflict in Korea. With a political stalemate evident at Lake Success, Stone, at the behest of *Compass* editor Thackrey, left on a fact-finding trip to India, the Middle East, and Europe. In his own words, the purpose of the trip was "to see whether it was possible to form some neutral bloc or 'Third Force' which might keep the two great powers from each other's throats." According to Thackrey, the "Third Force" idea had been discussed at numerous editorial conferences at the *Compass* since the paper's inception in May 1949. The Korean situation afforded Stone and Thackrey, the most energetic advocates of this approach, a unique opportunity to test its possibilities.[18]

Between the time Stone left the United States in mid-August 1950 and the time he took up residence in Paris in mid-November as the *Compass'* chief European correspondent, events were rapidly changing the complexion and meaning of the Korean war. Within two weeks of the initial outbreak of the war, General MacArthur had established a beachhead at Pusan, thus averting the threatened liquidation of the retreating South Korean armies. American reinforcements and supplies aided in securing the area, and by early August MacArthur began to unravel his own plan for a counteroffensive. This plan, involving an amphibious assault behind enemy lines aimed at capturing Inchon and Seoul, was launched on September 15. Within two short weeks the general's strategy had turned the tide of the war against the North Koreans.[19]

The momentum engendered by MacArthur's military heroics necessitated a re-evaluation of America's war aims. Shortly after the outbreak of the war, Secretary of State Acheson had stated that the United Nations was fighting "solely for the purpose of restoring the republic of Korea to its status prior to the invasion from the North." [20] Thus, by late September 1950, with the last remnants of the North Korean army retreating north of the 38th parallel, the essential goals of the United Nations had been achieved.

But not according to President Truman, who recalled some years later that "I had already [September 27] given approval to new instructions . . . transmitted to MacArthur in which he was told that his military objective was 'the destruction of the North Korean Armed Forces.' " This decision was subsequently ratified by the United Nations General Assembly on October 7, 1950. One can question both the wisdom and propriety of the decision which led to eventual Chinese involvement in the war.[21]

Although Peking had warned since late September 1950 that it would deploy "volunteers" should North Korean territory be attacked, no one, least of all MacArthur, gave the warnings much credence. As UN forces advanced toward the Yalu River deep into North Korea, Chinese forces began to filter across the border. The intervention, according to one author, "was initially cautious and limited" and taken only after "all political means had been exhausted." [22] Nevertheless, by early November the Chinese entry had once again transformed the nature of the conflict.

While the world's attention had been riveted on the fighting in Korea, events of monumental significance were taking place on the political and diplomatic front. Secretary Acheson announced on September 12 that in addition to America's willingness to provide NATO with a supreme commander and substantial numbers of American soldiers, the United States proposed the creation of ten German divisions. While it can be maintained that the Korean War was not the only factor in this decision, it certainly would have been very difficult to secure either congressional or allied approval of such a measure without the exigencies brought on by the war. Only three days later, on September 15, State Department adviser John Foster Dulles publicly stated that the United States did not intend to restrict Japanese rearmament in the peace treaty on which he was working. Dulles believed that the Korean crisis would intensify the Japanese desire to remain in the orbit of the Western powers, and thus it was imperative that the treaty be concluded as soon as possible.[23]

As the outline of a powerful international coalition of anticommunist nations grew sharper, President Truman pressed Congress to triple defense expenditures to approximately $50 billion. At the same time, plans were drawn up projecting a 30 per cent increase in military manpower. In late June 1950, Truman decided to resume a direct role in the Chinese civil war by ordering the Seventh Fleet to the Formosa Straits. Thus the outbreak of the Korean War had convinced the administration to meet the threat of communist expansion head-on. Even with the enunciation of the Truman Doctrine and the Berlin blockade, for example, defense expenditures had been kept under $15 billion. To I. F. Stone, Korea could not be understood without taking these other developments into account.[24]

Stone's original doubts about the wisdom of a policy that tied America's fortunes to those of Chiang Kai-shek and Syngman Rhee was compounded by the cavalier attitude of General MacArthur and his apparent reluctance to follow the instructions of his civilian superiors. Stone contended in a dispatch from Paris on December 7 that MacArthur's famous "home-by-Christmas" offensive was anything but that. Demonstrating that the original large-scale contact with Chinese forces on November 6 had miraculously receded as the United Nations advance halted, Stone interpreted this to mean that China "acted to save her border." MacArthur's subsequent offensive "may prove to have started World War III," but at the least it was designed, according to Stone, to coincide with the appearance of the Chinese at Lake Success. Referring to a dispatch in the *New York Herald Tribune,* Stone claimed that an agreement between Great Britain and the United States calling for the creation of a "buffer zone" along the frontier between North Korea and Manchuria had been worked out in principle. This step, Stone felt, could have been the harbinger of a possible settlement. As tenuous as this assertion may have been at the time, there can be no denying Stone's claim that while MacArthur's "end-the-war" offensive did not end the war, it did cut short the talks at the United Nations.

Military historian Stephen Ambrose supports Stone's contention that MacArthur's actions forestalled the possibility of diplomatic agreement at Lake Success.[25]

Stone would subsequently amplify his allegations concerning both the timing and validity of MacArthur's action of late 1950 and early 1951 in his study *Hidden History of the Korean War* (1952). Expanding upon his *Compass* articles and still relying on such reliable sources as the *New York Times,* the *Herald Tribune,* the (London) *Times* and the (London) *Observer,* along with other respected English- and French-language dailies, Stone pointed out the considerable number of contradictions emanating from headquarters in Tokyo. The impression had been given that MacArthur's offensive had run into stiff resistance in the form of vast hordes of Chinese infantrymen sweeping across the border from Manchuria. The term "Chinese aggression" became a familiar part of America's political vocabulary in the next few months, but again Stone pointed out the vacuity of the phrase. A synopsis of dispatches from the battlefield convinced him "that the MacArthur forces seemed in a great hurry to withdraw while the communist forces seemed in no hurry to attack." [26]

Throughout December, as the United Nations retreated to positions south of the 38th parallel, the barrage of communiqués establishing the existence of an overwhelming communist force continued unabated from Tokyo. Stone believed that MacArthur was issuing these alarmist and exaggerated statistics in order to obtain permission to bomb China, a step that the general viewed as a prelude to the return of Chiang to the mainland.[27] Truman, fearing a possible world war, and despite intense pressure from elements in Congress, refused to accede and insisted at his press conference on January 4, 1951, that the United States would not bomb China, and that such a decision could be taken only after consultation with Congress and the United Nations.

MacArthur, whose desire to enlarge the war by going into China had been rebuffed by the administration and the Joint Chiefs of Staff, now claimed that his position in Korea was "eventually untenable." According to Stone, the desperate situation conveyed by MacArthur in his communiqués and in press releases was not only misleading but downright false. The visit to Korea by Generals

J. Lawton Collins and Hoyt Vandenberg of the Joint Chiefs of Staff substantiated Stone's contentions, as their report sharply contrasted with MacArthur's tales of woe. Within a matter of weeks the UN retreat was suddenly halted and a new offensive launched.[28]

In a series of reports in the *Compass* that began on February 13, 1951, Stone prepared an in-depth analysis of United Nations military strategy. He declared in the initial article that MacArthur had been "waging a phony war for six weeks, creating the necessary headlines for the condemnation of China as an aggressor . . . and keeping up the illusion of large-scale fighting . . . to whip up public opinion against China." He also took strong issue with what he called MacArthur's "scorched earth" policy, asking, "What right do we as Americans have to treat another people's country and countryside so wantonly?" Stone also pleaded for an end to indiscriminate saturation bombings by "rockets, napalm, and machine guns" of villages suspected to be "enemy-occupied." [29]

By the end of February, Stone's harsh criticisms of America's handling of the war had stimulated him to reassess the war's origin. Stone had certainly been aware of the guerrilla warfare and border raids initiated by both North and South Korean forces in the two years preceding the events of June 25, 1950. He knew also of the bellicose statements of South Korean President Rhee, who on more than one occasion had threatened to unify Korea by force. Nevertheless, not until this time did Stone begin to re-examine carefully the circumstances surrounding the war's initial phase.[30]

This re-examination, often raised in the form of questions, has in many people's minds unfortunately detracted from Stone's credibility as a commentator on the Korean War. Essentially his reconstruction of the events surrounding the June 25 crossing of the 38th parallel revolves around the precarious political status of both Syngman Rhee and Chiang Kai-shek before that date. Chiang had been driven from the mainland by the Communists, and it had been disclosed in January 1950 that the United States would not intervene on his behalf if his new stronghold on Formosa should suffer the same fate. In South Korea, Rhee, on the other hand, had been under increasing American pressure in the early months of 1950 to hold long-delayed elections. These elections, held on May 30, 1950, witnessed the emergence of a new National Assembly whose composition was at least 60 per cent independent. If not opposed outright to Rhee's intransigent refusal to negotiate the unification issue with the North Korean Communists, certainly the Korean legislators were more receptive to accommodations aimed at ultimate resolution of the problem. Then, too, the Japanese elections in early June had shown a majority hostile to continued American occupation and bases as well as to the concept of a separate peace treaty with the United States. At the same time, the admission of Communist China into the United Nations was gaining support and, according to observers at Lake Success, Secretary General Trygve Lie was soliciting votes for such action.[31]

Truman's action on June 27, 1950, establishing a protectorate over Formosa and providing aid for the Philippines and to the French in Indo-China, as well as to South Korea, not only transported the "containment" policy to the Far East but, in Stone's words, "he outbreak of war in Korea set in motion all that . . . the China Lobby, the rebuild Germany and Japan crowd and the advocates of preventive war wanted. In less than a year it started the mobilization of America . . . opened the prospect of American aid for the reestablishment of Chiang and brought closer a preventive war against Red China and Soviet Russia." [32]

Certainly these were the results of the steps taken by the Truman administration. But Stone went to far as to suggest that President Rhee in collusion with Chiang Kai-shek had deliberately provoked the North Koreans into attacking. He furthermore implied that certain high military officials, including General MacArthur, were aware of these machinations.[33]

While Stone expressed reservations regarding his own hypotheses about the war's origins, particularly because of the coordination and scope of the North Korean attack, he still felt that far too many important questions remained unanswered. He called for a congressional investigation of the circumstances surrounding the outbreak of the war and for answers to the following questions: Why did General MacArthur's headquarters receive a message to the effect that South Korea had attacked North Korea? What was the nature of the Dulles mission to South Korea in mid-June 1950? What was discussed during the talks held between General Omar Bradley, Secretary of Defense Louis Johnson, and MacArthur the

week before hostilities erupted? Why had the North Koreans attacked in June when according to MacArthur's own intelligence
staff's report of July 30, 1950, the North Korean army had only
six divisions of a projected thirteen ready for combat? [34]

Equally if not more important in Stone's mind were the questions
of why the Chinese entered the war and which side was responsible
for prolonging it. Regardless of what prompted American involvement, the thrust of United States policy had been radically transformed during the war. To Stone, whose initial response to the
war's horrors had brought pleas for mediation and resolution, it
became clear that the administration feared peace almost as much
as it feared a broadened war.

In his memoirs, Truman viewed the North Korean action as part
of a Russian grand design for taking over the world in piecemeal
fashion. Seen in this perspective, Truman argued, American inaction would have demonstrated American weakness and would have
meant that in the future "no small nation would have the courage
to resist threats and aggression by stronger communist neighbors."
Thus Korea was much more than an isolated incident; it was part
of the world-wide struggle against a Moscow-directed campaign of
conquest. Initially almost everyone, including I. F. Stone, believed
that Russia had instigated the Korean conflict. Subsequently, however, Stone revised this notion, claiming that "the failure of Malik
to show up at the Security Council suggests that the Russians were
taken unaware." This contention has had few advocates but is supported by Wilbur W. Hitchcock, a former member of the United
States Military Government in Korea. After analyzing all the possible effects of the North Korean attack on East-West relations and
the international balance of power, Hitchcock concluded "that the
Soviet Union in fact did not initiate the war, that the Soviet Union,
far from throwing the switch, was just as surprised as was the Western world when the North Koreans threw the switch!" [35]

Viewing the origins of the war in this new light, Stone, while
recognizing the President's political courage in firing General Mac-
Arthur, asked rather sardonically, "What is Mr. Truman going to
do about Mr. Truman?" There was little change, he pointed out, in
the American attitude toward China, little shift in the plans to rearm Germany and Japan, and little chance for peace in Korea.

Stone cogently argued in April 1951 that the Cold War psychology and its concomitant military expenditures "depend on some way to keep people terrified," and that "if there were no Korea . . . it would be necessary to find one." Stone would reiterate this theme over and over again during the next eighteen months. Not only was Truman fearful of political repercussions should the war be settled, but a settlement "would relax the tension on which [the] military program depends," and thus the dream of "negotiating from strength" would be shattered.[36]

Stone agreed that "President Truman's desire to avoid a [wider] war is undeniable," but Stone's own view of history had demonstrated that "increased tension, hate, propaganda and rearmament had always led to war in the past and almost certainly will in the future." In re-enacting these steps, "Mr. Truman and MacArthur have been going in the same direction, but at a different pace." This continuing criticism of administration policy was not without Stone's pleas to entertain seriously peace feelers from the other side.[37]

Attempts to resolve the Korean situation had been going on under the auspices of the United Nations since December 1950. Most of the proposals provided for Peking's admission to the United Nations, a step the United States was totally unwilling to accept, for, in the words of the administration, this would be tantamount "to offering a reward for aggression." A January 13, 1951, United Nations resolution introduced by the British, Canadian, and Indian delegations proposed five principles for a peaceful settlement of the conflict: (1) a cease-fire; (2) a political meeting for restoring peace; (3) a withdrawal by stages of all foreign forces; (4) arrangement for an immediate administration of all Korea; (5) a conference, after a cease-fire, of the great powers, including the Chinese Communists, to discuss Far Eastern problems. The administration reluctantly supported this resolution, according to Secretary Acheson, "in the fervent hope and belief that the Chinese would reject it (and they did) and that our allies would then return . . . to comparative sanity and follow us in censuring the Chinese as aggressors."[38]

In fact, most of America's efforts at Lake Success during this period were geared toward drumming up support for a resolution that would brand China as an "aggressor." Such a resolution was adopted on February 1, 1951, by a vote of 44 to 7, with nine abstentions. The resolution also provided for the establishment of a Good Offices Committee which was to continue the search for a peaceful solution to the dispute. It was this proviso and the assurance that the committee would be more than a pro-forma body that helped marshal the support of many nations, including both France and Great Britain, who by the time were becoming wary of American intransigence over the China issue.[39]

On March 20, 1951, after much of South Korea had once more been liberated, MacArthur was informed of the President's decision to attempt to begin peace talks with the communists. This decision, as Dean Acheson recalls, was made in response to "an idea strongly held in the General Assembly that further diplomatic efforts towards settlement should be made before major forces moved north of the parallel" once more. But before the President's intentions were made public, General MacArthur had put forth his own plan which undercut the President's proposed initiative. It included several threats of carrying the war into China should the Chinese field commander fail to surrender.[40]

In his memoirs, Truman claimed that MacArthur's deliberate undermining of presidential authority left him no choice but to fire the general. "I could no longer tolerate his insubordination," he later wrote. Still, it was not until two and a half weeks later, with the public release of MacArthur's anti-administration letter to House Republican leader Joseph Martin, that Truman finally acted. To I. F. Stone the delay was just more evidence that Truman was not serious in his desire for peace. He claimed that Truman "was prepared to forgive the truce offer by which MacArthur upset the applecart. . . . He was prepared to forgive that because the administration is reluctant to approve any proposals which went beyond vague generalities and banalities—to a concrete statement of aims opening the door to new peace talks." [41]

Peace talks finally got underway in early July 1951, in response to Malik's call on June 23 for an armistice. This proposal was soon accepted by the Chinese, and on June 30, at the direction of the President, General Matthew Ridgway, who had replaced MacArthur, broadcast to the Chinese high command American willingness to send representatives to discuss an armistice. The terms of a settlement acceptable to the administration had been presented by Secretary Acheson in testimony before the House Foreign Affairs Committee on June 26, 1951, when he emphasized that the United States would be willing to accept boundaries as they had existed before the outbreak of the Korean conflict.[42]

Stone was unenthusiastic, however, because he noted that General Ridgway was beginning "to act like MacArthur." Ridgway's late June visit with President Rhee, who had denounced the Russian peace offer and who for many months had actively opposed the Truman-Acheson policy of accepting the military realities of a divided Korea, seemed to Stone to be another example of the military trying to undercut chances for peace. Stone asserted that "Ridgway has taken over MacArthur's role as Rhee's High Protector" at a time when Rhee was declaring "that anything short of complete control of all Korea would be 'appeasement.' " [43]

While United Nations forces launched no new major offensives, by November limited forays by units of General James Van Fleet's Eighth Army had secured strong defensive positions in areas north of the 38th parallel. Difficulties in the negotiations certainly could have been anticipated, but no one expected the talks to drag on for two years. The initial obstacle was the location of the cease-fire line. The communists, in accordance with Acheson's statements, insisted on the 38th parallel, while the American position now demanded that the line reflect military realities. General Ridgway claimed subsequently that this important change had "Washington's full backing" and that "to have withdrawn our troops [south] to the 38th parallel, placing them along a line that could not have been held, would have been indeed a surrender." [44]

As it became obvious that the peace talks were not moving rapidly toward consummation, Stone reiterated his belief that the administration was prolonging the war in order to maintain high levels of military spending and forge ahead with the political goals it had often enumerated—the creation of an anti-communist coalition of nations that was to include a newly rearmed Germany, Japan, and Formosa, as well as America's NATO allies. His most caustic denunciation of the military came in response to an Associated Press interview with General Van Fleet in which the general was quoted as saying, "Thank God for Korea." The general's position was that Korea had been the catalyst that brought on American mobilization. "Where would we be," he asked, "if we hadn't had something like this to shock our people into action?" Stone solemnly answered, "At peace. . . . The dead would be alive. The maimed would be whole. The napalm-burned villages would be preparing for the harvest. We would have something for which to thank God." [45]

By early November the communists agreed to withdraw their insistence on the 38th parallel as the cease-fire line and accepted the American suggestion that the battle line should serve as the demarcation point. Stone, taking cognizance of the significance of the changed communist posture, called for the appointment by the United Nations of an intermediary to help resolve remaining problems. Claiming that "there is no need to go on with the killing of men on both sides while the exchange of prisoners, supervision of the truce and the political recommendations are being argued," he asserted "that both sides are so close" not only on Korea but on general arms reductions as well, that a "mediator of stature" could clarify the issues and bring the war to an early end.[46]

Much to the chagrin of General Ridgway and Admiral C. Turner Joy, chief United States negotiator, the administration ordered a truce line established. It conformed to the battle line and was to hold for thirty days, during which time it was hoped that an armistice could be concluded.[47] The truce talks, however, bogged down in an endless wrangle over air bases and prisoners of war, and by December 27 the thirty-day cease-fire period had elapsed and fighting was once more resumed.

Although some commentators claimed that the Chinese had signed the truce agreement merely to use the thirty-day breathing space to construct an impregnable fourteen-mile-deep defense network, Stone maintained that the United States was just as unwilling to bargain in good faith. "The fear of peace has been seeping from every pore of the government," Stone wrote on November 30, 1951. Peace which would bring a "relaxation of tensions" was what Washington seemed to fear most, for if tension relaxed how could the administration "get Universal Military Training and a 140 group air force and more money for the rearmament of Europe . . . push England and France into accepting more rearmament . . . , make them swallow the still hateful dose of German and Japanese rearmament if the guns die down and mankind relaxes . . . , [and] keep Red China out of the United Nations and the Seventh Fleet outside Formosa with the Republicans hot on the trail of that next election?" [48]

By far the most difficult issue at the peace talks was the question of prisoners of war. As President Truman has stated, "On January 1, 1952, our side proposed that all prisoners of war *who wished to be returned* [italics added] should be exchanged. . . . It was here, also, that I insisted that we could not give ground. . . . We will not buy armistice by turning over human beings for slaughter." While there were obvious humanitarian overtones implicit in the American position, Stone, quoting *New York Times* Tokyo correspondent Lindsay Parrott, claimed that the proposal represented "a new departure in the history of warfare." Stone pointed out that just a month before the enunciation of the new plan, Admiral Joy, General Ridgway, and Secretary Acheson had been feverishly denouncing the brutality of the communists toward our own prisoners. Stone surmised that the disappearance of the atrocity claims and the introduction of the concept of "voluntary repatriation" was another in the long line of ploys used in "delaying a settlement." [49]

The communists refused to concede on the repatriation issue, and Stone subsequently claimed that their position was well within the stipulations of the Geneva Convention which provided that "prisoners of war should be released and repatriated without delay after the cessation of hostilities." Stone concluded, after analyzing the statements of Admiral Ruthven Libby, one of the American negotiators, that the government was less motivated by humanitarian concern than by fear that the exchanged prisoners would shift the precarious military balance. American fears were perhaps justified considering the fact that as of December 1951 the Chinese claimed to be holding only eleven thousand prisoners, while 132,000 prisoners were being held by United Nations forces.[50]

By the end of April 1952 the truce talks had collapsed over the repatriation issue. The United States claimed that of the almost 170,000 prisoners it held, only seventy thousand desired repatriation. This figure was based on a screening process about which little information was publicly divulged. Stone called for the establishment of a "neutral commission of inquiry to investigate our camps and the methods used in screening prisoners." This same commission would act in a similar manner in the communist prison camps.[51]

Stone was still fearful of what he considered the military establishment's desire to "widen the war." Any breakdown in the peace talks could serve as just such a catalyst. He pointed out that Admiral Arthur Radford, commander of the Pacific Fleet, had on May 3 stated "that if the truce talks broke down, a naval blockade of China 'might be a way of stabilizing things out here.' " Stone's fears became more a reality with the replacement of General Ridgway, who became Allied Commander in Europe, by General Mark Clark in May 1952. As Clark recalls, his aim was "to make the stalemate more expensive for the Communists than for us, to hit them where it hurts, to worry them, to convince them by force that the price tag on an armistice was going up, not down." [52]

Within this framework the decision was made with Washington's approval to expand air attacks on North Korea. The most important target chosen for destruction was the Suiho Dam on the Yalu River, the largest hydroelectric complex in the Far East and North Korea's major source of power. The decimation of these facilities in a massive air raid of five hundred planes on June 23, 1952, was bound, in Stone's mind, to place another impediment in the way of a peaceful settlement. Pointing out that even in the early days of MacArthur's drive to the Yalu the hydroelectric installations had been respected, Stone contended that the bombing could only result in prolonging the war and intensifying the difficulties of the negotiations.[53]

As the 1952 presidential campaign unfolded, it seemed as if peace in Korea was an impossibility. The Democrats, wary of being called appeasers, could not resolve the dispute, while General Dwight D. Eisenhower, the Republican nominee, on more than one occasion had spoken in concert with the conservative MacArthur-Taft wing of the party. By October, however, Eisenhower began to concentrate on the issue of Korea. The climax of his appeal came on October 24, 1952, in a speech at Detroit's Cobo Hall, when the general pledged that if elected he would go to Korea in a personal search for a peaceful solution to the conflict.[54]

To Stone, this was just the green light the Democrats needed, for whether Eisenhower was sincere or not the Republicans were on record as advocating a peaceful settlement of the dispute. Thus the Democrats could not be considered "appeasers" if they implemented what Eisenhower advocated. In late October, Stone pointed out that "the gap between the Communists and the American military at Panmunjom is a narrow one," and with that in mind he proposed the following: "An immediate cease-fire . . . , and those prisoners of war whom our military list as not wishing to go home be turned over to a committee of Asian powers for rescreening and repatriation." He suggested that Pakistan, India, Indonesia, and the Philippines be given the task of settling the prisoner-of-war question. Three days before the election, Stone continued to advocate this approach, claiming that it would be difficult for the communists to turn it down while at the same time "it would show America's friends in Asia that we thought enough of them to use them as peacemakers." But, more important, it would demonstrate that "the Democrats really wanted to end the war." Such a plan was not forthcoming, and it is certainly doubtful that even its publication could have prevented Eisenhower's overwhelming victory.[55]

In addition to witnessing a debacle for the Democratic party, Tuesday, November 4, 1952, saw the demise of the *Daily Compass*. In financial straits since its inception, it simply ran out of money, and I. F. Stone found himself unemployed for the first time in his long journalistic career. His anti–Cold War orientation, combined with his ringing denunciations of Truman and Acheson at a time when liberals were lauding the two for their heroic efforts in firing MacArthur and in preventing the war from spreading, made Stone a journalistic liability to any paper in the jaundiced intellectual climate created by Senator Joseph McCarthy and his followers.

Stone decided that he would try to fall back on the fairly substantial personal following he had built in the previous decade and a half, and sell his reporting through the mails in his own four-page newsweekly. With only $3,500 in the bank (severance pay from the *Compass*) and various subscription lists to work from, by January 1953 he had rounded up five thousand subscribers. Stone promised the readers of the *Weekly* "a sober analysis of facts too often left out or buried on the back pages of the commercial newspaper." He would continue to employ the same techniques of reportage he had used in the past. He continued to denounce the stalled truce talks at Panmunjom and to call for an immediate cease-fire. Unwilling to be tied to views and opinions expressed in the past, Stone came more and more to have confidence in Eisenhower's quest for peace. (While today he realizes that only an Eisenhower, with his enormous prestige and personal popularity, could have resolved the conflict, Stone did not feel that way during the election campaign.) By mid-June 1953 he issued what he called a "challenge to the left" to "back Ike for Peace." [56]

Eisenhower did secure the armistice that Stone had so long desired. The Cold War was by no means over—the gigantic military budgets had in fact just begun. American-communist rivalry for domination in the Pacific was only in its incipient stages, but on July 27, 1953, the guns fell silent in the Korean hills and the shooting war had ended.

Throughout the Korean War, I. F. Stone's words went largely unread. The *Daily Compass* was always struggling to maintain a readership of about thirty thousand. In addition, Stone had a difficult time getting the *Hidden History of the Korean War* published. After a futile search in England and an unrealized promise of aid from Jean-Paul Sartre, it was only by accident that he secured a publisher. Walking in Central Park in New York City in July 1951, after his return from Paris, Stone ran into Leo Huberman, his old colleague on *PM,* and Paul Sweezy. The two veterans of the independent left had recently founded Monthly Review Press and were interested in publishing something on the Korean conflict from a radical perspective. When they asked Stone if he was aware of any possibilities he suggested they look over his own manuscript. Thus by sheer coincidence he found a publisher. The book appeared in the late spring of 1952 and was for the most part ignored. Only the *New Republic,* the *Nation,* and the *New Statesman* chose to review it. The intellectual climate of the day was, to say the least, not very conducive to a leftist critique of the administration. McCarthyism was rampant, and the only acceptable criticism of Truman embodied the notion that Truman was an appeaser who had rejected "victory" and accepted stalemate in Korea. Liberals such as Richard Rovere, Arthur M. Schlesinger, Jr., and James A.

Wechsler rallied to Truman's defense and embraced his doctrine of "limited war."

To Stone and the small minority who rejected the precepts of the Cold War to begin with, the issue was not one of "enlarging" the Korean War or "limiting" it, but of how to end both it and the Cold War of which it was a part. The war had intensified the rivalry between capitalism and communism, and had solidified the Pentagon's grip on American society. Only a complete rejection of the containment policy would satisfy Stone.

His own efforts toward achieving that goal were Herculean, given the obstacles that one outside of the mainstream of American politics faced in those tumultuous years. His sense of historical perspective never deserted him. Stone's main contribution to an understanding not only of the Korean War but of American politics as well may rest in the fact, as Murray Kempton has reminded us, that Stone "always remembers the official lie of last month which is contradicted by the official lie of today." [57]

Certainly some of Stone's contentions regarding the war's origins may be questioned, though there can be little doubt that the outbreak of hostilities and America's subsequent response enormously pleased MacArthur, Rhee, and Chiang Kai-shek. But in his analysis of the actual conduct of the war, the truce talks, and the war's political and diplomatic ramifications, Stone was at his penetrating best. This may have been due to his increasing reliance on documentary evidence in tandem with dispatches appearing in the West's most respected journals, rather than to his own appraisal of the motives and intentions of political leaders.

Admittedly, Stone did not subject communist conduct to anything approaching his rigorous scrutiny of American policy. Nor did he really offer any long-range blueprint for American policymakers to follow once the fighting ceased. Nevertheless, as Stephen Ambrose has recently written, Stone's work "remains the most carefully researched and ably presented history of the Korean War." At the very least, as one commentator has succinctly stated, "Stone certainly presents a case that should go to a jury." [58]

I. F. Stone has continued to hammer away at injustices associated with the continuation of the Cold War. In the 1960's he emerged as one of the most articulate opponents of the increasingly unpopular Vietnam War. The recognition so long denied him has finally come. To many, Stone personifies the spirit of independence and free inquiry which lie at the very heart of a democratic society. Perhaps, as historian Joseph Conlin has recently written, "If the world survives the conflagration which I. F. Stone fears and wields his pen to avoid, he will probably be remembered as the greatest journalist of his era." [59]

Notes

1. Henry Steele Commager, "Common Sense," *New York Review of Books,* XI (December 5, 1968), 3.

2. *Newsweek,* LXXI (January 22, 1968), 52. As Stone later recalled, the small monthly paper "was printed at the local weekly's job shop and it carried ads solicited on bicycle trips. . . ." See I. F. Stone, *The Truman Era* (New York, 1953), p. xii. Stone was a poor student by his own admission, having finished forty-ninth in a high school class of fifty-two. However, the University of Pennsylvania, according to Stone, was "obligated . . . to take graduates of high schools in neighboring communities no matter how ill-fitted." The description of Stone's college career is found in *I. F. Stone's Weekly,* May 19, 1969.

3. Personal interview, May 21, 1969, Washington, D.C. For Stone's written appraisals of Roosevelt, see *PM,* April 13, 1945, and "Farewell to F.D.R.," *Nation,* CLX (April 21, 1945), 436–437.

4. I. F. Stone, *The Court Disposes* (New York, 1937), pp. 12, 114.

5. I. F. Stone, "1937 Is Not 1914," *Nation,* CXLV (November 6, 1937), 495–497.

6. Stone had become Washington editor of the *Nation* in 1939; in 1940 he also became affiliated with the newspaper *PM.* For his account of the failures of the defense program, see I. F. Stone, *Business as Usual* (New York, 1941), pp. 8–9, 265–266.

7. I. F. Stone, "Planning and Socialism," *Nation,* CLIX (October 21, 1944), 493. See also I. F. Stone, "F.D.R.'s Post-War Program," *ibid.* (November 11, 1944), 578–579.

8. See *PM,* April 17, 1945, and I. F. Stone, "Farewell to F.D.R.," *Nation,* CLX (April 21, 1945), 437.

9. See *PM,* May 4, 1945; I. F. Stone, "Anti-Russian Undertow," *Nation,* CLX (May 12, 1945), 534–535; "Pie in the Frisco Sky," *ibid.* (May 19, 1945), 561–562, and "Trieste and San Francisco," *ibid.* (May 26, 1945), 589–590. Stone's assertions are substantiated in Gabriel Kolko, *The Politics of War* (New York, 1968), pp. 467–469.

10. I. F. Stone, "U.S. and U.S.S.R.," *Nation,* CLXII (March 16, 1946), 306–307. The Russian desire for security on her western borders is considered by a number of recent studies as the most important factor in Soviet post–World War II diplomacy. See Fred Warner Neal, "The Cold War in

Europe: 1945–1967," in Neal D. Houghton, ed., *Struggle Against History* (New York, 1968), pp. 25–27; Louis Halle, *The Cold War as History* (New York, 1967), pp. 10–19; and Adam Ulam, *Expansion and Coexistence* (New York, 1968), p. 383.

11. *New York Star,* August 25, 1948. Stone had serious reservations about Henry Wallace's ability to provide the Progressive party with strong and effective leadership.

12. Ted O. Thackrey, "The Compass Story—Some Lessons Learned in Failure," *Editor and Publisher,* LXXXVI (December 26, 1953), 50.

13. *New York Star,* January 21, 1949.

14. For an extended discussion of the factors surrounding President Truman's decision of June 27 to send American naval and air units to aid the South Koreans, and his decision of June 30 to commit American ground forces for the same purpose, see Glenn D. Paige, *The Korean Decision* (New York, 1968), *passim.* For Stone's views on the early phases of the war, see *Daily Compass,* June 27 and 28, and August 4, 1950.

15. *Daily Compass,* June 28, 1950.

16. *Ibid.,* July 2, 1950.

17. Leland Goodrich, *Korea: A Study of U.S. Policy in the United Nations* (New York, 1956), pp. 122–123. Stone's suggestion is found in the *Daily Compass,* July 9, 1950; Acheson's response is contained in Dean Acheson, *Present at the Creation* (New York, 1969), p. 419.

18. *Daily Compass,* October 3, 1950. A telephone interview with Ted Thackrey on October 27, 1969, provided additional information on Stone's trip.

19. Carl Berger, *The Korean Knot* (Philadelphia, 1964), pp. 114–119.

20. *Department of State Bulletin,* XXIII (July 10, 1950), 46.

21. Harry S. Truman, *Memoirs* (New York, 1965, 2 vols.), II, 411. Full text of the UN resolution is found in John W. Spanier, *The Truman-MacArthur Controversy and the Korean War* (Cambridge, Mass., 1959), p. 88.

22. Allen S. Whiting, *China Crosses the Yalu* (New York, 1960), pp. 117, 122.

23. See Martin Lichterman, "To the Yalu and Back," in Harold Stein, ed., *American Civil-Military Decisions* (Tuscaloosa, Ala., 1963), p. 645, for a discussion of the factors involved in the Secretary's announcement. For the background of Mr. Dulles' initiatives, see Frederick S. Dunn, *Peace-Making and the Settlement with Japan* (Princeton, 1963), pp. 105–108.

24. The increased expenditure would bring the armed forces to a level of 3.5 million men. See Cabell Phillips, *The Truman Presidency* (New York, 1966), pp. 330–331, and Edward A. Kolodziej, *The Uncommon Defense and Congress, 1945–1963* (Columbus, Ohio, 1966), p. 65.

25. *Daily Compass,* December 7 and 8, 1950. In the *Daily Compass,* Stone referred to British parliamentary debates in which spokesmen of both the left and the right had asserted that General MacArthur had violated instructions approved by both the British government and the State Department. For Ambrose's review, see Stephen Ambrose, "Destined to Be Ignored," *Baltimore Sun,* September 14, 1969.

26. I. F. Stone, *The Hidden History of the Korean War* (New York, 1952), p. 213.

27. *Ibid.*, p. 229.

28. *Ibid.*, pp. 248–249.

29. *Daily Compass,* February 13, 16, and 18, 1951.

30. See *Daily Compass,* June 27 and July 16, 1950. See also Richard Barnet, *Intervention and Revolution* (New York, 1968), pp. 66–67.

31. *Daily Compass,* March 6, 1951.

32. *Ibid.*, February 27, 1951. In a recent study, Walter LaFeber maintains that the Korean War cannot be understood without taking into account the administration's world-wide military and diplomatic maneuvers. Utilizing the statements of Secretary of State Acheson, LaFeber demonstrates that the Korean War provided a justification for the creation of alliances aimed at thwarting the perceived communist menace. A rearmed Germany was to be one of the cornerstones of this system. See Walter LaFeber, *American, Russia, and the Cold War, 1945–1966* (New York, 1967), pp. 101–103.

33. Stone, *Hidden History,* p. 52. In our interview, Stone agreed that the size and coordination of the North Korean attack tends to introduce limitations to his own hypothesis, which he nevertheless still accepts. Also see *Daily Compass,* March 13, 1951, and I. F. Stone, "Les Origines de la Guerre de Corée," *L'Observateur,* March 8, 1951, pp. 12–14.

34. I. F. Stone, "New Facts on Korea," *Nation,* CLXXIII (December 15, 1951), 517.

35. President Truman's comments are found in Truman, *Memoirs,* II, 379, 384. Stone's view that Russia did not bear responsibility for the outbreak of the war is found in *Daily Compass,* August 4, 1950. Hitchcock's conclusion is found in Wilbur W. Hitchcock, "North Korea Jumps the Gun," *Current History,* XX (March 1951), 142.

36. *Daily Compass,* April 16, 1951.

37. *Daily Compass,* April 17 and 22, 1951.

38. Spanier, *Truman-MacArthur Controversy,* pp. 180–193, and Acheson, *Present at the Creation,* p. 513.

39. Spanier, *ibid.*, pp. 196–197.

40. For material on the second liberation of Korea, see I. F. Stone, "Le Mystère Coréen: Combat contre un Fantôme?," *L'Observateur,* February 15, 1951, pp. 6–7. Acheson's statement is found in Acheson, *Present at the Creation,* pp. 518–519. MacArthur's machinations are described in Richard H. Rovere and Arthur M. Schlesinger, Jr., *The MacArthur Controversy and American Foreign Policy* (New York, 1951, 1965), p. 168.

41. Truman's claim is found in Truman, *Memoirs,* II, 501–509, while Stone's reaction is found in the *Daily Compass,* April 17, 1951. Stone was perhaps being kind calling MacArthur's statement a "truce offer."

42. See Truman, *Memoirs,* II, 516–517, 519. Also see Matthew B. Ridgway, *The Korean War* (Garden City, 1967), p. 182. A synopsis of Secretary Acheson's testimony is found in McGeorge Bundy, ed., *The Pattern of Responsibility* (Boston, 1952), pp. 284–285.

43. *Daily Compass,* June 27 and 28, 1951.

44. Ridgway, *The Korean War,* pp. 183–190, 203, and David Rees, *Korea: The Limited War* (New York, 1964), pp. 297–300. For a book that conveys the difficulties of the negotiations, see C. Turner Joy, *How Communists Negotiate* (New York, 1955), *passim.*

45. For articles accusing the administration of deliberately prolonging the

war, see the *Daily Compass,* July 30 and 31, August 1, 10, 21, 22, 23, and 26, September 6 and October 5, 1951. For Stone's specific response to the Van Fleet interview, see *Daily Compass,* August 27, 1951.

46. *Ibid.,* November 9, 1951.

47. Joy, *How Communists Negotiate,* p. 129.

48. *Daily Compass,* November 30, 1951.

49. Truman's views on the prisoner-of-war question are found in Truman, *Memoirs,* II, 521; Stone's response to the voluntary repatriation idea is found in *Daily Compass,* February 27, 1952.

50. *Daily Compass,* April 22 and 23, 1952. The prisoner-of-war figures are available in Rees, *Korea,* pp. 316–317.

51. *Daily Compass,* May 14, 1952. Stone subsequently pointed out in the *Daily Compass,* October 28, 1952, that the Chinese would have been willing to accept 110,000 as the number of prisoners to be repatriated.

52. *Ibid.,* May 6, 1952. General Clark's views are contained in Mark W. Clark, *From the Danube to the Yalu* (New York, 1954), p. 69.

53. *Daily Compass,* June 27, 1952.

54. See *New York Times,* September 5, 1952, for an account of General Eisenhower's Philadelphia speech. A comprehensive discussion of the Eisenhower campaign and its relation to the Korean question is available in Ronald Caridi, *The Korean War and American Politics* (Philadelphia, 1969), pp. 209–246.

55. *Daily Compass,* October 28 and 31, 1952. Stone, like many on the left, feared John Foster Dulles and the impact that he would have on the nation's foreign policy in a Republican administration. And while he recognized Adlai Stevenson's liabilities, he supported his candidacy rather than that of Progressive party nominee Vincent Hallinan. See the *Daily Compass,* September 30, October 1 and 2, 1952, for an interesting debate between Stone, advocating support for Stevenson, and former Congressman Vito Marcantonio, supporting Hallinan.

56. Sol Stern, "I. F. Stone: The Journalist as Pamphleteer," *Ramparts,* VI (February 1968), 53–55, contains material on the founding of the *Weekly.* The subscription list now numbers close to fifty thousand, making Stone, in his own words, "a practitioner of free enterprise" and an "honest independent capitalist." For Stone's comments on the war in the early part of 1953, see *I. F. Stone's Weekly,* January 24, February 7, March 7, April 4, May 3, 16, and 30, 1953. On his support of President Eisenhower's peace moves, see *ibid.,* June 13, 1953.

57. Murray Kempton, "Introduction," to I. F. Stone, *In a Time of Torment* (New York, 1968), p. ix.

58. See Stephen Ambrose, "Destined to Be Ignored," *Baltimore Sun,* September 14, 1969, and W. MacMahon Ball, "Some Questions on Korea," *Nation,* CLXXV (July 5, 1952), 15.

59. Joseph R. Conlin, *American Anti-War Movements* (Beverly Hills, Calif., 1968), p. 85.

by Athan Theoharis

The Threat to Civil Liberties

In the years immediately after World War II, the American people came to accept the federal government's right to restrict civil liberties in "national security" cases. Where federal powers with regard to civil liberties had been well defined and limited, the Truman administration in 1947 instituted a permanent federal employee loyalty program. Intended to avert acts of sabotage and espionage, and to satisfy exaggerated fears, the program was directed at the more nebulous issue of "subversion." It reviewed the political beliefs and associations of federal employees as one basis for ascertaining their "potential disloyalty." By resorting to a "national security" rationale, the Truman administration would after 1947 extend the scope of the program step by step.

Under the loyalty program, all federal employees, regardless of the sensitivity of their position, were first subjected to a preliminary loyalty check. If derogatory information was found, the individual would then be more fully investigated. On the basis of this investigation, departmental loyalty boards would determine whether or not to dismiss the employee. This decision would then be subject to review by a central board within the Civil Service Commission, the Loyalty Review Board. By March 1952, 20,733 employees had undergone this full field investigation. Of these, 2,490 left the federal service before their cases were reviewed; 11,679 were subsequently cleared; 384 were dismissed; and 2,293 cases were still pending. In addition, 2,756 employees who had initially been cleared were being reviewed as the result of Truman's April 1951 revision of the dismissal standard.[1]

The amount of energy and resources expended to secure the dismissal of 384 employees is striking when the reasons for dismissal are examined. The most controversial case involved that of John Stewart Service, a Foreign Service officer, who was denied clearance on December 12, 1951. Service had earlier been cleared seven times by the State Department loyalty board and by the Loyalty Review Board. The dismissal finding of 1951 was not based on evidence of Service's disloyalty but on a past association. Similarly, on December 15, 1952, the State Department loyalty board recommended the dismissal of John Carter Vincent on grounds of suspicion of his loyalty. At the time, the board conceded that it lacked evidence to find Vincent "guilty of disloyalty," but it justified its decision on the basis of Vincent's studied praise for the Chinese Communists and his criticism of Chiang Kai-shek during his World War II duty in China; his association with persons whom he should have known to be or had reason to believe were communists or communist sympathizers; and his failure, when head of the Far Eastern desk at State, to adequately supervise classified documents. The board concluded: "To say that Mr. Vincent's whole course of conduct in connection with Chinese affairs does not raise a reasonable doubt as to his loyalty would, we are forced to think, be an unwarranted interpretation of the evidence." [2]

The executive branch also tried during the postwar period to secure broader investigative authority for the Federal Bureau of Investigation, and to obtain legislation providing for the registration of the Communist party, elimination of the statute of limitations in espionage cases, waiver of an individual's right to claim immunity on the basis of the Fifth Amendment in national security hearings, and authority for wiretapping by the FBI in "national security" cases. All this added up to an increasing federal encroachment upon individual liberties. The powerful rationale for these actions—the need to safeguard national security—subverted traditional restraints on federal authority.[3]

The growing federal challenge to civil liberties in the postwar period was not inevitable, nor a product of an irrational body politic seeking security from Soviet espionage, nor the result of the impact of McCarthyism on American politics. The impetus to these procedures emanated from the Truman administration itself; the inception of the loyalty program in 1947 antedated McCarthy's emergence to national prominence.

Even if there was a need for a counterespionage program, could

the President have used procedures that would not have subverted
individual liberties? Or, conversely, why did Truman reject alternatives suggested by critics within the administration which could
have achieved security without unduly restricting individual liberties?

This essay will examine alternative proposals to and criticisms of
the Truman administration's loyalty procedures, advanced between
1946 and 1952. It will concentrate narrowly on criticisms from
within the administration, ignoring the more substantive and searching critiques leveled by the press, liberal congressmen, and civil
libertarians. A review of the decision-making process will help explain the nature of Truman's loyalty program and his rationale for
rejecting alternatives.

World War II, like World War I, had aroused anxiety among
Americans about existing federal safeguards against subversion and
espionage. Capitalizing on these anxieties, on July 2, 1946, a subcommittee of the House Civil Service Committee began an investigation of the federal government's loyalty and employment
practices. After hurried hearings the subcommittee concluded in
late July that existing federal procedures were inadequate and that
the problem required further study. On July 25, 1946, Congressman Jennings Randolph (Democrat of West Virginia), chairman
of the parent committee, submitted the subcommittee's report to
the President and recommended that he appoint a commission to
review federal procedures and standards to ensure "adequate protection to the government against individuals not primarily loyal to
the United States Government." [4]

The subcommittee's investigation had coincided with disclosures
in the *Amerasia* case and by a Canadian Royal Commission, both
of which dramatized the problem of Soviet espionage.* Attorney

---

* *Amerasia* was a journal of Far Eastern affairs edited by a prominent
radical, Philip Jaffe. In late 1945, under orders from the President, the FBI
had raided the offices and homes of the journal's editors and had discovered
reams of classified State and War Department documents. In 1946 a Canadian Royal Commission, after a study of security procedures during the
wartime atomic bomb program, documented successful Soviet espionage attempts that had relied on the Canadian Communist party to secure information about the program and its military secrets.

General Tom Clark and Civil Service Commissioner Arthur Flemming, in particular, by exploiting the subcommittee's report and this atmosphere of alarm tried to pressure Truman to authorize a commission study. Between July and November 1946, Truman temporized. He directed the White House staff to study the issue and assured Randolph, Flemming, and Clark of his serious interest in the matter. During this four-month period, available records indicate little evidence of opposition within the White House to the idea that additional safeguards were needed. Presidential assistant George Elsey did voice reservations in August about the ramifications of a proposed executive order establishing such a commission study, which had been drafted by the Civil Service Commission. The draft order, Elsey argued, was too broad in scope because it would grant to the proposed inter-departmental commission authority "to study questions which have little or nothing to do with the problem of disloyalty among government employees."

Political exigencies undercut Truman's apparent indecision. The principal factors were the Republicans' success in the November congressional elections and the likelihood that the Republican-controlled 80th Congress, exploiting the *Amerasia* case and Canadian Royal Commission report, would initiate a hostile congressional investigation of the executive branch's security procedures. On November 25, 1946, the President issued Executive Order 9806 establishing the inter-agency Temporary Commission on Employee Loyalty, and directing it to consider the findings and recommendations of the House Civil Service Subcommittee. The commission, whose membership was confined to administration personnel,* was specifically authorized to inquire into the existing standards, procedures, and organizational provisions for the investigation of federal employees.[5]

Limited by the specific questions posed in the President's executive order, and composed of individuals with an investigative back-

---

* The members included A. Devitt Vanech (Justice), John Peurifoy (State), Edward Foley (Treasury), Kenneth Royall (War), John L. Sullivan (Navy), and Harry Mitchell (Civil Service). The commission advisers included L. V. Meloy (Civil Service), Harold Baynton (Justice), Stanley Goodrich (State), Stephen Spingarn (Treasury), Kenneth Johnson (War), Marvin Ottilie (Navy), Lieutenant Colonel Innes Randolph (War), and Rear Admiral P. B. Niebecher (Navy).

ground, the commission never questioned the need for a loyalty program. It saw its purpose as devising procedures to ensure more adequate security.[6] The commission's principal sources of information were security-oriented; the only witnesses invited to testify before it were representatives from investigatory agencies (Department of Justice, FBI, military and naval intelligence, and President Roosevelt's Wartime Interdepartmental Committee on Employee Investigations) and two members of the subcommittee of the House Civil Service Committee. With the exception of Herbert Gaston, the chairman of Roosevelt's Wartime Committee, these witnesses maintained that a far-reaching, centralized loyalty program was gravely needed.

Based on his administrative experience as head of the wartime investigation, Gaston testified that the Civil Service Commission and the various department heads should attempt to screen out the "subversive, the dishonest, the incompetent and the unambitious." But Gaston warned against an overzealous program which concentrated on the political opinions of incumbent or prospective employees:

Examinations and investigations intended to exclude advocates of violent revolution from employment . . . are essential, but they need to be conducted with extreme care and wisdom lest they should have the effect of setting up bars against the employment of those who conscientiously advocate constitutional and peaceful changes in forms or methods of government. To give a screening agency power to refuse candidates or to an investigating agency power to exclude from the Federal service those who sincerely hold political views not consonant with those of the examiners and investigators would be to set up an intolerable tyranny. . . .

The past several years have seen a determined effort to confuse these matters and to attempt to coerce agencies of the government into enforcing unlawful standards of employment based on condemnation of political ideas. This is a dangerous trend—in my opinion far more dangerous than the slackness or ignorance that might permit the employment of a few advocates of revolution.

Gaston further belittled threats of revolution or internal subversion. In those few cases where employees were members of organizations "judged to be subversive," he observed, they "never presented any substantial danger to our government." Only at "critical" times,

Gaston said, would the employment of such persons entail real risks that warranted surveillance of their activities. He did recommend the establishment of two boards to ensure an adequate and fair appraisal of charges of subversive membership and advocacy— "one for advice and coordination, another to sit as a court of review. The latter could appropriately be composed of persons of judicial experience who would serve part time by holding occasional hearings for review of accumulated cases." [7]

Gaston's recommendations could have proven workable had they been tried, and they could have prevented the kind of pilfering of documents that had occurred in the *Amerasia* case. Gaston's plan would not have eliminated individuals who might have been susceptible of leaking information, but his emphasis was strictly on overt acts, not suspicions about possible actions. In addition, his recommended review board of "persons of judicial experience" would have avoided the conservative bias of Truman's Loyalty Review Board. Gaston's intent to remove the board from partisan pressures and to ensure fair treatment and not absolute security would have avoided the Loyalty Review Board's fears of conservative criticisms centering on the adequacy of the program and its purposes.

Gaston's recommendations were for the most part ignored by Truman's Temporary Commission. In its report to the President, the recommendations of which Truman incorporated in his Executive Order 9835 of March 22, 1947, establishing the loyalty program, the commission concluded that existing procedures were not sufficient to prevent persons of "questioned loyalty" from securing federal employment. It proposed pre- and post-employment checks, departmental loyalty boards to decide on dismissals on the basis of these investigations, and a supervisory, central board within the Civil Service Commission to review the decisions of these departmental boards. The commission also sought to balance security provisions by protecting the individual from unfounded charges and averting liberal suspicions of an FBI-directed loyalty program. Accordingly, it stipulated that the ultimate responsibility for denial of clearance should be vested in the department, and that the department or the Civil Service Commission should assume the primary investigatory role.

Truman's executive order specified this departmental responsibility and limited the FBI's function to checking the names of employees against its records. But the order did not specifically deny the FBI responsibility for conducting the full field investigation if derogatory information was uncovered during the preliminary departmental check. The order did stipulate that an accused employee would have the right to counsel during his loyalty hearing and would be provided with a list of charges in sufficient time and detail to permit the preparation of a defense. Investigating agencies were required to provide department heads with all investigative material and information, although they were permitted to refuse to disclose the names of confidential informants when "essential to the protection of the informants or to the investigation of other cases. . . . Investigative agencies shall not use this discretion to decline to reveal sources of information when such action is not essential." [8]

To ensure fair treatment to the individual, these proposed safeguards would have to be enforced. Significantly, the commitment to granting individual liberties priority over "security" considerations was not shared by Tom Clark, Truman's influential Attorney General. The establishment of the loyalty program, moreover, had provided an opening that was utilized by the Department of Justice and the FBI to maximize their influence and authority. Thus the Attorney General immediately sought approval for all field investigations under the new program to be conducted by the FBI. This objective conflicted with provisions of Truman's executive order and encroached upon the delegated prerogatives of the Civil Service Commission. As a result, Justice's procedure elicited protests from Stephen Spingarn (then Assistant General Counsel of the Treasury Department and a member of Treasury's loyalty board, who had been Treasury's representative on the Temporary Commission) and from Civil Service Commissioners Harry Mitchell (who also had served on the Temporary Commission) and Frances Perkins.

Spingarn saw the FBI tactic as a repudiation of the "carefully considered and much discussed decision of the Temporary Commission" and an attempt by the Bureau to increase its investigative funds at the expense of other investigatory agencies. Spingarn thereby recommended to his superior at Treasury, Edward Foley, that this matter be discussed at the "top level." There is no evidence to confirm that Spingarn's recommendation was considered by Foley or referred to the White House.[9]

Mitchell and Perkins, after repeated efforts, managed to see the President to protest this total delegation of investigative authority to the FBI. Although they based their arguments on the provisions of Truman's executive order itself, Mitchell and Perkins nevertheless failed to convince the President. A compromise was worked out, however, that provided for technical adherence to the order's provisions: departmental investigative requests would be directed to Civil Service for reference to the FBI for action.

Mitchell and Perkins had found little support for their position within the administration. Instead they had encountered the spirited opposition of the Attorney General, the director of the Bureau of the Budget, James Webb, and presidential assistant Clark Clifford, whose main counterarguments had been the FBI's superior efficiency. Webb also had favored delegating full authority to the FBI on budgetary grounds, noting that the Bureau already investigated all incumbent federal employees to determine if they complied with the noncommunist membership provision of the Hatch Act. Clifford had further advised the President:

I am fully cognizant of the dangers to our Civil Rights which we face in the matter of loyalty investigations, and I share your feelings of concern. It is precisely because of the dangers involved that I believe that the FBI is a better agency than Civil Service to conduct loyalty investigations for new employees; the more highly trained, organized and administered an agency is, the higher should be its standards.[10]

While these events were taking place within the administration, the new loyalty program was being criticized by liberals on grounds that it would violate individual liberties. On April 14, 1947, Philip Murray, president of the Congress of Industrial Organizations, protested direct to Truman that his executive order failed to ensure due process by not providing for the specification of charges against the accused employee or the opportunity for the employee to confront and cross-examine his accusers. Murray also expressed alarm at the provision empowering the Attorney General to list organizations as subversive without clearly defining that term. What grave emergency, he asked Truman, necessitated this order, for existing legislation had apparently provided ample security during World War II. In reply, Truman dismissed Murray's fears as unfounded and alarmist, and affirmed that the executive order had been carefully drafted to ensure that civil liberties would not be violated.[11] Murray had correctly pinpointed the adequacy of wartime safeguards, but his protest ignored what had been another of the President's primary objectives—to avert the Republicans' partisan use of possible cases of disloyalty.

Acting more indirectly than Murray, Robert Carr, the executive secretary of the President's Committee on Civil Rights,* on September 24, 1947, wrote the Attorney General about a section of the committee's forthcoming report dealing with safeguards for the "civil rights" of government employees. Conceding the necessity for a federal employee loyalty program, Carr also emphasized the need to ensure that individual liberties would not thereby be violated. The Civil Rights Committee, Carr reported, had drafted a section specifying:

> It is also important that the procedures by which the loyalty of an accused worker is determined be a fair, consistently applied, stated "due process." Specific rules of evidence should be laid down. Each employee should have the right to a bill of particular accusations, representation by counsel at all examinations or hearings, the right to subpoena witnesses and documents, a stenographic report of proceedings, a written decision, and time to prepare a written brief for an appeal. Responsible, competent, and judicious people should have the responsibility for administering the program.

Carr requested that Attorney General Clark draft a statement, to be included in the committee's final report, affirming his recognition of "the importance of each of the safeguards mentioned . . . and that it is your intention in so far as you have any control over the present loyalty program to see that each of these specific rights are safeguarded." Clark replied but sidestepped Carr's indirect criticisms of the established loyalty procedures. The Attorney Gen-

---

* A committee appointed by Truman on December 5, 1946, to investigate federal, state, and local law enforcement procedures and to recommend ways to strengthen law enforcement in order to safeguard civil rights. The committee submitted its report to the President on October 29, 1947.

eral did affirm his intent to require "substantial observance" of these recommendations, but he also added:

I recognize each of the listed rights and procedures to be very important to the protection of the civil rights of Federal employees in connection with the current loyalty program. It must be pointed out, however, that the right to subpoena witnesses and documents would require legislative implementation.[12]

Clark's response evaded the real issue of whether the FBI should be permitted to protect the confidentiality of its informers. This procedure had elicited protests from many officials within the administration and was the basis for objections raised by Assistant Secretary of the Interior C. Girard Davidson in a letter to Clark Clifford dated December 29, 1947. This letter was subsequently leaked to the press in early January 1948.

In his communication, Davidson conceded the need for a loyalty program, but not if basic civil liberties were sacrificed or an atmosphere of fear and intimidation created. Davidson saw no reason why court procedures requiring due process should not apply during the proceedings conducted under the loyalty program. An accused individual, Davidson thus argued, should be afforded the opportunity both to confront his detractors and to examine the government's evidence. In those cases where the FBI refused to disclose its sources or to permit its informants to testify, the department should be allowed to conduct its own investigation into the facts of the case. Davidson admitted that these procedures might lead to the employment of some disloyal persons. Yet the loyalty order must "not undermine the security of the individual and the integrity of the government service." [13]

Because Davidson's letter had been sent with the full knowledge of Secretary of the Interior Julius A. Krug, Clifford could not ignore this criticism of established loyalty procedures. He referred the matter to presidential assistant Donald Dawson, who subsequently informed Clifford that it had earlier been announced at Cabinet meetings that the FBI would be the only agency permitted to conduct loyalty investigations. When the loyalty program had been established, Dawson further reported, it had been recognized that the complete specification of charges, involving the revelation of confidential sources and the confrontation of witnesses, "would not be possible in all cases." Dawson defended this confidentiality as essential to the FBI's effective operation. He recommended that Clifford advise Davidson that the loyalty program could not function if its investigative machinery was "destroyed," and that all those responsible for the conduct of the program were committed to protecting individual liberties.[14] No revisionary action was taken; confidentiality remained the established procedure.

Rebuffed in this attempt to amend the confidentiality restriction, Davidson nonetheless retained his concern over the program's procedures. In early 1949 he wrote directly to Seth Richardson, chairman of the Loyalty Review Board, and suggested that the operation of the program over the past year had revealed the need for certain changes to safeguard individual liberties, minimize embarrassment to the individual, and expedite the conduct of the hearings. Davidson specifically proposed that after an individual had been cleared by investigation, his record should be wiped clean of any reference to it. Davidson asked further whether current loyalty investigative procedures should properly be terminated, arguing that they were intimidating individuals who held liberal views from entering the federal service. Specifically citing cases of improper investigations and interrogations by FBI agents, he also questioned whether the FBI should continue to conduct loyalty investigations or if this responsibility should better be delegated to the departments themselves. Finally, Davidson asked whether the Attorney General's list of subversive organizations should remain a criterion for evaluating individual disloyalty.

In reply, Richardson criticized Davidson's suggestions as impugning the wisdom of, and thereby opposing, the President's policies. Richardson defended the need for the program and emphasized the importance of the FBI's investigative work. Persons who opposed FBI investigations, he added, should properly be investigated on loyalty grounds. In response to Davidson's citation of FBI investigations into political questions, Richardson conceded that there had been unavoidable cases, but they were the exception. He advised Davidson not "to hamper or nullify the express aims of the President in relation to his Executive policies." (Strange to say, Richardson had at this time recommended a series of revisions to the established loyalty procedures. These included amending the standard for dismissal, increasing the Loyalty Review Board's review authority, and deleting that section of the executive order requiring the institution of a full review if it were discovered that persons had sought to deny constitutional rights to others by force or violence because the section was "foreign to the spirit and purpose of the loyalty program.") [15]

In a different vein, Secretary of the Treasury John Snyder had on April 15, 1948, protested a memorandum issued by the Loyalty Review Board on April 3, advising all executive departments "not to contact an employee under investigation, either orally, in writing, or by interrogatories" before the issuance of formal charges against the employee. Snyder requested an interview between Richardson and Treasury representative Stephen Spingarn for the purpose of reconsidering the memorandum.

By the board's proposed procedure, Snyder observed, the fact that charges had been made would remain on the employee's record even though he might subsequently be cleared. An employee might better be interrogated under oath before charges were made, Snyder affirmed, because "in some cases" this procedure might clear up doubts raised in the preliminary check and thereby foreclose further investigation. Treasury's practice, Snyder wrote, had been to keep a stenographic record of such an interrogation, to submit a copy to the employee, and to allow him a "reasonable period of time" to present additional material. Snyder added that Treasury did not object to permitting employees to bring counsel to such interrogations. The Secretary also informed Richardson that many other major agencies had "informally advised" Treasury of their interest in joining a request for reconsideration of the memorandum. Apprised of this interest, Snyder wrote, Richardson might wish to circularize all the major agencies to determine whether some might wish to discuss this matter with the Loyalty Review Board. Snyder concluded that his department intended to continue its established procedure until final action on his demand for reconsideration had been taken. Whether such a meeting was held cannot be determined on the basis of available documents. In fact, the memorandum remained in force but, significantly, Treasury alone of the various executive departments was not required to comply with its provisions.[16]

Stephen Spingarn meanwhile had his own doubts about the

loyalty program. As a special assistant to Truman for the 1948 campaign, with responsibilities for preparing position papers and coordinating internal security procedures, Spingarn had to deal with an internal security proposal by Secretary of Defense James Forrestal. He used the opportunity to appraise the conduct of loyalty investigations. Spingarn first advised the President to make a noncommittal reply to Forrestal's report; then he outlined his own views of the "major problem in the internal security field"—the FBI's ineffectiveness in dealing with communist subversion and espionage. This weakness, Spingarn argued, stemmed from the FBI's failure to recruit agents capable of infiltrating communist organizations, forcing the Bureau to rely on paid or volunteer informants. Spingarn also criticized the FBI's "unrealistic" conception of security in refusing to provide full and uncensored information about loyalty matters to government agencies. Accordingly, Spingarn urged Truman to appoint a task force of competent experts to appraise the effectiveness of the FBI's work and with the authority to review all FBI records and sources of information. "Such a mission," he observed, "should result in restoring control of the FBI to the Department of Justice and the Executive Branch where it belongs. Among other benefits, this would have the effect of suppressing further leakage of FBI reports to Congressional Committees in search of scare headlines." There is no evidence that Truman seriously considered Spingarn's recommendation. The proposal could have tightened control over FBI activities, and improved them, but it would undoubtedly have resulted in a confrontation between Truman and the Bureau and its conservative proponents in Congress and the news media.[17]

The question of reconsidering established loyalty procedures was raised anew in 1949 in response to specific investigative actions undertaken by the Justice Department and the FBI. The disclosure during the Judith Coplon case * that FBI agents had resorted to

---

* Judith Coplon had been an employee in the Department of Justice and had been arrested in early 1949 on the charge that she had given departmental secrets to a Soviet agent, Valentin Gubitschev. Miss Coplon was never formally convicted. After a lengthy trial and appeal, she was released on procedural grounds. The court held that the evidence resulting in her conviction had been illegally obtained through wiretapping. As one result, during the 1950's various congressmen would press for the enactment of legislation authorizing the resort to wiretapping in "national security" cases.

wiretapping, and the publication in open court of the contents of FBI investigative reports dramatizing the Bureau's reliance on hearsay testimony and gossip, created a public furor and resulted in demands by civil libertarians (the American Civil Liberties Union and the Americans for Democratic Action, among others) for an investigation of FBI and Justice Department practices. In this context, a suggestion that the President appoint a special commission to investigate the procedures and conduct of the loyalty program, advanced in 1948 and again in 1949 by Walter White (National Association for the Advancement of Colored People), Leon Henderson (ADA), Hugh Wolfe (Federation of Atomic Scientists), and Norman Thomas (Socialist party and Post–World War Council), was promoted by the White House staff. Another important impetus to the staff's support for this idea was a resolution proposed by Senator Harley Kilgore (Democrat of West Virginia) that directed Congress to establish a special commission to review executive loyalty proceedings.[18]

Picking up Kilgore's suggestion, on May 5, 1949, Spingarn (by then a presidential assistant, having been permanently transferred from the Treasury Department) wrote Clifford recommending that the President appoint a commission of outstanding citizens to review the loyalty program. Spingarn stressed the timeliness of such a review in light of the virtual completion of loyalty investigations of incumbent federal employees and the desirability of averting an inquiry by a congressionally appointed commission. Spingarn also emphasized the need to ensure a balance between freedom and security, adding that many liberals had consistently protested "flaws" in the loyalty procedures. He had already discussed this matter with Dawson. Dawson had concurred that certain changes were required and had recommended that Harry Mitchell of Civil Service discuss these changes with the Attorney General. As yet, Spingarn observed, Clark had not replied, but had agreed after further pressure from Dawson to expedite the matter and to make recommendations to the President. In view of the possibility that a presidential commission would soon be appointed, Spingarn urged someone— and not necessarily the President—to talk with Kilgore to convince him not to introduce his resolution.

There is no evidence that this meeting with Kilgore took place or that further consideration was given to establishing a presidential commission—a proposal opposed by both the Justice Department and the Loyalty Review Board. In fact, no commission was appointed in 1949. And in a June 16, 1949, press conference, Truman refused to comment on the suggestion that he appoint a commission to study the practices of the FBI; nor would he say whether he thought unsubstantiated allegations ought to be deleted from the loyalty files, though he did respond under questioning that "[J. Edgar] Hoover has done a good job." [19]

In December 1949 Spingarn again raised the idea of a presidential commission. The catalyst for his renewed suggestion was the administration's difficulty in securing clearance for the appointment of David Lasser to the Economic Cooperation Administration. Spingarn this time stressed the need for the Attorney General to note the time when he judged an organization "subversive." Present procedures, Spingarn noted, merely listed subversive organizations and did not delineate the time of this finding. Many organizations on the Attorney General's list had not originally been subversive. (Lasser's security clearance problem had stemmed from his having formerly been a member of an organization then on the Attorney General's list.) But the suggested commission study was again not implemented.[20]

During 1950 the commission idea was broached anew, though in quite different circumstances. The impact of Senator Joseph McCarthy's sensational charges of "communists in the State Department," the failure of the Tydings Committee * to disarm these charges (its report and investigation were dismissed by some as a partisan defense of a Democratic administration), and the increased popularity of "internal security" legislation brought about by the Korean War—these events led White House staff members to renew pressure on the President to appoint a special commission on "internal security and individual rights." The staff's recommendation received more serious study in 1950 than it had in 1949, being the subject of a special meeting at Blair House on June 22. The announcement of the appointment of such a commission was also

---

* An investigation conducted by the Senate Foreign Relations Committee, under the chairmanship of Millard Tydings (Democrat of Maryland), into the validity of McCarthy's contention that he had evidence confirming the existence of eighty-one known communists in the State Department.

considered in September during the drafting of a presidential veto message on the McCarran Internal Security Act.

In 1950 the rationale for establishing a commission differed from the objective of commission proponents in 1949. The main intent now was not to safeguard individual liberties from abuse but to rebut congressional and popular charges that the President's program was inadequate and ineffective. Owing to opposition from the Democratic congressional leadership, from the Loyalty Review Board, and from the Department of Justice, no action was taken to establish a commission until late November 1950. Then, obviously influenced by the demonstrated impact of McCarthyism during the congressional elections, particularly in the Illinois, California, and Maryland senatorial campaigns, the White House began serious consideration of such a commission. In January 1951 the President formally announced its establishment, to be headed by Admiral Chester Nimitz.[21]

Whereas the Justice Department had successfully averted a commission study in early 1950, it had also successfully stymied State Department recommendations to the administration for responding to Senator McCarthy. After McCarthy's February charges, State had urged the President to take the initiative and to recommend that Congress investigate the Senator's charges. Subsequently, State recommended that the President permit the Tydings Committee access to the confidential loyalty files of the eighty-one individuals that Senator McCarthy had specifically accused of being communists. Truman rejected both suggestions. Initially he dismissed the effectiveness of the McCarthy charges, and he consistently refused to create any precedent that might undercut the confidentiality of the loyalty files.[22]

Truman's directives to the Nimitz Commission, the character of its membership, and the actions and interests of the commission during its abortive existence reveal clearly that the President was more interested in ensuring "adequate" security than in safeguarding individual liberties. Despite rhetoric about the need to balance internal security and individual rights, the commission's operative premise was to remove public doubts about the President's commitment to an effective loyalty program. Thus, in his directive of January 23, 1951, establishing the commission, Truman stipulated that "the Commission shall examine the laws, practices and procedures concerning protection against treason, sabotage, espionage, and other matters affecting the internal security of the Nation; and the Commission shall consider the operation of and need for changes in such laws, practices, and procedures."

A second indication of this commitment was the timing of Truman's decision to amend the loyalty program's standard for dismissal.* In February 1951 Truman had refrained from accepting the Loyalty Review Board's recommended revision of the standard, arguing that before he would make any decision he would wait for the Nimitz Commission's report of the effect of this new procedure on individual liberties. An April 20, 1951, letter from Deputy Attorney General Peyton Ford to the President's general counsel, Charles Murphy, captured the sense of priorities that led Truman to change his mind and to revise this earlier procedure. (The President formally announced the revision of the loyalty dismissal standard on April 28, 1951.) Ford wrote:

In view of the considerable discussion regarding the proposed change and the implications that failure to act on this proposal is impeding the progress of the loyalty program, I believe further that fairly prompt action is desirable. Prompt action on this particular question is probably more important than a recommendation from Admiral Nimitz's Commission.

The membership of the Nimitz Commission was distinctly conservative, being composed of prominent clergymen, businessmen, and citizens of unquestioned anti-communist views.† This conservatism was illustrated in the commission's decisions to seek co-

---

* Thus, instead of the original requirement that dismissal be based on the existence of "reasonable grounds" for believing that the individual was "disloyal," the 1951 revision provided for dismissal if "reasonable doubt" existed for believing that the individual was not "loyal."

† These included Chester W. Nimitz (a retired admiral), John A. Danaher (a conservative Republican, formerly senator from Connecticut), Russell C. Leffingwell (executive, J. P. Morgan & Co.), Charles Silver (executive, American Woolen Co.), Harvey S. Firestone, Jr. (executive, Firestone Tire and Rubber Co.), Emmet M. Walsh (Catholic bishop, South Carolina), Karl M. Block (Episcopalian bishop, California), and Anna Lord Strauss (past president, League of Women Voters).

operative relations with the House Committee on Un-American Activities and the Americanism Commission of the American Legion (but not the ACLU or the ADA), to secure information from the major industrial corporations about their security programs, and to accept uncritically the Loyalty Review Board's recommended revision of the standard for dismissal. A further insight into this conservatism and the members' primary commitment to security considerations as opposed to individual liberties is a March 20, 1951, letter from commission member R. C. Leffingwell to Nimitz:

I think employee tenure and civil rights generally have to be subordinated to the right of the nation to defend itself against Russia. . . . Freedom of speech and freedom of thought do not include freedom for those who have surrendered their freedom of thought and speech to the Kremlin, to parrot the teachings of the Kremlin in our schools and colleges and newspapers and over the air. . . . [I] will not change my mind about the primary right and duty of the nation to defend its security in the present emergency even though that necessitates infringement of our cherished civil liberties.[23]

Truman's hesitancy to establish a commission in 1949 or 1950, and his subsequent handling of the Nimitz Commission, were consistent with his unwillingness to expend political capital simply to protect individual liberties. Such an opportunity had occurred in 1949 when Senator Joseph O'Mahoney (Democrat of Wyoming) had proposed to amend the Independent Offices Appropriation Bill to preclude the awarding of Atomic Energy Commission fellowships to any person not cleared by an FBI loyalty investigation. O'Mahoney's amendment would have extended existing clearance requirements to include non-secret research. Reacting to this proposal, Spingarn had urged Clifford to have the President during his July 28 press conference formally express opposition to this "dangerous" amendment, symptomatic of an "almost hysterical" unreason on loyalty and security matters. The passage of the amendment, Spingarn had warned, would create a dangerous precedent that could be extended to other non-secret federal programs. But the President made no such comment during his July 28, August 4, August 11, or August 18 press conferences. There is no evidence that Clifford informed Truman about Spingarn's suggestion, or that Spingarn's fears were shared within the administration. O'Mahoney's amendment was eventually approved by the Senate, accepted by the House, and signed into law by the President on August 24, 1949.[24]

Of far greater substance and complexity was a confrontation between the White House staff and the Department of Justice which emerged in early 1950. It concerned the department's actions in two spheres: first, the department's efforts to secure congressional passage of an alien deportation bill (H.R. 10), and, second, the White House staff's uncovering of the process by which Attorney General Clark had earlier obtained presidential approval for an extension of FBI wiretapping authority.

The wiretapping issue surfaced again when disclosures during the Judith Coplon case indicated that FBI agents had wiretapped Miss Coplon's telephone before and after her arrest—but then had denied resorting to wiretapping when under oath before the grand jury, and inexplicably had destroyed the records of the taps during the interim. Civil libertarians had vociferously condemned these practices as unconstitutional and in violation of Section 605 of the Communications Act of 1934.

Attorney General J. Howard McGrath, Clark's successor, attempted to neutralize these criticisms in January 1950. He defended the FBI's resort to wiretapping as necessary to national security, denied that there had been any concealment except "in limited cases with the express approval of the Attorney General," and emphasized that the Justice Department had simply followed the policy and procedures established by President Roosevelt. At the same time, Assistant Attorney General Peyton Ford asked Truman to permit the Department of Justice to publish the text of Roosevelt's May 21, 1940, memorandum to Attorney General Jackson authorizing FBI agents to wiretap during investigations of subversive activities. Publication of the Roosevelt directive, Ford stated, would be useful in answering critics who had accused the FBI of wiretapping without proper authority. Ford urged Truman not to publish his own much broader wiretapping directive of 1946, arguing that by releasing only Roosevelt's memorandum Truman would "protect" himself and avoid having to make public his own directive.

Ford's request led presidential assistant George Elsey to investigate the matter more fully. After studying the records, he advised Truman that FBI wiretapping practices had been criticized in the past, yet it had not been necessary to publish confidential directives. More important, current FBI wiretapping practices had been conducted pursuant to Truman's broader directive of 1946 and not the one of 1940. Elsey further reported that when Attorney General Clark had first secured Truman's assent to the 1946 directive, he had failed to include a key sentence in his quote from Roosevelt's 1940 directive, and that the language of Truman's order was "a very far cry" from Roosevelt's. Elsey submitted for the President's consideration the texts of the 1940 and 1946 directives. He directed Truman's attention to the first paragraph of Clark's letter, which quoted from Roosevelt's directive, and contrasted this with Roosevelt's order, noting the omission of the final sentence, italicized below:

You are, therefore, authorized and directed in such cases as you may approve, after investigation of the record in each case, to authorize the necessary investigating agents that they are at liberty to secure information by listening devices direct to the conversation or other communications of persons suspected of subversive activities against the Government of the United States including suspected spies. *You are requested furthermore to limit these investigations so conducted to a minimum and to limit them insofar as possible to aliens.*

On the basis of this discovery, Elsey advised Truman to deny Justice's request for permission to release the Roosevelt directive, to refuse to comment on wiretapping at any press conference but to refer all questions to the Attorney General, and to consider rescinding his 1946 directive.

In response to this report, the President asked Elsey and Murphy on February 2, 1950, to prepare a directive to the Attorney General canceling the current wiretapping authorization and returning to the 1940 authorization. Murphy appointed Elsey and Spingarn to implement the President's request.[25] We cannot determine if Truman's February 2 recommendation was acted upon and the 1946 directive rescinded. If so, the document remains classified. But the President might also have reconsidered his February 2 decision, sensing adverse congressional reaction or pressure from the Department of Justice.

The issue of Justice's wiretap policy coincided with another controversy of early 1950 over the department's pressure for passage of H.R. 10. This bill, introduced in 1949 by Congressman Samuel Hobbs (Democrat of Alabama), provided for the forced detention of aliens against whom warrants of deportation had been issued. Until informed of the President's opposition, on grounds of the bill's infringement of individual liberties, the department had independently endorsed the bill. Even when apprised in February 1950 of presidential opposition, the department continued to support the bill and moreover pressed for reconsideration of the President's opposition. On May 16, 1950, Spingarn and Murphy, in light of their earlier conflicts with Justice over the department's internal security recommendations and outspoken opposition by prominent liberals to H.R. 10, urged Truman to review Justice's internal security policies. They advised the President:

Justice policy on internal security legislation normally originates in the security branches of the Department, the FBI and the Immigration Service. . . . their outlook is naturally and properly limited to the security field in which they work. They are inclined to resolve all doubts in favor of security. . . .

In the light of the above considerations, we suggest that you call in the Attorney General and Peyton Ford and tell them:

. . . 3) Your wish that all internal security proposals be carefully scrutinized by the civil rights branch of Justice (or other appropriate Justice personnel) as well as by the security branches, and that the Attorney General satisfy himself that a proper balance has been struck between internal security and individual rights before Justice sponsors or approves any internal security measure.

The President accepted this recommendation, motivated in part by his distress over Justice's continued support for H.R. 10 and the wiretapping issue. He instructed Matthew Connelly, his appointments secretary, to contact McGrath and arrange an interview between the Attorney General and Spingarn. This meeting was held on May 19. As a result, McGrath acceded to the Spingarn-Murphy recommendations.[26]

For a time this procedure was effective. Thus on May 23, 1950, Peyton Ford advised Congressman Emanuel Celler (Democrat of New York), chairman of the House Judiciary Committee, that although the Justice Department had long supported legislation along the lines of H.R. 10, "in view of certain recent decisions of the courts, the Department is now giving [the matter] further consideration." Ford advised Celler that Justice intended to study the whole problem of subversion and undesirable aliens and report its findings to the committee by the following January. Ford sent a copy of this letter to Murphy for clearance. In response, Murphy and Spingarn advised him to add a section stating specifically that consideration of H.R. 10 should be deferred pending the conclusion of the Justice study.[27]

The outbreak of the Korean War accentuated congressional and popular anxieties about internal security and stymied this restraint. Thus, on July 17, Spingarn learned from Congressman John McCormack (Democrat of Massachusetts), the Democratic majority whip, that H.R. 10 had passed the House. When Spingarn informed McCormack that the President opposed the measure, McCormack expressed surprise. He thought Truman had approved the bill. Spingarn expressed irritation, as Justice had been instructed to "take steps to kill the bill." The bill, amended somewhat in the Senate, eventually passed and was signed by the President in August 1950.[28]

After June 1950 the White House staff did little more than protest the activities of the Justice Department, despite assurances of presidential support. Although opposed to what it considered vague and sweeping Justice-sponsored legislation, the staff was unable to impose effective constraints on the department's legislative activities. Uneasy, yet feeling impotent, the White House staff simply sought to hold the line. Presidential assistant Richard Neustadt forcefully conveyed this resignation in a memorandum commenting on proposed additions to the administration's urgent list of legislation. The outbreak of the Korean War had led the White House staff to consult various executive departments to determine if they wished to upgrade or revise old measures or introduce new proposals. Reporting having contacted State, Defense, Budget, Treasury, and the National Security Resources Board, Neustadt added:

I would let it [the urgent list] rest for the time being. I have not checked Justice for fear they *would* want to upgrade the priority of one or another of the internal security bills. (Congress will do enough of that on Justice's urging, if any, without White House intervention.)

Roger Jones, of the Bureau of the Budget, echoed these sentiments. Commenting on a proposed Justice Department bill which waived the right of bail in national security cases, Jones admitted that his initial reaction had been to "recoil from the proposal as being inconsistent with our traditions and our heritage." But no one, he added, wanted to challenge Justice by opposing the legislation. Jones urged Murphy to consult with Peyton Ford about reconsidering the proposal. Subsequently, Ford agreed to defer action "in light of the imminence" of the establishment of the Nimitz Commission and the commission's proposed responsibility for reviewing such questions.[29]

The anxieties over security procedures increased significantly during 1951 and contributed to the administration's reappraisal of current classification policies. From July on, the President had under study a draft executive order extending classification restrictions to nonsecurity federal agencies. The impetus for this proposed extension had been the frequency of leaks to the press by department personnel of what many administration officials considered critical national security information. Truman eventually issued this order on September 25, 1951, aware of the inevitability of protests from the press and Congress. In defense of the order, he emphasized the need "to strengthen our safeguards against divulging to potential enemies information harmful to the security of the United States."[30]

Almost immediately the leadership and a majority of Senate Republicans protested this "censorship" and pledged their support to any federal employee who might be victimized "as a result of the exercise of his constitutional right of freedom of speech." In a more temperate protest, the Associated Press Managing Editors' Association adopted a resolution criticizing the order's restrictions on freedom of the press and the public's right to information. The editors' resolution specifically condemned the order's failure to define classification terms, its absence of clear guidelines by which employees could govern their actions, its cession of review powers to the National Security Council, and its failure to discourage abuses by executive officials. The executive order, the resolution added, "has been issued without showing any necessity . . . without the careful public discussion and honest debate that ought to precede any departure from demonstrated methods." The editors urged the President to rescind his order and, if the need for more rigorous classification could subsequently be "demonstrated," institute within the civilian departments "a system of security consistent with the right of the people to be informed fully about their government." [31]

Truman responded to the editors' resolution and righteously defended the order as an honest attempt to resolve "a problem that is important to the survival of the United States." He dismissed these criticisms as misrepresentations and reprimanded the editors for passing up "this opportunity to serve the cause of freedom of information in the dangerous days when the safety of our country and the freedoms for which it stands are in peril." [32]

Meanwhile, another public furor was building over the administration's revised loyalty dismissal standard. The specific catalyst was a December 1951 announcement by the Loyalty Review Board. The board advised the various executive departments that it intended to review those cases of employees who had formerly been cleared, on the basis of the 1947 dismissal standard, when their clearance resulted from the board's reversal of a department dismissal decision. Presidential assistant Donald Hansen was instructed to study the basis for the board's December directive.

In his report, Hansen noted that in February 1951 the Loyalty Review Board had recommended the revision of the 1947 dismissal standard, but at the time had not given any explanation "other than to cite the war in Korea and the President's declaration of emergency." On April 20, 1951, Hansen reported, Deputy Attorney General Peyton Ford had also urged adoption of this new standard. Ford had affirmed that the new standard would not change the decisions in loyalty cases but "would provide greater uniformity of loyalty decisions." Hansen then expressed his own concern about the vagueness of the revised standard's reference to "reasonable doubt" as the criterion for dismissal. He specifically contrasted the adverse application of the "reasonable doubt" standard in loyalty dismissal hearings (whereby small areas of doubt prevailed over overwhelming evidence of loyalty) to criminal proceedings where doubt was resolved in favor of the accused. Hansen added that the Loyalty Review Board had not justified its December 1951 directive, and had inaccurately implied that President Roosevelt had instituted a similar procedure during the conduct of his wartime loyalty program. Hansen urged the President to take advantage of the John Stewart Service case to appoint a panel of distinguished jurists to study the "reasonable doubt" standard. He did not, however, advise the President to tighten loyalty procedures as he recognized the political ramifications of such a decision: "As to the loyalty program, I believe quite coldly that no White House action should be taken pending any developments which would make such action desirable, propitious, and timely from a public relations standpoint." [33]

In essence, the President followed this advice. Thus, when asked at his January 31, 1952, press conference about the change in the dismissal standard, and whether he had intended automatically to reopen all cases that had been cleared on appeal, Truman evaded these questions. The changed standard, he stated, had been adopted pursuant to the recommendation of the Loyalty Review Board and the Civil Service Commission. He tersely advised reporters to read the press release issued at the time of the announcement of the revised standard.[34]

This strategy of presidential inaction proved politically untenable. In April 1952 the White House received another Loyalty Review Board request to extend the loyalty check procedures to include presidential appointees to advisory boards (civil aviation, international development, and so forth). These appointees were generally prominent civilian experts and had been exempt from the loyalty program's requirements that all federal employees be fingerprinted and subjected to investigation before assuming office. Appraising this recommended change, Hansen described the requirement of a complete loyalty investigation as a "waste of time and money" and an "unnecessary nuisance and source of embarrassment." He feared that such distinguished citizens, who already had to be importuned, might be even less willing to accept presidential appointment because of this requirement and its implied insult. Hansen supported a pre-employment check into the character and qualifications of the appointee, but opposed a follow-up investigation unless requested by the White House. He maintained that the responsibility for these investigations should be confined to the White House loyalty board. The only reason for a loyalty investigation of presidential appointees, Hansen argued, would be to "protect" the President and the appointee from "smear attacks." [35]

The Loyalty Review Board again raised the issue of presidential appointees in November 1952. Hiram Bingham, Richardson's successor as chairman of the board, requested a meeting between Dawson and representatives from Civil Service, Justice, the FBI, and the Loyalty Review Board to discuss extending the coverage of the loyalty proceedings to include presidential consultants. Under the President's Executive Order 9835, Bingham emphasized, all federal employees were to have been covered, and thus "consultants who have any contact with policy making or with scientific or technical studies having any relationship to the national defense should not be excluded from the investigative requirements of the loyalty program." Dawson acceded to the suggestion. Accordingly, he advised Bingham to terminate these exclusions and conduct the necessary investigations.[36]

By 1953 a loyalty program had evolved that was distinctly different from what had existed in 1947—one vastly more restrictive of individual liberties. President Eisenhower would subsequently extend these procedures by Executive Order 10450 of April 27, 1953. His order would direct the attention of investigators and reviewers toward "any behavior, activities, or associations which tend to show that the individual is not reliable or trustworthy." It would also extend the right of summary dismissal from "sensitive" departments (Defense and State) to "all other" departments and agencies, and provide for the denial of clearance if an investigation found that an individual's employment was not "clearly consistent with the interests of national security." The vague and sweeping nature of these proscriptions would increase areas of abuse and create a stifling, repressive atmosphere within the federal service.[37]

The form and extension of the Truman administration's loyalty program partially resulted from the President's failure to consider seriously libertarian criticisms of the loyalty procedures. Critics within the administration were reluctant to press for the adoption of their recommendations. But why were their criticisms, which correctly pinpointed the adverse effect of established loyalty procedures on individual liberties (as scholars Eleanor Bontecou, Thomas Emerson, Ralph Brown, William Berman, and Harold Chase have demonstrated),[38] not considered or implemented? Why didn't the President and his principal White House staff advisers, Clark Clifford through 1949 and Charles Murphy thereafter, when informed of the program's abuses—by Carr in 1947, Davidson in 1948 and 1949, Spingarn in 1947, 1948, 1949, and 1950, and Hansen in 1952—institute corrective measures, reappraise procedures, or end certain practices? Indeed, as Hansen noted in 1952, the John Stewart Service case had provided an opportunity for reviewing the "doubtful loyalty" standard, yet no serious attempt was made to alter the direction of the program. Moreover, the dismissal of Service on loyalty grounds indirectly lent support to Senator McCarthy's charges of administration laxity. (Service had been one of the eighty-one State Department employees whom McCarthy in 1950 had identified as being communists before the Tydings Committee and on the floor of the Senate.)

This failure can be attributed partly to inefficient or indifferent staff work, especially during the early years of Truman's presidency from 1945 through 1948. During this period the Department of Justice had been able to secure adoption of its recommendations on wiretapping and loyalty investigation. A capable, vigilant staff might have kept the President better informed about these practices and about the ramifications of particular decisions for individual liberties. From 1945 to 1948, moreover, there was no real champion of civil liberties within the immediate White House staff or Truman's close circle of advisers. After 1948 a more efficient staff was developed, and because of the inclusion of Stephen Spingarn it was more concerned about civil liberties. By then, however, the outbreak of the Korean War and the momentum of procedures established earlier was too great to reverse.

Of far greater importance in the adoption of repressive policies were the shortsightedness and priorities of the President and, less so, his staff advisers. Pragmatists, concerned about partisan criticisms, and hesitating to confront the Department of Justice and the FBI, the President and his staff temporized and more often opted for security measures than safeguards for individual liberties. Under pressure they seemed more interested in firmly establishing their anti-communism than in promoting controversial measures that would have preserved civil liberties. At the same time, when they did act, and despite their rhetorical expressions of concern about civil liberties, their reason was political expediency and their objective to restore public confidence in the administration's commitment to effective loyalty measures. This is pointedly reflected in the timing of presidential decisions to appoint the Temporary Commission in 1946, the Nimitz Commission in 1951, or to impose confidentiality on congressional requests for employee loyalty files in 1948.

The President, and even his more liberal advisers, never questioned the need for a loyalty program, and consistently sought to blunt criticisms of the administration's commitment by taking "preventive" action. The extension of the loyalty program to cover consultants and presidential appointees in 1952, and the revision of the dismissal standard in 1951 are good cases in point. Nor was the President willing to risk political injury by forcefully defending individual liberties.

Despite the furor precipitated by congressional conservatives who since the 1930's had assailed the loyalty of federal personnel, there is serious doubt that any loyalty program was needed during the Cold War period. The anxieties about Soviet espionage aroused by the *Amerasia* case could have been effectively resolved by tighter administrative control of classified information. Gaston's suggestion of an alert counterintelligence service would have met the real threat of Soviet espionage. Since the 1930's the FBI had surveyed the political activities and associations of federal employees. Should there have been any attempt to pass government secrets to Soviet agents, as Judith Coplon presumably had, the individual could have been apprehended and the information intercepted. The Coplon case also dramatizes the limited effectiveness even of Truman's more extended program, for Miss Coplon had been cleared under the President's established loyalty procedures.

In sum, then, a parochial, pragmatic, and partisan administration, lacking in commitment, indecisive under pressure, failed to provide the leadership during the post–World War II years necessary to thwarting conservative demands for restrictions on individual liberties, or to averting the discrediting of radicalism and reform. It purposefully ignored or rejected alternatives intended to improve the loyalty program. Eventually, Truman's leadership contributed to a repressive political climate and some of the most hideous moments of the Cold War at home.

Notes

The author expresses his appreciation to the Truman Institute for National and International Affairs for support of his research, to Marquette University for typing assistance, particularly Miss Ann Koenig, and to Thomas Paterson, Ivan Dee, and Nancy Theoharis for editorial assistance.

1. U.S. Civil Service Commission, Loyalty Review Board Report on Loyalty Program, March 31, 1952, Loyalty Review Board, Martin Friedman Files, Truman Library.

2. Ralph Brown, *Loyalty and Security: Employment Tests in the United States* (New Haven, 1958), p. 368. Press Release, Department of State, December 15, 1952, China File, Charles Murphy Papers, Truman Library.

3. For a detailed discussion of the development of the loyalty program, see my "The Escalation of the Loyalty Program," in Barton J. Bernstein, ed., *Politics and Policies of the Truman Administration* (Chicago, 1970), and *Seeds of Repression: Harry S. Truman and the Origins of McCarthyism* (Chicago, 1971). See also Eleanor Bontecou, *The Federal Loyalty-Security Program* (Ithaca, N.Y., 1953); Brown, *Loyalty and Security;* Harold Chase, *Security and Liberty: The Problem of Native Communists, 1947–1955* (Garden City, 1955); and William Berman, "Civil Rights and Civil Liberties," in Richard Kirkendall, ed., *The Truman Period as a Research Field* (Columbia, Mo., 1967).

4. Randolph to Truman, July 25, 1946, OF252-I, Truman Papers, Truman Library. (Henceforth all OF citations refer to Truman Papers, Truman Library.) Thomas Emerson and David Helfeld, "Loyalty Among Government Employees," *Yale Law Journal,* LVIII (December 1948).

5. Elsey to Clark Clifford, August 16, 1946; Arthur Flemming to Attorney General Clark, July 22, 1946; Telephone Call, John Steelman to Mr. Latta, August 21, 1946; John Collet to Steelman, September 18, 1946; Executive Order 9806, November 25, 1946; James Webb to Clark, November 20, 1946, all in OF252-I. Harry Mitchell to Truman, September 9, 1946, OF2 (1945–1946). Matthew Connelly, October 1, 1946, OF482.

6. See Executive Order 9806, November 25, 1946; also sample letters, A. Devitt Vanech (chairman, Temporary Commission) to FBI, Office of Naval Intelligence, Military Intelligence Division; and the fifty executive agencies, departments, and commissions, December 26, 1946, OF252-I.

7. Statement, Herbert Gaston, no date, OF252-I.

8. Concluding quote from Executive Order 9835, March 22, 1947; see also Report of the President's Temporary Commission on Employee Loyalty, n.d., both in Loyalty, Murphy Files. Berman, "Civil Rights and Civil Liberties," p. 200.

9. Spingarn to Foley, April 9, 1947, General Loyalty File, Spingarn Papers, Truman Library.

10. Clifford to Truman, May 7, 1947, OF252-K. Memo for the President, April 7, 1947; Telephone Memo, April 10, 1947, OF252-I. Mitchell and Perkins to Truman, April 25, 1947; Webb to Truman, April 30, 1947; Clark to Truman, May 1, 1947; Clifford to Truman, May 9, 1947; Truman to Mitchell, May 9, 1947, all in OF252-K.

11. Murray to Truman, April 14, 1947, and reply April 15, 1947, OF252-K (1945–1947).

12. Carr to Clark, September 24, 1947, and reply September 30, 1947, President's Committee on Civil Rights, Truman Papers.

13. Davidson to Clifford, December 29, 1947, Loyalty, Murphy Files. *Washington Post,* January 8, 1948. When the issue of permitting confrontation of witnesses was discussed within the Loyalty Review Board, FBI Director J. Edgar Hoover made it abundantly clear to Seth Richardson, board chairman, that the FBI would not cooperate with the board "unless the facts received in confidence by the investigation can be kept entirely confidential at all times and under all conditions." *New York Times,* December 28, 1947, p. 28.

14. Dawson to Clifford, January 7, 1948, OF252-K (1948).

15. Richardson to Davidson, January 3, 1949; L. A. Moyer (executive director and chief examiner, Civil Service Loyalty Board) to Civil Service Commission, February 2, 1949, OF252-K (1949).

16. Snyder to Richardson, April 15, 1948, Personnel 1946–1952, Snyder Papers, Truman Library. Spingarn to Clark, September 9, 1948, and reply, White House Assignment, Spingarn Papers.

17. Spingarn to Truman, October 15, 1948, White House Assignment, Spingarn Papers.

18. Press Release, Department of Justice, March 31 and July 1, 1949, Department of Justice Library. Morris Ernst to Connelly, April 28, 1949, Federal Loyalty Program, Spingarn Papers. Henderson to Truman, September 27, 1948; and White to Truman, November 26, 1948; OF252-K (1948). Thomas to Truman, June 24, 1949, OF562. Wolfe to Truman, July 8, 1949, General Loyalty File, Spingarn Papers.

19. President's News Conference, June 16, 1949, *Public Papers of the Presidents: Harry S. Truman, 1949* (Washington, D.C., 1964), pp. 292–296 (henceforth referred to as *Public Papers.*) Spingarn to Clifford, May 5, 1949; Spingarn to Dawson, June 17, 1949, all in Federal Loyalty Program, Spingarn Papers.

20. Spingarn to Clifford, December 30, 1949, Chronological File, Spingarn Papers.

21. Charles Maylon to Murphy, March 28, 1950; Murphy to Spingarn, April 1, 1950; Spingarn to Murphy, April 27, 1950; Meeting, May 23, 1950; Draft Executive Order, President's Commission on Internal Security and Individual Rights, June 1, 1950; State Department to Murphy, June 1, 1950;

Suggestions for a Committee Report of the Tydings Committee, May 26, 1950; Murphy and Spingarn to Truman, May 24, 1950; Spingarn to Murphy, June 19, 1950; Spingarn, June 26, 1950; Spingarn to Murphy, Dawson, Elsey, July 20, 1950, all in Loyalty, Murphy Files. Connelly to Truman, January 3, 1951; Truman to Nimitz, January 4, 1951, and reply January 9, 1951, all in OF2750-A. Tydings to Truman, July 24, 1950, OF252-K (1950). Senator Harley Kilgore to Truman, September 14, 1950; and Congresswoman Helen Gahagan Douglas to Truman, September 20, 1950; OF2750-C. Theodore Tannenwald to W. Averell Harriman, July 27, 1950, Chronological File, Tannenwald Papers, Truman Library. Draft Executive Order, President's Commission on Internal Security and Individual Rights, July 25, 1950; David Bell to Murphy, November 14, 1950; Murphy to Truman, November 15, 1950; Elsey to Murphy, November 22, 1950, all in Internal Security, Murphy Files. Max Kampleman to Murphy, November 20, 1950, K, Murphy Papers. Spingarn, June 20, 1950, Loyalty, Communism and Civil Rights, Spingarn Papers. Draft Memo, Murphy to Truman, February 1, 1950, Federal Loyalty Program, Spingarn Papers. Spingarn, May 22, 1950; Spingarn to Dawson, September 30, 1950; Spingarn, June 23, 1950; Bell to Murphy, June 23, 1950; Murphy, Elsey, and Spingarn to Truman, July 11, 1950; Spingarn, July 12, 1950; Spingarn, August 15, 1950, all in National Defense—Internal Security and Individual Rights, Spingarn Papers. Spingarn, September 19, 1950; and Draft Statement by President, September 18, 1950; Philleo Nash Papers, Truman Library.

22. President's News Conference, March 12, 1950; Letters Regarding Disclosure of Confidential Files, March 28, 1950; Letter to Senator Tydings, April 3, 1950; *Public Papers, 1950*, pp. 181–185, 229–232, 240–241. J. Edgar Hoover to Attorney General McGrath, February 24, 1950; Draft Memo to Truman, February 27, 1950; Murphy to Truman, June 5, 1950; all in Loyalty, Murphy Files. Adrian Fisher (Legal Adviser, State Department) to Dawson, March 8, 1950; Tydings to Acheson, March 22, 1950, and reply March 27, 1950; McGrath to Truman, March 17, 1950; Richardson to Dawson, June 26, 1950; all in OF419-K.

23. Quote from Executive Order 10207 Establishing Nimitz Commission, January 23, 1951, RG220, Truman Papers. Ford to Murphy, April 20, 1951, OF252-K (January–April 1951). Leffingwell to Nimitz, March 20, 1951, RG220. See also Nimitz to Truman, February 14, 1951, OF2750-A. Hiram Bingham (chairman, Loyalty Review Board) to Mitchell, February 15, 1951; and Bingham to All Heads of Departments and Agencies, May 23, 1951; OF252-K. Statement upon Establishing Nimitz Commission, January 23, 1951; and Remarks at Swearing In of President's Commission, February 12, 1951; *Public Papers, 1951*, pp. 119–121, 152–153. John Danaher (commission member) to Nimitz, February 5, 1951; Press Release, February 15, 1951; Nimitz to Bingham, February 16, 1951; Connelly to Nimitz, February 21, 1951; Danaher to George Jacoby (General Motors Corp.), February 28, 1951; Danaher to Nimitz, March 1, 1951, and reply March 4, 1951; Bingham to Nimitz, March 12, 1951, and reply March 16, 1951; Truman to Nimitz, April 28, 1951, all in RG220. Draft Memo, Elsey to Truman, October 5, 1951, Loyalty, Communism and Civil Rights, Spingarn Papers.

24. Spingarn to Clifford, July 27, 1949, Federal Loyalty Program, Spingarn Papers.

25. Directive quoted in Roosevelt to Jackson, May 21, 1940; the Truman directive cited in Clark to Truman, July 17, 1946; and the Elsey review and report on President's response in Elsey to Truman, February 2, 1950; and Elsey to Spingarn, February 2, 1950, all in National Defense—Internal Security, Spingarn Papers. See also Press Release, Department of Justice, January 8, 1950, Department of Justice Library. For a more thorough discussion of this matter, see my articles "Attorney General Clark, Internal Security and the Truman Administration," *New University Thought*, VI (Spring 1968), 16–23, and "The 'National Security' Justification for Electronic Eavesdropping: An Elusive Exception," *Wayne Law Review*, XIV (Summer 1968), 749–771.

26. Murphy and Spingarn quotes in Murphy and Spingarn to Truman, May 16, 1950, National Defense—Internal Security and Individual Rights, Spingarn Papers. Spingarn, January 27, 1950; David Lloyd to Spingarn, February 1, 1950; Spingarn to Murphy, February 1, 1950; Spingarn, May 6, 1950; Spingarn Notes for May 19, 1950, Talk with Attorney General, May 18, 1950; Truman to McGrath, May 19, 1950; Spingarn, May 20, 1950, all in National Defense—Internal Security and Individual Rights, Spingarn Papers.

27. Ford to Celler, May 23, 1950, National Defense—Internal Security, Deportation and Exclusion of Aliens, Spingarn Papers.

28. Spingarn, July 17, 1950, National Defense—Internal Security and Individual Rights, Spingarn Papers.

29. Jones to Murphy, October 13, 1950, OF41. Neustadt to Spingarn, July 3, 1950, National Defense—Internal Security and Individual Rights, Spingarn Papers. Italics in original. See also Ford to Murphy, August 2, 1950; Ford, August 3, 1950; Spingarn to Murphy, August 10, 1950; Lloyd to Spingarn, August 10, 1950; Spingarn, August 11, 1950; Lloyd to Spingarn, August 17, 1950; all in National Defense—Internal Security and Individual Rights, Spingarn Papers. Ford to Murphy, September 12, 1950; Murphy to Jones, September 28, 1950; Murphy, October 13, 1950, all in OF41.

30. Statement, September 25, 1951, *Public Papers, 1951*, pp. 535–537. See also James Pope (managing editor, *Louisville Courier-Journal*) to Joseph Short (Truman's press secretary), July 13, 1951, OF484. Murphy to Truman, September 24, 1951, Memo—Big Four Meetings, Murphy Papers.

31. GOP statement quoted in *Washington Post*, October 1, 1951; editors' resolution quoted in *New York Times*, September 30, 1951.

32. President's News Conference, October 4, 1951; and Letter to the President of the Associated Press Managing Editors' Association, December 18, 1951, all in *Public Papers, 1951*, pp. 554–563, 648–649.

33. Hansen, January 3, 1952, Loyalty, Communism and Civil Rights, Spingarn Papers.

34. President's News Conference, January 31, 1952, *Public Papers, 1952*, pp. 130–136.

35. Dawson to Murphy, April 8, 1952; and Hansen to Murphy, April 14, 1952; Dawson, Donald, Murphy Papers. Murphy to Dawson, April 16, 1952, Chronological File, Murphy Papers. Dawson to Robert Ramspect (Civil Service Commission), September 17, 1952, Loyalty Review Board, Friedman Papers.

36. Bingham to Dawson, November 28, 1952, OF252-K (1952–1953).

See also Dawson to Bingham, December 8, 1952, Loyalty-Security Program, Friedman Papers.

37. Brown, *Loyalty and Security*, p. 262. *Congress and the Nation, 1945–1964* (Washington, D.C.: Congressional Quarterly, 1965), p. 1665.

38. See Brown, *Loyalty and Security;* Bontecou, *Federal Loyalty-Security Program;* Chase, *Security and Liberty;* and Berman, "Civil Rights and Civil Liberties." For additional studies critical of the loyalty program, written during the tenure of Truman's administration, see Alan Barth, *The Loyalty of Free Men* (New York, 1951); American Civil Liberties Union, *Our Uncertain Liberties, 1947–1948* (New York, 1949); Francis Biddle, *The Fear of Freedom* (New York, 1951); Thomas Emerson and David Helfeld, "Loyalty Among Government Employees," *Yale Law Journal* (December 1948); Walter Gellhorn, *Security, Loyalty and Science* (Ithaca, N.Y., 1950); John Lord O'Brian, "Loyalty Tests and Guilt by Association," *Harvard Law Review* (April 1948) and "New Encroachments on Individual Freedom," *Harvard Law Review* (November 1952); Arthur Sutherland, "Freedom and Internal Security," *Harvard Law Review* (January 1951); and Clair Wilcox, ed., *Civil Liberties Under Attack* (Philadelphia, 1951).

Index

Index

A Note on the Contributors

HENRY W. BERGER, Assistant Professor of History at Washington University, St. Louis, has contributed to David Horowitz's *Containment and Revolution* (1967), *The Nation, Science and Society,* and *Labor History*. He is writing a book on the foreign policy of American labor and contributing to a forthcoming history of American diplomacy, edited by William A. Williams. Mr. Berger did his graduate work at the University of Wisconsin (Ph.D. 1966).

WILLIAM C. BERMAN, Associate Professor of History at the University of Toronto, has written *The Politics of Civil Rights in the Truman Administration* (1970), and has contributed to Richard Kirkendall's *The Truman Period as a Research Field* (1967), the *American Journal of Legal History,* and the *Canadian Historical Review*. He is preparing a history of the Democratic Advisory Council, 1957–1961. Mr. Berman received his Ph.D. from Ohio State University in 1963.

BARTON J. BERNSTEIN, Associate Professor of History at Stanford University, has edited *Politics and Policies of the Truman Administration* (1970), *Towards a New Past: Dissenting Essays in American History* (1968), and, with Allen Matusow, *The Truman Administration: A Documentary History* (1966). He has also contributed articles to the *Journal of American History, Mid-America,* and the *Bulletin of Atomic Scientists,* among many others, and is preparing a study of the Truman administration. Mr. Bernstein received his Ph.D. from Harvard University in 1963.

NORMAN KANER, Assistant Professor of History at Temple University, is at work on a study of I. F. Stone and preparing a volume of documents

311

on political opposition to war in American history. He received his Ph.D. in 1968 from Rutgers University.

LEONARD P. LIGGIO, Lecturer in History at the City College of New York, has contributed to the *Catholic Historical Review, The Progressive,* and *Viet-Report.* He is completing an essay on Cold War politics and a larger study of American isolationism in the twentieth century. He received his Master's degree from Fordham University in 1959, and is now a Ph.D. candidate there.

THOMAS G. PATERSON, Associate Professor of History at the University of Connecticut, has edited *The Origins of the Cold War* (1970) and has contributed to the *Business History Review, The Nation,* the *Journal of American History,* the *American Historical Review,* and Bernstein's *Politics and Policies of the Truman Administration* (1970), among others. He is at work on a study of American economic foreign policy and the origins of the Cold War, and a collection of essays on American imperialism and anti-imperialism. He earned his Ph.D. at the University of California, Berkeley, in 1968.

WILLIAM C. PRATT, Assistant Professor of History at the University of Nebraska at Omaha, has contributed to *The Nation,* the *Pacific Northwest Quarterly,* and the *Journal of Southern History.* He is completing a book on the Socialist Movement of Reading, Pennsylvania. He received his Ph.D. at Emory University in 1969.

RONALD RADOSH, Assistant Professor of History at Queensborough Community College (CUNY), has written *American Labor and United States Foreign Policy* (1970) and, with Louis Menashe, has edited *Teach-Ins U.S.A.: Reports, Opinions, Documents* (1967). He has also contributed to *The Nation, Liberation,* Julius Jacobson's *The Negro and the American Labor Movement* (1968), the *Journal of American History,* and *Studies on the Left,* among others. He is preparing a collection of essays on Eugene V. Debs, and, with Murray N. Rothbard, is editing *Roots of the American Corporate State.* He studied at the University of Wisconsin (Ph.D. 1967).

MARK SOLOMON, Assistant Professor of History at Simmons College, has contributed to *Labor Today* and *The Minority of One.* He is preparing a study of white radicals and the Afro-American community, as well as shorter analyses of McCarthyism and the Negro, American student radicalism, and the historiography of Christopher Lasch. He received his Ph.D. from Harvard University in 1970.

ATHAN THEOHARIS, Associate Professor of History at Marquette University, is co-author of *Anatomy of Anti-Communism* (1969) and author of *Seeds of Repression: Harry S. Truman and the Origins of McCarthyism* (1971) and *The Yalta Myths: An Issue in U.S. Politics, 1945–1955* (1970). He has contributed to the *Political Science Quarterly*, the *Wayne Law Review, New University Thought,* Melvin Small's *Public Opinion and Historians* (1970), and Bernstein's *Politics and Policies of the Truman Administration* (1970). The University of Chicago awarded him the Ph.D. in 1965.